Normandy to Berlin: The Trek to Honor The Legacies

JAMES JOSEPH PELOSI

ISBN:1548065994
ISBN-13:9781548065997

DEDICATION

I dedicate this book to my father, James Vincent Pelosi (1923 – 1996), who, in 1944, served as a First Lieutenant in the United States Army Air Corps flying B-17 and B-24 bomber aircraft in support of the Allied landings at Normandy, France, and who, between 1948 and 1949, served as a Captain in the newly-formed United States Air Force flying C-47 and C-54 cargo aircraft in support of the Berlin Airlift. I wrote this story with a sentiment shared by the Greek poet Pindar who wrote that "unsung, the noblest deed will die."

CONTENTS

APPENDICIES

ACKNOWLEDGMENTS

Because of everything which transpired throughout the events of The TREK I feel that I truly am blessed. I am very grateful to everyone who supported me as I planned and conducted The TREK and to many of those same people and others who helped me as I struggled to describe and share the experience.

Here I will try my best to express my thanks knowing that I may not write about everyone who helped me and everything which was done for me.

Ms. Helen Irene Schenck, the closest member of my extended family, was the first to hear of my plan to walk across Europe as a physical demonstration of support for our veterans, especially those who served during World War II, the Berlin Airlift and in Berlin before the fall of the Berlin Wall in November 1989, three of the four Legacy events. She provided me constant encouragement; helped me to plan, organize and conduct my research; managed all my personal affairs during my four month absence in Europe; and critiqued all the draft and final versions of the text. In addition to supplying me with home-baked brownies, she did more than anyone else to help ensure the success of this effort.

Once I made the decision to undertake this project my next door neighbor, Richard R. Arnold, and his family were a consistent source of inspiration and motivation. Ricky and I worked together for seven years in Clear Lake for the government organization where at one time the expression "failure is not an option" was a dictum. We discussed all of my work in detail as I progressed with the planning and there was not a suggestion nor a recommendation that I did not consider valid and that I did not adopt. The Arnold family actually kicked off The TREK for me by hosting a farewell party with our neighbors and friends. On June 3, 2014, Ricky drove me to the airport for my flight to France.

I always had planned to generate a book based upon my experiences during The TREK. In the fall of 1980, I met Bob and Julie Davey when I enrolled at Pepperdine University. At that time, Dr. Bob Davey, PhD, my Pepperdine MBA classmate, was a Professor of Aerospace Engineering at Caltech. In 1997 Bob published his first novel, The Moon War, a futuristic adventure sometimes too true to reality. Julie was a college writing professor with the reputation of encouraging her students and me to "write about what you know." In 2012, she published, Cry Wolf, a psychological thriller inspired by actual events and packed with adventure and emotion. We exchanged numerous messages and telephone calls before, during and after The TREK. Over-generous with their time and attention to me, they provided me invaluable support with reading, editing, formatting, recommendations for revisions, and sources within their personal and professional circle of friends

i

for supplemental help and technical support. On several occasions they hosted me at their Laguna Niguel home and, when not entertaining or feeding me, we conducted strategy sessions with the goal of publishing this book. I am most grateful to them for the time and attention they gave to support me in this effort but, most of all, for their 35-plus year friendship.

A major task for me was to generate interest in the project and to obtain support for the resources essential to its success. I knew that I needed to create a website. The website, "Honoring the Legacies," was designed and managed by Mr. Tom Raines, a U.S. Navy veteran. Within the website, the map he created, which showed every city, town or village along The TREK route between Normandy, France and Berlin, Germany, helped to give the residents there a better understanding of the scope of this adventure at those times when my oversized backpack, sweaty torso and deficient language skills sparked interest and conversation.

Dr. Gary Boetticher, PhD, Professor of Computer Science at the University of Houston, Clear Lake, Texas, helped provide the structure and the format which Tom included in the website. He read and reviewed all the contents of the website as well as the drafts of the text, and provided suggestions for revision which were especially helpful to me. A man of many skills, he also designed The TREK patch "Normandy to Berlin Honoring the Legacies." The image of the patch which he created is within the text at Appendix 1.

To my close friend and professional associate with whom I shared five duty assignments over the course of our careers beginning in Berlin in 1973 Colonel Gerald "Jerry" Lechliter, United States Army, Retired, I owe a very special "Thanks." I sent Jerry each chapter and separately each of the nine stories about Berlin within the second chapter. Although he was extremely busy advocating environmental and community standards within his hometown of Lewes, Delaware he returned every document with detailed comments which made the content more accurate with respect to the Legacy histories and military topics and the text more easily readable.

Miss Yvette Orozco, a reporter for the Clear Lake newspaper, *The Citizen*, wrote two front-page stories about The TREK, the first before my departure and the second after my return. Scott Knoll, an investigative reporter for KHOU 11 News, who had read Yvette's first story, broadcast a three-minute report on the evening news. This publicity steered supporters to the website which added to the credibility and reputation of The TREK.

As a member of the American Legion's Post 490 in Houston, Texas, I sought support from my fellow Legionnaires to help me defray the anticipated $10,000 cost of the project. The American Legion not only provided significant financial support but also published a story about The TREK which appeared nationally in *The Legion* magazine: https://www.legion.org/stories/family-legacy/veteran-walks-844-miles-between-normandy-and-berlin-honor-father. The Veterans of Foreign Wars

(VFW) post, which is collocated with the American Legion Post 490 at the Ellington Field facility, matched the financial contribution from the American Legion. A third veteran's group which meets at the same facility, The Submariner Veterans, provided the funds to purchase all the flags which I placed on 120 gravesites at the American Cemetery at Normandy on June 5th 2014.

For additional support I sent more than 120 letters to the cadet and midshipman unit commanders of the 2014 graduating classes at the four Service Academies. The sole response was from Cadet Company Commander Rommel Claude Verano, Cadet Company D-2, at West Point who, within an extremely polite letter one week before graduation, provided a cash contribution from the members of his cadet company. I know that the soldiers whom he commands are serving with a truly dedicated professional.

I reached out to more than 200 key executives and Hollywood celebrities many of whom were veterans or who played a role as a service member in a film or television show. Only two senior executives responded which was two more than anyone from Hollywood.

I wrote Mr. Kendall J. Powell, Chairman and Chief Executive Officer for General Mills. I told him that during my training I was consuming daily one of his company's "Nature Valley Protein Chewy Bars, Peanut Butter Dark Chocolate" at the cost of a dollar a bar. For The TREK I would need two bars a day or 112 bars for the projected length of The TREK and I asked for a donation. Within three days I received a letter from his executive assistant, Ms. Kari Perreault, who sent me 240 bars in two cases, twice the number that I needed. So very grateful, I will continue to grocery shop for General Mills products.

For years, I have used a small, four-inch microbrush to supplement my oral hygiene care beyond brushing and flossing. These microbrushes are made by Microbrush International, in Grafton, Wisconsin. I wrote and requested a donation of one tube containing 100 microbrushes. Immediately I received a response from the team of Ms. Anne Klein and her colleague Heather who sent not one but four tubes of the microbrushes, a year's supply, to my home.

My West Point 1973 "Proud and Free" classmate, Lieutenant Colonel Richard Wilson served as a Military Police officer until his retirement. He entered the seminary in Houston close to my home and we reestablished contact after more than 35 years. In 2015, I attended his ordination in South Carolina. He wrote the group of three prayers the first of which I would say at Normandy, the second daily during The TREK and the third at my arrival at the Brandenburg Gate in Berlin. Like others, I am better as a person for knowing Father Rich. In spirit he was walking alongside me as I recited those prayers.

The second chapter, which is one-fifth of this book, describes several of my experiences throughout my tour of duty in Berlin. More than 40 years later I still consider those 39 months in Berlin to be the happiest days of my life: great duty, regular paychecks, free public mass transit, hundreds of quality bars and restaurants many of which never closed, and, most importantly, a contingent of dedicated professional soldiers with whom it was an honor to serve. It is here where I most regret any unintentional omissions when I say "Thanks for your service with me" to those who taught me more than I taught them:

Second Platoon, Bravo Company, 3rd Battalion, 6th Infantry Regiment, Berlin Brigade: Rifleman and "Team Womack" member Specialist 4th Class James Chiew; Platoon Sergeant Robert Cunningham; Second Squad Leader Staff Sergeant "Red" Edmondson; Weapons Squad Leader Staff Sergeant "Jack" Jackson; Radio Operator Specialist 4th Class Bruce Laukitis; Third Squad Leader Staff Sergeant Eugene "Badass" Middleton; Rifleman Private First Class Carlos Soto; Platoon Sergeant George Wertin; First Squad Leader and Commander "Team Womack" Staff Sergeant Sammie Womack.

Bravo Company, 3rd Battalion, 6th Infantry Regiment, Berlin Brigade: Mortar Platoon crewmember Specialist 4th Class Stephen Alloway; Mortar Platoon Leader Lieutenant Archibald Arnold; Company Commander Captain Mercer Dorsey; Company Commander Robert Harmon; Rifleman Specialist 4th Class David Hensley; Platoon Leader Lieutenant Jeffrey Jenkins; Company Commander Cecil Kiilehua; Mortar Platoon crewmember Specialist 4th Class James Klein; First Sergeant Jesse Meekins; Training Sergeant Douglas Stefek; Rifleman Specialist 4th Class David Westbrook; Platoon Leader Lieutenant Gary Wright; Team Leader Sergeant Nicholas Vone.

Combat Support Company, 3rd Battalion, 6th Infantry Regiment, Berlin Brigade: Ammunition carrier and driver Private First Class Thomas Bolmer; TOW Gun Commander Sergeant R. Haney; TOW gunner Private First Class Jeffrey Langdon; Platoon Sergeant William Pulliam; Company Commander Lloyd "Sonny" Ray; TOW gunner Private First Class David Shifflet.

3rd Battalion, 6th Infantry Regiment, Berlin Brigade: Lieutenant Michael Fankell (USMA 1972, deceased 1992); Lieutenant Thomas Kelley; Lieutenant Gary Loberg; Battalion Commander Lieutenant Colonel Don Phillips; Lieutenant Ronald Rowley (USMA 1973, deceased 2009); Lieutenant Patrick Sinnot; Lieutenant Jeffrey Stacer.

Headquarters and Headquarters Company Commander Captain Joseph Finch; Battalion Commander Lieutenant Colonel Bruce Gard; First Sergeant Bruce Harmon; Company Commander Captain Gary Jones; Supply Technician Specialist 4th Class Barbara Mahoney; Supply Sergeant Staff Sergeant Samuels.

Berlin Brigade: Inspector General Lieutenant Colonel Capps; Deputy Brigade Commander Colonel Richard Kattar; Lieutenant Bill Jockheck; Lieutenant Tom Mason.

Mentors and very special friends: Command Sergeant Major Mario Estrella; Lieutenant Jeffrey Kallman; Colonel William S. McArthur; Sergeant Major James Vining, Lieutenant Colonel John "Jack" Francis Whalen.

The four chapters relating my experiences in France, Belgium, Luxembourg and Germany describe the daily thrill of this adventure. Part of my motivation to succeed was due to the people whom I encountered by chance throughout The TREK. Many are my friends now. Many I see each year when I return to Europe. All of them have a special place in my heart for the attention, affection and support they gave me when we were together.

In Mery-Corbon, France, Roland Francois, his wife Florence and their daughter Elise rescued me after a bad fall in a shopping center parking lot. The family owns and manages the company "Normandy Ambulances" located across the street from where I fell. After Roland's employees treated the wounds at my knee, lower leg and arm Roland brought me to his home where I met his wife and daughter. The family hosted me as "the liberator" at an all-night party with their friends and neighbors. At breakfast, Director Francois presented me with a black chapeau displaying the multi-colored Normandy regional crest which I wore until my arrival in Berlin.

In Evreux, France, Mrs. Juana Bargot observed me standing in the middle of a plaza studying and orienting a map. She introduced herself and offered to help me with directions. After hearing about my plan for The TREK, she made a telephone call and then walked me through Evreux to the home of Colonel James Callahan, United States Army, Retired. I spent much of the next two days with Jim and his wife Marie-France residing at their home, exchanging stories throughout the day, dining al fresco in their patio garden and traveling with them between Evreux and Paris. The 99th birthday party for Marie-France's father in Paris was an honor for me to experience.

Mrs. Monique Comard, in St. Brice Courcelles, France dragged me into her home and kept me as a pseudo-prisoner after I complimented her on her beautiful garden while walking past her home. She asked about the backpack and then learned about The TREK. I was wined and dined and regaled with stories about events in France, especially those in the local area, for more than half a day. Spirited and supportive, Mrs. Comard puts a smile on my face every time I recall our time together.

I was blessed to meet Karl Pettit in Virton, Belgium and spend an evening with him at his home and later two days in Bastogne. He taught me much about the history of Belgium during and after both world wars and made me proud to be an American having credited the American military with the liberation of Belgium.

Father Pierre at Saint Donat's Catholic Church in Arlon, Belgium provided me exceptionally comfortable lodging and outstanding full breakfast meals as my host in what had once been a dormitory for the priests of his parish. He offered the daily masses which I attended for me and for the success of The TREK.

Environmental engineer Derek Sinnot, from Ireland, met me in Arlon and introduced me to Father Pierre. He hosted me at the University of Liege where, for a day and a half, I observed representatives from 30 European countries of the European Cooperation in Science and Technology discuss energy and environmental issues. My eyes opened to the efforts which Europe is making to reduce the global carbon footprint. But they were hard to keep open after Derek helped me gain a greater appreciation for Irish beer and ale none of which I had tasted before I met him.

Almost half way through The TREK, my restaurant encounter with Dr. Alex (Colonel, British Army Medical Corps) and his wife Margaret was a chance event which greatly improved my ability to finish The TREK. In addition to the camaraderie which we shared as military officers and the combat-related stories which we exchanged, I received invaluable professional medical treatment and advice identical to how his soldiers patrol in Afghanistan that aided me greatly for the remainder of my walk.

Marion Schwartz in Hahnenklee, the staff at the Braunschweig Klinikum and Dr. Rainer Baumann in Osterode am Harz saved my eyesight. If not for their efforts the TREK would not have been completed. After I accidentally blinded myself while a guest at the Hotel Blackcom Erika, owned and managed by Marion and Ralph Schwartz, Marion drove me ten miles to a doctor at the closest clinic and then another 60 miles to the Klinikum where I remained for four days. With my sight almost completely restored, although compromised with respect to my ability to distinguish colors, the medical team gave me the go-ahead to continue The TREK. Without the efforts of these compassionate professionals I would have been physically unable to continue.

During my rehabilitation in The Harz, I met young Sven Küppers after I tripped and stumbled into the ice cream shop where he was working. By chance, we met again the following day when he was with his mother and sister and they brought me to their home. After meeting Sven's father Steffen, I was invited to spend the weekend as their guest. For three years we have kept in touch at least monthly through electronic messages and long-distance telephone calls. Except for Steffen, all of the Küppers family have visited me in the United States. I always have been treated as if I were part of their family.

During the time of my eye trauma and my rehabilitation, my long-term friends from Berlin, Detlev and Ilona Gebhard, drove the 200 miles to The Harz to offer their support including escorting and interpreting for me during my examinations with Dr. Baumann. Detlev prepared a modified route for the remaining walk to Berlin consistent with the conditions demanded by the medical teams. They were on hand to meet me at the Brandenburg Gate when I arrived in Berlin. With each of us holding a glass of champagne Detlev raised his glass to "one crazy man."

Finally, in the fictitious movie, *Saving Private Ryan*, the final scene shows the actor portraying a former World War II United States Army Private James Ryan at the American Cemetery, Normandy standing in front of the gravesite of Captain John Miller who led the team to "save" him and who, before he died of his wounds, encouraged him to live a long and productive life in health and happiness. With his children and grandchildren standing behind him, Mr. Ryan kneels and speaks softly toward the tombstone saying, "Every day I think of what you said to me that day on the bridge. I hope that in your eyes I have earned what all of you have done for me." Not a day goes by since I completed The TREK on August 15, 2014 that I do not think about our veterans and our military still serving in combat arenas throughout the world that I do not thank them and wish them all a long and productive life in health and happiness."

JAMES JOSEPH PELOSI

In life, character is the indispensable basis of enduring success.

1. Introduction.

All life is precious. Historically, throughout our lifetime, many of us aspire to know, once and for all, the sum of our lives: who we are, what we are, why we are, and where we are.

There is a sense that the increasing number of internet websites which support a person's search of his ancestry is due, in large part, to a quest to learn about when and where some family member lived. In some part, it is also a quest to understand better the political, social, and economic conditions under which that family member lived. This historical family information provides the data which may help someone to understand the sum of his life.

I am a member of the Baby Boom generation. My father was 17 years old when the Japanese attacked Pearl Harbor on December 7, 1941. He turned 18 four days later, enlisted in the Army, was selected for flight training, earned his wings, and served as a pilot of B-17 and B-24 bomber aircraft throughout the war. His parents and my mother's parents, all of European descent, were born at the beginning of the Twentieth Century when only six percent of Americans were graduated from high school and the average American lived to be only 46 years old.

My grandfathers were too young to serve during World War I. But after the war, they each married and started families, sadly only a few years before the Stock Market crash in 1929. Each breadwinner struggled to support his family of four throughout the years of the Great Depression, when more than 30 million Americans had no income of any kind. Then they faced another challenge: World War II.

Although my grandparents and their children were relatively poor, their lives were extraordinarily rich in history beginning in the early 1900's. That World War I Generation later sired The Greatest Generation, those men and women who fought and won World War II.

As a child, my grandparents and parents taught me the history of the significant periods of their lives: the events of World War I; the crash of the stock market; the Great Depression; the rise of fascism in Europe; World War II, and the decades-long Cold War. Later, as a student, I read as much as I could to learn and try to comprehend how the United States and these two generations of my family struggled and survived. What were the reasons why life had been so difficult for my family then but seemingly so simple and easy for me now?

During the summer of 2013, years after my grandparents and parents had died, I read a biography of President Franklin Delano Roosevelt. From the history within the text of that book, I realized that the next year, 2014, would be an historic year for many Americans and Europeans. It would herald four significant anniversaries of events which highlighted the Twentieth Century and which affected millions of people of all ages, races, creeds, and occupations.

- July 28th 2014 would be the 100th anniversary of the start of World War I. During that war, trench warfare took an average of 150,000 lives a week. When the war ended in 1918 more than 35 million people had perished.

- June 6th 2014 would mark the 70th anniversary of the Allied landings at Normandy, France. More than 160,000 American, British, and Canadian soldiers supported by more than 200,000 Allied naval personnel landed on the beaches.

- September 30th 2014 would be the 65th anniversary of the end of The Berlin Airlift. For eleven months in 1948-49, the Soviets blocked the Allied rail, road, and canal access into West Berlin.

- November 9th 2014 would be the 25th anniversary of the fall of the Berlin Wall. For 28 years between 1961 and 1989, the "Wall of Shame" isolated West Berlin from East Berlin and East Germany.

The loss of treasure, as a result of World War I and World War I, both in human life and economic devastation, defies comprehension. Statistics to date, which are being refined continuously, estimate that more than 35 million people perished as a result of the four years of World War I (1914–1918), and another 70 million as a result of the seven years of World War II (1939–1945). All humanity should mourn the loss of so many potentially great political and spiritual leaders, doctors, scientists, engineers, inventors and entrepreneurs.

In that summer of 2013, I had been living for 62 years, approximately 22,630 days. I calculated that the 105 million people lost during the 11 years of the World Wars represented the deaths of approximately slightly more than 4,400 people for every day that I had been alive. In the course of probably each and every day of my life to date, every person with whom I ever had come into contact that day at play, at school or at work, indoors or outdoors, by day or by night, symbolically represented a casualty of war. Never, throughout every one of those 22,630 days, could I ever have encountered, or even seen, 4,400 other human beings.

With less than a year until the dates of the calendar year 2014 anniversary events, I decided to do something to recognize the sacrifices of the men and women who had served during the legacy events of World War I (1914–1918), World War II (1939 – 1945), the Berlin Airlift (1948-1949) and the Era of the Berlin Wall (1961-1989). My intent was to make an effort to bring attention to these anniversaries as well as to the legacies that they represented by honoring the contributions of the military of all ranks in all services, their families, and the civilian population which supported their efforts to win World War I, defeat fascism in World War II, end the Soviet blockade of Berlin, bring down the Berlin War, and reunite Germany. The Greek poet Pindar wrote: "Unsung, the noblest deed will die."

In 1944, my father, James Vincent Pelosi, served as a First Lieutenant in the Army Air Corps, flying B-17 and B-24 bomber aircraft in support of the Allied landings at Normandy, France. Later, in 1948 and 1949, he served as a Captain in the newly-formed United States Air Force, flying C-47 and C-54 cargo aircraft in support of the Berlin Airlift. In 1973, after my graduation from the United States Military Academy at West Point, I served as a Lieutenant of Infantry in the 3rd Battalion, 6th Infantry and Headquarters, Special Troops with the Berlin Brigade in Berlin, Germany.

I decided to walk the 895 miles between Omaha Beach at Normandy, France and the Brandenburg Gate in Berlin, Germany over the battlefields and through the cities and towns in which the two World Wars were fought, and along the corridors by which Berlin was supplied during the Airlift. "Normandy to Berlin: The TREK to Honor the Legacies" would begin on June 6, 2014, the 70th Anniversary of the Allied landings at Normandy.

I had almost one year to plan and prepare for "The TREK." The narrative which follows describes some of the history of the events leading up to World War I as well as the highlights of the history of World War I and World War II as they were fought in Western Europe. Although World War I was fought also on Fronts in Eastern Europe, Serbia, Italy, and Turkey, including the Dardanelles, Mesopotamia, and Palestine; and, although World War II was fought also on Fronts in Eastern Europe, the Balkans, North Africa, Sicily, Italy, and Japan, this narrative does not include historical highlights of the wars on those other Fronts.

The reason is simple. The historical narratives describe battles which were fought along the air corridors and over the terrain for missions flown by my father as a 21-year old bomber pilot in 1944. His missions were in support of the Allied landings at Normandy, France and the ground combat operations into Germany. The narratives also describe air and ground operations along the air corridors through which he flew four years later as a cargo pilot during the Berlin Airlift. "The TREK" route follows those central air corridors and the ground routes through locations in Europe in which the U.S. Army fought to liberate Europe and end the war.

"The TREK" route, 895 miles beginning at Omaha Beach in Normandy, France and ending at the Brandenburg Gate in Berlin, Germany, was exclusive to Western Europe.

"I hope that some young foreigner may fall in love with Berlin and that he someday will write what happened to him there."

– Christopher Isherwood, Author, The Berlin Stories, and resident in the Schoneberg District of Berlin, 1929-1932.

2. Lieutenant James J. Pelosi, Berlin Brigade, 1973-1976.

If I were successful in completing The TREK route then I would end the walk at the Brandenburg Gate in the center of Berlin. Forty-one years earlier, at only 22 years of age, I fell in love with Berlin immediately upon my arrival in the fall of 1973. The TREK would provide the opportunity to return to Berlin after so long an absence and to see how much I remembered and how much had changed.

Arrival, 1973.

The Army officer who was assigned as my sponsor met me that Friday morning at Templehof Airport, and drove me the short distance to my bachelor quarters in the Dahlem District, one of the more affluent sections of the city.

The street address was 3A Flanagan Strasse, named after Father Flanagan, the founder of Boys Town. From the front door of the apartment I could step out into the Grunewald Forest and walk or run along its numerous lakes, ponds, parks, and trails within its more than 7,500 acres.

Travel within the walled city of Berlin was made possible by an extensive system of public transportation routes that included trains, subways, trolleys, and buses. This system was free to all members of the Allied military who were assigned to duty in Berlin and who traveled while in uniform or could produce an identification card if traveling in civilian clothes. Off duty, I intended to use much of my free time riding public transportation and exploring the attractions of Berlin. Within this 735-year-old city there were war monuments, churches, museums, art galleries, libraries, theaters, shops, boutiques, restaurants, outdoor cafes, night clubs, pubs, and sporting fields and arenas. Before my arrival, I had read about many of these attractions. Soon I hoped to have the opportunity to visit them.

More importantly, on duty in my first assignment in the Army, I intended to work as hard as I could to be the best second lieutenant in the Berlin Brigade.

The Berlin Brigade was composed of members of the United States Army serving as a part of the United States Armed Forces which occupied Berlin after World War II. Among the four armed services with a presence inside Berlin, the Army's Berlin Brigade had the largest representation and the greatest visibility. This army command had a variety of names between 1945 and 1961. Then, during the height of the Berlin Wall Crisis, the Commander-in-Chief, United States Army Europe, General Bruce Clarke, ordered that the Army's Command be titled "United States Army Berlin Brigade." The name remained until the Berlin Brigade was deactivated in September 1994, almost five years after the fall of the wall.

I was assigned to the 3rd Battalion, 6th Infantry as a rifle platoon leader in Bravo Company. The battalion was one of three infantry battalions located at McNair Barracks, named after U.S. Army Lieutenant General Leslie McNair. General McNair was killed by friendly fire on July 25, 1944, near St-Lo in Normandy, France, when a bomb from an American aircraft exploded near his foxhole.

At the apartment, my sponsor recommended that I sleep off the jet lag after the nine-hour flight and six-hour time zone change, and then explore Berlin with what would remain of Friday and the weekend. On a table in the living room he left maps and guides to the military facilities and to the attractions in Berlin.

At first light on Monday morning, he would return to drive me to McNair Barracks where I would meet my commander, my fellow officers in the company, and the 40 enlisted members of my platoon. His wife had stocked the refrigerator with enough provisions for a week. I made a sandwich, washed it down with a Schultheiss beer, my first, and fell asleep on the living room sofa.

The time was just shy of 8 p.m. when I awoke fully refreshed after nearly six hours sleep. Berlin is located at about the same northern latitude as London and Moscow. Then, in the middle of October, I dressed in a heavy coat and watch cap as if it were winter, and left the apartment to explore my neighborhood. On my side of the street, one block away to the east was another apartment identical in size, shape, and color to the apartment in which I was residing. It housed the senior enlisted members of the American military and their families. My new neighborhood included one of the many housing areas which were provided for the Americans and their families who were assigned in any capacity to Berlin.

In addition to the military, there also were U.S. State Department personnel, Department of Defense Dependent Schools (DoDDS) school teachers and administrators, and other U.S. government employees among the residents. One more block east was the inter-faith U.S. Army Chapel, Berlin. Next to the Chapel was the DoDDS elementary school for dependent children, who were referred to in military slang as "brats." Across the street from all this were the three sports complexes: an outdoor tennis facility; an indoor, multi-lane, lap swimming pool; and, a two-story gymnasium.

Both the tennis facility and the swimming pool were closed because of the late hour. The gymnasium was open and I toured the second-floor weight room, the first-floor basketball court, and the basement bowling alley which was reached by walking down a metal-railed circular staircase. Beyond the staircase and inside the door to the bowling alley was an attendant who checked identification cards to validate privileges for use of the facility. I produced my ID card and walked around. The bowling alley was full. The air-filtration system wasn't working well enough to clear the cloud of smoke and I left.

From the bowling alley, I had a short, 200-yard walk to find the Oskar-Helene-Heim U-Bahn station on Clay Allee, from which I planned to discover Berlin the following morning. About 50 yards away, I saw a young man walking towards me wearing only a white T-shirt, jeans, and sneakers. I thought that he must be freezing. He had a strange expression on his face and a far-away look in his eyes as we exchanged glances when we passed each other. Then, to my rear, I heard someone shout, "Hey Mario, Mario." I kept walking and heard another shout, "Hey Mario, Mario. Come here."

I turned around and looked, and the same young man I just had passed now was walking towards me. When we reached each other, he said, "Mario, I just scored some horse. You wanna shoot some?"

He was telling me that he just had obtained some heroin that he was willing to share, and he was asking me if I wanted to use it with him. I guess he mistook me for his pal Mario.

I told him, "Sure," then added, "but first I have to pee. Let's go in the bowling alley real quick."

He followed me into the sports complex and down the circular staircase. I turned to look at him to make sure he was following me and saw him blink and squeeze his eyes as he tried to adjust to the brighter light in the stairway. At the base of the staircase, he followed me through the entrance to the bowling alley, and walked by the attendant towards the men's room.

Before the attendant could call to him I threw my ID card on the desk and said, "Call the MP's. Tell them to get here immediately. I think this guy is dealing drugs."

When I got into the restroom, he was standing at a urinal, holding the flush handle to keep his balance, breathing slowly and deeply, and trying to focus his vision.

In the very bright light of such a small enclosure he fixed his eyes on me and said, "Hey, you're not Mario!"

He struggled to button up his jeans, gave up on that effort and then bolted from the restroom.

I was right behind him when he passed the attendant's desk and I asked the attendant as I passed him, "Did you call the MP's?"

He said, "Yes, Sir. They're on the way."

I did not want this guy to be out of the facility and on the street. At the base of the staircase, I stopped him and he resisted. He was somewhat shorter than my 5'11" and slightly heavier than my 145 pounds. We struggled, fell, and tumbled around on the tile floor, neither of us having an immediate advantage over the other. While we were rolling, I heard a click, looked, and saw an open switchblade knife moving toward my face about six inches from my forehead. I knocked the blade from his hand and we kept grappling and exchanging body blows.

I heard screaming from some female patrons at the top of the staircase. As I looked up at them, I saw a pistol come across his body. As the sounds of the screaming got louder I managed to knock the pistol away from him, fortunately for me, more because of his state of impairment than my superior physical prowess. Amid the chaos and confusion I sensed a lot more hands and arms around my body. Several military policemen were doing an outstanding job separating the two of us. They were equally as proficient applying handcuffs. The bowling alley attendant rushed over to where I was lying prostrate on the floor beneath the weight of at least one MP. He gave him my ID card and said, "Not him. He's the lieutenant!"

For the next hour or so, I completed the paperwork which described the incident. Then I went across the street to my quarters. I fell asleep thinking that I had not even been 12 hours in Berlin and already I had been in a knife fight with an American druggie. What would it be like when I met the British, the French, and, most eerily, the Russians?

But before that would happen I wanted to meet the Berliners. I awoke early the next morning, hoping for a calmer second day in Berlin. I was about to enter the bathroom and shower when I heard a knock at my door. Wearing only my Hanes, 28"-30" white briefs, which my mother had continued to buy me every year for my birthday, I answered the door. Standing there was a very distinguished looking, middle-aged man who asked, "Lieutenant Pelosi?"

I responded, "Yes."

"I'm General Tiner. Good job last night."

I quickly straightened my posture, stood more erectly, and moved more visibly from behind the door to face the Commanding General.

"Yes, Sir! Thank you, Sir!"

General Tiner asked me, "Can you get dressed and meet me in about 30 minutes in the cafeteria at the PX?"

"Yes, Sir,"

"Fine. I want to talk to you about what happened at the bowling alley."

"Yes, Sir," was becoming my standard response. Then I came to my senses. I said, "Excuse me, Sir, but I don't know where the cafeteria or the PX is."

He laughed, and told me, "Get dressed. My aide will take me there now and then he will come back and get you."

When I met the General, I immediately apologized for my lack of proper dress at our first meeting. He said that he had noticed some bruises on my arms and upper torso and he asked me if I had sought any medical attention. I told him that I had not and that I felt fine. He suggested that I get myself checked at a base clinic or the hospital.

General Tiner told me that the Command's teams of law-enforcement agents had been working for almost two years to "snag this guy," and that I had managed to snag him less than eight hours after I had arrived in Berlin.

"Just a coincidence, Sir."

"Coincidence or not, when he was strip searched we found 57 packets of extremely dangerous heroin taped to his body. He'll be off the street and away for a long time."

I never was told and I never asked the identity of the soldier.

As promised, my sponsor met me at the apartment Monday morning.

"Did you get to see any of Berlin?"

"I did."

I told him that I toured most of the weekend and that I cut short my day on Sunday so that I could hit the rack early and be ready for whatever anyone had planned for me today in the unit.

Then he asked, "Did you do anything Friday night?"

"Well, sort of. . ." I began.

I finished the story with his car stopped and parked at the PX gas station and my sponsor wide-eyed and staring at me in disbelief.

He asked me, "Does the CO (Commanding Officer for my company) or the colonel (CO for my battalion) know anything about this?"

"I don't know. I didn't tell anyone except you just now."

Not knowing how the Army functions after incidents like this, I added, "Maybe the General said something to one of them."

Second Platoon.

That Monday morning, my very first day in the unit, when I was introduced to the Second Platoon, there were 40 soldiers all with looks on their faces trying to figure out the real identity of the Criminal Investigation Division (CID) agent who was assigned to their platoon and was pretending to be an infantry lieutenant.

Activities related to in-processing consumed all of the first week and much of the first month. In addition to the members of the Second Platoon, I met the other officers and senior non-commissioned officers (NCO's) within my company, many of those within the four other companies of the battalion, and those assigned to the battalion staff. Of the six officers in Bravo Company, only the CO was a combat veteran who had served in Vietnam. However, the First Sergeant, all four of the platoon sergeants, (Sergeants First Class (SFC), E-7), more than half of the 16 squad leaders and support NCO's such as the armorer and the communications chief, (Staff Sergeants (SSG),

E-6), and perhaps ten percent of the more junior-enlisted men were Vietnam veterans.

There was an acute awareness of the irony of a younger man with no combat experience assigned by the Army in a position senior to and responsible for the combat training of older, more-experienced veterans. These soldiers were not only exceptionally respectful, but they also were highly motivated and willing to share their combat lessons. Over time, I realized that I was learning much more from them about my job than I was able to teach them about theirs.

By the end of my first month, I had drawn my field uniforms and TA-50 gear (helmet, flak vest, rucksack, cold-weather clothing, and winter boots). I also had signed for a weapon and a protective mask. The armorer attempted to issue me a 45-caliber pistol which he said was the weapon that had been assigned to the five other officers in the unit. I told him that, during training on the marksmanship ranges, I had been an absolutely ineffective marksman with the 45. The only way I would be effective with a 45 as a weapon would be if I were able to throw it at someone at very close range, hit him in the head, and either knock him out or kill him. I asked for an M-16 rifle and was issued one without any further discussion. With the M-16 I was respectably proficient as a marksman. I did hope to be equally proficient if the balloon went up in Berlin and my skills as marksman were needed.

During that first month I sat through classes about the "History of Berlin," "Respect due our Allies," "The Berlin Local Transportation System," "Customs and Courtesies in Europe and Germany," and "Do's and Don'ts While Wearing the Uniform in Public." We took a bus tour in duty uniforms of the several bases and the support facilities within the Berlin Brigade and the Allied units within West Berlin. There also was a second bus tour, with everyone wearing Dress Green uniforms, of Checkpoint Charlie and East Berlin. The contrast with West Berlin was startling.

The Commanding General had directed that all newly-assigned officers who did not speak German enroll in German-language classes and attain a minimum Level II proficiency (conversational). Classes were conducted twice a week in the evenings at the Army Education Center. I enrolled and enjoyed a laugh when the men from the deep south would say, in their heavily accented drawls, "Good day, Sir" as "Goaten Tauwk, Maynah Hayeah."

The club system was separated into facilities which hosted officers and those which hosted enlisted men. Fraternization among the ranks on a regular basis when alcohol was involved was frowned upon and considered potentially detrimental to the good order and discipline of a unit. As often as once a month, however, the Enlisted Club would host a "Bring Your Boss Night" when members could host their officers, and the Officers' Club would reciprocate and host an "NCO Appreciation Night" when members could host their non-commissioned officers.

The platoon sergeant and squad leaders invited me to one such function on "Payday Friday," the last Friday of my first month in Berlin. The effects of some great-tasting German beer and some mystery meat from the buffet table tempered much of the strict formality among the ranks when on duty and at the unit. By the end of evening, the senior sergeants were well convinced that I was a genuine infantry lieutenant and not an agent for the CID as several of the junior-enlisted soldiers kept insisting. However, there were two junior sergeants, team-leader Sergeants (SGT) E-5, who, after everyone else had left, pretended to be not so sure about my status.

Nicholas from Pennsylvania and Stephen from Virginia both were in their early 20's. Instead of waiting to be drafted for a two-year term of service, and probably sent to combat duty in Vietnam, each had decided to enlist for three years, and each had been offered his choice of either a duty position or a duty location. Both wanted to see Europe. Both chose Berlin. Both were assigned to the infantry.

They were intelligent, made rank quickly, and had no intention of making the Army a career. When their terms of enlistment were completed, they both planned to return to their hometowns and use the GI Bill to fund a college education.

We drank two more rounds of beer which they bought. The third round was on me. I knew that I was nearing my limit of alcohol when the mystery meat began to taste good. It took a little time before one of them offered to tell me the history of the "New Officer Induction" ritual into the unit. According to them there was a tradition that all newly-assigned officers had to experience before the enlisted men under their command would accept them, trust them and follow them into hell.`

"Oh, really? What might that tradition entail?"

"Actually sir, it's more like a test. There are three parts that you have to pass with one of us as a witness."

"Three parts to one test? Okay, tell me. What are they?"

"Well, first you have to take us out with the platoon and not get lost. Then you have to go out with us, drink Jägermeister and not puke. Last, and this is the best part, you have to go out on a date with us and some girls, and go all the way with the girl who we find for you."

"Is that all?"

"Yes, sir. That's it."

"Do I get to veto the girl if I think that she's not too attractive or not my type?"

Rather quickly one of them responded, "Sir, you've been in Berlin long enough to know there aren't any nasty-ass girls in this city. They're all keepers. But you have to go out with one of the girls who's with us.

Then I asked, "So you say this is a regular tradition in the company?

"Yes, Sir."

"And the CO", (whom the troops affectionately referred to as "Mad Merc"), "and Lieutenant Pallone", (a Mormon who drank only water and herbal tea), "all have done this and passed?"

"Yes, Sir."

I decided to play along and ask when we could get started. I also asked if I would earn a diploma or a certificate of completion if I passed. They hadn't thought about that so I didn't get an answer.

The land-navigation patrol in the training area within Berlin's Grunewald was easy, although no maps were entirely accurate. Throughout the woods, there were soft trails and paved paths that were longer and wider than the marked, hard-surface roads. It was easy to get lost without the combined use of a map, compass, dead reckoning, and a pace count.

Jägermeister, which in German means "Master of Hunter," is an herbal liqueur, 70 percent proof, made from more than 50 ingredients of herbs, fruits, roots, and spices. It has a dark brown color and consistency of motor oil, and exactly the same taste for a non-German, first-time drinker. All three of us put up brave fronts, but none of us could get past three shots and three strong beers to chase down the terrible taste. Since we all three failed, I was credited with a pass.

I was a stranger to the three girls whom we met one Friday night. They all were well known to my two companions for more than a year. All three had been well briefed about the details of how the night should develop and end. Poor Monika must have drawn the short straw and ended up with me as her companion. She was very attractive with shoulder-length brown hair, deep green eyes, and a perfect complexion absent any make-up. When she smiled, her whole face lit up. Monika was exceptionally gracious and polite. She never criticized my beginner's-level German except to say "They do not teach you in school how we really speak German on the street. They are too formal."

The next morning on the way back to the base, I dodged all the questions about how my evening and night developed. Before we parted company, Sergeants Nicholas and Stephen for some much-needed rest in the barracks and I for the same reason back at my quarters, I heard one of them say, "Hey Sir, we always knew you weren't a CID agent. The diploma is in the mail."

Team Womack.

The second month in Berlin brought additional surprises and challenges for me. The McNair Kaserne and the facilities within it may have been among the best-built and well-maintained buildings which hosted the American military in Europe. The funds paid to build and maintain the structures were provided primarily by the German taxpayers who supported the majority of the expenses of the Allied forces that were deployed in an occupation status.

The barracks where the soldiers lived were shared by sergeants and junior-enlisted men on duty in a bachelor status, that is, single or married but deployed without their families. A large bay for the junior-enlisted men in the ranks of Private E-1 (PV1) through Specialist E-4 (SP4) was furnished with between six and eight beds and wall lockers, and one writing desk and chair. A slightly smaller bay for non-commissioned officers in the ranks of Corporal (CPL) E4 through Sergeant First Class (SFC) E7 was furnished with between two and four beds and wall lockers, and one or two writing desks and chairs. Every attempt was made to billet non-commissioned officers in shared bays with other non-commissioned officers of the same rank or within one rank senior or junior. The most-senior non-commissioned officers, Master Sergeant (MSG) E-8 and Sergeant Major (SGM) E-9, deployed in a bachelor status were provided private quarters in the off-base housing areas.

At 5 a.m. on a duty morning the junior non-commissioned officers, corporals and sergeants, would pass through the junior-enlisted bays and wake the soldiers to start the duty day. At 6 a.m., the entire company would form for Physical Readiness Training (PT) which consisted of calisthenics and a run usually between two and three miles. Before assembly for formation, soldiers would attend to their personal hygiene, dress in their PT uniforms, make their bunks, and arrange their personal property in their wall lockers. After PT the soldiers would shower then hustle off to the mess hall for breakfast. Morning training usually began at 8 a.m.

In garrison, the Second Platoon sergeant and I often had breakfast together. One morning, he asked me if we could alter the routine slightly and have three of my four squad leaders join us. At the table, everyone focused on me when Staff Sergeant Ed Edmundson, a red-haired country boy from Arkansas said, "Sir, you have to help us."

Sergeant Edmundson continued, "Sir, it's Sergeant Womack," referring to Staff Sergeant (SSG) Sammie Womack, the weapons squad leader. Before he joined the Army, Sammie Norman Womack was a Farmville, Virginia neighborhood basketball player who stood 6'5" and weighed 250 pounds.

"I don't know if you know that Sergeant Womack was a POW (Prisoner of War) in Vietnam. We don't know how long ago that was or how long he was a POW. But we know that the VC (Vietcong) kept marching him from place to place and chaining him to a tree every night when they slept. They were afraid of him because he was so big. One night, the VC didn't secure him too tightly and he broke free from the chains. He told us that he roared like a lion and ran away from the VC. He said that the VC, weapons and all, ran in the opposite direction. But he was recaptured a day or two later."

"Sir, Sergeant Womack has these terrible nightmares almost every night. He starts screaming in his sleep; wakes himself up; gets out of the bed covered in sweat; and, leaves the room. Sometimes he comes back right away. Sometimes he's gone for a few hours. Sometimes he's gone until morning formation. We can't get any sleep. Whatever is happening can't be any good for him. We don't even know why he's still in the Army. Can you help us and do something for him?"

Part of the story about SSG Sammie Womack as a prisoner of the Vietcong is described in Neil Sheehan's 1989 Pulitzer Prize winning book, "A Bright Shining Lie. John Paul Vann and America in Vietnam," an engrossing history of almost everything good and bad, but considered normal in every war. It describes in detail the effects on the nations that prosecuted the war and on those people who fought it.

Born on August 8, 1944, Staff Sergeant E-6 Womack was a Sergeant E-5 squad leader in 1966, on duty in Vietnam in Charlie Company, 2d Battalion, 27th Infantry, 25th Infantry Division. He was 22 years old and in an area near Tan Son Nhut Airfield on October 22, 1966, when his company was surprised and ambushed as it moved through an open area in a series of rice paddies. The unit was wiped out by a numerically superior Vietcong force. Sergeant Womack was captured and marched north.

He arrived at a VC POW camp and was imprisoned there together with three other Americans: an Army Private and a Marine Corps Captain who had been captured two years earlier in December 1964, and a civilian USAID worker who had been captured in January 1966. These four men were moved almost daily among several way stations and camps hidden in the dense jungle of South Vietnam close to the border with Cambodia. At night they were roped together beneath bamboo lean-to's, chained, or enclosed in bamboo cages known as "tiger cages."

Prior to the Vietnamese Lunar New Year of Tet, in 1967, the Vietcong made a goodwill gesture and released Staff Sergeant Womack, a black POW, together with Private Charles E. Crafts, a white POW, who had been held for 787 days. Before obtaining his freedom after four months in captivity, the wounded and injured Sergeant Womack had been tortured, starved with a diet of water, manioc, bamboo shoots and rats, and stricken with malaria. SSG Womack's status as a member of Second Platoon immediately became my first priority of work. I spoke with him at length. His stories about his time in Vietnam came very reluctantly. He never talked about his fear or his bravery. It wasn't until early afternoon when I was able to describe what I knew about SSG Womack to my company commander.

With the Commander's help we were able to relocate him and all of his personal property to an unused storage room with a private entrance and a window. Two problems remained. The first was not having anyone as a companion at night with SSG Womack who could monitor any serious disturbances and react if necessary. The second was understanding his physical and mental condition and determining what his future should be with whatever time he had remaining in the Army.

The next morning some help arrived. A Chinese-American junior enlisted man, Specialist E-4 James Chiew, was assigned to the company and sent to Second Platoon. The platoon was short one 90 mm recoilless rifle (RR) team of two persons: the gunner and the loader-ammunition carrier. The crew was part of the eight-man weapons squad which was led by SSG Womack. The other six members of his squad were the second recoilless rifle team and two M-60 machine gun teams each consisting of one gunner and one loader-ammunition carrier. In training and in combat, the teams within the weapons squad are detached and assigned to the three maneuver rifle squads within the platoon. The weapons squad leader acts in support of the platoon sergeant and the rifle squad leaders wherever he may be most needed.

Within an infantry platoon, a 90 mm recoilless rifle is a formidable crew-served weapon as valuable as a machine gun. It is an anti-tank, bunker-busting weapon with a length of almost five feet and a weight of almost 40 pounds. One round of ammunition weighs almost 10 pounds.

Specialist Chiew was born on May 2, 1947. He enlisted in the Army on March 14, 1968 and was sent to Vietnam. He arrived just after the Tet offensive on January 30, 1968, when more than 80,000 North Vietnamese Army regulars and Vietcong attacked Saigon and more than 100 towns and cities. It was an event which changed the American perspective on the war. He was wounded on November 26, 1969 and medically evacuated through several facilities to Letterman Army Hospital in San Francisco. There he was awarded a Purple Heart, treated for his wounds, and discharged honorably. He came back into the Army with his rank of Specialist E-4 on March 25, 1972. After a short period of training, reduced in scope for prior-service personnel, he was assigned to Berlin.

SP4 Chiew stood only 5'6" and may have weighed 125 pounds. He was small and thin, not wiry and not muscled. He was dwarfed by SSG Womack at 6'5" and 215 pounds. SP4 Chiew was only six inches taller than the length of a 90 mm. recoilless rifle which was one-third his weight.

Within Second Platoon there were no vacancies for rifleman within the three rifle squads. A rifleman was armed with an M-16 which weighs seven pounds and which fires a small 5.56 mm round of ammunition weighing only four ounces. No rifleman was willing to exchange positions with SP4 Chiew and trade his M-16 weighing only seven pounds for a recoilless rifle weighing almost 40 pounds.

In the vernacular of the military, I made a "command decision." With the entire Second Platoon assembled I related the story of SSG Womack's combat experiences in Vietnam and his time in captivity as a prisoner of the Vietcong. I told them all that, in my opinion, SSG Womack had served his time as a soldier in war and training for war. Those days now are over. His duty, for as long as I continued to command the Second Platoon, would be to spend his time building SP4 Chiew into his physical image: muscled and powerful. Both SSG Womack and SP4 Chiew would form "Team Womack." They would be excused from all platoon training for Special Duty.

SP4 Chiew was ordered to follow SSG Womack in the chow line for breakfast and put on his mess tray the same food items that SSG Womack selected. After a full and sufficient meal they could rest and plan their day. Their next team task was to hit the gym where SSG Womack would act as the personal trainer for SP4 Chiew five days a week between 9 and 11 a.m. Following weight training, SP4 Chiew again would shadow SSG Womack in the chow line at lunch and load his mess tray similarly. Mid-afternoons, between 2 and 4 p.m., were dedicated to forced-march conditioning. SSG Womack, in duty uniform, would lead SP4 Chiew, in duty uniform and carrying a rucksack, on conditioning marches. Each week, the weight in the rucksack and the distance walked would increase slightly as SP4 Chiew gained weight, built muscle, and grew stronger. Supper, under conditions the same as breakfast and lunch, ended the day for the two-member Team Womack.

The members of Second Platoon always shouted encouragement to Team Womack whenever we passed each other. The troops chuckled at the image of huge SSG Womack alongside the barely visible SP4 Chiew as they walked on base or did pushups and sit-ups on the sports fields. Within a year, SP4 Chiew had added 20 pounds of solid muscle. Team Womack was deactivated. At the time of this narrative, Second Platoon and Team Womack were an experience 41 years in my past. Almost every week of every month of every year since then, I have received a letter from Mr. James Chiew, now retired and living with his family in Vancouver, Washington. His letters all end with the same words, "You are always in my thoughts and prayers, James."

Special Duty.

The duty of an infantry second lieutenant in peacetime is not limited to training soldiers to close with and destroy the enemy by means of fire and maneuver. There always are additional duties within the unit, such as safety, motor, training, voting, assistance, and income tax assistance officer.

In my third month in Berlin and just before Christmas my company commander ordered me to report to the battalion adjutant for special duty. The adjutant informed me that I would serve as the representative of the battalion commander as his survivor assistance officer to support the family of a junior-enlisted soldier who just died. Private Michael Castor was found dead in his bunk in the barracks as a result of an overdose of heroin. A tourniquet, syringe, needle, and residue were found at his bedside. Private Castor was 19 years old.

His body was removed from the barracks and prepared for return to his family in the United States. His commander and other members of his immediate chain of command inventoried and secured his property. My job was to confirm the inventory and prepare the property for shipment to his family.

Consistent with Army procedures for the performance of this duty, I sent out a notice within the Berlin Command announcing the death of Private Castor. The notice included a request that I be contacted by anyone in possession of any of his personal property, anyone who may have loaned property to Private Castor, or anyone to whom Private Castor may have incurred a debt. At the end of two weeks, I had not received any responses, and I noted that on the summary sheet detailing my activities in chronological order.

From his commander, I obtained access to Private Castor's personal effects. After I confirmed the inventory, and again in accordance with Army procedures, I scanned or read everything which was written and was contained within his effects. I scanned books and magazines for anything pornographic or profane. There was nothing. I read notebooks and mail for any content that would be offensive if read by his family. Again, there was nothing.

Next, I brought all his uniforms and personal clothing to a laundry where the items were washed, folded, and ironed, if appropriate. His dress uniforms and dress clothing such as suits, sport coats, shirts, ties, and slacks were dry cleaned. I cleaned and shined his military boots and shoes and washed his personal footwear. After I had completed these tasks I made arrangements through the command transportation office to pack and deliver Private Castor's personal effects to his family.

The packers contacted me the day after I made the request and informed me that they would arrive at Private Castor's unit the following morning at 9 a.m. That morning, I arrived at the unit at 6 a.m. to pick up the property and to make a final confirmation of the inventory. In my rush, I had skipped breakfast.

The packing crew arrived exactly at 9 a.m. The crew was composed of three German contract laborers none of whom spoke English. Here was an opportunity to practice my Level II conversational German. The boss, "Chef" in German, used my inventory but prepared his own copy on which half the words were in German. The other crew members selected the items for packing, identified them for the inventory, then placed them carefully into the cardboard containers. The process went slower than I would have expected, first, because of the care with which the effects were packed, and second, because of difficulty I had translating the items on my inventory into German. I had not thought to bring an English-German dictionary and I did not want to leave the packers while they were working to find one.

The crew finished the inventory and the packing at about the same time that the mess hall was closing after lunch. There still was one more

formality which had to be completed. After the cardboard boxes had been taped closed, the procedures specified that all six sides of each box must be labeled with the words, "Effects of Deceased Personnel." I did my best to use all my Level II German language skills and describe that formal requirement to the "Chef."

Then, I told him that while he and his crew were labeling the six sides of the eight boxes, I would excuse myself for no more than five minutes to run downstairs to the mess hall to grab a sandwich before it closed. I should have eaten breakfast.

In the mess hall, I met the battalion commander. He had seen the government moving van outside, and he asked me how my special duty assignment was progressing. I described the events of the morning to him.

He said, "Sounds good. Let's go take a look."

Upstairs the team was finishing the labeling on the eighth box. On six sides of the seven other boxes, which within two weeks would be delivered to the grieving parents of Private Castor, was handwritten in thick, black magic-marker letters, "PERSON IST DED."

Oops!

The battalion commander and I each looked at one another with the same expression of surprise and shock on our faces.

I said to my commander, "Well, Sir. I guess my Level II German is not **as good as I thought it was."**

Spandau Prison.

Six months into my assignment, in March 1974, my commander informed me that Second Platoon would support a duty assignment next month in April at Spandau Prison in the British sector of Berlin. Spandau Prison was built in 1876 as a military prison. In 1919, offenders from the civilian community also were imprisoned there. After Hitler came to power in 1933, Spandau Prison added the enemies of the Third Reich to its inmates. After the end of World War II in 1945, and the end of the Nuremburg Trials in 1947, the four-nation Allies appropriated the facility to imprison the seven former senior members of the Third Reich found guilty of war crimes at Nuremberg.

Deputy Reichsführer Rudolf Hess was one of those seven prisoners.

Rudolf Hess was born on April 26, 1894, in Alexandria, Egypt. He was the son of a successful merchant who owned a trading firm. As a soldier in World War I, Hess was wounded several times and was discharged at the end of the war in 1918.

Two years later, his fellow World War I veteran, Adolf Hitler, who also had been wounded in the war, spoke at a Nazi Party rally in Munich. Hitler vilified the terms of the Treaty of Versailles and condemned the victorious Allies and certain segments of the German population, especially the communists and the Jews, for Germany's defeat and for the on-going recession. He promised reform and the rebirth of a new, vigorous, and glorious Germany through his leadership and the Nazi Party.

Sold on Hitler's philosophy and leadership, Rudolf Hess joined the Nazi Party and became Hitler's close friend as well as his personal and professional confidant. In 1933, after Hitler became Reich Chancellor and Führer he appointed Hess as his Deputy Reichsführer, the number-two man in Nazi Germany. Beginning in 1935, Hitler used the power of his office and the might of Germany's military to recover territory once controlled by Germany, and to seize territory that bordered on Germany and hosted large German populations sympathetic to the Nazi Party. Hitler's continued aggression started World War II after Germany invaded Poland on September 1, 1939.

By 1941, Hitler's Third Reich had marched its armies to a victorious war, and occupied most of Western Europe, half of Scandinavia, and parts of northern Africa. Hess knew of Hitler's plan to break Germany's non-aggression pact with the Soviet Union and the plans to invade her sometime in the summer of 1941. Fearing disastrous results for Germany, which after the invasion would be fighting a war on two over-extended fronts, Hess fled Germany.

He flew a twin-engine, Messerschmitt 110 E-1/N, an unarmed fighter-bomber from an airfield in Bavaria, located near the Messerschmitt headquarters, factories, and airfields, to England. There, he hoped to contact a person of influence in the British leadership and arrange for peace between Great Britain and Germany. Flying at night, Hess, a trained and skilled pilot, became disoriented. His aircraft ran out of fuel, and he was forced to parachute over Scotland before his plane crashed. He landed in a field and was captured by a local farmer who was armed with only a pitchfork. He marched Hess to his home where his mother offered him tea and aid for an injury to his leg, both of which Hess refused. The local Home Guard arrived and relieved the farmer of his prisoner.

Claiming to be Luftwaffe Captain Alfred Horn "with a message for the Duke of Hamilton," Hess was declared a prisoner of war and transferred among various units to several holding facilities until his true identity and mission could be verified.

Eventually, on June 26, 1942, Rudolf Hess was sent to Maindiff Court Hospital in Wales. He remained there under guard, but with opportunities for recreation, until after the end of World War II. On October 10, 1945, he was transported by the British to Nuremberg, Germany, to stand trial for war crimes.

In his role as Deputy Reichsführer, Rudolf Hess was found guilty of two of the four crimes with which he was charged. On October 1, 1946, Hess was sentenced to life imprisonment. He began serving that sentence in Spandau Prison on July 18, 1947.

In April 1974, Hess was the only inmate in a prison originally built to house 600 prisoners. He had been a prisoner there for nearly 27 years. He was guarded by soldiers from the four armies of the former World War II allies: France, Great Britain, the Soviet Union, and the United States. They performed this duty in a rotational order every month by providing a guard force composed of one officer and 37 enlisted men. This guard force composition conformed precisely to the protocol established by the Allies when they assumed control of Spandau Prison in 1947. The protocol provided for the guard force to be armed. Guards were armed with rifles and two three-round magazines, one of which was chambered when the guard was on duty.

Because Spandau prison was located in the free Western sector of Berlin, the Soviet guards were locked inside the prison immediately upon their arrival at the beginning of the month and released upon departure at the end of the month. The Soviets feared that the junior-enlisted men, armed with weapons and ammunition, would mutiny; shoot their officer; and seek asylum in the West. One dead Soviet officer and 37 defectors in the free West presented an unacceptable set of circumstances for the Soviet leadership in the East. The solution to preclude mutiny and murder was to guarantee no chance of escape for any potential traitors.

Soldiers from Great Britain served on guard duty in January, May, and September, then changed guard duty with the French who served in February, June, and October. The Soviets served in March, July, and November, then passed the duty to the Americans who served in April, August, and December.

The military forces of the Berlin Brigade included three infantry battalions. These three battalions performed what was termed, "Spandau Guard Duty," on a yearly rotational basis.

On April 1, 1974, one officer and 37 enlisted men, from the Berlin Brigade's Honor Guard and Ceremonial Detail changed guard at Spandau with an identical-sized force from a military unit of the Soviet Union assigned in the East. Later, the ceremonial detail was replaced by 38 members of the Second Platoon, Bravo Company, 3rd Battalion, 6th Infantry Regiment.

After the guard force was transitioned, I secured my property and went into the bowels of the administrative area of the prison to find my room and store my gear. The room was furnished with a single bed, wall locker, cabinet with shelves containing reading materials in the languages of the Allies, mini-fridge, and a writing desk at which was seated a Soviet senior lieutenant.

He rose when I entered and saluted me. I returned his salute. I was 23 years old and he probably was 10 years older than I and twice my size. In nearly perfect English he said, "Excuse me. I did not expect you so soon. I am now finishing report for administrator."

Then he asked me, "Do you speak Russian?"

"No, I do not. Sorry. Not one word."

He snickered and said, "I speak almost exactly English. I can pick up enemy radio on battlefield and use radio to direct enemy unit into Soviet fire and win battle."

I thought, "Well, that's a fine how do you do. So I'm the enemy, huh?"

The only response I could think of was, "Comrade, if you learned English just to be able to do that then you wasted your time. Please go ahead and finish your report."

I left and told myself that I never would be at that sort of disadvantage again. I decided to try to learn to speak Russian at the education center where I still was trying to learn to speak German.

The platoon's guard force was organized into one officer of the guard; two senior non-commissioned officers of the guard; five non-commissioned officers, sergeants of the guard; and, 30 junior-enlisted members of the guard.

Technically, I was on duty for 24 hours daily. I tended to my personal hygiene, ate, and slept whenever I was able. Fortunately for the enlisted men of all ranks, those soldiers in any unit who always bear the burden of the actual work, the daily schedule was not as rigorous. There was sufficient off-duty time for hygiene, meals, sleep, and recreation.

The platoon sergeant and weapons-squad leader served as the senior non-commissioned officers of the guard force. They were on duty daily for 12-hour shifts.

The three rifle squad leaders and their two senior team leaders served as the four sergeants of the guard in three consecutive shifts of three hours. They were on duty for nine hours and off duty for 21 hours. The fifth sergeant of the guard was a "roamer," serving wherever and whenever someone needed relief.

The 30 junior-enlisted men performed their duty in five squads of six men each. Each soldier served for three hours in one of the six guard towers that formed an elongated horseshoe around the prison. After their three-hour tour, the tower guards were off duty for 12 hours.

In addition to the details of our guard force mission, I taught these soldiers the history of Nazi Germany and the role and reputation of "Prisoner Number Seven." It also was important for me that, someday in the future, these young soldiers could tell their families that they had the opportunity to be up close, but not personal, with the man who once had been Hitler's deputy, close friend, and confidant. In the guard towers, less than 30 yards away from where Hess took his walks twice daily in the mornings and in the afternoons, the guards would be able to view a living relic who represented 45 years of Nazi history. Many of their fathers and close family relatives had fought in Europe during World War II against the war machine and the tyranny that this man had helped create.

Cameras were forbidden within the prison. There would be no photos. The guards would have only their memories from which to relate their stories. Before the end of April, every member of the guard force had the opportunity to see the once-proud, former Deputy Reichsführer at least twice.

During the day, a British warder managed the affairs for Hess: hygiene, meals, laundry, privileges, and communications. The warder was responsible for everything for which Hess was entitled according to the Allied protocol.

The primary responsibility of the officer of the guard was to supervise the guard force. However, there were several pseudo-official duties that supported the warder. One was the daily opportunity to inspect the trays containing the meals for Hess. An inspection sheet was provided on the tray to verify the contents which the warder delivered into the room for Hess, and to record what had been consumed after the tray was returned. The protocol required that Hess consume a specific number of calories daily and that the amount was recorded. His not eating, or eating less than what was provided, would be an indication of potential medical, physical, or mental problems that might require intervention and/or professional attention.

One morning, I inspected and verified the contents of his breakfast tray. Later, after the tray was returned I noticed that Hess had not eaten the soft boiled egg. The warder told me that Hess refused to eat it because "it was runny and not prepared properly."

I thought that his sentiment was inappropriately brazen for someone of his status. Hess was alive; he was eating and exercising; he could visit with his wife and son; all of this 28 years after seven of his co-defendants at Nuremberg had been hanged.

I took the egg off the tray, brought it to my room, and put it in my mini-fridge. That same evening, the contents of his dinner tray included a green salad. I took my issue bayonet and chopped up the formerly runny, and now hard-boiled, egg and sprinkled it on top of the salad. The warder brought the dinner tray in to Hess. Later, the tray was returned with all the food contents consumed.

When I saw that I said, under my breath, "Well I got you, you worthless Nazi! This month, like it or not, you'll eat everything that someone has prepared to keep you alive, and for what reason, I do not know."

Very soon, on April 26th, Hess would be 80 years old. For years the Western Allies, supported by a fair representation of the German population, had been negotiating with the Soviets for his release. They argued that Nuremberg established that:

(1) he fled Germany 18 months after World War II began and four years before it ended; (2) he had fled to seek peace before the war expanded; (3) he

had been imprisoned since 1941, more than 30 years; and, (4) he had paid his debt to the international community.

None of that mattered to the Soviets who had suffered the loss of more than 20 million citizens and the inestimable destruction of its major cities and motherland. Soviet statistics reflect that of all Soviet males born in 1923 an estimated 80 percent did not survive the war. Hess should and would die in Spandau.

His 80th birthday, a Friday, was a serious concern for the Western Allies in general and for the United States Army in Berlin in particular. The civilian and military leadership feared demonstrations to support the release of Hess had the potential to become violent. As a precaution, the guard force had ready reaction teams that were trained to reinforce the on-duty guards, enhance the security of the prison at key locations, and prepared to protect personnel and property.

In addition, the senior non-commissioned officers and I had been provided a four-inch by six-inch laminated card printed in German and English with a statement to be read to individuals and groups who might assemble at the prison on his birthday. When that happened, a guard would call to the command post, (our recreation room), using the telephone in his tower, and report the number of people assembled and give his assessment of the situation. Whatever the guard reported, I would decide on an appropriate course of action and act. There was not a history of violent protests in Berlin. I expected that either one of the two senior non-commissioned officers or I only would have to exit the prison and read the statement from the card to the persons assembled.

On the card was written:

1. Guten Tag.
   (Good day.)

2. Spandau Gefängnis ist eine Alliierte militärische Einrichtung
(Spandau Prison is an Allied military facility.)

3. Ich vertrete der Kommandant der Anlage.
   (I represent the Commander of the facility.)

4. Es ist verboten in diesem Bereich zu sammeln.
   (It is forbidden to assemble in this area.)

5. Bitte, gehen Sie nach Hause.
   (Please, return to your homes.)

6. Die Wachen sind befugt, zu schießen.
   (The guards are authorized to shoot.)

Just before lunch, while four senior non-commissioned officers and I were engaged heavily in a friendly game of cards, Private First Class Clayton Vount called from Tower One. He reported that about a dozen people had gathered on the sidewalk across the street from the prison, and that some had crossed the street. Now they were directly in front of the prison where they were trying to peer through the front gate. He added that many had cameras.

I asked one of the sergeants to pass me the card and I started to get up. Sergeant First Class (SFC) Jimmy Minot, my platoon sergeant and senior non-commissioned officer of the guard, stopped me.

He said, "Stay here and keep losing L.T," (informal soldier slang for "Lieutenant"). "I'll take care of this."

SFC Minot, in the image of Daniel Boone minus the facial hair, constantly bragged that he was born to be an infantryman. Hailing from Red Bay, Alabama, he told everyone that it took him "two terms to get through the eighth grade – Eisenhower's and Kennedy's," and that, "I joined the Army as soon as I turned 18. I tried to join when I turned 17, but I never could locate either of my parents to sign the permission."

On the Second Platoon's internal and unofficial personnel record, in the section, "Weapons with which you are Qualified," he had handwritten, "guns, anything that shoots, bow an arow, knifs, clubs, hands."

I stayed behind, remained playing cards, and kept losing. Time passed. I just had finished commenting that, "Sergeant Minot must be jaw-jacking with the locals. I wonder what he could be doing for so long?" Just then, the telephone rang.

Private First Class Vount sounded excited when he said, "Sir, you better come out here."

"What's wrong?"

"I don't rightly know, Sir. But every time Sergeant Minot reads that card the Germans break up laughing, grab and shake each other, then run and get more folks from inside that bar across the street. He reads the card again and they do the same damn thing. More people keep coming. I can't figure it out."

I told him, "I'll be right there," and left losing at cards to someone else.

I found SFC Minot standing in front of a group that now had swelled to about 30 persons. I asked him what was happening.

"The hell if I know, Sir. They think this whole thing is a joke. They're hootin' and hollerin' for no reason. Probably been drinkin' all mornin' and refuse to go home like the card says."

"Go ahead, Sergeant Minot, read the card again."

The reaction by those assembled was the same – raucous laughter – and this time, I was laughing too.

"Damn, Sir. What the foxtrot is the matter?"

SFC Minot, after more than two years in Berlin, did not know a single word in German, except for the word, "bier," which, when spoken, sounds exactly like "beer" in English.

At the last word of the last sentence, he was pronouncing the word, "schießen," which means "to shoot," as "scheißen," which translates "to sh*t."

He gave me the card and walked away complaining, "Why the hell would anyone want to live in a city with a wall around it?"

The rest of that day and our final four days on Spandau Guard Duty were uneventful.

All of us were happy to go home.

Second Platoon returned from Spandau Prison late morning, Tuesday, May 1, 1974. After accounting for all personnel, weapons, ammunition, and equipment, the platoon was dismissed on pass through the weekend. The company commander granted the returned guard force an extended training holiday beginning immediately and extending through Sunday, May 5th.

The married soldiers wasted no time exiting the barracks to drive to their quarters and be reunited with their families. The single soldiers showered then ate lunch in the mess hall where they found a far greater variety of food and beverages than what they had been consuming the past 30 days. After chow they either hit the rack for some much-needed rest or stormed the enlisted club to become reacquainted with the taste of alcohol after surviving a mandatory 30-day abstinence.

There, among their fellow soldiers who never had performed Spandau Guard Duty and never even heard of Spandau prison and its purpose, they let the alcohol help them invent stories of greater and greater fantasy about fighting with the Russians, confronting protesters, and harassing Hitler's best friend, Rudy.

I went nowhere.

The Airlift Anniversary.

The commander brought me into his office and informed me that the senior civilian and military leadership in West Germany and Berlin would celebrate the 25th anniversary of the formal end of the Berlin Airlift, 1948-1949, on Sunday, May 12, 1974. That was the date on which the Soviets formally ended their blockade of Berlin. (Not trusting the Soviets to reimpose the blockade, the Allies continued to fly aid into Berlin through September 30, 1949.)

Perhaps because my father, former U.S. Air Force Captain James V. Pelosi, had flown C-47 and C-54 cargo aircraft in support of the Airlift, I was selected to serve as an escort officer for Brigadier General Frank "Howlin" Howley, United States Army, retired, and his family. General Howley had served as the United States military governor and as the commandant of the American sector of Berlin from 1945 until 1949.

My commander read a message from the State Department through the Berlin Brigade's chain of command addressed to me. It contained very few specifics and a lot of unknowns. I concluded that the reason for the paucity of information was because the message had been prepared by the dilatory State Department and not by the time-on-target military.

At a time to be determined on Sunday, May 12, 1974, there would be an official wreath–laying ceremony for a mostly-private, limited number of invitees at the Airlift Memorial at Berlin's Templehof Airport. The ceremony would be followed by a much larger 25th anniversary event open to everyone. An unknown number of unnamed representatives from the Federal Republic of Germany, the former Western Allies civilian and military leadership, and the City of Berlin would speak. The current Governing Mayor of Berlin was the only person identified by name. The area at Templehof Airport within which the anniversary event was to take place would be converted to an "Open House." Work was in progress to locate sources for heritage equipment, photographs, and other memorabilia. With only 11 days until the anniversary it seemed to me as if the organizers still had a mountain of work ahead of them.

The final part of the message concerned me specifically. I was directed to contact representatives in the command's protocol and public affairs offices as soon as possible after my return from Spandau.

"Jim, if you have nothing else to do here today then I suggest you get on this right away. Oh, by the way, there's a reason why General Howley has the nickname, 'Howlin Howley.' He has a reputation for being about as independent and as direct as you sometimes are. You two should get along just fine."

"Yes, Sir."

The commander's "right away" would be tomorrow. First, I wanted to get back to my apartment, clean up, dress in something other than a uniform, and call my parents, six time zones earlier, on the east coast of the United States. I was hoping that I could convince them to come to Berlin for the anniversary events. If my dad had not been invited to the ceremonies and receptions, I felt certain that I could help him crash the events. We all would have a good time.

I also needed to get a good night's sleep. As I drove up to my building, I could see my apartment. All of my indoor potted plants with a southern exposure from the windows had wilted. They were near death from a lack of water and nutrients after a month's neglect. From the street, my apartment looked like something from somewhere in Ethiopia.

I still was soaking in the tub when the telephone operator called and told me that she had made the connection to my party in the United States. My father, at age 50, still was working, and he took the call from his office. He told me that he would make flight arrangements for a one-week visit that would bracket the anniversary events. I reminded him to pack something formal for him and my mother. I asked him to bring his leather flight jacket, and any Airlift memorabilia that he could find.

The following morning at 8 a.m., I arrived at the headquarters building which contained the protocol and public affairs offices. Both offices were closed. There was no indication when anyone would arrive. For half an hour I walked between the two offices waiting for someone. A senior officer recognized me and asked me what I was doing "slumming around the head shed.." I told him and he said, "Come with me."

He took me to his office suite and, while I waited in the reception area, he went into his private office to make a telephone call.

"Come on in and sit down. Someone will be here shortly. While you wait, tell me, how was duty at Spandau?"

"Great learning experience, Sir, and a lot of history. I met a Russian lieutenant who says he's ready to go war with us."

The Colonel smiled and said, "Really? Maybe I should call his boss and tell him what he said. In a week he'll be freezing his ass off in Siberia looking at about a million Chinese infantry. He'll have to flush his English and learn Chinese."

There was a knock at his door and another field grade officer, junior to the Colonel, peeked in and said, "I'll take it from here, Sir. Come with me, Lieutenant Pelosi."

I looked at the Colonel. He nodded. I stood up, said, "Thank you, Sir," saluted and left.

Among his other duties, this officer had the responsibility for coordinating the itineraries and logistics of the general officers, their wives and families, and the officers assigned to escort them for the anniversary events. In addition to Brigadier General Howley, Lieutenant General William Tunner, former Commander of the United States Air Forces Europe and the Military Air Command; and, General Lucius Clay, Commander-in-Chief, United States Forces Europe and Military Governor, U.S. Occupation Forces, Germany, were expected to attend.

"Colonel Bonbon," more correctly, Gail Halvorsen, Colonel, United States Air Force, retired, whose aircraft dropped chocolates and candy in mini parachutes to the children in Berlin, had been invited together with an unknown number of American Airlift pilots.

For almost two hours, I was briefed on the plan and my duties to support each of the five days of the anniversary celebration. I would be occupied for almost a week with multiple trips to airports, hotels, government buildings, military bases, reception facilities, and the private residences of Berlin's most-distinguished citizens. There would be three military vehicles and drivers dedicated around the clock exclusively to me. Two were to transport General Howley, his wife and four children. No one knew if the children would attend and, if they did, whether or not they would bring their families. The third vehicle was available for "unexpected additional family and friends." Since my father had not received an invitation, I decided that he and my mother qualified as "unexpected additional family."

I was excused with the comments, "If you can read and follow instructions, Lieutenant, then your job will be easy and it all should run smoothly. Leave the drinking to the guests."

The hell with him and that last comment. My troops had taught me that I not only could drink German beer without issue but that I also could swig a Jägermeister or two or three and still function.

My parents arrived in Berlin on Wednesday, May 8, 1974. I met them at the airport and drove them the short distance to my quarters. Just as I did after my arrival in Berlin, they both took long naps to sleep off the rigors of the travel and the jetlag. The next morning, I took them on a tour of my neighborhood, McNair Barracks where I worked, and through the city past Berlin's most prominent attractions: The Reichstag, Brandenburg Gate, Checkpoint Charlie, Victory Angel, Charlottenburg Palace, The Kaiser Wilhelm Memorial Church, and the Kurfürstendamm (Ku'damm), its two-mile long famous boulevard.

One block off the Kurfürstendamm still stands the Hotel Kempinski where reservations had been made for several of the distinguished visitors and their families, and where several receptions were being planned. Reservations notwithstanding, the organizers expected some of the dignitaries to accept private invitations and reside in the homes of their friends and professional associates.

At the end of our driving tour, I checked my parents into the Kempinski. There they would have the possibility to be among the men and their families with whom my father had served. For the week my parents would be in Berlin, they would have access to a five-star, luxury hotel with exceptional amenities. They would be located a half-block from Berlin's equivalent of Paris' Champs-Élysées which boasted many of Berlin's attractions, best restaurants, high-end shops, and boutiques. Berlin would be theirs to enjoy while I was busy on duty.

"Chaotic" was the term I heard most often to describe the time as May 12th neared. The German government, the City of Berlin, and each of the three Western Allies had their own recommendations for the priority of the anniversary events, their locations, the schedules, and the list of personnel to be invited. They all kept tweaking the master plan through the morning of Friday, May 10th. The Berlin newspapers were publishing a different schedule of events, their locations, and the times every day during the anniversary week. On the morning of Sunday, May 12th, the travel plans for the dignitaries still were incomplete or changing.

With the same stubborn determination that made the Berlin Airlift a success, the organizers triumphed. The 25th Anniversary of the Berlin Airlift was an outstanding success.

General Howley and his family were a treat. My commander was right. We got along fine. The presence of my father helped considerably. They both were die-hard New York Yankee fans.

Celebrants of all ages from the dozen countries that had supported the airlift shared sentiments of pride, endearment, camaraderie, joy, and, at the wreath-laying ceremony, sorrow.

"Berlin bleibt doch Berlin." "Berlin remains Berlin" was the city motto at that time.

That same Sunday was Mothers' Day. I am sure that watching me perform dutifully in my first real job was as much a gift to my mother as was the bouquet of flowers I had appropriated for her the day before from the Protocol Office.

My parents returned to the United States and I returned to the Second Platoon on Wednesday, May 15, 1974. The bill from the Kempinski at the checkout for my parents read like a page from the budget for the Defense Department.

Transfer.

My troops knew before I did. In the barracks, as we were preparing to assemble for PT, a few of my sergeants gathered around me and asked, "Hey, Sir, is it true? Are you really leaving us?"

"What. . .what are you talking about. . .leaving you? "Well, Sir, while you were playin' hooky, the First Sergeant told Sergeant Minot that you're going over to Combat Support Company to get a platoon there. He told him that, until we get a new lieutenant, he'd been running the platoon."

I told them that I had not heard anything from anyone about leaving and, if it were true, then someone, probably the company commander, would tell me. We ran PT.

After PT, as I was entering the barracks, the CO stopped me. He asked me to drop by his office after I showered and had breakfast. Some of the same sergeants who had alerted me to my possible departure witnessed that short conversation.

"See, Sir, what did we tell you? Are we right? Are you leaving us? Tell him you don't want to go."

"I have to see him after chow. You'll be the first to know if he tells me anything about leaving."

In the chow hall the sergeants from Second Platoon who were there crowded around my table. I sensed that they would not be too happy if I were to leave. I had been with them only eight months and our shared experiences brought me very close to all of them. Within military life, there is an attachment, even an affection, among the men who share life-changing experiences together. On the lighter side, one sergeant said, "Sir, if you do go, please take Sergeant Minot with you."

We all laughed.

"You guys know you couldn't get along without Sergeant Minot. Y'all need each other. If you have time for lunch, be back here at 12:30, and I'll tell you everything that the CO tells me. Make sure that you bring Sergeant Minot with you!"

In the CO's office, my commander asked me if I had enjoyed the escort duty for the Airlift anniversary and the leave time with my parents.

"Yes, Sir. Everything was just fine. I think my father had the best time of all of us."

Then I listened to a mini-lecture about officers' careers in the Army. He told me that the career path for all officers is the same: "Move up or move out."

Although I still had another 13 months as a second lieutenant, he and the battalion commander believed that I was ready to move up. On Monday, May 20th, I would be reassigned to Combat Support Company (CSC) to command a new platoon. He said that he did not want to lose me but that the Battalion Commander selected me. He told me to make an appointment to meet my new commander who would provide me the details of my new assignment.

"Yes, Sir. Thank you, Sir."

As I was opening his door he said, don't let too much daylight burn away before you get back and tell Second Platoon."

"Yes, Sir."

As if they all didn't already know.

Captain Raines was far more enthusiastic to see me than I was to see him. He, too, was a West Point graduate, eight years ahead of me in the Class of 1965. A great many of his classmates had served in combat in Vietnam and many of them had died very young in their 20's. His wife was sterling. As the mother of two grade-school age boys, she possessed the instincts and talents to make the young, newly-assigned, bachelor officers in the battalion feel both welcomed and loved.

In his office, Captain Raines voiced many of the same opinions about a career that my CO had told me earlier. He gave me a brief description of the mission and components of his company.

Unlike a rifle company, which was composed of three rifle platoons and one weapons platoon, CSC was composed of four independent platoons each with very different missions. The lieutenants who commanded these platoons usually had the freedom to plan and conduct their platoon training separately from the rest of the company. There were exceptions for company training such as PT, safety, and weapons qualifications.

The Heavy Mortar Platoon was the most-critical support platoon within CSC. Its mission was to provide indirect fire support for the battalion. The senior first lieutenant in the company normally commanded this platoon. The Scout Platoon patrolled within the American sector around the Berlin wall in nine jeeps. Its mission was to "show the flag" and to obtain low-grade intelligence information about the status of the wall and the East German soldiers and border troops who guarded it. The TOW Platoon, (TOW: Tube-launched, Optically-sighted, Wire-guided missile), provided anti-tank support to the battalion. It employed another nine jeeps on which were mounted the TOW missile weapon system. The mission of the TOW platoon was to destroy tanks, armored vehicles, and bunkers. The Redeye Platoon provided anti-aircraft defense for the battalion through the use of surface-to-air Redeye missiles. The missiles were effective against airborne targets up to a distance of 4,500 yards. Usually an Air Defense Artillery officer, not an Infantry officer, commanded the Redeye Platoon.

Captain Raines offered me the command of the TOW Platoon which I accepted immediately. He took me on a short tour of the company headquarters, the barracks, and the motor pool where the vehicles assigned to his company were maintained.

At the end of our meeting, he told me to use the remainder of the week to out-process from Bravo Company and to report for duty on Monday morning. After PT, he would introduce me to the other officers in the company, his non-commissioned officer training and support staff, and the enlisted members of my new platoon.

All of the NCO's from Second Platoon were waiting for me in the mess hall when I arrived just shy of 12:30 p.m. I had no appetite now that it was time to inform the platoon about my pending departure. When I met them, I noticed that no one had a lunch tray in front of him. Before I took the one vacant seat that had been set aside for me I asked, "Do y'all want to get some chow before we start?"

No one responded. There were a few short, negative shakes of the head, then Platoon Sergeant Minot said, "No one's hungry, Sir. We'll wait 'til later."

I told them what they had expected to hear. Their words of congratulations were genuine, but their facial expressions belied them. For me, that was the most miserable half hour that I had spent with these men in the eight months of our association. The mood could not have been more somber if there had been flowers, a coffin, and a body on view next to us.

Platoon Sergeant Minot announced that he would assemble the troops at the end of the duty day and that I could repeat to the junior-enlisted men what I had just told them. Before we returned to duty I said that I was inviting myself to the NCO Club in the afternoon where we could review the bidding in a more relaxed atmosphere. I added that I had made arrangements for two trucks and drivers from the battalion to take the entire platoon to Lake Wannsee, Berlin's largest lake, on Friday.

The weather was supposed to be good. I had reserved a 40-person tour boat and guide from which we would see the sights of Berlin while drinking beer and eating wurst.

I asked Sergeant Minot to compile a headcount so that I could order the beer and food. The monstrously large SSG Womack said, "Everyone will be there, Sir. I'll make sure of that."

On Monday morning, Captain Raines introduced me to the company before we ran PT. I ran alongside the members of my new platoon. After a shower and breakfast, the platoon assembled in the company day room for an informal meeting with me. Compared to Second Platoon which had a force of 11 NCO's and 28 junior-enlisted men, the TOW platoon had ten fewer men: only seven NCO's and 22 junior-enlisted men.

I introduced myself. After only 11 months as an officer and only eight months in the battalion, I had not accomplished anything unique or exceptional. I described my former duties with Second Platoon, and concluded by saying that I was very proud and happy to be serving with them.

My platoon sergeant, Sergeant First Class (SFC) E-7 William Poule, was a combat veteran with three tours of duty in Vietnam. He had been wounded on each of those three tours. The other six non-commissioned officers included three staff sergeants (SSG) E-6, one of whom was a combat veteran with duty in Vietnam, and three sergeants (SGT) E-5, none of whom had seen combat.

SFC Poule had been leading the TOW platoon for five months since the promotion and reassignment of its officer platoon leader. Now, similar to SFC Minot, SFC Poule's duties would be to run the platoon in garrison and supervise administrative matters.

Each of the other non-commission officers led the four-man TOW gun crew. Besides himself, a TOW gun crew included a jeep driver, a gunner, and an assistant gunner-missile loader all of whom were required to be cross-trained in each other's duties. The remaining two enlisted men, the most-junior in rank, were assigned as the ammunition team, responsible to drive and maintain the seventh gun jeep, and to transport and distribute the ammunition. One of them would be my driver.

During the platoon introductions, the non-commissioned officers did not say much more than their names, how long they had been in the Army, where they had served, and that they were glad to have me on board. None had any questions for me.

But it was entirely different when the younger, junior-enlisted men had their turn. Over the weekend some of them had made an effort to check me out with their buddies from Second Platoon. After they introduced themselves all that these teenagers, mostly brand-new to the Army, did was ask me questions related to stories they must have heard from those motor mouths in Second Platoon.

"Sir, when you first got to Berlin did some of those idiots like Private Paben in your old platoon think you were a CID agent?"

"Sir, did Sergeant Womack ever tell you any cool stories about being a POW in Vietnam and escaping? Did they really feed him rats?"

"That Jägermeister really is some nasty stuff isn't it, Sir?"

"Sir, how was Spandau guard duty? Did you get to see Hitler's friend real close? How come the Russians won't let him out?"

The chances were remote that I ever would get to know as much about any of them as they already seemed to know about me.

The next day I found out one of the reasons why I had been reassigned so quickly. Every year, in the late spring or early summer, the three Western Allies conducted a week-long field exercise to demonstrate Allied solidarity and the ability to defend Berlin against an attack. The maneuvers this year would begin Monday, June 10th and end Friday, June 14th in time for many of the men to celebrate Fathers' Day with their families.

Within the 7,500 acres of Berlin's Grunewald, a task force composed of a battalion of American infantry and a company of British and French infantry, augmented by a company of American tanks, would simulate combat against a second task force composed of a battalion of British infantry and a company of American and French infantry, augmented by a company of British tanks. The young soldiers joked that the reason the French contingent was so small was that no one would notice when they quit early and went home.

Combat Support Company would support this training exercise. Except for the TOW platoon, the three other platoons would be detached from the company and assigned within the battalion. The TOW platoon would perform "command and control duty."

We would be responsible to ensure that the maneuver of the two task forces remained within the boundaries of the exercise; to assist with the relocation of units which maneuvered outside the boundaries; to assist units which were lost; to deliver food and fuel to units which failed to be resupplied; to assist with medical evacuations and emergency situations; to help the Berlin law enforcement and safety officials prevent curious Berliners, especially children, from entering the maneuver area; and, perhaps most importantly, to locate, remove, and secure the pyrotechnics which failed to detonate during the simulated combat.

We deployed into the Grunewald one week ahead of the task forces. During the week of June 3rd to 7th, the entire TOW platoon of 30 members assembled daily in our nine jeeps and drove in a convoy at first light from McNair Barracks to the exercise area where we trained until dark. The mess hall had made special arrangements for us to eat early breakfast at 5:00 a.m., and late supper at 7 p.m. For lunch we ate C-rations.

The first day within the Grunewald, we drove along the miles of major paved roads which marked the boundaries and enclosed the maneuver area of the exercise. We made detailed notes of every recognizable terrain feature, landmark, and structure that would aid in route recognition and land navigation. We annotated every one of our 39 maps with exactly the same details so that maps could be exchanged without confusion. There was one map for each member of the platoon and one map for each jeep.

The second day, inside the maneuver area, we drove along the minor paved roads, trails, and paths for the same purpose. We reconnoitered all the north-south routes in the morning, then all the east-west routes in the afternoon.

For the next three days, we conducted practical exercises. SFC Poule and I split the six TOW gun crews into two teams of three gun crews each: primary, alternate, and backup. We assembled the teams at a base area. Then we each left for two different locations and called by radio to our gun crews to rendezvous with us. We simulated a maneuver unit that needed assistance. The primary crew had the mission to complete the rendezvous. The alternate and backup crews traveled behind the primary crew to learn what they did right or wrong in navigating. They only could observe, not assist, with the navigation. Each rendezvous mission was timed and critiqued. Then the crews rotated positions: primary moving to back-up; alternate moving to primary; backup moving to alternate. Navigation for each gun crew was the primary responsibility of the non-commissioned officer leader.

At the end of the first week, each gun crew had two trained navigators and drivers all of whom were familiar with the exercise area.

Friday evening, I informed my commander that the platoon was prepared to support the exercise beginning on Monday. I was surprised when he informed me that the task forces would be in "tactical configuration." This would be a requirement for us also. That meant that we would have to strip the canvas tops and doors from the jeeps, and cover their insignia and identification numbers. In the event of inclement weather, we would not have the protection of an enclosed jeep and would be vulnerable to the elements.

This unexpected information required us to work Saturday to prepare the vehicles and collect additional equipment. We needed rain and cold-weather gear, waterproof clothing bags, sleeping bags, and air mattresses. We also needed extra ponchos to use as lean-tos.

On Monday, June 10th, the first day of the exercise, the platoon assembled, had early breakfast, and deployed to nine locations in the Grunewald by 7 a.m. The exercise was planned to start at 9 a.m.

Just when it should have been getting light at about 7:30 a.m., I noticed that it was getting darker. We all heard the first clasps of thunder about 8 a.m. It rained continuously for four and a half days.

Anything that could go wrong, did. Fortunately, there was no loss of life, no physical injuries and no serious damages to any vehicles except those which were bumped accidentally by tanks. A "bump" from a tank tends to "total" a vehicle. On four occasions, we led military tow trucks into the maneuver area to recover vehicles.

In a strange reenactment with historical significance, the French quit early and went home on Thursday. My troops asked me why it took so long for them to "surrender."

On Friday the 14th, the exercise ended at first light. The rain stopped about two hours later. We saw the sun for the first time in a week. The task forces left the exercise area. Everyone headed home except the members of the TOW platoon.

As soon as the exercise ended, the platoon formed on line along the roads. We swept the maneuver area for anything which had been left behind unintentionally, trash, and unexploded pyrotechnics. Within the boundaries of the exercise area, the gun crews in their six jeeps and SFC Poule and I in our two jeeps swept the maneuver area. We used each driver to search to his front; each passenger to search to his rear, and the remaining gun-crew members to walk astride the slow-moving jeeps and search five to 10 yards inside the forest. We made multiple passes in all directions filling every jeep with items such as clothing, field gear, maps, food, trash, and unexploded pyrotechnics.

It was close to 3 p.m. when I called and declared the mission complete. I instructed everyone to drive safely back to the barracks, hose down the vehicles, and clean and secure their gear. All work should be finished to allow for time for a shower and a hot meal, the first in five days, before the mess hall closed.

While my driver waited to enter the high-speed autobahn from a side rode in the Grunewald I looked over at him and said, "What a week! I guess we get to do it all again next year."

Then a horn blared from a vehicle stopped behind us. We both turned around and looked.

From his side of a shiny, white, four-door, Mercedes taxi, a driver had his left arm out the window and the middle finger of his hand raised. He was shaking his arm and hand emphasizing a very familiar obscene gesture.

We heard him shout, "Hey Amerikaner. Ficken Sie, Amerikaner. Amerika ist Scheiße. Ficken Sie."

That was enough for me. From the rear of the jeep that was stuffed with unexploded pyrotechnics, I grabbed two smoke grenades and put one in each trouser pocket. Then I stepped out of the jeep and walked to the taxi. I retrieved one grenade, pulled the pin, and threw it inside the open window from which he had been gesturing. This time it exploded. Smoke grenades burn far too hot to be retrieved by hand. While the driver jumped out of his taxi, I jumped back into my jeep.

I looked at my driver and said, "Bolmer, step on it."

He could not have had a wider grin on his face when he responded, "Yes, Sir!"

In Friday rush-hour traffic, Private First Class Thomas Bolmer kept looking over at me and grinning. I had to tell him more than once to watch the road.

"Yes, Sir. Sorry, Sir."

I think that I had settled down when I said in my best, command voice, slowly and deliberately, "Bolmer, now pay attention to me."

Immediately Bolmer responded, "It's okay, Sir. I know what you're gonna tell me. That German had it coming to him. We've been freezin' our asses off out here in the woods for two weeks, this whole friggin' week in the cold and rain. All for these friggin' people. For what? No, sir. He deserved it. It's okay."

I let Bolmer's comments sink in then said, "Bolmer, pull into the right lane and drive a little slower."

"Yes, Sir."

While he was driving I turned and leaned toward him with my face just inches from his.

"Bolmer, I either will be out of the Army or in jail or both if anyone finds out what I just did."

"Yes, Sir!

"Shut up and listen to me."

"Yes, Sir!"

Now, we still have some camouflage on our faces and the jeep still has no ID on it."

"Yes, Sir, that sure works out great."

"Bolmer!"

"Yes, Sir. Sorry, Sir, I promise I'll be quiet."

"Bolmer, this goes for both of us: not one word to anyone ever, got it?"

"Sir, you can count on me."

After we entered McNair Barracks I told PFC Bolmer to drive to the motor pool. I would help him wash the jeep and clean up our gear. From the motor pool we walked together to the company. Before we started up the steps into the company I said, "Remember, Bolmer."

"Yes Sir, I know, not one word."

At the top of the stairs, before we turned away from each other to our separate shower areas, PFC Bolmer looked at me and said, "Sir, did you see the look on that guy's face when he was standing next to his Mercedes - all four doors open and the mess of green smoke pouring from it?"

I remembered from psychology classes at the Academy how expressive and predictive are body attitude and facial expressions. Right then, as I looked at Bolmer, grinning and shaking his head, I knew I was going to jail.

I debriefed my commander who had waited for me to return. He congratulated the platoon and me on the work that we did. He said that Monday would start a light work week with only routine cleaning and maintenance of our vehicles and equipment. Friday would be a training holiday. We would have a long weekend.

After I finished showering and dressing there were only 10 minutes left before the mess hall closed. When I entered, I was the only one in the chow line. The mess sergeant said, "Your driver told us that you were coming, Sir, so we stayed open for you."

Hmmm . .my driver . .told someone . .something . .about me.

I thanked him and he filled my tray.

I walked from the enclosed serving area of the chow line into the open area of the mess hall and general seating. As soon as I came into view, the mess hall erupted. The sound of applause was diminished only slightly by shouts of "Hurray, Lieutenant Pelosi." "Hey, good job, Sir." "Way to go, Lieutenant Pelosi."

Some of my former soldiers from Second Platoon rushed up to me, started slapping me on the back and petting my arms and shoulders.

"Boy, Sir, we sure miss you." "Good job, Sir." "Wish I'd been there, Sir."

I made a quick glance around the mess hall as more of the troops started to come up to me. I saw a wiry figure with Bolmer's shape and dark hair dash out the side door. I passed my tray to the soldier closest to me and said, "Hold this, please. I'll be right back."

PFC Bolmer ignored my repeated shouts of "Freeze, Bolmer."

We would be court-martialed together. I, for about a dozen charges, not the least of which would be attempted murder, aggravated assault, arson, felony destruction of private property, fleeing the scene of a crime, conduct unbecoming an officer. Bolmer for failure to obey a direct verbal order.

He slowed down. When he sensed that I was directly behind him, he turned around and fell to his knees. He folded his hands against his chest in the manner of someone praying. He looked up at me with an expression that begged for mercy.

"Sir, I swear, Sir, I told only one person in the shower. That's it. One person. I don't how the hell everyone else found out."

I reassured him that everything was okay and that if there were a problem then the problem was mine, not his.

In the mess hall, I retrieved my tray from the dutiful soldier standing guard by it on the empty table where he placed it. I said to everyone who came up to me while I was eating, "Private Bolmer has been with me out in the cold and rain for two weeks, way too long. Anything you may have heard from him is pure fantasy and hallucination."

In 1981, I attended the wedding of Thomas Jefferson Bolmer and Linda Elaine Wagman in Salinas, California. At the reception, he introduced me to his family and friends by saying, "Remember the lieutenant in Berlin I told you about who blew up the German taxi."

Live Fire.

The weather cleared nicely over the weekend. With only a few days until the start of summer, the temperatures began to warm as the sun was shining. Conditions were ideal for the start of an abbreviated duty week during which only cleaning, maintenance and inspections were scheduled.

After morning PT, the non-commissioned officers showered and went to the mess hall. Most of the junior-enlisted men splashed some water on their hands, arms and faces and went straight to breakfast. Showering made no sense if they were going to get wet and grungy again washing and working on their vehicles.

The noncommissioned officers rotated supervising the junior enlisted men whom Platoon Sergeant Poule referred to as the platoon's "terrible TOWS." His semi-sarcastic, clever play on words, associated them and their antics with distracted, inattentive, misbehaving children in their "terrible twos."

After only an hour, more water had been hosed on the soldiers than on the jeeps. After another hour of more play than work, the soldiers were shining with sweat having stripped shirtless to soak up the sun and even out the distinctive farmers' tans on their young, muscled torsos. The entire day, originally dedicated to the cleaning and maintenance of personal gear and vehicles, ended up as a day of fun in the sun.

The troops started the next morning applying touch-up paint where needed on the jeeps and, where not wanted, on each other. After the paint dried, they waxed the jeeps, re-blackened the tires, and took the jeeps out for a spin. The purpose of the drive, through the base and around the surrounding neighborhood, was to listen for strange noises and check for rough handling. It also provided an opportunity to show off their vehicles and themselves. These test drives always included a detour by way of an outdoor café that they knew was popular with the local girls.

I did my best to stay even further away from the troops than Platoon Sergeant Poule did when they were pretending to work. At lunch, my commander asked if I had time in the afternoon to go along with him for a training briefing by the staff at battalion headquarters. It was the sort of question, phrased with certain words and expressed with certain mannerisms, that a senior officer always can ask a junior officer and know that the answer assuredly will be, "Yes, Sir."

That afternoon, I learned a second reason why I was reassigned from Second Platoon. At the end of June and sometime in July, the TOW platoons from the other two infantry battalions in the brigade, 2/6 Infantry and 4/6 Infantry, would travel to the "Zone," the military's slang term for West Germany. My platoon would travel last in August. The purpose for travel was to conduct annual maneuver training, weapons qualifications, and live-missile firing. All live-fire training required the physical presence of an officer on the range and the written signature of that officer on a safety certificate. I had been reassigned to the TOW platoon in time to learn enough to support the travel, training, and live-missile firing.

The Zone hosted three huge U.S. Army bases with maneuver areas and firing ranges large enough to support the training and gunnery which were restricted in areas where many smaller bases were located. Berlin was a perfect example. Nothing larger than a 7.62 mm. round of ammunition for an M-60 machine gun could be fired on the gunnery ranges within Berlin.

Each TOW platoon would train with simulators first in Berlin and again in the zone. The most proficient of the three junior enlisted men of a TOW gun crew would merit the opportunity to fire a live missile. After he launched the missile, the gunner would watch $3,000 of taxpayer money fly away in less than 10 seconds. The platoon's six best gunners would watch $18,000 of taxpayer money burn up in under a minute.

There were eight weeks until our travel and training. I intended to train the platoon, especially the gun crews, to a standard that would guarantee gunnery skills worthy of the taxpayers' burden.

In a combat unit, soldiering and weapons proficiency come first. Leaders of combat units know that it is rare to lead an effective unit with soldiers who are not nearly entirely compatible. Anyone who has read the book by Stephen Ambrose about Easy Company's "Band of Brothers," the company that fought together during World War II after parachuting into France on D-Day in June 1944, and fighting in Western Europe until the end of World War II in May 1945, clearly understands that principle. The platoon-training program for the next eight weeks would hone soldier skills, develop expert gunners, and build esprit de corps.

Three of the 24 junior-enlisted men would begin training on Sunday. After lunch on Thursday, as the start of the long training holiday weekend was nearing, I asked for three volunteers from the junior-enlisted men to go out on the town and train with me on Sunday. There were no takers. I added that, unless anyone had plans for a three-day weekend, the day should be fun, and I would restore their lost three-day weekend the following week.

One soldier asked, "Sir, how can training on Sunday be fun?"

I knew he really wanted to ask, "Sir, how can training with you on Sunday be fun?"

I answered, "My vehicle has room for me as the driver and three passengers. For the next eight weeks on Sunday, three of you, each week, will dress in Class A's (the Army's Dress Green uniform) and meet me here at 9 a.m. sharp."

"We'll drive to the Ku'damm, eat breakfast in a fancy restaurant, the Konditerei Schilling, for about an hour. Then we'll walk across the street and watch a two-hour, black and white documentary, *The Battle of Berlin*, which is the history of the Soviet assault on Berlin in May 1945."

"After the movie, we'll drive to Checkpoint Charlie and into East Berlin. We'll visit the Soviet war museum, and you can climb all over the Soviet tanks and the rest of the vehicles that are on display there. Bring your camera or borrow one."

"We'll stop at East Berlin's version of Bloomingdales and you can buy your mom or girlfriend something really sweet for about a dollar in East marks which I'll have with me. Then we'll have an early dinner at a first-class restaurant near the State Opera House where you can eat and drink whatever you want. I will pay for everything for everyone, except any gifts you buy at the Bloomingdales Bazaar. That dollar comes out of your own pocket."

"Sunday is mandatory platoon training. Three of you will learn about tank warfare and Soviet tanks. Knowing how to kill tanks is our business and I want business to be fun. Over the next eight Sundays and before we leave for the Zone all of you, three at a time, will do this. Who's going to be first?"

There were more than enough volunteers. As I expected, they volunteered in the same groups of three that formed the gun crews. Platoon Sergeant Poule and the gun-crew team leaders would schedule a duty roster for the remaining Sundays.

The threat to NATO in Europe was the Warsaw Pact led by the Soviet Union. After PT on Monday mornings, every week for eight weeks, the platoon trained to identify the armored vehicles of the seven-nation members of the Warsaw Pact: Bulgaria, Czechoslovakia, East Germany, Hungary, Poland, Romania, and its leader the Soviet Union. The last hour of each four-hour training session was dedicated to a review of Soviet armor.

After PT on Friday mornings, I used a half day every week for eight weeks to teach the platoon the history of eight major tank battles fought between the start of World War II, when German armor led the ground attack on Poland on September 1, 1939, and the end of the Yom Kippur Arab-Israeli War in October 1973.

My lectures were reinforced with movies, actual combat footage, and photographs. References, primarily books about the battles, were available in the platoon's meeting and recreation room. Within the history, I emphasized the traits of the leaders who won and lost battles. The platoon studied tactics, the employment of armor in offensive and defensive maneuvers, and the events in which tanks played the decisive role in achieving a victory. Every class ended with a discussion of each battle, critiquing what was right and what worked, what was wrong and what did not work, and where leaders were confused or missed opportunities.

At the end of the eight weeks, the soldiers understood better what most people know: except for politicians and taxi cab drivers, most people get better at their jobs with experience. That was true for leaders and their soldiers in combat.

Mid-week, between the classroom training in garrison, the platoon trained at the weapons range or within the Grunewald. At the range the TOW missile training simulator was used to fire a 5.56 mm. round, the same round used as ammunition for an M-16 rifle, at paper targets only 100 yards away. The distance represented only three percent of the ideal range of 3,000 yards at which a live missile should be fired at enemy armor in combat. With no other training resource available, this technique served the purpose to train gunners to sight targets and fire. In addition to firing from a fixed position along the firing line, we practiced racing the gun jeep from one side of the range, stopping, turning to face and engage the target, then race off again much like we would do with Soviet armor approaching. Not surprisingly, we ran afoul of the Range Safety Sergeant who had not seen a unit move-shoot-move before.

Since we were compliant with the regulation to fire at or behind the firing line from a stationary position, we continued to train as we would fight.

A week before the deployment, my company commander and I reported to the battalion commander for a meeting with him and his primary staff about the readiness of the platoon. My commander gave a brief summary and stated that the platoon was ready to travel and live fire. I described in detail the past eight weeks of training in garrison, in the Grunewald, and at the weapons range.

After I concluded, the battalion commander commented, "Sounds good to me."

He asked his staff if anyone had any questions. No one did.

Then he said to me, "Lieutenant Pelosi, do you know what your standard is?"

"Standard? No, Sir. I don't."

"Well, you know that the TOW platoons in the two other battalions deployed and fired in June and July."

"Yes, sir."

"Do you know how they did?"

"No, Sir, I don't."

"Well, four out of six, and five out of six. Make sure your best gunners aim well."

The battalion commander was telling me that, when it came time to fire the live missiles, he expected my gunners to score kills on no less than five of six targets. The standard was to score at least as well, if not better, than the higher-scoring TOW platoon in the battalion of his two rival commanders.

We departed Berlin late Sunday night on the military duty train and arrived in West Germany early Monday morning. In less than an hour, the jeeps were unloaded from the train and packed with the members of the platoon, their weapons, and gear. Few of us ate the C-rations which had been issued for breakfast. When we drove by a grocery store we stopped for food and drinks.

At the base, we found our cantonment area. It included a barracks, mess hall, storage buildings, parking area, and sports field. Platoon Sergeant Poule departed in one jeep with a gun-crew leader and the two ammunition specialists to confirm the support requirements and arrange for messing. I departed in a second jeep with three gun-crew leaders to locate and study the range, and confirm our training and live-fire schedules. The remaining two gun-crew leaders supervised the junior-enlisted men organizing the billeting, checking the functionality of the equipment within the billets and mess hall, and upgrading the cleanliness of our temporary facilities.

The range non-commissioned officer, Sergeant First Class Watton, had been on duty at that base and that range for 10 years. Injuries that he sustained in Vietnam forced his reclassification out of the infantry. There was not a detail about that range that he did not know. It was dedicated to the platoon for the week for whenever we wanted to have it. Subject to any changes I wished to make, his schedule provided time for us to train the remainder of Monday and Tuesday, live fire on either Wednesday or Thursday, and stand down from the cantonment area before departure on Friday.

As soon as I saw and studied the range, I knew that his schedule would not work for us.

Across the 100 yard width of the range and down the 4,000yard depth of the range there was an array of targets. They included heritage and newer vehicles such as tanks, tank hulls, personnel carriers, trucks and trailers of all sizes, jeeps and, surprisingly, field ambulances. Most of these targets were former NATO military equipment recycled for use as targets because they were obsolete or non-functional. There also was an impressive amount of Soviet armor. It had been provided by the Soviets to the Arabs, and was disabled or captured intact by the Israelis during the Yom Kippur War nine months earlier. It's nice to have an ally.

The targets downrange at 100 and 200 yards all were obliterated. What remained were only mounds of twisted iron, shells, and hulks. The targets much further away at 1000, 1500, 2000, 2500, and 3000 yards were pristine.

With the three gun-crew leaders listening attentively, I asked SFC Watton why the training schedule set aside two full days to live fire six missiles which, if fired rapidly in succession, would take only a minute or two.

"Well, Sir. What other units usually do is fire on the day when the best weather is projected. Usually, they get out here in the morning, have the gunners take several practice rounds using the simulator, then, when they think they're ready, they live fire. Live fire takes a lot more than a couple of minutes, maybe about a half an hour, because a lot of the troops get battle-rattled from the roar of the missiles and the explosions on impact."

I asked SFC Watton if the reason why all the targets were positioned at their greatest vulnerability, fully exposed from the side instead of head-on as if they were attacking, was to make them easier to hit.

"Yes, Sir,"

"Does anyone ever ask to have some targets moved so that they appear head on and not laterally?"

"No, Sir. Not since I've been here. Ten years."

Then I asked SFC Watton if the reason that I was looking at what once were targets and now were only unidentifiable masses of metal at the 100 and 200-yard ranges was that the close-in targets were chosen to help guarantee a hit.

"Yes, Sir. Exactly."

"Then I can assume that the reason the most distant targets out at 1000 yards and beyond are untouched is that they never have been engaged."

"Yes, Sir. Why take a chance like that and miss?"

"My comrades-in-arms from the other two battalions came here this past June and July. Were you here?"

"Yes, Sir. This is my range. I don't want anyone else running it or else something gets screwed up."

"Two more questions, please, Sergeant Watton. If they fired during daylight in ideal weather conditions at only these up front targets then how could they miss?"

"Well, Sir, like I said, some gunners get jumpy when the missiles are fired. When they jump, they lose control of the optical tracking. The missiles are traveling at 300 yards a second. They're already passed the targets before the gunners recover. So they miss. That's what all those craters are around these targets. The missiles impacted wherever the gunners were sighting after they got spooked."

"Sergeant Watton you've got to be kidding me!"

"Sir, I don't even know you. Why would I kid you?"

"Last question now, Sergeant Watton, I promise. What about night?"

"What do you mean, Sir, what about night?"

"Does anyone ever live fire for record at night?"

"Now you're the one kidding me, Sir. For record? No way!"

I thanked SFC Watton for his time, help and information. I told him that I would return with my platoon in nine jeeps after lunch and, before the end of the day, I would tweak the training and live-fire schedules that he had shown me.

As we were walking away from SFC Watton, one of the gun-crew leaders looked at me and asked, "What's so funny, Sir?" On the seven-mile trip back to the cantonment area, I traded my front passenger seat for one in the back and leaned forward among the gun-crew leaders so that they all could hear me.

"Does anyone here think that if the Soviets ever attack it will be at high noon on a bright sunny day? And does anyone here think that we'll wait until we can see their faces and the red star on their uniforms before we shoot at them? I think that the answer is 'No' to both questions."

"When we get back we'll grab chow. Then the whole platoon will convoy back out here. We'll show them the range and the targets. I'll tell them everything we just heard from Sergeant Watton and more. Then we'll plan the training and the live fire."

After viewing the range even the most junior and inexperienced young soldiers knew that it did not reflect the image of a battlefield. Not one distant target had been engaged. I changed the schedules to give us time to prepare and stage a simulated battlefield for when we live fired.

Tuesday morning, two gun-crew leaders supervised the junior enlisted men in the cantonment area for meals and pick-up games of baseball and soccer. Platoon Sergeant Poule and I each took two gun-crew leaders to get support for our live fire. By the end of the day, Platoon Sergeant Poule's team had secured a sound truck from a Signal Corps unit on base. My team had secured two tanks and an eight-man squad of infantrymen.

On Wednesday morning, SFC Watton did not permit us to use the jeeps and their tow cables to turn any target from a profile to a head-on position. He feared that there might be unexploded ordnance downrange. Exactly as we had trained in Berlin, the gun crews drilled all day in the move-shoot-move routines. They fired using the simulator at fixed targets but now over far greater distances. After supper the platoon returned to the range and repeated the drills. At night, it was difficult to see and hit targets up to 1000 yards. Beyond 1,500 yards it was almost impossible.

By mid-day Thursday, all the gunners had trained maneuvering, identifying targets, and firing the simulator. Throughout most of the day many of the eager gunners wanted to know when on Friday they would live fire. Platoon Sergeant Poule and I said that we did not know until we could confirm that all our support requirements were available. As they went to bed, they still did not know.

Friday, at 4 a.m., we went to war. Platoon Sergeant Poule, his six NCO's, and I were awake and dressed in full combat gear.

The troops were hustled out of their bunks with shakes and shouts of "Let's go! Let's go! The balloon's gone up! Berlin is under attack! We're at war with the Russians!"

By 4:30 a.m., we all were racing to the range. According to a script that the leadership kept secret from the junior men, six jeeps halted at different distances behind the firing line and formed three, two-jeep simulated fighting positions.

As the troops dismounted and took cover behind the fighting positions, the tanks on either side of the range opened fire blanketing the long-distance targets in smoke. The tank fire was the signal for the sound-truck team to begin, blaring from its mounted speakers, the sounds of aircraft flying close air support and artillery rounds exploding. A squad of infantrymen began throwing explosive pyrotechnics on the range.

Platoon Sergeant Poule arrived at the first gun-team location with a jeep prepared for live fire. Following the commands of the gun-crew team leader, the assistant gunner loaded one of the six live rounds delivered in the ammunition jeep. The team leader shouted to a gunner he selected, "Tank in the open. Two thousand yards. Two o'clock. Fire when ready."

Specialist Langdon took aim, fired and missed.

At the command, "Move out!" the TOW missile jeep, followed by the ammunition jeep, raced to a second firing position. There, another target was identified and attacked. A second gunner aimed and fired. Another miss.

The war raged on. Two new targets, two new gunners, two more live missiles fired long-distance downrange. The fifth and sixth live firings were executed with everyone wearing protective masks.

In less than an hour, it still was dark when the Soviets chose to withdraw having lost only one tank. SFC Watton completed his range live fire report which was sent by message to Berlin.

"Six missiles fired. One recorded hit. No incidents or safety violations. Range secured at 0530."

Back in the cantonment area, the troops were elated. Non-stop talk and all smiles. No one really cared that only one missile hit its target.

"Gee, Sir, that was fun!"

"Where did those tanks come from?"

"I couldn't hear anything Sergeant Hanes was yelling at me, and I was hiding right behind him."

The troops learned that war is serious business; that chaos and confusion dominate a battlefield; and, most importantly, that their training serves a purpose.

Private Webster from Pontrain, Mississippi, told everyone, "Them other guys didn't do sh*t. Them targets they shot at were so friggin' close I could hit 'em with a chaw of my chewin' tobacco. We did it for real!"

SFC Watton found us at the train station as we were boarding. He had a message from Berlin. Upon arrival Saturday morning, Platoon Sergeant Poule was to return everyone and everything to the company.

"Sir, you're supposed to take a jeep and meet your CO at brigade headquarters. He'll be waiting for you."

"Thank you, Sergeant Watton. Good job with everything."

"Thank you, Sir. Never did anything like that before. That was fun."

"Yeah, so I heard. My troops told me exactly the same thing. Fun."

When I arrived, I was at receiving end of a lot of questions from many officers all of whom outranked me.

"What went wrong?"

"Didn't you have enough time to train?"

"Didn't the gunners have enough rest before they fired?"

"Did you pick the wrong gunners to fire?"

I didn't get a chance to say anything to anyone before someone said, "The CG (Commanding General) is free. Go on in."

Everyone entered his office and saluted.

The general said, "Good day, gentlemen. So, what have we got?"

The brigade training officer gave an overview of what someone told him was my length of duty and experience with the platoon. He made a few training-related comments and concluded saying, "There was every reasonable expectation that the score should have been higher."

Both my battalion and company commanders said that they did not know many details because I just had returned. They added that they thought I would score at least as well if not better than the two other platoons from the brigade which fired ahead of mine.

Then the commanding general said, "Lieutenant Pelosi."

I told the general and everyone assembled everything that we all did from the minute I first saw the range and spoke with Sergeant Watton until we pulled off our protective masks at the end of the live fire exercise. I took advantage of an easel in his office to draw a representation of the range showing targets as black ovals at distances from 100 to 3,000 yards.

As I crossed out the closer targets with a red "X" I explained why I thought they had been selected. As I circled the distant targets with a green "0" I explained why I thought that they had not been selected.

I scribbled "tank," "sound trk," and "inf squad" and indicated their positions. The more detailed the drawing of the range became and the longer I spoke, the easier it became for the general to keep smiling.

I concluded saying that, if I had to do everything all over again, I would not do anything any differently.

The general said, "Good job, Lieutenant Pelosi. I am extremely happy to have a warrior and not a bean-counter leading that platoon."

"Yes, Sir."

"Go on back to your platoon and see if you're needed. Everyone else, standby."

"Yes, Sir." I saluted and left.

When I got back to the platoon I told them where I had been and what was said.

Then I added, "I'm pretty sure I still have my job."

Lifesaving.

My closest friend at West Point, one year behind me in the Class of 1974, was Jeffrey Kallman. His younger brother, Scott, was a member of the Class of 1976. As cadets, Jeff and I took a four-day leave together over Easter and vacationed in Acapulco. We enjoyed the sun and surf but not the beggars, widespread poverty, and the abhorrent spectacle of bullfighting.

Recently Jeff had married. In March 1976, he invited me to his home in Bad Hersfeld, West Germany to meet his wife.

Second Lieutenant Jeffery Thomas Kallman commanded an Air Defense Artillery unit which was deployed nearby in the strategic Fulda Gap. Bad Hersfeld is located approximately 250 miles southwest of Berlin. I had estimated that the trip would take between five and six hours given the weather and road conditions in the winter; the time to process at the two border checkpoints between West Berlin and West Germany; the condition of the 110 mile East German autobahn and the strictly-enforced 50 mile per hour speed limit; and, the 140-mile drive through the scenic towns and villages of the Fulda Gap.

I was awake at 4 a.m. I wanted to start the long drive from Berlin at the border checkpoint not later than 5 a.m. Outside my apartment it was cold and windy, and the rain was starting to turn to snow.

My troops knew that I would be absent for a three-day weekend. They knew also that I was traveling to West Germany by vehicle. That meant that I would have to process through two Soviet checkpoints twice during the round trip. There would be four opportunities for me to obtain souvenirs from the Soviets for them. For years, Americans had been using their vehicles to trade with the Soviets at the checkpoints.

The autobahn between West Berlin and Helmstedt, West Germany, was the only authorized route for travel by members of the U.S. military through the Soviet-controlled zone of East Germany. Strict procedures governed the travel. The U.S. checkpoint in West Berlin, Checkpoint Bravo, was manned by the Military Police. Inside the checkpoint, one member of a detail inspected the special travel orders which included a copy translated into Russian, and read the formal rules of the road: no contact with any East German military, police or civilians; no travel on roads other than the autobahn; vehicle speed not to exceed 50 miles per hour; and, travel to be completed in not less than 2.5 hours and not more than four hours. Failure to arrive at the U.S. checkpoint at Helmstedt, Checkpoint Alpha, within four hours would trigger a search by the military police.

Outside, a second member of the detail inspected the traveler's vehicle for a full tank of fuel, a fully-inflated spare tire, and standard tire-changing equipment. He recorded the "start" mileage. If everything were in order then the traveler was directed to proceed to the Soviet checkpoint about 200 yards away.

At the Soviet checkpoint, the traveler stopped to continue processing. Before exiting his vehicle, anyone who wished to trade something with the Soviets would leave a copy of Playboy or another magazine with equally stimulating contents, a bottle of smooth American bourbon, (Jim Beam was the favorite), or both, on the passenger seat. Car doors never were locked.

Inside the Soviet facility, which lacked heating and air conditioning, the travel orders were presented to a Soviet soldier. He was hidden within an enclosed cubicle. When exchanging the documents, only his hands and the sleeves of his uniform shirt were exposed. While he inspected and copied the documents, the traveler had his picture taken from cameras supposedly hidden inside the eyes of the pictures of Marx, Engels, Lenin, Stalin, and the Soviet five-star Marshals who won the Great Patriotic War in 1945. The processing time always was long enough for a trade to take place unwitnessed by the traveler.

Usually, for each item left behind in the vehicle, the Soviets reciprocated with one item: an army brown leather belt or army brass belt buckle inscribed with the crest, five-pointed star, hammer and sickle. Swapping had gone on for so long that the Soviets knew to return one complete army belt and buckle for any two items that were left in the vehicle. My troops had provided me with what must have been every copy of Playboy from the PX (Post Exchange) and every bottle of Jim Beam from the Class VI store to "get as much as you can, Sir."

For this opportunity, and there should be three more, I had left behind two magazines and two bottles. When I returned there was only one belt and buckle. Although both magazines were gone, only one of the two bottles of bourbon had been exchanged. Given the Russian propensity to consume alcohol, I was surprised. The entry's "nachalnik" (boss) must have shown up unexpectedly and interrupted the exchange process.

Friday, March 19, 1976, must have been one of the most miserable travel days on record between Berlin and Helmstedt. The temperature was well below freezing. There was a fierce arctic wind blowing strongly from the northwest. The freezing rain had turned to snow. Black ice had formed in isolated patches on the road. Visibility was no greater than 30 to 50 yards.

My thermal underwear, layered clothing, wool sweater, ski cap, and insulated wet-weather parka provided little relief inside the unheated Soviet structure and almost no protection outside. Inside my vehicle, only two years new and perfectly operational, the heater at full blast was not enough to keep me warm.

I had been driving for about half an hour and had travelled about 20 miles when I realized that there was an unopened bottle of bourbon on the seat next to me. There were a dozen more in the trunk to trade later. Now I needed to get warm. I unscrewed the cap and took a little swig. It tasted terrible but had the effect I wanted. My stomach was on fire. I waited for the fire to spread and warm my feet and hands. After 15 or 20 minutes, the flames started to die down and parts of me still felt cold. I decided to restoke my internal furnace and took a second swig.

It was only beginning to get light. The storm continued and visibility remained poor. After a quick glance to ensure that the bourbon was secure on the passenger seat, I looked back at the road. Suddenly, rolling across the highway directly in the path of my vehicle was the biggest self-propelled tire I ever had seen. I applied the brakes slowly, but firmly, to avoid skidding. The car fishtailed a bit and came to a stop on the road and shoulder. I watched the tire roll by and crash into the trees.

While I was stopped, I leaned to my right, rolled down the passenger window, and threw away the bottle of bourbon. I vowed not just to give up drinking and driving but to give up alcohol entirely. Two short swigs of anything that brings on hallucinations such as a self-propelled tire traveling on the road with me could not be good for the mind or body.

I was not hallucinating. Fifty yards ahead I discovered the source of the tire. It had fallen from a huge, East German transport truck heading west. The truck had crashed head-on into a sedan traveling east.

For three seasons, travel on the autobahn moved east and west on two-lane roads with a 40 yard grass median between the four lanes. But during the long winters, to save money and wear and tear on the autobahn surface, with far less vehicular travel, the East German government closed one side. What had been a two-lane, one-way road was converted to a two-lane road with travel in both directions. Breaks in the median permitted local travelers to enter and exit the autobahn. The open and closed sides were rotated every year.

There were any number of reasons for the cause of the accident but none of them concerned me. What did concern me was the fact that the wreckage was blocking any further travel in both directions. I got out of my car and ran to the two vehicles. I counted four passengers none of whom appeared to be conscious. In those days, no one wore seat belts because none of the vehicles was equipped with any.

In the transport truck, the force of the impact had propelled the driver partially over the steering wheel, which was gnarled beneath the mass of his body, and into the windshield which shattered almost completely. The only part of the windshield still intact was a huge shard extending from the top of the windshield frame into the driver's forehead which was split open.

Some of the contents in the cargo bay had caught fire. If the driver were not already dead, then he would be after his vehicle exploded. I climbed into the cab on the passenger's side and extracted the shard and smaller fragments from his forehead. Then I leaned him back off the steering wheel. From the looks of the steering wheel, I assumed he also had suffered severe internal injuries and possibly was dead. Dead or alive, I ran around to his side of the cab and opened the door. I stood on the step and struggled to turn him. From the ground I tugged at his body. He tilted 45 degrees and fell into and on top of me. As I wiggled to get out from under him, I heard him moan. That was good. At least he was not dead.

I dragged him by his upper body to a distance that I thought was safe if there were an explosion. Then I ran to my car and took a blanket from the trunk. I placed him on the blanket, removed my cold-weather parka and covered him. Half an hour earlier I needed two swigs of bourbon to keep warm. Now I was sweating.

The situation was more challenging at the sedan. It looked as if the sedan had been impacted directly to its front, knocked backwards from the impact and spun around on the ice which had increased the damage. The front of the sedan must have impacted the truck below its higher bumper. The sedan's engine compartment, windshield, and the front half of the roof were crushed in and down toward the passenger compartment. The front two doors were folded inward and were impossible for me to open. I was able to open one of the back doors. Inside were three men all wearing Soviet Army uniforms: two younger men in the front, and one much older man in the back.

From my auto, I retrieved the pillow, blanket and linens that I had packed to use at the Kallman residence. I had not wanted my hosts for the weekend to have to do laundry because I had been their overnight guest.

After I opened the back door, I reached under the arms of the older man and pulled him from the sedan. I dragged him away, and placed him on the ground over the linens and half the blanket with his head on the pillow. Then I covered him with the other half of the blanket.

Back at the sedan there was nothing that could be done for the two passengers in the front. The vehicle was so mangled, as were their bodies, that I was unable to reach either of them or touch a wrist or throat to feel for a pulse. I could neither see nor hear any signs of life.

Inside the sedan, I saw three radios which looked similar to those used by the U.S. military. One was wedged between the roof of the sedan and the console between the front seats. Two others were on the floor in the rear. Also on the floor was a thick, black-leather briefcase. I assumed that the briefcase and radios were for use by the older man now lying on the ground next to the sedan. The two individuals in front probably were his driver and his aide or assistant.

I did not know how to operate the radios nor did I know if they would work. Regardless, I used the push-to-talk handsets on each of the three radios and called for help. First in English I said, "This is Lieutenant James Pelosi, United States Army. I am at the scene of serious accident involving a truck and a sedan in which this radio is located. There are four men who are injured seriously. I need medical help. I think I am near mile marker number 50 traveling to the west on the Berlin to Helmstedt autobahn."

Without waiting for a response, I used all three radios to make the same request for help again using my Level II German. (Thank you, Berlin Brigade commanding general, for requiring that I learn the language.) Again, no response.

Finally, I tried a third time, now in Russian. (Thank you, Soviet Senior Lieutenant, Spandau Prison Officer of the Guard, for shaming me into learning Russian.)

Still with no response, I left to check on the two men lying on the ground. No one else had arrived at the accident site. I went first to the truck driver, He had a pulse and was breathing. I took a pillow case, dampened it in the snow and used half to clean the gaping wound at his forehead and the blood from his face. Then I left him to check on the passenger from the sedan. He, too, was breathing and had a pulse. I used the clean half of the pillowcase to wash his face hoping that the cold sensation would revive him. It did not.

Much to my surprise, the radios suddenly came alive. All at the same time, voices from two or three radios in two or three languages were asking questions and making comments.

In Russian, "Is this American officer?"

In English, "Where are you in location? What is health of passengers?"

I responded, first in English then Russian if I could, to as many questions that I could understand which were asked in English and Russian. The questions were coming on two radios faster than I could answer on the third.

It was hard for me to hear and understand anything from the back of the sedan with all the chatter from the radios. It became much harder when I heard the roar of engines. I left the sedan and looked up and out past the accident site. What I saw I thought I had to be imagining.

In the air were half a dozen Soviet Army helicopters. On the ground racing down the autobahn and travelling cross-country were a variety of Soviet Army vehicles. I expected to see tanks at any time.

Two of the Soviet helicopters were medevac platforms. The remaining four contained soldiers carrying AK-47 rifles who deployed around the accident site and secured the area from everyone and everything.

Two of the Soviet ground vehicles were ambulances; one was a communications van; three or four others were troop carriers which deployed additional squads of soldiers to support those who had arrived by air and to reinforce the security of the area.

I knew from his face that the old man was not General Secretary Brezhnev nor was he any member of the Soviet Politburo whom I could recognize. But whoever he was, he wasn't very far down the chain of command to rate this sort of response.

A Soviet army major escorted by two junior officers and a squad of soldiers with their AK-47's at the ready found me immediately. I was the only person standing there who was not wearing a Soviet army uniform.

In nearly perfect English he asked, "Are you American army Lieutenant?"

Recognizing his rank, I saluted and answered, "Yes, Sir."

I showed him my ID card and gave him my copy of the travel orders which had been certified by the Soviets at Checkpoint Bravo.

The medical personnel had removed and evacuated the old man and the truck driver. Others succeeded prying open the doors to the sedan, removing and evacuating the two front-seat occupants.

Next, I was asked, "How did this happen?"

I told him that I did not know, and that, having seen the rolling tire, I was the next and only car along almost immediately after the accident had occurred.

I described my actions. One of the junior officers with him was taking notes as I spoke.

When I finished he said, "Thank you. What about documents?"

"What documents?" I said with surprise.

"You saw briefcase in back seat near passenger. Did you read documents?"

"I saw the briefcase and I saw four injured people. I had no interest in the briefcase or its contents, and I still don't. I never touched the briefcase. All I touched besides the passengers were the three radios to call for help."

"Thank you. Please wait here."

Where was I to go? There was a Soviet vehicle on every side of my 1973 Chevrolet Malibu and a squad of armed Soviet soldiers walking around it and looking inside. The autobahn still was blocked by Soviet and now East German personnel and their equipment which were loading the accident vehicles on to flatbed trailers.

When the Major returned he asked me, "Do you require medical attention?"

"No, Sir, Thank you," I answered.

"Do you want to go Helmstedt or return Berlin?"

"I would like to go Helmstedt. I mean I want to go to Helmstedt."

"We are ready now."

He and a soldier walked me to my vehicle. The soldier opened the car's door. This was probably the first and only time in his life that he would put his hands on an American-made automobile. I got in and a Soviet army sedan pulled in front of me. Before I closed my door I heard the words, "Please follow me."

There were another 50 miles to travel to get to the Soviet checkpoint at Helmstedt. From my rear-view mirror I could see another sedan, what I thought was the communications van, and a troop transport vehicle, all behind me.

When we arrived after about an hour on the road, the Major gestured with him arm and hand for me to pull up behind him. The three vehicles following me pulled alongside our two vehicles. The Major sent a soldier into the checkpoint and he returned with a detail to whom he issued orders.

The Major told me that processing through the checkpoint was waived and I that could proceed directly to the American checkpoint. We saluted each other and shook hands. All this was witnessed by an ever-increasing number of U.S. military policemen at Checkpoint Alpha. I arrived five hours later than the four-hour maximum time limit for transit.

Private E-2 Nixon greeted me with "Good afternoon, Sir, you are late! You are banned from further travel on the autobahn."

I didn't have time to command, "Find me an officer ASAP, Private," when four officers suddenly appeared. They all outranked me. The two company-grade officers were assigned to the checkpoint security force. The two field grade officers were assigned to the Military Liaison Mission in East Germany.

I knew to expect dozens of questions and be expected to complete reams of paperwork. I was asked to produce my ID card and my leave orders, which I did. After that someone said, "Come with us, Lieutenant."

"Sir I would like to clean up and use the telephone first."

"That can wait!"

"No Sir, it can't. I want to call my commander in Berlin. If you don't let me do that then I'll say and do nothing until you let me. Right now, I'm the good guy in all this. If you treat me as if I'm the bad guy, then you'll get nothing from me. My commanders in Berlin will get involved and I will not end up the loser."

After some hesitation and consultation, one of the more senior officers said to me, "Do what you have to do, Lieutenant."

I called my commander and told him everything that had happened.

He asked me if I was alright and if I wanted to return to Berlin. If I wanted to return, then he would send a team to travel with me or drive back my car. I told him that I was expected at a belated wedding reception in Bad Hersfeld and that I was already six hours late. I wanted to continue my leave.

I made sure that I was overheard telling him that I felt as if I were being harassed, having been banned from the autobahn and not being permitted to use the restroom or the telephone. My commander told me to stay where I was, close to a telephone and not to say or do anything until after he got back in touch with me. I reported this to the officers who had been monitoring the conversation. Then I excused myself to wash the blood from my hands, arms, and clothing.

Within an hour, a call came from Berlin. I was instructed to provide only information concerning the details of the accident. I could provide information concerning my comments and actions with the Soviet Major only with respect to the accident and my involvement in rendering aid and seeking help. Anything else that I saw, said, or did with the Soviet military I would report after I returned to Berlin. I complied, answered their questions, and completed their paperwork.

Two hours later, I departed Checkpoint Alpha and arrived at the Kallman residence. I was nine hours late. They did not believe one word I told them about why I was delayed.

The next morning, Jeff came into the spare bedroom and drew back the covers. He sat on the edge of the bed and woke me more gently than the sergeants who wake their troops when they want them up and active. He was eager to tell me that Tina had heard on both German and AFN (Armed Forces Network) radio stations a story about the accident on the autobahn.

Apparently something really did happen to delay my visit to them.

We shared a pleasant two-day visit. I toured Jeff's Air Defense Artillery unit and Hawk surface-to-air missile site locations. The highlight for me was Tina's two home-cooked meals.

Early Sunday afternoon I was back at Checkpoint Alpha. Private Nixon's statement that I had been banned from further travel on the autobahn was overruled. I processed through the American segment routinely. At the Soviet checkpoint, my vehicle was waved to the side by a Soviet sentry who saluted.

"Strange," I thought to myself.

As I pulled over, I saw the Major with whom I had worked two days earlier at the accident site. I exited the car to greet him. We exchanged salutes and shook hands. He told me that processing was waived again for me and that I could proceed directly to Berlin.

"Fsee-oh horow-shevah." (Good luck.)

The Soviet sentries were on alert for my vehicle as I approached Checkpoint Bravo. One sentry opened the barrier. The second sentry waved me through. Both sentries saluted crisply as I passed them.

Through no fault of my own, I had missed three opportunities to trade magazines and bourbon for belts and buckles. My troops would be disappointed.

In Berlin, on duty Monday, my soldiers were waiting outside the barracks and rushed to greet me as I drove up for morning PT. They had heard the story on the Armed Forces Radio network and also read some embellished details in "The Stars and Stripes" newspaper. Specialist Hensley said, "Damn, Sir, we just asked you to trade for the belts and buckles! We didn't want you to kill anyone to get them for us."

For what was described as an heroic life-saving event, I received commendations from the President of the United States, Gerald Ford; the Governor of New York where I was an absentee resident; the Chairman of the National Association of the Red Cross; and, several veterans organizations. I also received a life-saving medal from the army and a commendation from the Chairman of the Joint Chiefs of Staff with endorsements through six levels down to my company commander.

I am most proud of the commendation that I received from the government of the Soviet Union and the "Medal of Merit" from the four-star Commanding General, Group Soviet Forces Germany.

We were supposed to be enemies.

If you don't know where you are going, you'll end up someplace else."
– Yogi Berra, New York Yankees baseball player and team manager.

3. Concept and Plan.

The driving distance between the parking lot at the American Cemetery overlooking Omaha Beach in Normandy, France, and the traffic circle in front of the Brandenburg Gate, Berlin, Germany, is approximately 825 miles. The ground route along which American soldiers fought during World War II between the battles at Omaha Beach on D-Day, June 6, 1944, and their entrance into Berlin in May 1945, was approximately 1,000 miles. I planned my walking route for "The TREK" to be as close as possible to the route taken by the soldiers in the American infantry divisions which fought in Europe during the war. Matching those divisions with their lines of advance generated a convergent route that was approximately 900 miles.

I dedicated two months to completing "The TREK." I would need to walk an average of 15 miles a day. My plan was to arrive in France and find lodging as close as possible to Omaha Beach before the 70th anniversary of the landings on June 6, 2014.

Before then, I wanted to walk the length of the five beaches which the Allies assaulted: Utah, Omaha, Gold, Juno, and Sword; and imagine if I could, the sights that the soldiers must have seen from the water. In whatever peace there might be along that walk, I sought to sense the experience of young men still in their teens and early 20's suffering the horrors of combat – many of them for the first time. Could it be possible to picture witnessing friends and fellow soldiers being blown apart, dismembered, incinerated, and drowned? Could it be possible to imagine a scene more chaotic or confusing? More importantly to me personally, would I be able to envision what I would have done had I been there?

Finally, I hoped to be able to visit the American and British cemeteries before they became flooded with veterans and their families, tourists, dignitaries surrounded by security teams, and the international media.

On the morning of June 6, 2014, far from the crowds of the anniversary celebrants, I would start walking inland and east through France, Belgium, Luxemburg, and Germany, finishing two months later in Berlin. The soldiers did not sleep in hotels, motels, or campsites; neither would I. The soldiers did not eat in restaurants or outdoor cafes; neither would I. The soldiers drank mostly coffee, tea, and water; so would I. The soldiers lived for days and weeks in a minimum amount of the same clothing; so would I. The soldiers washed their clothing and bathed infrequently; so would I. At least that was my plan before I started. Everyone who has ever experienced a long-distance walk, hike or bicycle trip knows that there are an unlimited number of things that can go wrong and how important it is to plan and do everything right.

The remainder of this section is dedicated to the details of the planning, organizing, scheduling, supplying, and funding "The TREK."

"Camping is nature's way of promoting the motel business."
- Dave Barry, Author.

4. Hiking and Camping.

Planning a daily, 15-mile walk through four countries and camping overnight wherever I stopped presented the first set of problems for planning the route. For reasons of comfort, health, and safety I wanted to start and end each day near or within a city or town. I would have an opportunity to obtain drinking water, and to buy coffee, fresh fruit, and bread to supplement the military "Meals Ready to Eat" (MRE) which I would carry. There also would be access to law enforcement and medical services in case of an emergency.

With very slight variations, I was able to mesh these concerns with the routes of the American infantry divisions as they fought east across France into Germany. I would walk for 59 days: 22 days through France, five days through Belgium, one day through Luxembourg, and 31 days through Germany. Like the many other American infantrymen who had never seen Paris before they liberated it, I had never seen Paris and planned a re-liberation. Under fire, the American infantrymen took 71 days to reach Paris on August 25, 1944. Hoping that no one would be shooting at me as I walked, I planned to reach Paris in 11 days on June 16, 2014. I would re-liberate the City of Lights for three days.

Ten days later, I planned a second, one-day rest stop in Reims, France, where the armistice which ended World War II was signed on May 7, 1945. There would be a third, one-day stop, in Bastogne, Belgium, the focus of the epic Battle of the Bulge in December 1944.

The final rest stop would be one day in the Harz Mountains in Germany, 170 miles from Berlin. I frequently had vacationed there 40 years earlier during my assignment in Berlin and occasionally in later years.

There was a volume of information about camping throughout Europe in books, travel magazines, tourist brochures, and on the internet. Much of it described camping in the summer at the height of the tourist season between May and September. That fit perfectly with my schedule. The descriptions included campsite locations, facilities and amenities, and distances to the ocean, lakes, mountains, hill country, and tourist attractions. All of the nationally registered and recognized campsites charged fees for sites and amenities. Almost all of them offered showers with hot water, toilets and equipment washing areas. Unfortunately, there were no campsites that were close to "The TREK" route in France, Belgium and Luxembourg. All were located more than five miles away which presented an unacceptable ten-mile detour. There was only one campsite in Germany. In Koblenz, there was a four-star facility along the water at the intersection of the Rhine and Moselle rivers and within a short walk to the 2,000 year old city.

I was forced to plan to camp off-road in the forests, fields, and roadside rest stops. Several sources stated that many farmers in remote locations supported overnight camping to supplement their income. For additional fees, a camper might be able to obtain a shower and breakfast. Reservations for these opportunities were made exclusively through the internet. Without such a reservation, campers were strongly encouraged to secure permission from the landowner to avoid issues of trespassing. As a courtesy, campers were expected to remove their trash and restore the campsite.

I would be traveling with a minimum of camping gear: a two-man tent, sleeping bag, and air mattress. After a brief introduction and description of "The TREK," supported by a copy of the route and pictures of my father's combat photographs, I felt confident that I could obtain permission from landowners in France, Belgium and Luxembourg. Germany would be different and perhaps more difficult. There, I would describe only "The TREK" route and my father's duty as a pilot in support of the Berlin airlift. Almost all of the references cautioned that the laws concerning hiking, cross-country land navigation, and camping on land in other than recognized campsites were different in every country. There was not one European Union standard for hiking and camping. France was represented as the least restrictive of the four countries.

Paris is located at nearly the same latitude as Vancouver, British Columbia, and Volgograd, Russia. Berlin is slightly further north, close to the same latitude as Birmingham, England. In summer, from the beginning of June through the middle of August, there would be between 15 and 16 hours of daylight. For most of my life, I have been able to walk comfortably at a pace of three miles an hour. The daily 15-mile walk would require five hours. During "The TREK" the sun would rise between 5:30 and 6:00, and would set at Omaha Beach at 10:03; Paris at 9:57; Bastogne at 9:49; Koblenz at 9:38; the Harz at 9:20; and, Berlin at 8:55. I expected to be able to walk every day with plenty of light to sightsee and to explore locally in the early evening after I had stopped and set up camp.

I needed to develop a routine that would support walking almost 900 miles through 56 cities and towns. In addition to dedicating a minimum of five hours to walk the 15 miles, I had to schedule time to eat, set-up and tear-down the campsite, tour by day, explore by night, rest, and sleep.

I created a draft daily schedule. Before I departed for Europe, I would train for two months to test the schedule and tweak it until I was satisfied that it would work.

The schedule provided for:

0600-0700: Wake. Hygiene. Breakfast.
0700-0730: Stretch. Decamp.
0730-1100: TREK: nine miles.

1100-1400: Lunch. Rest.
1400-1700: TREK: six miles.
1700-1800: Encamp.
1800-2100: Dinner. Explore.
2100-2200: Journal.
2200-0600: Sleep.

The sources for information about the cities and towns through which I would pass came almost entirely from the internet. Except for Paris, I would not be anywhere long enough for any leisure as a tourist. In the other towns, I was interested in the history and the places where I might explore historical sites, battlefields, war memorials, military cemeteries, museums, and churches. The internet also provided valuable information about local annual, seasonal, and holiday events and celebrations. If I were not too tired at the end of each day, then I hoped to participate in any festive occasion.

Throughout 26 days in France, and in addition to the four nights and three days that I planned to tour Paris as a belated liberator, I wanted to see, in Bayeux, the centuries-old, huge, embroidered tapestry which depicted the Norman invasion of England in 1066; the war memorial in Caen, the Sanctuary of St. Theresa in Lisieux, the Cathedral of Notre Dame in Evreux, and the World War II Surrender Museum in Reims.

With only four days to pass through Belgium, I would make time to see the Church of St. Lawrence in Virton, the ancient Roman architecture and baths in Arlon, and the monuments and museums of Bastogne. If I stayed on schedule then I would be in Bastogne to celebrate the Fourth of July with the locals. That promised to be festive. Weather permitting, I hoped to walk through the gardens and visit the Abbey of Cinqfontaines in Troisvierges, Luxembourg.

Much of West Germany I had seen when I was assigned there on three tours of duty between 1973-1976, 1983-1985, and 1988-1989. In 2014, the former cities of East Germany would be open to me, and I would pass through at least 10 of them. In the very remote and rural areas there may not be much that would have changed. But I expected to see great changes for the better in the cities where, for more than 25 years, I had seen only drab pictures of a dull and dreary existence.

"A sound logistics plan is the foundation upon which any operation should be based."
 - Admiral Raymond A. Spruance, Commander-in-Chief, U.S. Forces, Pacific.

5. Logistics.

Experienced hikers and backpackers, the professional and recreational organizations which support them, and the medical community strongly recommend that when backpacking an individual carry a weight not to exceed one-third his body weight. That recommendation is tempered by several factors such as the hiker's health and experience, his equipment, the terrain, seasonal climatic conditions, and the daily weather in the area. There is no ideal weight to recommend. Over time, a hiker will determine it for himself. In the literature, the backpack weight carried by the most experienced, long-duration hikers averaged, at the high end, between one-fourth to one-third of their body weight.

I am just shy of six feet tall. For about 45 years I have weighed 150 pounds varying only a pound or two either side of 150. I decided to limit the weight of the camping gear, clothing, food, personal hygiene items, and supplementals to one-third my weight, 50 pounds. I reduced that weight further by ten percent and settled on a backpack and contents not to exceed 45 pounds. I made the fudge factor reduction arbitrarily assuming that I would weaken physically over time, and a weight reduction would help me.

Everything that I would need for the 59-day length of "The TREK" I would carry with me. It was important to select items that served the greatest purpose but weighed the least. The priority for items which I considered essential was first, backpacking gear and camping equipment; next, clothing; third, food; and last, personal hygiene items.

The internet again provided the most useful and convenient method to research backpacking gear and camping equipment, none of which I owned. My 40-year old Army rucksack was too bulky, small, and tattered to serve any purpose. In addition to the internet, magazines such as *Backpacker* and *Outdoor Life* were most helpful. Some editions of *Men's Health*, a health and fitness magazine, contained articles with relevant information.

Everything which I needed for hiking and camping I found in one store in Houston, Texas. Recreational Equipment, Incorporated. REI, as it is more commonly known, is an American-owned outdoor recreation, sporting goods, and clothing store. A membership is required to make a purchase. On my first visit to the store all I did was describe "The TREK" in detail and ask several sales representatives in the different departments what their professional recommendations would be for the equipment that I thought I would need. One salesman recommended against the purchase of a pillow, saying that it would add unnecessary bulk to the backpack. No one whom I had known in the Army ever included a pillow among his field gear. He suggested that I wrap my T-shirts and underwear in a pillowcase to form a pillow.

At home, I researched the product information for all of the recommended items. I returned to the store and purchased an "Osprey Atmos 65, Medium" backpack for $249.95; a "Quarter Dome T2 Plus" two-man tent for $249.73; a "Kelty Cosmic Down, Regular, Right" sleeping bag for $129.95; a "Big Agnes, Insulated Air Core, Regular" air mattress for $89.95; two pairs of "Salomon XA Pro 3D Ultra Mid, Size 12" walking shoes for $145. a pair; and one pair of lightweight convertible, (full-length to shorts) trousers for $85.20. After my credit card bill arrived, it made little difference to the balance in my bank account that I had saved $24.50 by not buying a pillow.

I owned all of the clothing that I knew I needed: baseball cap, wool watch cap, sunglasses, poncho, windbreaker, sweater, long-sleeve dress shirt, two T-shirts, six pairs of briefs and socks, one pair of jeans, a belt, and two pairs of shorts. Everything was easily replaceable if anything were lost or stolen.

After my arrival in France, I planned to buy and carry two one-pint plastic bottles of water. I would add to or refill one bottle with water from public sources as I drank. The second bottle would serve as a spare. The MRE's would provide the bulk of my daily diet. For my first 12 years in the Army I had eaten canned C-rations. The taste was tolerable and they served their purpose. MRE's came into the military inventory in 1981. I thought that the taste was as good as, if not better than, the C-rations which they replaced, although not all the members of the military agreed. Some of their slang terms for the acronym, MRE, included, "Meals Rejected by Everyone," "Meals Rejected by the Enemy," and, most disparagingly, "Meals Rejected by Ethiopians." I am not fussy about the taste of food when I am hungry.

An MRE provided approximately 1,200 calories. I estimated that I ate 3,000 calories daily. The weight of one MRE was between 1 and 1.5 pounds, depending upon the menu selection. I could reduce that weight by up to six ounces a meal by discarding the cardboard container, plastic wrapping and non-essential items, such as plastic ware and candy. Instead of plastic ware, I would use metal utensils that I could wash after each use.

At the start at Normandy, and then every seven days into "The TREK," I would carry 14 meals and consume two each day. Additional calories would be provided by snack bars (two a day), and bread and fresh fruit that I could buy. Each day, the weight of the backpack would be reduced ever so slightly by about two to three pounds. By the end of the week, that daily reduction would amount to almost 20 pounds. I hoped to complete each seven-day resupply at hotels or guesthouses located near or within the towns through which I would pass. Two months before the start of "The TREK," I wrote to multiple hoteliers in both English and their native language. I asked if I could send a package of freeze-dried food, weighing about 12 to 15 pounds,(20 to

25 kilograms), addressed to me at their lodging facility. I provided a one-page description of "The TREK," the route, photos of my father and me, and my anticipated date of arrival.

Within a month, I had acknowledged and accepted the support of seven hoteliers. The seven packages containing 15 MRE's (one spare) would be mailed in early May. There is a maxim within the military that "you win wars by planning to lose them." In the event of a lost package, I would purchase my food locally until I reached the next resupply location.

The last logistical concern for me was communications. In 2014, I had owned a simple cellular telephone for 14 years. It did nothing more than make and receive calls – exactly the reason why I owned it. I kept it in my automobile to use for only emergencies. I had purchased it in January 2000, after I accepted a job at NASA's Johnson Space Center in Houston. By day at work, I expected to be contacted in person and by electronic mail or the landline at my desk. Since I would not provide my personal cell phone number, NASA provided and funded a pager for me. After pagers were discontinued, NASA refused to provide and fund a cellular telephone for me. Blackberrys were state of the art technology then. Over time, Smart Phones continued to evolve, but I had no interest in them, never bought one, and kept my primitive cell phone. I did own a computer to communicate electronically. I also owned a first class, 35mm camera with a variety of quality lenses. The camera was purchased for me by the State Department when I was assigned to embassy duty in Helsinki and Moscow in the 1980's.

My friends tried to convince me that investing in a Smart phone would be a valuable resource throughout "The TREK." First, it would provide valuable Global Positioning System (GPS) navigation. That would eliminate the need for bulky maps and a compass. One neighbor, convinced that I was the only employee at NASA who did not own a Smart phone, told me that I would not have to carry my heavy sextant and parchments of hand-drawn maps. Next, a Smart phone would include a camera that could produce not only still photos but also videos with sound. The still photos could be tagged with locations, dates, and times as a record. Hundreds of photos could be stored using only a minimum amount of memory.

In April 2014, at the local Apple store I examined an I-Phone 5S which was for sale at $700. The technician who was describing and demonstrating the phone did not believe that I worked for NASA and did not own a Smart phone or know how one worked. The astronaut who was standing next to us told the rep that I was more comfortable with two cans and a string.

The Apple store tech explained the basic functions. He was astute enough to inform me that the phone would not work in Europe without a special phone card. The phone card and fees would be different for each country. From his personal experience, he told me that cell phone coverage in many parts of Europe was unreliable. Cell phone towers are not located as densely in

Europe as they are in the United States. They provide coverage only in limited areas near the big cities with large populations. Coverage, where it does exist, often is blocked by the centuries-old, massive, concrete structures within the cities. He suggested that I look for groups of high school and college-age students and other groups of young people. Most probably they would be congregating with their cell phones in areas where coverage was available. I was about to pay more than $700. for an electronic device that I was not sure I could use for anything other than a camera. But I decided to take a chance. I consider myself a skilled navigator and intended to pack a compass if GPS were not available. It proved to be a smart decision. Even though I had no plans to call anyone during "The TREK," I thought that I had a telephone which might work.

"I've spent most of my money on women and beer. The rest I just wasted."
– Overheard in a confessional, St. Clare of Assisi Roman Catholic Church, Clear Lake, Texas.

6. Budgeting.

Just before midnight on September 30, 2013, an order from the Director of the Federal Government's Office of Management and Budget closed down the government effective 12:01 a.m. on October 1, 2013. It was the first shutdown of the federal government in 17 years and lasted for 16 days. More than a million federal workers who had been declared "essential" were ordered to work without pay. Hundreds of thousands of their non-essential coworkers were furloughed. Federal buildings, offices, facilities, national parks, and monuments were closed. Many Americans were upset and frustrated. The shutdown cost two billion dollars. Not surprisingly, there was absolutely nothing productive to show for it. Many tourists were inconvenienced and forced to change schedules, plans, and reservations.

But many American veterans were enraged. Closed not only were the sites that they considered sacred in the United States, such as Arlington Cemetery, and the Pearl Harbor and Iwo Jima Memorials, but also the 20 American National Cemeteries in Europe. Many World War II veterans in their late 80s and 90s, who fought at Normandy on June 6, 1944, when they were in their late teens and early 20's, had traveled to Europe. Some were escorted by their families. Some traveled as members of veterans organizations. They had traveled for perhaps their last opportunity to reflect and pay their respects to other veterans.

More loathsome than the closings was the fact that money was spent and work expended to erect barricades at these hallowed sites. The barricades blocked the access for veterans to the gravesites of other veterans who had given their lives for their country. Stranded at Normandy and other national cemeteries in Europe, the veterans' disdain for the current commander in chief, was reported in hundreds of international news media sources and echoed within the membership of thousands of veterans organizations. The shared sentiment was that a non-veteran, with a schemer's reputation for signing executive orders that violated the Constitution, did not issue an order to open these sites. Veterans and others felt certain that Democrats, such as Harry Truman and John Kennedy, and Republicans, such as Dwight Eisenhower, Ronald Reagan, George H. W. Bush and George W. Bush, would not have tolerated this national disgrace and insult to the veterans.

When the extent of this travesty was exposed, I vowed that I would conduct "The TREK" with a redoubled effort. It became more important to succeed in this project to honor the veterans. I named the project, "Normandy to Berlin: The TREK to Honor the Legacies."

The cost of the project would be considerable if I were able to accomplish everything which I hoped to do. I wanted to succeed in the 900 mile walk along a route that had historical significance for all our veterans, especially those who served in Europe during the two world wars and the cold war which followed. If I were successful then I planned to write a book based upon my experiences. Any funds from the sale of this book would be donated directly to wounded warriors. I never have been interested in supporting any organization where the majority of donated funds are used for unconscionable executive salaries, travel expenses, huge offices with lavish furnishings, mass mailings, and infrastructure costs. Any profits from a book would be donated directly to a veteran in need whom I knew personally.

In 2011, I donated $5,000. to a blind marine who lost his sight as a result of an Improvised Explosive Device (IED) explosion while on patrol in Afghanistan. With that money, he purchased a German shepherd guide dog and the services of a professional dog handler and trainer. The money funded the dog for life and four months' training. The trainer stayed in the marine's home with him and his dog every day for the first month; three to five days for the second month; one to three days for the third month; and, was on call every day for any amount of time during the fourth month. The marine's rent and his other living expenses were paid, in part, by a Veterans' Administration (VA) disability check.

My expenses would be considerably less if I were able to obtain the financial support of sponsors with deep pockets who shared my sentiments. I generated a list of almost 500 potential donors more than 400 of whom were veterans. High tax rates in Europe are tolerated because "caring is sharing."

In the United States there are 16 billionaires who are veterans. To each person I wrote a personal letter with a generic theme which described the purpose and plan of "The TREK." I included background information about my father's service in World War II and the Berlin Airlift, and my service in the Army and Berlin. I wrote that I had hoped to publish a book about "The TREK." I emphasized that I planned to donate all profits from the sales of that book to individual wounded warriors for whom the Veterans Administration (VA) is unable to provide the complete care which they need.

I started with actor Richard Thomas who portrayed me in a 1975 made-for-television movie, "*The Silence*," about an unfortunate experience for me, the Corps and the Academy while I was a cadet at West Point. No response.

Next I wrote to Denzel Washington, who starred in the movie, "*Crimson Tide*," which was filmed aboard the Italian Navy submarine, "SKS Salvatore Pelosi," named after grandfather Salvatore Pelosi, Italian Navy Gold Medal winner. I sent him two photos: one of him and one of me on the SKS Salvatore Pelosi at different times. No response.

I sent letters to two of the media's talking heads who frequently advocate for veterans issues on their broadcasts. First on that list was Bill O'Reilly followed by Rush Limbaugh. No response.

I wrote a shorter letter to each of three former presidents: President Jimmy Carter; President George H. W. Bush; President George W. Bush; and, billionaire presidential candidate H. Ross Perot. All veterans. No response.

But I did receive an electronic response from half-billionaire, former presidential primary candidate, Steve Forbes. I wrote to him at "sforbes@forbes.com." The response: "Rejected: Message goes Against Email Policies." It didn't read as the sort of response, favorable or unfavorable, which I would have expected from a potential president. I am sure that the quality of the punctuation does not reflect on the quality of the man. Personally, I try to be attentive to anything that is produced in my name and over my signature.

More than 120 letters were sent to the cadet and midshipman unit commanders of the graduating classes at the four Service Academies: The United States Air Force Academy at Colorado Springs, Colorado; The United States Coast Guard Academy at New London, Connecticut; The United States Military Academy at West Point, New York; and The United States Naval Academy at Annapolis, Maryland. In the letter, I described "The TREK" and asked for support from only the members of the graduating class who, within two months, would be joining the officer ranks and following those who had served during the legacy events.

There were no responses from anyone at the Coast Guard Academy. Nor were there any from anyone at the Naval Academy. From the United States Air Force Academy, a field grade officer wrote to inform me that that all requests for support from the Academy must be routed first through the public affairs office. But not one of the 40 letters had been addressed to him.

The sole response was from West Point Cadet Company Commander Rommel Claude Verano, Company D-2, at the Academy. In an extremely polite letter, this native Texan informed me of his support. A week before graduation for his West Point Class of 2014, I received a second equally polite and supportive letter. Enclosed was his company's donation in cash.

Thank you very much, Second Lieutenant Rommel Verano, United States Army.

Finally, I wrote 300 members of the Hollywood fame and shame community who had produced, directed, or starred in films and television shows which had a military theme. At the top of that list was director Steven Spielberg and actor Tom Hanks, both so very much responsible for the success of the 1998 film, "*Saving Private Ryan*," about the D-Day landings and combat in western Europe. Other Hollywood's celebrities to whom I sent letters included veterans such as Mel Brooks, a corporal in World War II who fought at the Battle of the Bulge; Bill Cosby who served as a Navy Corpsman; Dennis Franz, Army; Gene Hackman, Marines; Harvey Keitel, Marines; J.R. Martinez, Army; Rob Riggle, Marines; Tom Selleck, California National Guard; and,

Montel Williams, Navy.

Although almost all of the 300 letters were addressed and mailed to the individuals and to their agents, I failed to receive a single response.

The price for round-trip airfare between Houston and Paris on United Airlines in the summer of 2014 was approximately $1,500. I purchased the ticket, in part, using frequent flyer miles and charged only $99.60 to my credit card. I wrote a personal letter to Mr. Jeff Smisek, Chairman and Chief Executive Officer at United Airlines. The letter contained much of the same information which I provided to others from whom I was seeking financial support. I asked if he would rebate the $99.60 as a donation.

Two months later, I received a polite "Thank you, but No" response from someone in his office. I thought that over those two months, the number of staffers who handled my letter and the others who wrote, reviewed, and approved the negative reply must have cost Smisek ten times more than my Franklin. His deep pockets must have been sewn by Chinese slave labor. United Airlines does not need my business and will not get it.

At the same time, I wrote a man with the same title and very similar responsibilities, Mr. Kendall J. Powell, Chairman and Chief Executive Officer, General Mills. I told him about The TREK, and said that, as I was training, I was consuming one of his company's "Nature Valley Protein Chewy Bars, Peanut Butter Dark Chocolate" daily. I was buying them for a dollar a bar at the candy store. I added that I would need 112 bars, two for each day of the 56-day walk. I asked if he would donate them to me.

Within three days I received an electronic mail message from Ms. Kari Perreault, his executive assistant. She wrote that "we would be happy to help by donating the product to you," and she asked me to confirm my home address. Within two weeks, two cases containing 240 protein bars arrived at my home. Mr. Powell and his team donated more than twice the number of protein bars that I needed and had requested.

Thank you, Mr. Powell and Miss Kari.

Regardless of the cost, I grocery shop for products made only by General Mills. As an aside, "Chex Mix" is a snack which is available for purchase on certain United Airlines (-) flights. It is made by General Mills (+).

For years I have used a small, four-inch microbrush to supplement my oral hygiene care beyond brushing and flossing. Microbrush International, in Grafton, Wisconsin, produces tubes with these brushes in three sizes. I wrote and requested a donation of one tube containing 100 microbrushes explaining that the brushes would be especially helpful at times when I might have limited opportunity for proper dental hygiene. Immediately I received a response from the team of Ms. Anne Klein and her colleague, Heather. They sent not one but four tubes of the microbrushes, a year's supply, to my home.

Thank you, Miss Anne and Miss Heather.

The majority of the expenses for "The TREK" fell into 10 categories:

1. Administration. Passport fees; TREK logo design and production; research; postage stamps, and parcel post.
2. Clothing. All-weather gear; hiking boots; and shoes.
3. Communications. Smart phone with international service plans.
4. Equipment. Backpack; tent; sleeping bag; air mattress; tools.
5. Food. MRE's; snack bars; local supplements; restaurant meals.
6. Financial. Fees: ATM; currency exchange; wire transfers.
7. Legal. Pre-TREK counsel; intellectual property documentation.
8. Lodging. Normandy, two nights; Paris, four nights; Bastogne one night; The Harz, one night.
9. Insurance. Flight; international short-term medical and dental; personal property.
10. Travel. Round-trip flight between Houston and Paris; locally in Normandy, Paris, Bastogne and The Harz.

The guesstimated expenses were $7,000. I expected that round-trip air fare and the lodging in the summer, especially at Normandy during the D-Day anniversary celebrations and Paris in June, would be expensive. I knew the costs of the backpacking and camping gear, and also the Apple Smart phone. I was surprised that a single MRE cost $7.36 at the military commissary. I would need 112 MRES's at a cost of over $800. I was more surprised that a 20-pound parcel, containing 15 MRE's and one toothbrush, mailed parcel post between Houston and seven towns in France, Belgium and Germany, would cost an average of $50. a parcel.

I was prepared financially to fund the entire cost of "The TREK."

"Be a yardstick of quality. Some people are not used to an environment where excellence is expected."
  - Steve Jobs, Co-founder, Chairman and CEO of Apple, Inc. 1955-2011.

7. Public Affairs.

Much of an individual's reputation is based on his character and the quality of work that he produces. Character takes shape during childhood and usually defines a person by the time he is 25. The quality of a person's work at any age reflects his intelligence, aptitudes, ethics, and pride.

I do not consider anything that I have done in my life to be of inferior quality. But everything that I have done pales in comparison to the achievements of the veterans who fought and won World War II and saved their former enemies from starvation three years later during the Berlin Airlift. The 2014 anniversary celebrations recognizing the legacy events of the end of World War I, the D-Day landings at Normandy during World War II, the end of the Berlin Airlift, and the fall of the Berlin wall all were celebrated, for the most part, as individual events during May, June and November throughout much of Europe and elsewhere. "The TREK" was planned as a demonstration to link these four legacy events with one area: the single route stretching almost 1,000 miles between Omaha Beach in Normandy, France, and the Brandenburg Gate Berlin, Germany.

Along that route had marched the armies of the nations that fought in both world wars. Over that route had flown the air forces of the nations that fed Berliners and kept them alive. Across that route moved the people, technology, resources, and wealth of the free nations which helped to bring down the wall.

As an event, the two-month TREK along the same route would accomplish nothing of value to anyone other than me. But the opportunity to relate and share the reasons for "The TREK" as an event of historical significance offered the potential to raise an awareness of veterans and to promote support for issues important to the veterans.

I needed to bring attention to "The TREK."

I started in January 2014 in Houston. The publicity from that broadcast generated a front-page story by Yvette Orozco in one of Houston's local newspapers, *The Citizen*, in which she described the purpose and plan for "The TREK."

I made personal presentations to several Houston veterans organizations three of which provided more than $500. in donations.

My expectations of expanded publicity and national attention were lowered considerably when none of the talking heads, any of the country's more famous citizens and no one from the Hollywood community responded to my letters and appeals.

Internationally, I wrote to the Public Affairs Section at the American embassies in all four countries. In two of them, France and Germany, I would pass through Paris and Berlin where the American embassies are located. In my letters, I provided a list of each city and town, and the dates on which I expected to pass through them. I asked for the embassy's support to provide the local media with "The TREK" information. Included within each letter was my e-mail address for contact if any news source or organization were interested in scheduling a media event or interview. Given the fallout from the adverse publicity after barriers were erected at the American National cemeteries during the government shutdown, I suspected that I would not receive any response and I was correct.

Before my departure for Europe, I knew that I would have to generate my own publicity through the contacts I might make while walking and from the book I hoped to write after I had finished.

"An army marches on its stomach."
–   Attributed to Napoleon and Frederick the Great.

8. Training and Diet.

On June 3, 2014, I would fly from George Bush International airport in Houston and arrive on the morning of June 4th at Charles de Gaulle Airport in Paris. From there I would travel by train to Bayeux where I would settle in to a hotel to prepare to begin the walk two days later on June 6th.

For most of my life I have had a very active lifestyle that has included some form of physical activity between 60 and 90 minutes daily no more than six days a week. Except for yardwork, which I do not consider to be labor, Sunday always is work-free. That includes no electronics of any kind.

For 46 years I have weighed between 145 and 150 pounds. A personal review of my diet, and activities as a test subject in volunteer medical studies at the University of Texas Medical Branch, Galveston, Texas, over a period of eight years, have established that I have maintained that weight with a diet of approximately 3,000 calories daily. During my planning for "The TREK," I recorded and studied my daily activity schedule of work, exercise, diet and rest which required the 3,000 calories. Then I combined the rather relaxed work and light exercise routines, and added the demands of walking every day for an average of 15 miles over nine hours while carrying a 45-pound backpack for approximately 60 consecutive days. I calculated that I needed approximately 4,000 calories a day to maintain my weight.

At home I eat five meals daily: a light breakfast almost immediately after waking, a full breakfast after an hour of light weight lifting in my home gym, a full and sufficient lunch after an hour's swim in a 50-yard lap pool, a mid-afternoon snack, and a light dinner about two hours before my usual bedtime at 10. While walking, I planned to adhere to a schedule which would provide time for five meals daily but with changes to the times and volume of food which I would eat at each meal.

One MRE contains 1250 calories of which 13 percent is protein, 36 percent is fat, and 51 percent are carbohydrates. It also contains one-third of the Military Recommended Daily Allowance of vitamins and minerals which was unimportant to me. Two MRE's daily, or an MRE-equivalent meal on the economy, would provide approximately 2500 calories. Each Nature Valley protein bar contains 190 calories. Fruit provides about 100 calories a serving. A roll with meat or cheese or a small panini could contain roughly 200 calories. European beer or ale or a glass of wine would another 100 calories per serving.

After waking, I would eat an MRE. During the walk for the first three hours or nine miles, I would eat a piece of fruit and a Nature Valley protein bar and stop for a roll if I passed by a bakery. At lunch I would eat half of a second MRE. After a rest for about an hour, I would continue walking another two hours or six miles and eat either another piece of fruit or a protein bar until I stopped for the evening. Dinner would be the last half of the second MRE and whatever snack item was remaining. My expectation was that this schedule and diet should sustain me.

From the notes I made during "The TREK," I realized that if I drank alcohol in the evening I often had two servings. After walking 15 miles, the first beer usually was consumed too quickly for me to taste. The second beer, which I nursed, served to remind me that European beer has a real flavor vastly superior to most American beers containing government-mandated, taste-inhibiting preservatives.

For two weeks between Sunday, May 11th and Saturday, May 24, 2014, I planned to walk a 15-mile route daily throughout my neighborhood while carrying a 45-pound backpack, and then camp in my yard at night. The purpose would be to test my endurance and the ability of this diet to sustain me. I knew that the heat and humidity in Houston in late May would place far more stress on me physically than would the heat and humidity anywhere along the route between France and Germany. The difference in stress might be compensated by the differences in the terrain. My neighborhood is relatively flat. The terrain in Belgium and Germany would include rolling hills and mountainous regions.

The test went well. I was satisfied with the schedule, the routine of splitting the walk into two segments of nine and six miles, and the five meals during the day. There was a minor degree of boredom associated with trying to vary a 15-mile route through residential neighborhoods and along safe roads in the Clear Lake area of Houston where I live. Boredom would not be a factor when I was in Europe. During the training most of my neighbors looked at me as if they thought I could find something less demanding and more pleasant to do during the day.

"I'm not telling you it's going to be easy. I'm telling you it's going to be worth it."
–   From a United States Marine Corps recruiting poster.

9. Training. Strength Training Exercise.

Between 1969 and 1996, I served on duty with the United States Departments of Defense and State at military bases and embassies in the United States, Europe, Latin America and the former Soviet Union. All of the bases and embassies had extremely well-equipped gymnasiums. In addition to machines for cardio exercise, there always was a variety of weight-lifting equipment, including free weights and machines that provided a good strength training workout for lightweights like me at 150 pounds, across the physique spectrum to heavyweights at 220 pounds or more. Duty schedules, travel, field training exercises, and remote deployments frequently presented challenges to a workout regimen such as three days a week with weights and three days a week at cardio. The military and civilians with whom I served and who were genuinely concerned about their personal physical fitness managed to adapt and adjust their fitness routines to their changes in duty schedules.

During the time that I was researching, planning and organizing to conduct "The TREK," I thought that my level of physical fitness was sufficient to the task of walking an average of 15 miles a day with a 45-pound backpack. However, I also thought that a better level fitness, one at which I was physically stronger, would be an advantage and would help to guarantee my success.

I wanted to strengthen my legs to increase my stamina and endurance especially for walking over rugged and mountainous terrain, and I needed strong arms, shoulders and back to do the work of lifting and carrying the weighted backpack. I did not want to gain muscle, bulk up or add weight. I only wanted to tone my current physique and condition my body to the regimen of lifting, walking, and resting two or three times within a 16-hour day.

Over time, I grew tired and disillusioned with gyms and fitness centers. Patrons failed to replace the equipment they used, unseen "monsters" dripped sweat over everything and failed to clean up after themselves, equipment was unavailable while folks romanced each other when pretending to exercise, children and their parents were a nuisance, and the socially-challenged sick spread their germs over everything they touched.

I assembled a gym in my home with equipment I scrounged from fitness centers that were modernizing or going out of business, from yard sales, and from donations. One room, approximately 21 x 27 feet, hosts a cable crossover machine with two, 150-pound weight stacks and the attachments to support a variety of exercises, a Smith machine with a long bar which can support 300 pounds, 500 pounds of free-weight plates, and dumbbells in five-pound sets between 5 and 50 pounds. There are two 45-pound long bars and two curling bars, an incline-flat-decline bench, a curling bench, and an abs bench.

For eight weeks in April and May 2014, I trained aerobically in the mornings and afternoons, and then trained with weights after I returned home mid to late-afternoons. I trained only one body part each day, six days a week: chest, back, shoulders, triceps and biceps, legs and abs.

Each week I scrambled the order in which I exercised. I started with weights so light, reps so few, and an abs routine so simple that I barely felt any stress. Over the eight weeks, I added weight and reps until I reached the weight where I could perform three sets of eight reps without straining at the last rep of the last set. The theory was that anything I did which was load-bearing was to my benefit. The bottom line was that I was not going to risk an injury while exercising. The strength training exercise routines following the daily walks also served to increase my appetite.

During "The TREK," I expected to be tired and hungry at the end of each day. I began to eat more and add calories to my diet. Toward the end of the eight-week training period I estimated that I was consuming close to 4,000 calories while my weight remained at between 148 and 150 pounds.

"The men are walking. They are fifty feet apart, for dispersal. Their walk is slow, for they are dead weary, as you can tell even when looking at them from behind. Every line and sag of their bodies speaks their inhuman exhaustion."
- Ernie Pyle. Pulitzer-Prize-winner. American journalist. War correspondent. Killed during the Battle of Okinawa, April 18, 1945.

10. Training. Aerobic.

The quotation from war correspondent, Ernie Pyle, describes his observations of American military members moving in combat formation during World War II. It does not matter if they are moving into battle or away from it. His description could apply equally to combatants in any army at any time in history: Hannibal's soldiers crossing the Alps, Napoleon's army retreating from Russia, the German military abandoning Stalingrad, Allied prisoners driven with bayonets and rifles into camps by reprehensible Japanese during the Bataan Death March, North Vietnamese and Vietcong irregulars infiltrating along the Ho Chi Minh Trail to invade South Vietnam.

Because of the planning which designed "The TREK's" route, established the daily distances, and set aside times for meals and rest, I did not expect at any time to be that tired or anywhere close to a state of exhaustion. Regardless, knowing how individuals, especially the military in combat, are capable of extraordinary feats of strength and stamina, I was motivated to train to a standard which would guarantee success while honoring those to whom I was paying tribute.

In the same two months of April and May 2014, during which I would begin the eight-week period of strength training, I created a schedule for aerobic training. There would be a major difference between my strength training and aerobic training schedules. The strength training would be conducted six days a week, Monday through Saturday, in the late afternoons or early evenings, indoors in my air-conditioned home gym. My aerobic training would be in progress seven days a week, beginning at 7 a.m., outdoors, in all weather conditions. Those whom I was honoring did not select their conditions, nor would I.

My plan was to begin slowly, walking a short distance and carrying a light weight, and then gradually add distance and weight. At the seventh week, I planned to be walking 15 miles a day, carrying a full 45-pound back, and camping in my yard at night. The 15-mile walk would be split into a first leg of nine miles, a break for a meal and rest, and the second leg of six miles. I planned the final eighth week to walk 15 miles and carry 45 pounds having made corrections to the load and schedule based upon the seventh week's experiences.

Near my home in Clear Lake is a machine shop with an annex containing precision scales which can measure weights between one ounce and two tons. I drove there with my backpack containing the contents of everything I expected to carry: camping equipment; support equipment such as the cell phone, binoculars, and tools; all-weather clothing; items for personal hygiene; notebooks, maps, and food. After I told the shop manager about "The TREK" and my need to weigh my equipment and provisions, he gave me unlimited access to the annex and his scales at no charge. I weighed everything separately. When the total weight exceeded 45 pounds, I discarded items such as an extra T-shirt, pair of socks or briefs, or spare tube of sunscreen to make weight.

I wanted the weight, which would be increasing weekly in the backpack until it reached 45 pounds, to be made up of the items I intended to carry so that the bulk in the pack would be representative of my ultimate load. The weight would have to be distributed with ease of access to the more frequently used and useful items such as the tent, sleeping bag, air mattress, washcloth, toothbrush and toothpaste, food and water, and reference materials. With easy access to useful items as the first factor for packing, the next factor was storing the infrequently-used items, such as the rain poncho and binoculars, and the extra items, such as clothing and food, so that the pack was balanced on my hips, back and shoulders while I was walking.

To achieve this, I loaded the heaviest and least useful items at the bottom of the backpack. Above them, and in the middle of the backpack, I loaded the tent, sleeping bag and air mattress. On one side of these camping items I packed my clothing; on the other side I packed the daily food, water, and hygiene items.

For the first training week I planned to walk six miles and carry 10 pounds. The second week's plan was to walk nine miles with 20 pounds. I would walk 12 miles during the third and fourth weeks beginning with 25 pounds in the third week and 30 pounds in the fourth. That would increase to 15 miles in the fifth and sixth weeks with a weight of 30 pounds in the fifth week and 35 pounds in the sixth. The final two weeks I would walk 15 miles with the maximum weight of 45 pounds. Finally, I would camp out only during the seventh week and use that week to evaluate my physical effort, meal and rest schedule, and the ease and comfort with which gear could be carried, de-stowed for camping, then re-packed for the next day's walk. I planned to make any necessary modifications during the eighth week. At the conclusion of the two month's training, I gave myself 10 days to rest before I left Houston for Paris and the start of The TREK."

"Whenever I get the urge to exercise I lay down until it goes away."
–   Woody Allen (among others), At Large, USA

11. Training. The Routine.

The comment by comedian Wood Allen is not a sentiment that I share with him. My father used to tell his children, "Everything in moderation." For most of my life I have enjoyed a moderate amount of exercise mostly in the form of participating in team sports such as baseball and swimming and individual sports such as cross-country running and orienteering. For all of the physical activities in which I competed or participated I worked out hard enough to be proficient at the skills I needed and harder than I often had the energy or strength for in order to win. But, whatever the intensity of the training event or sports activity was, I almost always provided for adequate rest and recuperation after performing and before my next event or activity.

For most sports during high school and at the Academy, I would train five or six days a week throughout the year and compete once a week in the sport that was in season. When I entered the Army at age 21, I continued to train and exercise, but I no longer belonged to any team that competed in any seasonally scheduled competitions. The soldiers and I participated in daily Physical Readiness Training (PRT), which consisted of a series of warm-up exercises, calisthenics, and a two-or-three-mile run. After duty, we would organize occasionally into "grab-ass" teams to play baseball, basketball, or soccer. In peacetime, during training, whatever rest or sleep I got at home or in the field always was sufficient to begin a new day feeling rested and refreshed. That was not often the case in simulated combat training exercises or actual combat. The amount of rest or sleep that a leader of any rank obtained in combat training exercises or in combat was inversely related to the number and complexity of the tasks that the leader was responsible to accomplish. Leaders in any organization, not just in the military, do not make good or competent decisions when they are stressed and over-tired. Both the brain and the body need an adequate amount of rest to regenerate their ability to function.

As described earlier in this narrative, I did not think that "The TREK" route and daily routine would challenge me to the point of exhaustion. I did know that the effects of the daily activities would be cumulative. Perhaps, over time, I would start to lose weight, experience muscle strain or cramping, develop blisters on my feet, or not be able to sleep soundly at night or when I rested. I did not predict accidents or serious injuries and did not actually expect any.

Between June and August there would be between 15 and 16 hours of daylight every day along the route of "The TREK." During the planning and training I had calculated that I was able to walk an average of one mile every

20 minutes or three miles an hour. At that rate, my daily objective of an average of covering 15 miles a day would require only five hours. That left 10 hours of daylight during which I could continue to walk to meet the daily objective if my schedule were interrupted because I had been slowed down by an illness or injury, or because I sensed the need for additional rest while I was walking.

Also, during the planning phase, I had selected the route to be consistent with the movement of American Army ground forces during World War II between Omaha Beach and Berlin. But I planned the walk so that I would start and end each day in or within sight of a town in the event that I became ill or was injured and required medical attention. I did not want to aggravate further any condition that would compromise my goal of completing "The TREK." The best way that I knew to guarantee the success of this project was to maintain a routine and do everything in moderation: walk, eat, rest, walk some more, eat again, and rest again.

"I have tried to lift France out of the mud. But she will return to her errors. I cannot prevent the French from being French."
  - Charles de Gaulle. Brigadier General, Leader of Free France 1940-1944, President of France, 1958-1969.

12. France.

On Sunday, June 1st, my neighbor and his family hosted a farewell barbecue for our friends and me at his home. The summer heat and humidity had not yet arrived and the day was perfect to be outdoors. The Arnolds had stocked a cooler with beer from France and Germany and ale from Belgium. In Houston, there is not much demand for beer from Luxembourg and they could not locate any. They substituted Peroni which is my all-time favorite beer from Italy. A local bakery provided a sheet cake decorated with "The TREK" logo.

Everyone had a good understanding of many of the details of "The TREK." The men had several suggestions about how and where to spend a less-rigorous and more relaxing time on any future two-month trip to Europe. The women expressed concern about my comfort, my having to eat meals on the ground in the woods, and creepy creatures walking around inside the tent and hiding in the contents of my backpack, not to be discovered until I was about to put on my socks and underwear.

Ricky drove me to George Bush International Airport on Tuesday morning, June 3rd. The flight was full. In coach, there were several families who were traveling to France for the D-Day anniversary events. There was also a group of middle-school and high-school-age children from San Antonio's Texas Children's Choir who had been invited to perform at the ceremony at the American Cemetery. The very late decision by the president to attend had upset the schedule for almost all of the performers. On the morning of June 4th, as we landed at Charles de Gaulle Airport in Paris, the group's leaders and chaperones still did not know if the choir would perform two days later. Their coworkers back in San Antonio also did not know. Schedules were being changed to accommodate the demands of the White House.

While we waited for our luggage, I asked if the choir would entertain the travelers gathered at baggage claim and sing one of the songs that it had rehearsed for its performance. The students were enthusiastic and their voices rang throughout the terminal. Their singing earned a well-deserved round of applause from the other travelers, airport security and facility workers. Following the improvised mini-concert, I spoke with the choir members. I told them about my father's service during World War II and his recollections about the air and land combat 70 years earlier. Many of the students told me, "My great-grandfather was in that war, too." They could have told me that their elder relatives had served with my father at The Alamo, (their San Antonio hometown memorial). I began to feel uncomfortably older for reasons other than travel and jet lag.

The train ride from Paris to Bayeux took just over two hours. I arrived at noon on a cool day, brilliant with sunshine and a panorama of flowers and trees in full bloom. Adjacent to the train station was a small outdoor café. All the tables were occupied, but there was an open seat at one of them. In French, I asked the gentleman seated there, in a uniform which I did not recognize, if the seat were taken.

"No. S'il vous plait," he answered and gestured for me to take the seat.

I thanked him and said that I spoke only a little French. I told him that I was visiting for the liberation anniversary. In near-perfect English he commented that many Americans already had arrived. Some had been in Bayeux and the Normandy area for more than one week. He asked me from where I had traveled. I told him that I had come from Houston in Texas

"We all know about Texas from John Wayne and George Bush. You may discover that many French think they are the same person."

I asked him about his uniform insignia and learned that he was a senior member of an explosive ordnance unit, part of the French national security forces. He was at the station to meet other members from the unit who would arrive shortly from Paris. Lieutenant Montreaux listened to my plan for "The TREK" and told me that traveling through France would be difficult without GPS because many roads in rural and remote areas are not marked. "We do not have street signs on every corner, as you have in the USA."

I showed him the photos of my father and his crew in a B-24 Liberator bomber flying over Normandy in support of the Allied landings. I explained that he was born in December 1923, and was only a 20-year-old pilot in June 1944, which was about the same age as most of the crew.

"I am glad that he survived for you to tell me this story. You will see at the cemetery that it was not to be for many others," he said.

That I knew.

He offered to buy me a beer and I accepted. I did not have time to buy him back something before his team arrived. As we parted he told me, "In the cities, at the restaurants and pubs they will know from your accent that you are not French. Make sure that you check your bill, especially if you drink. Some persons, especially in crowded places, may try to cheat you."

That didn't sound like fun – having to sober up, read the bill in French, and do arithmetic. For the hour or so that I had been sharing company with Lieutenant Montreaux, I had been watching three or four taxis wait for trains to arrive. They would meet passengers and then drive them into town. The round-trip ride took only about 10 minutes. From the station, I could see the taller buildings in Bayeux. In two days I would start walking an average of 15 miles a day. Given the favorable weather, it seemed like a good idea to work off the jet lag, get some exercise after the long flight, train ride, and beer, and walk the four or five miles into town to the hotel.

There are only a few main streets in Bayeux. The hotel at which I had a reservation was at the intersection of two them. The management failed to provide adequate staff to accommodate the number of guests arriving or to answer questions from them and other guests about the hotel, its amenities, meal hours, the town attractions and anniversary celebrations. Apparently, the management also failed to appreciate the fact that the majority of the guests would be native English speakers or other Europeans who could speak English but not French. The two young receptionists possessed only a halting command of English. They were helped by guests who answered questions for other guests.

The center of town was a few blocks away. Half the parking lot adjacent to the town hall and central administration buildings was filled with campers, automobiles, motorcycles, and scooters bearing license plates from England, Denmark, Holland, Belgium, and Germany. I saw one plate from Italy. Plates from France almost all were exclusively from the regions outside of Normandy.

The other half of the parking lot was filled with World War II era vehicles, most of which had been used by the Allies. The American M-151 jeep was the most popular. About half of those had trailers attached to them. The trailers contained five-gallon cans painted olive drab, camouflage nets, and coolers full of beer and bottled water. I saw mostly beer. There were three-quarter-ton vehicles used during the war for troop transport and supplies and some ambulances. They came in handy for transporting reveler casualties from the local bars to their hotels. Without exception, all the vehicles were restored to appear as if they were competing for prizes. Coats of wax made the fresh paint shine. Repeated applications of "tire black" left tracks along the streets and in the parking lots. Anything metal glistened. Mirrors and glass were pristine. Absent were any tracked or armored vehicles such as tanks, tank-killers or self-propelled weapons.

Most of the drivers and their passengers were wearing American, British, Dutch, or French uniforms from both world wars. I saw one German-made motorcycle with an attached sidecar painted in black and silver. It lacked any military markings. Its driver and passenger wore matching black leather jackets, flight caps, aviator goggles, and white scarves in the style of the Red Baron. They were neighbors from Denmark.

Although much attention had been placed on the precise details of the vehicle markings, such as the location, size, and color of the stenciling, the British spelled the word Armoured with the extra letter "u" on American jeeps. They were identified as "4th Armoured Division," a unit in Patton's Third Army. When I mentioned the irregularity to one owner he replied, "Aye

Mate, I shouldn't a bin swiggin' those Kiplings when I was stencilin'. I'll fix it for next year." Kipling is the name for a popular, pale English ale.

I wanted to see the beach and cemeteries ahead of the crowds which were expected in two days for the 70th anniversary. But I was having too good a time making merry with the celebrants. Almost everyone whom I met was traveling with a spouse, family member, friend, or as part of a group. Many visitors had been attending annually for years. The Channel Tunnel (Chunnel), which began operation in 1994, made the 25-mile crossing between England and France simple and economical for passengers using either the vehicle shuttle or the railway systems.

Midday through late in the evening on June 4th, there was not an empty seat at any bar or an empty chair at any table in the two outdoor and three indoor establishments that I visited. Food service took more than an hour but no one seemed to care. I heard one Tommy all decked out in his field uniform including spats ask his mate, "Is this what I ordered? Oh, well, who cares? Want some? Have a taste. It's not bad."

An American couple, seated on stools at the corner of the bar, offered me a place between them. At the intersection, there was just enough room to set my map and a mug.

The man who identified himself as Roger said, "We just ordered. As soon as he brings our drinks, yell for something. Otherwise you'll wait half an hour before he gets back this way. You here for D-Day?"

I told him that I was, and I showed him the photos of my father and the route of "The TREK." I was talking when two mugs of beer arrived. Roger told the waiter quickly, "One more for him, please, and put it on our bill."

He and his wife, Gloria, explained that they had been traveling through Holland and France since late May. They decided to stay one week longer after they learned that the D-Day landing ceremonies would be in honor of the 70th anniversary. Sadly, they would be the first of many Americans and others whom I met in Normandy who expressed displeasure that our president was expected to attend. Initially, I thought that the Americans and other tourists would be bothered by the potential for huge traffic jams, additional delays caused by security lines and personal property inspections, and the possibility that the American Cemetery might be closed temporarily for security reasons for an unspecified amount of time during his visit.

But I was wrong. The common sentiment seemed to be that, after five years in office, there was little evidence of his respect or support for the military. Compared to the presence at the British Cemetery of Queen Elizabeth and Prince Philip, who would wear his full dress uniform and military decorations at the ceremony, this president would seem out of place. Roger shocked me slightly when, in a veiled reference to the comment the president made after the death of Trayvon Martin, he said, "I wouldn't be surprised to hear him say, If I had a son he wouldn't be buried here." Ouch.

On Thursday, June 5th, I rose at 4 a.m., an hour before sunrise. I showered and dressed in slacks and a collared shirt which I decided would be appropriate and respectful at the cemetery.

In a small knapsack, I carried a hat, sunglasses, snack bars, a bottle of water, and 120 small American flags which had been donated by the American Legion Post 490 in Houston. My father had kept his class books from his Army basic training and Army Air Corps flight training at Napier Field and Maxwell Air Force Base. In them he had noted his classmates who either had washed out of flight training or who, as pilots, had been killed on active duty. I had the grave locations at Normandy for 15 of his classmates and two of his former instructors. I planned to place another flag at the gravesite of Lieutenant General Leslie McNair after whom the base at which I had served in Berlin was named. The remainder of the flags I intended to place at the gravesites marked:

HERE RESTS IN HONORED GLORY

A COMRADE IN ARMS

KNOWN BUT TO GOD

The sun was rising as I started to walk the 10-mile mile distance along the shoulder of the road enroute to Omaha Beach. I wanted to be on the beach at or slightly past dawn – the time when the Allied forces had landed. I planned to walk the length of the five beaches and climb the hill to be among the first at the American Cemetery when it opened at 9 a.m.

On my walk to the beach, an M-151 jeep pulled over and stopped ahead of me. A passenger with a heavy English accent turned back to ask me if I was headed to the beach and if I wanted a ride. I answered "yes" to both questions. In the jeep, I was offered and drank not tea but coffee. The two men from England, both grade-school friends and now school teachers on holiday for the summer, were headed to the beach to take photographs. The hobbies that they share together are photography and restoring and maintaining the American M-151 jeep. More than 30 years ago, they had purchased the jeep and its trailer from an American in Iowa. They left the trailer in England for two reasons. First, from previous trips to Normandy in June they expected the crowds this year would be larger and the traffic more congested. Their ability to avoid delays and detour cross country would be much easier without the trailer. The second reason: "the trailer is too damn easy for some frog farmer to steal."

The sun began to break through the early morning clouds. The view from the interior toward the Atlantic Ocean is to the west. In 1944, observation would have been more favorable for the defenders. The Allies would have the sun in their faces as they attacked over the beaches, up the hills, and into the countryside. They did not need one more tactical disadvantage that day. This day, there was no one on the beach except one middle-age jogger. The tourists had not yet arrived. Many of the revelers who I had left at the bar just before midnight appeared to be in no rush to leave. They would be lucky to be sober and functioning for the anniversary ceremonies on the 6th.

Access to the American Cemetery was possible from the beach before 9 a.m. There were no barriers and all of the security personnel were busy with last-day preparations. The main entrance was clogged with vehicles and people seemingly more confused than the Germans must have been when they viewed the assaulting allied armada.

The media made a mess of everything. Without any respect for the sanctity of the cemetery, they drove their news-broadcast and support vehicles across the manicured lawns and over the small gardens of seasonal flowers. Workers rushed to build tents, awnings, and platforms to support the international dignitaries, and to cordon off areas for private and public events. Almost a sixth of the cemetery, containing gravesites at the southwest section opposite the bronze statue, "Spirit of American Youth Rising from the Waves," was closed.

Staffers still were completing the task of placing one American and one French national flag at each gravesite. When the work was finished, with the exception of the clutter generated by the media, the atmosphere was solemn, dignified and respectful. I was able to find a senior administrator kind enough to link me with an escort. Together we located the 17 specific gravesites at which I placed a second American flag. As I had intended before I arrived, I walked past and touched every tombstone. I placed all of the remaining flags that I carried at the gravesites of the unknown. I did not bring enough flags.

I departed after having seen a ceremonial detail from a U.S. Army Honor Guard unit from Germany practice its movements and cannon firings from three artillery pieces set outside of the cemetery on the west side along the ocean. Crowds of tourists passed down the walking paths, around the barriers and across the gravesites with about as much respect as if they were moving between attractions at Disneyland: talking, eating, and shouting to stragglers. The small signs placed at judicious locations throughout Arlington National Cemetery which read, "Silence and Respect," would have served a valuable purpose at this American Cemetery, Normandy, France.

Back in Bayeux that night, I learned that, for security reasons, all roadways leading into the American Cemetery would be closed from as far away as two miles beginning at 4 a.m. on the 6th. I would need to arrange for a taxi or hope for a late-night reveler to take me as close as possible to the beach so I could begin at dawn on the first day of "The TREK." In the pubs, most of the conversation that I heard from the American community concerned the lack of available information about the schedule of events at the cemetery and the concerns about the number of restrictions, all because of the scheduled visit by the president.

None of that concerned me. On the 6th I would begin day one of 59 from the beach and detour around the American Cemetery to the British Cemetery where I would observe the anniversary ceremonies. There would be far fewer security restrictions, and the British tourists with whom I had spoken seemed far more excited to see the Queen in her role as Head of State and Head of the Armed Forces than the American tourists were to see their president.

Very early on the morning of the 6th, as I was checking out of the hotel, some of the revelers just were arriving after another night on the town. They had difficulty remembering their room numbers to obtain their keys. I left my backpack in the hotel's storage room. At night, when I returned, I would retrieve it and camp in a small garden adjacent to the hotel used as a break area for the staff during the day. The driver of a cab that just had deposited this group of nocturnal celebrants took me to the beach without charge. I had brought him a fresh cup of coffee and he was headed home in the same direction.

Just after dawn, on Omaha Beach, I skirted the American Cemetery and walked back toward town. At 9:15 a.m., Prince Charles and his wife, Camilla, were expected to attend a service in the Bayeux Cathedral. Doors would be closed to everyone other than the royal family and their escorts at 8 a.m. I would not arrive on time from the beach and would not be dressed properly to attend, but I watched from the side of the cathedral as everyone departed at the end of the service. Plain-clothed security personnel and British military of all services exited first. Prince Charles and his wife followed. It took more than an hour for the cathedral to empty as the royal guests paused to acknowledge and greet the bystanders.

From the cathedral, I walked back past the hotel and ate an early lunch at an outdoor café along the route to the British War Cemetery. The crowd was as large as what I had seen the day before and that morning at the American Cemetery. The striking difference was the standard of dress. Most of the men were attired in blue or dark blazers, white shirts and ties with a variety of the colors red, white and blue. Many wore berets with embroidered tabs or pins representing military units or veterans' organizations. The women all wore dresses mostly in dark or earth-tone colors. The young girls all wore dresses in bright pastel colors. The Queen arrived wearing a suit of soft pastel green. Prince Philip wore his full-dress uniform. Seated inside their Rolls Royce limousine or walking to their places for the ceremony, they received hearty applause from the onlookers. Both the President of France, François Hollande, and the Queen spoke at the start of the formal ceremony.

The American National Cemetery hosts 9,387 gravesites in which rest the remains of 307 men "Known but to God." The British War Cemetery hosts 4,648 gravesites in which rest 338 men "Known but to God." Across the street from the British cemetery is a monument to an additional 1,800 members of the British Commonwealth who were killed in combat between Normandy and Paris and who have no known grave.

In Bayeux, my third and last night, the atmosphere still was festive but tempered by a full day of memorial events hosted by the American, British, and French governments, and dozens of international veterans' organizations. I spoke at length with the Johnson family, father Roy and son Paul. Roy is a "Berlin Brat," the son of an American serviceman assigned in Berlin between 1968 and 1971. He had served in the Navy as a submariner in a nuclear boomer between 1986 and 1993. I mentioned my experience of hearing so many Americans express resentment at the president's presence that day. They echoed the sentiment saying simply that it was just bad timing for all concerned.

I was rested enough after only a 10-mile walk from Omaha Beach back into Bayeux, and then some short-distance walks between the anniversary events, to get an early start to Caen the next morning. The weather had worsened. Clouds were forming and there were forecasts for rain. The walk to the town center would be a tenth or two more than 17 miles. I had sewn a cloth four-inch by six-inch American flag on the upper rear portion of my backpack. Next to it I had sewn an identical-sized French flag. I had not walked two miles from the improvised campsite in the garden at the hotel when I had an offer of a ride. The thought of an 895-mile walk ahead of me made the offer enticing to accept; however, I refused, realizing that it would set a bad precedent and would be inconsistent with the way most soldiers moved between Bayeux and Caen during the war.

Midday, as I stopped for lunch and a rest having walked about 10 miles, the rain began. Light at first, the rain fell heavier as the sky darkened. Again, along the road, I received and refused two more offers for a ride. The temperatures dropped as the rain continued. When I found an isolated area to camp the temperature was below 60 degrees.

My first campsite in an isolated area would be impossible to secure when I walked back into town to explore and visit the war museum and men's and women's abbeys. On the outside of my tent I had sewn cloth patches of the flags of the four countries of "The TREK." I thought that a sense and spirit of nationalism might help discourage any potential mischief makers. I secured my valuables and departed for a tour ready to accept the loss of any or all of my property. When I returned early in the evening it was overcast and dark, although the sun had not yet set. None of my property had been disturbed. Tired after the first long walk and a few more miles added for touring, I quickly made some notes on a half-page of the journal. I fell asleep easily listening to the sounds of the rain smacking the top and sides of the tent.

When I awoke the next morning, it did not appear as if the rain had abated. The surface on which I had set the tent was flat, but only a few feet away were small pools of water and a field of mud. I would have to break down the campsite and pack everything standing in place on the once-dry ground where the tent floor had rested. My personal hygiene items and clothing had been wrapped in one-gallon plastic freezer bags and stacked within my backpack. Items that I needed daily and most often were at the top or in the four side compartments. The decampment took longer than I had expected, but everything stayed dry except the tent, rain fly, poles, and pegs. Those were rolled into separate bags and stored under a flap of the backpack away from everything that was dry.

The temperature was in the low 40's but the driving rain made it feel colder. In less an hour, I had walked more than two miles and found a bakery where I stopped to buy a cup of coffee and two rolls. I entered the small shop through a single door. Off to one side was a person standing and drinking his coffee. There were no places to sit. As I moved away from the door I removed my rain hat and backpack. I think that I may have shivered. After I ordered, I heard the clerk say something to her friend and use the word, "chien," French for "dog," commenting about me, my backpack or both. I didn't care. All that was important to me was that the coffee was hot and the roll was not stale. Even if she overcharged me, I still would not have cared. After I had finished the coffee and one of the two rolls, I thanked her and left an extra euro, about $1.40. Maybe she would not be so quick to insult the next non-French customer who visited.

It was mid-afternoon when I reached the town of Mery-Corbon. Although thick, black clouds still threatened, the rain had diminished to an annoying drizzle. Down one side street, I saw the town market. I detoured and went inside for some time out of the rain and the opportunity to buy bread and fruit for the next morning. After I left and was walking through the parking lot I failed to see the small, slightly elevated iron base bracket in which rested the poles for the security gates when the parking lot and market were closed. I tripped and took a hard fall to my front, falling on to the cobblestone on my right side. Only my right hand and forearm were scuffed, but the impact to my right knee was more severe. My thin, convertible trousers provided no protection. They tore at the knee and exposed a gash which had started to bleed. I rolled on to my back, undid the backpack and stood up. I tried to walk but my knee hurt badly and I only limped. From across the street, two men had seen me stumble and fall. They were leaving work at the end of the day and came to help me. One spoke English very well. He told me that they worked at a vehicle dispatch company and that there were linens and a first aid kit there to clean and bandage my knee. There also was ice which I could apply to my knee. We crossed the street together, one man carrying my pack and the other holding my arm and guiding me over the curbs and into their building. They offered me a lounge chair and placed my backpack next to me. Then they disappeared into the back of the building.

They returned with the owner of the company and two women, one of whom carried a plastic container of ice, and the other, a first aid kit. Each of the women had a good command of English. After I cleaned the wound, and while I was holding an ice pack on my knee, I told them about "The TREK" and my walk, 70 kilometers, (42 miles), since D-Day. From the backpack, I removed and showed everyone the photos of my father. As the photos were circulated among the group, I explained his service during World War II and the Airlift.

Everyone told me a story about their families' experiences in the military, as partisans or as supporters during the war in 1940, the occupation, and the fight for liberation after the D-Day landings. The owner of the company, "Normandy Ambulances," called home to his wife and told her and his family to expect a guest. As he stood next to me, he used his cell phone to place several calls. I heard him say, "Jacques est suis américain." (James is an American.)

"Il est le fils d'un libérateur." (He is the son of a liberator.)

"Il est ici avec moi maintenant." (He is with me now.)

Two hours later Mr. Roland Francois brought me to his home to meet his wife, Florence, and his teenage daughter, Elise. Only Elise, a tenth grade student, could speak some English. I learned that I had been invited to have dinner and to spend the evening as their guest. Before then, Elise would show me the shower where I could wash and re-bandage the wound. After I had showered, I returned to the kitchen. Roland passed me a cold beer. Florence offered me trays of food. Elise and I struggled with words in both French and English. Physically, Roland is in the image of baseball legend Babe Ruth, large, broad and powerful. Every time he hugged me he nearly took away my breath. When he patted me on the arm, shoulder or back, it felt as if I had been swatted by a grizzly bear.

Then the guests started to arrive. The first man who entered carrying several bottles of wine asked, "Où en est le libérateur?"(Where is the liberator?)

To each of the more than 20 guests Roland was proud to introduce me as "James, the liberator." I drank wine to be polite. Each time my glass appeared half-full it was replenished. Elise served me plates of food prepared by her mother and brought by the guests. She told me what each plate contained and in what region in France the food was produced. Throughout much of the evening I regretted not having included "Learn conversational French" as a task to accomplish before starting "The TREK."

The document protectors which contained the four-page route of "The TREK" and the photos of my father and the Normandy landscape between June 5-25, 1944, were circulated and explained among the guests. Elise provided me the names and e-mail addresses of guests who had asked for copies of the route and pictures.

The fest ended when Roland walked the last four of his friends to their cars all parked in the oversized yard on his acres of property. It was almost 2 a.m. The family invited me for breakfast at 8 a.m. so that Roland would be on time for work and Elise on time for school at 9 a.m.

The next morning, while we were eating, Roland presented me with a black chapeau embroidered with the coat of arms of Normandy: two yellow lions with blue claws on a background of red. I wore it every day through France, Belgium and Luxembourg. I removed and stored it only after I crossed into Germany. I did not want to lose my first gift and souvenir.

A further 15 miles beyond Mery-Corbon and still in the region of Lower Normandy is the city of Lisieux, the second most popular religious retreat area in France after Lourdes. It hosts the Basilica of St. Thérèse built to honor a Carmelite nun who died at the age of 24 and was canonized a saint in 1925. If I kept to my routine and schedule I would be able to visit the basilica in the late afternoon.

Arriving in a larger, more populated city might provide the opportunity to find an electronics store in which I could purchase a phone card that would work within France. I had discovered that many of the streets along which I had been walking were not identified conveniently for navigation and many changed names. On several occasions, in very rural areas, I was forced to find someone from whom I could obtain directions when I arrived at an unnamed intersection. Where unidentified intersections joined roads oriented north and east, or south and east, I always chose east as the general direction between Normandy and Berlin. However, when the roads at an unidentified forked intersection were oriented northeast and southeast then I was in a quandary. These roads often were too small to be designated on maps. Having GPS navigation might provide the opportunity to resolve my problem.

I arrived at a store in the center of the city. Two of the three clerks spoke English and among the three of us I was able to explain what I needed and why. I purchased a card which would work within France for one month, more than 10 days longer than I expected to be in the country. One of the clerks inserted the card into my Smart phone, used only as a camera until then, and explained the GPS feature for me. Then he led me outside where he demonstrated the navigation system emphasizing the built-in compass, and the satellite or map options. I paid 30 euros, ($42.), for the card with a one month data plan.

I did not need any aid to locate the basilica. There were signs all throughout the town, a strong indication of its popularity as a tourist attraction. Both the basilica and the grounds were beautiful. Set within the city for easy access, the basilica is surrounded by a small forest. I paid a small fee to check my backpack and toured for more than two hours. I noticed that the tourists of all faiths were more respectful of the sanctity of the church facility and property than were the visitors I encountered at the American Cemetery in Normandy. I concluded that the reason was the difference in atmosphere between indoor and outdoor memorials.

The forest provided an excellent location to camp. The next morning, I awoke refreshed and began walking to Bernay. At more than 17 miles away I would have an extra hour of walking ahead of me.

Still within the Normandy region, Bernay is located within rich farm country. A town with about 10,000 residents, it is famous for its cloth industry. On Saturdays. the town center hosts a market where linens, other cloth items and fresh produce from the region are sold. I would be there on a Tuesday. Again I arrived at a forked intersection, again the roads were not named, and again they diverted northeast and southeast. At the center of the intersection, in front of a pasture which expanded between the two roads, was a large wooden crucifix set in concrete at the top of a seven-step platform. Around the platform and on three of the steps were baskets of fresh flowers all in bloom. Visitors had written prayer requests and attached some at the base of the crucifix. They had deposited others within the baskets of flowers.

Here I had my first opportunity to use the GPS. I selected the southeast fork. As shown on the map, that road led in the direction of Bernay and the next two towns on my route, Barc and Evreux. The satellite image zoomed in close enough to view exactly where I was standing and showed the image of the platform and crucifix. I thought that I had made a good investment. I was wrong.

Despite the additional distance, the bright skies, warmer temperatures, and the relatively flat farmland made the walk not too difficult. The scenery was diverse. There were a variety of fruit trees and vegetables at different stages of growth. I walked past acres of some kind of thick-leafed vegetable which I did not recognize. A taste test of one of the green and purple leaves did not help. Later in the day, when the traffic coming toward me increased, I knew that I was close to town. The locals were on their way home from work. At the outskirts, I saw an older farmer inspecting a drainage ditch which ran between the road and his farmland. I introduced myself and told him that over the last five days I had walked from Normandy beach just over 100 kilometers away and had been camping at night. I asked him if he knew of a campsite, park, or off-road area where I might be able to camp. He told me that beyond the field where we were standing was an enclosed horse pasture which he owned. From the far east end of that pasture I would be able to see the town only a half-mile away. He said that I was welcome to camp anywhere on the property and advised me that some of the horses may stray over to visit. I thought that would be fun. In the horse pasture, with the town in view, I set up camp. I felt as if I had an added amount of security camping on private property enclosed by a fence and guarded by horses. I undressed, used the spare bottle of water to take a sponge bath, and changed my shirt, briefs, and socks. Everything that I had been wearing I placed on the inflated air mattress outside the tent.

In Bernay, I found two pubs and visited both of them; the first, for only a beer, and the second for a beer and sandwich. At the small grocery store, I purchased two baguettes and fruit. I saw the three horses before I saw my tent. From the road about 200 yards away, they were standing near where I had set the tent and air mattress. They hardly moved when I climbed through the space between the horizontal fence slats. Throughout the night, they stayed nearby, close enough for me to hear their occasional snorting and wheezing.

The road 12 miles to the southeast would lead to Barc, the smallest town in which I planned to stop with a population of only 1,000. I hoped to use some of the time saved from the shorter walk to clean and re-bandage my knee and to consolidate the contents of my backpack. The lower right section of my torn convertible trousers needed additional stitching. After my fall, I did not have the opportunity to repair the tear correctly. The convertibles were serving a dual purpose as my dress trousers. The hasty stitching was very obvious. Beyond Barc, three of the four more towns before Paris were at distances greater than 15 miles. The closer I came to Paris, the more difficult I expected the walk to become because of the potential danger from more cars on a complex network of roads and highways.

Barc was so small a town that it appeared as if the residents had no need for street signs. The tourists did not need signs because there were no tourists. Non-residents just drove through down the main street heading someplace else. Here was my second chance to use my new GPS. It worked fine at the first unmarked intersection. But, when I needed it again, it failed. The phone had a fairly full charge. The instructions were very helpful for troubleshooting, but I could not make the GPS feature work. Then I remembered the Apple tech's caution that the phone may not work in rural, low-populated areas. I shut down the phone and relied upon my compass and directions from the residents. In Barc, I was able to accomplish my first resupply, adding about 10 pounds of MRE's which would sustain me until I reached Paris.

What a surprise when I arrived in Evreux! Still in the Normandy region, Evreux is an almost equidistant drive to Paris or to the ocean. I arrived mid-afternoon on a spectacular day only one week before the start of summer. In the center of town, near the expansive, historic government center and public library, were dozens of people enjoying a late lunch or snack on the steps of many office buildings. Basking in the warmth of the sun, the men had removed their suit jackets and rolled up their shirt sleeves; the women sat with their shoes off. Twice as many people were seated comfortably at the outdoor cafes. Their dress was summer casual. Most of the tourists, those folks standing by statues, sitting by the fountains,, and posing for pictures, wore short-sleeved shirts and shorts. Two rednecks, shooting range buddies who must have had "visit Europe" on their spittoon list, hadn't a clue about the attention they attracted wearing twin baseball caps ("Proud member of the NRA"), wife beaters, and humongous belt buckles shaped like banjos. The packets of Red Man protruding from their back pockets made me think that sales at Walmart back in their hometown might be slipping.

I had obtained a city map from the front of the town hall and was studying it when I heard a woman's voice ask, "May I help you find something?"

To my side was a very attractive, well-dressed, young lady whose striking chestnut-brown hair and broad smile enhanced her attractiveness.

I returned the smile and answered, "Yes, please. But first tell me how you knew to ask me in English."

"Oh, easy. The French don't carry backpacks with an American flag. If they do then they probably are in America. Also, your "Follow Me" patch above the flags was another giveaway. My name is Juana Bargot. I'm also American. I'm married to a Brazilian who works here. We live in Evreux."

I asked her if she had time for a coffee some place nearby and, if so, if she would have time for a chat. As we walked to a café, Juana told me that her husband was a sales and quality control manager for a company which sells farm equipment. The adjoining French regions of Normandy and Ile-de-France contain vast tracts of fertile farmland. The climate is favorable for agriculture, and there are numerous rivers with excellent natural drainage. The Iton, a tributary of Eure, runs through Evreux.

Juana told me that it was rare to see backpackers pass through Evreux. Given its relative isolation, many backpackers hike through Normandy or areas closer to Paris. As I had done many times before, I explained "The TREK" and showed her the route and photos. She told me that she knew someone who lived close to where we were and who also had served in the Army. He and his wife lived nearby within walking distance. She called him and told me that we had been invited to visit.

Colonel James Callahan, United States Army, retired, and his French wife, Marie-France, were living in a beautiful four-story home not far from the center of town. The ground floor contains a foyer, living room, dining room, kitchen, and half-bath. On the three upper floors are dens, bedrooms, and baths. The kitchen overlooks a beautiful garden in which there is a patio with a large dining table and chairs. A sign within the garden displays the name for their home, "Safe Harbor." Adjacent to the garden is a one-car garage with the family vehicle, home and garden tools, volumes of books, two beer coolers, and a lifetime supply of bottles of wine.

We four took seats at the table in the garden. While Jim and I drank a cold beer, the women preferred water. Poor Juana had to endure me retelling the story about "The TREK" and how I arrived in Evreux. Jim had retired after a

30-year career in the Army serving in many of the same locations and at the same bases as I. We had the same dislike for careerists in the military, agreeing that the best officer in the Army is a full colonel who knows that he never will be a general. They always are passionate about their service. Their focus is on the soldier. They do not play politics or suck up to a boss hoping to pin on a star. Jim was especially happy to learn that, even though I was a graduate of Hudson High, a slightly disparaging term for West Point, only four-star general and president of the United States, Ulysses S. Grant, had graduated from the Academy with more demerits than I. I made the argument that, in my career experience, there was no proof of a direct relation between success as a cadet and success as an officer. It happened, but it was not guaranteed.

In addition to assignments with the 82nd Airborne Division, both Jim and I had served in assignments with the State Department and the alphabet agencies: CIA (Central Intelligence Agency), DIA (Defense Intelligence Agency), and the NSA (National Security Agency). Our paths had crossed with many of the same people who staffed those organizations.

After his retirement from the Army, Jim, fluent in French, was hired in a senior position within the French security forces. Having worked in the embassy in Paris, he had many contacts and knew much about the threats and issues. He mentioned that Americans were especially careless travelers outside of the United States. In Paris alone, the number of lost or stolen passports averaged 150 weekly.

Juana and Marie-France were patient listeners. Fortunately, both women, knowing Jim so very well and aware of his isolation in retirement from almost everyone and everything upon which he had built two successful careers, were happy to hear us share stories and sentiments. As Jim left the table to fetch a third round of beer, Marie-France excused herself to "bring out something from the kitchen." Juana stayed, and I told her how happy I was that we had met and that she had provided me the introduction to the Callahan family.

Jim was the first person whom I had met in Europe who truly understood and appreciated the four legacy events. As combat veterans, we loathed the senseless slaughter of the military and the noncombatants during both world wars. We discussed World War I and the technology which began with individual soldiers firing single-shot rifles and ended with machine gun teams and the first use of tanks and chemicals in warfare. Neither of us could understand nor justify trench warfare. It supported not a single tactical or strategic advantage, serving only to prolong the war.

We both agreed strongly that the vengeful terms of the Treaty of Versailles drove Hitler and his nationalist supporters to reject it completely. The early victories of the German army in World War II, before the United States and the Soviet Union entered as allies against their mutual enemy, gave strong evidence that Germany fielded an officer corps, especially generals, and noncommissioned officers superior to those of Allies. Hitler's foolish personal interference with military tactics was directly responsible for a number of battlefield losses that his generals could have won. German weapons, especially their tanks, self-propelled artillery, anti-aircraft guns, and heavy infantry weapons also were superior. It was the Allies' huge industrial base and their overwhelming superiority in resources, men, and materiel, which won the day. Each of us tried to outdo the other finding fault with British Field Marshal Bernard Montgomery. We traded pejorative adjectives to describe his leadership skills and reputation as a combat leader. We ended in a tie, Jim stating that he gambled the lives of his subordinates in a selfish quest for attention and glory. His failed Operation Market Garden ended after only nine days in September 1944, with 17,000 Allied casualties representing the loss of 2,000 men a day. At one bridge, heavily defended by the Germans in reinforced positions, the Allies lost 1,500 soldiers, equivalent to one man for each foot of the length of the bridge. I said simply that General Patton despised him and that was good enough for me.

Marie-France returned from the kitchen and began to set the table for a meal. Juana moved away to help. Jim and I did our part by clearing the six empty beer bottles from the table and selecting two bottles of wine. The meal was outstanding and included fresh vegetables, herbs, and fruit from their "Safe Harbor" garden.

During dinner, I commented that from the view of the structures around their home and enclosing the garden it appeared to me as if the Callahan family had one of the few outdoor patios and gardens in the neighborhood. I learned that their home was more than 100 years old and that, over the years, families had sold the land as the property values spiraled upward. Years earlier, not far from their home, a resident had sold a similar-size parcel of land. When the new owner's construction team broke ground to build a new home they discovered a surprising number of bones, decayed leather horse bridles, metal bits, armor, crushed shields, and helmets. The discovery forced a hold on further excavation and any new building while the French government and historical societies studied the site. The area was declared to be historic and worthy of preservation. Dating from the 16th or 17th century, it was either the site of a battle or a mass grave for humans and their horses. The land was claimed by the government under a law similar to eminent domain. Jim said that the deepest he now digs in their garden is the depth to plant petunias, vegetables and herbs.

In the early evening, Juana excused herself to be home in time to greet her husband. She left with the comment, "After four years in college, I never learned as much history as I heard over the last six hours."

The Callahan family invited me to stay the night and I readily accepted. After dinner, Jim took me on a tour of his home and showed me his extensive collection of military history books. Many were packed in cardboard boxes. He intended to donate them to the French Military Academy.

Away from Marie-France, who retired early to prepare for a busy Fathers' Day weekend, Jim assumed the role of peer-mentor and described his concerns about my personal security. His assumption that I was not traveling with a weapon was correct. He said that I would make a very easy target. The flag sewn on my backpack identified me as an American, and the bad guys knew that Americans are absolutely unaware of any threats to their safety outside of the United States. While carrying my backpack, I could be overpowered easily by two men. I told Jim that I was carrying a minimum of cash, had no watch, jewelry or other valuables, and was prepared to lose all my property, but not my life, in the event of a robbery.

Having studied the route, he said that the threat from the rogue gypsy community was significant not only in Paris but also on the city outskirts. Groups of gypsies, whose criminal activities included robbery, drugs, and prostitution, were organized in cells and operated from within Paris. They were controlled from as far away as Romania, Bulgaria, and Albania where money was sent from Paris and other large cities in France. Children between the ages of 12 and 16 did most of surveillance, robberies, and hustling. He was certain that I would be noticed, maybe followed, and possibly targeted. He gave me a non-lethal weapon to carry with me to dissuade an attacker. I kept it with me throughout "The TREK," but never had any occasion to consider using it.

At breakfast the next morning, I was invited to join the family for a Fathers' Day celebration at the Paris home of Marie-France's father. The day would also be the occasion of his 99th birthday. Jim and Marie-France would drive me to the party and bring me to a hotel in Paris. As I left, Jim reminded me that the World Cup Football championships would start that day and that I should try to make time to view some of the games. All of the champions since 1930, when the first World Cup championship games were played, qualified to be in this year's competition. They included teams from England, France, Germany, Italy, and Spain. The Netherlands was not among those champions but this year fielded a very strong team. Jim's final caution to me was, "Stay alert and stay on guard."

Paris would be a disappointment.

Beyond Evreux there were only three small towns and 45 miles before I reached Paris. Each of the towns was small with populations between 1,500 and 2500 residents. The towns themselves were rural, but the outskirts were a web of roads which networked into Paris. Never having visited Paris, I expected to be busy and take advantage of the 16 hours of daylight. As I walked toward Paris, my only planned activity in addition to sightseeing was to watch the World Cup Football championships.

In Breuilpont, on the first day of the World Cup, I sat at a bar among a group of men and watched the Netherlands decisively defeat Spain. The score was five to one. Everyone was rooting for the Netherlands. With every goal that the Dutch scored, the more poorly the players for Spain performed.

The next day, as I walked along a rural road enroute to Septuil, a French police sedan pulled in front of me and two gendarmes, a man and a woman, exited the vehicle and approached me. They greeted me in English and asked me my destination. I told them that I was heading to Septuil which I figured was about 20 kilometers or four hours away. They asked me what I planned to do there. I responded that I had been backpacking from Normandy and camping at night. Now I was heading to Paris where I would stay for four days, and Septuil is on the way. I showed them my copy of "The TREK" route to help me explain my status. My plan for the day was to arrive in Septuil, set up a campsite, then find a pub to watch the World Cup game between Italy and England.

The gendarmes told me that camping was not permitted in the area and that there were no authorized campsites in Septuil. There also were no hotels. I asked if I would be able to find a hotel if I walked further to the next town, Bois d'Arcy. The answer was yes.

Le gendarme masculin said, "Please wait one minute." While I waited le gendarme femelle asked me if I had been to France before, and how my trip was so far. As we were talking, the officer returned and ordered, "Please come with us." He walked to the sedan and opened the trunk.

"You may place your backpack in here."

He opened a rear door for me and I entered. This was the most polite way that I ever had been arrested. No pushing, no shoving, and no handcuffs. We drove for about 30 minutes. The sedan pulled to the front of the jail, with the sign, "P & S," which I guessed incorrectly stood for "Police and Security." The driver exited and went into the facility. When he returned he walked first to open the trunk and then the door for me. As I exited he told me, "There is a room for you here."

Ah, he said, "a room," not "a cell." That was a bit of a relief.

"You will be safe here tonight. Tomorrow you will have only a short walk to Paris."

I thanked them both and we shook hands before they departed. They had driven me to the "Park and Suites" hotel in Bois d'Arcy.

The hotelier greeted me as I entered. I placed my backpack at my feet and retrieved my passport and credit card. The hotelier told me that neither was necessary. The room had been paid for by the gendarme who had told him that I needed a quiet room to rest with a television to watch the football game.

I was asked to provide only my name and address on the registration card, and then I was given the key to my room. No wonder Jim had warned me that there were so many criminals in the area. It was fun to be arrested.

La vie en rose!

The game between Italy and England was as exciting as the game the day before, although the number of goals scored was only half. Italy defeated England two to one. I watched the first half of the game in my room and the second half in the hotel bar with the other guests. Everyone seemed interested in only a good match. I was not able to tell from their reactions whether Italy or England had been the favored team.

Sunday, June 15th, would be a full day for me and my first time to Paris. Jim and Marie-France planned to meet me at the hotel in the late morning. Together we would drive the 20 miles into Paris. The family wanted to take me on a driving tour of the sites of Paris before the combination Father's Day and birthday party at 2 p.m. In Paris, Jim drove along the Champs-Élysées and around the Arc de Triomphe which I recognized immediately. He took us past the Eiffel Tower, the Louvre, the Cathedral of Notre Dame, the Basilica of the Sacred Heart (Sacre Coeur), the Musee d'orsay, and the Pantheon, crossing the river Seine occasionally during the tour. For the next five days, all of these attractions and others would be easy to reach within a short walk from the dozens of metro stations within the city.

The birthday party was fabulous. There were seven of us in the home in the center of Paris. Very narrow, four stories tall, and perhaps 1500 square feet, it is valued at $2 million. Marie-France's sister and her husband were there. Also attending was a student in his mid-20's from the Far East for whom the family provides room and board in exchange for his care of their father. Every weekend one or both sisters visit their father. The guest of honor never was without a glass of red wine to which he attributes his longevity.

Before the meal, his daughters opened several bottles of champagne and we drank toasts to their father's health and happiness. My toast was a short comment that Papa had been a witness to all of the legacy events which brought me to Europe in time to celebrate Father's Day and his 99th birthday with his family. The meal was another exceptional home-cooked treat for me: fresh meats, chicken and fish, home-grown carrots, peas and other green vegetables, and potatoes. There were several selections of cakes and pies for dessert. I sampled a sliver of each. Papa began to fade late in the day.

While Marie-France and her sister worked in the kitchen, Jim drove me to my hotel in the southeast side of Paris about 100 yards from a metro station. Regardless of my experiences in Paris, I would return again if only to spend more time with this family.

As a child I occasionally watched my great-grandmother fall asleep after dinner in her soft, oversized chair while reading. Her daughter always would try to encourage her to get ready for bed. With renewed energy she would comment, "Mary, not now. There's plenty of time for sleep in the grave."

All that I needed in Paris for a hotel room was a comfortable bed in which to sleep for only a few hours, access to a hot shower to clean and refresh myself at least once during the day, and a toilet. To save money, I made a non-refundable reservation four months in advance through an internet travel service. I chose the least expensive lodging for five nights. I would be in the hotel only a quarter of the day. The rest of the day I would be commuting, walking, and touring.

Paris does not have any zero star hotels. If it did, the hotel I selected would head the list. The desk clerk was from somewhere in the Middle East. She spoke no English or any of the five European languages with which I felt comfortable communicating. I showed her the printout with the details of my reservation. She set it aside without looking at it. She handed me a registration card and gestured with one hand as people do with a waiter when they want to pay their bills. From under a paper plate with residual hummus, manakeesh, and falafel, she took a piece of paper and waved it at me. It had a picture of the front of a passport. I handed her mine. She matched the name in my passport with the name on the reservation. A checkmark next to my name on the internet confirmation completed the formal registration. She handed me a skeleton key and a piece of paper on which she had written the room number. The key probably opened every door in the hotel. I would try that later. Pointing over my head, she indicated that my room was somewhere upstairs.

There was no elevator. My room was on the uppermost, 5th floor. The room was small; actually, it was tiny. Apparently designed for only one person, in a single space was the bed, the shower, and the toilet. The bed linens were clean, but the shower and the toilet needed some housekeeping attention. There was one hand towel rolled like a sausage in a plastic bag at the foot of the bed.

From the window, I could see that the building next door was under construction. Opening my window would let in the dirt, dust, and debris from the construction, and possibly any of the workmen on the scaffolding who might need the use of the toilet. I undressed to shower. I was able to empty everything from my backpack and sort the contents on the bed before the water in the shower began to get hot. The final temperature was closer to warm than cold, and I was satisfied. This was my fourth shower in 11 days, twice as many as I had expected when I was still in Texas planning the logistics.

A short distance down the street, at a traffic circle with a metro station nearby, were several bars and restaurants. All were full, and the patrons were cheering. On the third day of the World Cup, France was playing Honduras and France was winning. After the slightly depressing experience at the hotel, I came alive with the spirit of the crowd. I decided to stay at the first pub I entered. I wiggled my way through the fans to get as close as I could to the bar and the wide-screen television. After France scored its second goal, my neighbor at the bar turned and gave me a powerful bear hug. His grip was so intense that I could not hear or understand what he was shouting at me. I recovered well enough to tell him, in French, that I was an American visiting France for the liberation ceremonies. Now I was in France to watch her team win the World Cup.

A science professor at one of the universities in Paris, Henri Guillen spoke English perfectly. Usually he attended the liberation ceremonies every year. This year his wife was ill. He regretted not being able to attend. During World War II, his father and uncles all served in the army and, after the fall of France in 1940, they fought as partisans. Two of his father's three brothers were killed in one attack. One was killed during the firefight. The other was captured and immediately executed. We changed the subject to enjoy what appeared to be a certain victory for France.

Henri reminded me that the United States was in the competition and asked if I were rooting for the team. I told him that, with the possible exception of college soccer teams, no one in the United States takes soccer seriously. I reminded him that one-third of Americans are obese; not fat, that's another third; but obese. I tried to explain that these Americans did not gain their girth by playing soccer. They did so by patronizing drive-through feeding troughs, drive-through banks, drive-through laundries, even drive through church services where it is possible to be anointed on Ash Wednesday. Teenagers would rather vegetate in their rooms surfing the net or texting, tweeting, twaddling, and tooting on their Smart phones. Soccer in the United States is promoted only by parents who need someone else to babysit their children so they can stay away from each other longer, and by "soccer moms" who need an excuse to leave work early.

I added that I would be in Europe for the duration of the games. I could not hope for someone to buy me a beer if I were rooting for the United States and not his national team. However, now that I am in France, I am rooting for the French team. This should give me a better chance to hustle a drink.

Henri responded, "When I am in Normandy I almost always meet an American and buy him a drink. We French are free because of the Americans, not because of the French and not because of the other Allies. Only because of the Americans. We never will forget that. I noticed that you were rooting for France before we spoke. Would you like another beer?"

"Henri, you have embarrassed me slightly, but I cannot say no. If I have one from you, then you must stay and have one from me."

Together with most of France, Henri and I watched as France defeated Honduras. The score was three to zero. Between 1986 and 1987, I served a tour of duty with the Army's Joint Task Force Bravo at Palmerola Air Force Base north of Tegucigalpa in Honduras. As part of the senior American staff there, I discovered how corrupt many of the officers were, steering U.S. government contracts to their families and friends, and protecting drug runners for kickbacks. Siphoning off funds intended for humanitarian purposes as part of the Reagan Contra Aid Program, they used their ill-gotten money to buy land and build lavish homes in the United States where their wives shopped and their children were educated. The State Department turned a blind eye. Honduras was needed as an ally to help support the Contras and defeat the Sandinistas in Nicaragua. I was glad that France had defeated Honduras in a shutout.

At 3 a.m., I was sound asleep when the walls started to shake, and I heard the sounds of banging and voices. Certainly no construction crews were starting work this early.

Out from bed and standing in the hallway, I studied these new, late-night arrivals. Despite the very late hour and the residual effects of World Cup revelry, I was able to recall data gleaned from documentaries which I viewed as a child and from reports by many of America's most reliable "I was there" news sources which I watched as an adult. Saturday afternoon matinees, featuring biographical films such as "Abbot and Costello Meet Frankenstein" and "The Bride of Dracula," combined with recent weekly broadcasts on cable television channels about nature and history, provided some clues. The ever-increasing pollution from communist China's factories has continued to drift over Japan. Overfishing in the East China Sea and the Sea of Japan by the nations of the Far East has depleted the region of its abundant resources.

With the intuition of Sherlock Holmes, I solved the puzzle. Seeking food, Godzilla again had risen out of the water and was devastating Tokyo, munching on its residents to satiate his hunger. Awakened from its peaceful hibernation and choking on China's toxic pollution, Rodan was buzzing through Japanese airspace in search of a healthier mountaintop on which to nest. What appeared as a butterfly insignia on the guests' luggage tags actually was the logo for Japan's national airline, Air Mothra. Heroically, its pilots were flying passengers to safety, all packed in its signature coach and cargo classes more tightly than passengers in a Tokyo subway. I would confirm this in tomorrow's L'Express and Le Monde. Now, though, I needed to make something happen so that I could get some more sleep.

Everything that these new guests needed for the time away from their honorable homeland was packed in huge, heavy suitcases. Without an elevator, the only way that these shocked, tired, and frail folks knew to move the suitcases up the stairs was by turning them end over end up each stair. That explained the banging and crashing. I employed several creative gestures using my hands and mouth to indicate that this time of night was quiet time. I picked up one suitcase and demonstrated using pseudo-volunteers how to carry a suitcase quietly between two people. On my floor, the intervention resolved the noise problem for me. On the floors below, the sounds continued for another hour.

The hotel fact sheet provided by the internet travel service stated that breakfast was available from six to eight. The reality was that breakfast could be available between those hours if someone were on duty for that purpose.

Chinese and Japanese were two more languages not spoken by anyone employed at the hotel. In the early morning, the chaos which rained in the lobby was almost humorous. I ate breakfast at a busy outdoor café only three short streets away. Then I returned to prepare for my first full day in Paris. The line of the late-night arrivals, now waiting for their breakfast, extended from the entrance to the dining area up two flights of stairs. The dining area, where still nothing was happening, contained only four tables and eight chairs two of which were occupied by cats. Had there been kitchens in any of the rooms the cats might have been prepared and eaten by these Asians. I got out of the hotel as fast as I could.

The Louvre is closed on Monday. The walk from there across the grounds, through the parks, and along the Seine, with its bridges and bookstalls, is full of history and beauty. I walked to the Tuileries Gardens, the Place de la Concorde and the far western end of the Champs-Élysées as far as the Arc de Triomphe. I found an outdoor café on a side street and treated myself to a glass of wine. I returned to the hotel early in the evening. Given the congestion there and the potential demand for warm water in the morning, I thought it prudent to shower early. I had snacked well during the day and stopped for a light meal in a crowded corner restaurant.

After I had ordered, and while I waiting for my meal, the World Cup game between Germany and Portugal began. I was unable to gauge the sentiment of the onlookers for their favored team. They cheered for all the good plays, groaned at all the missed goals, and booed all the questionable calls by the refs. I gave up my table to a family that was waiting. I stood with my glass of wine, and watched Germany defeat Portugal by a score of four to nothing. The Germans absolutely dominated the game.

Since the second half of "The TREK" would begin and end in Germany, I hoped that Germany might make it to the semi-finals. If Germany won, then I would be there as a fan when the team played in the finals. Wow! Wouldn't it be great to be in Germany when its team won the World Cup?

I bar-hopped until midnight when I took my place at a pub to cheer as the United States defeated Ghana two to zero. My hooting and hollering in English attracted some of the patrons to root with me. To those who stayed with me and loyal to TEAM USA until the final victory I expressed my gratitude and bought the last round. TEAM USA, Paris, closed the pub.

After much less sleep than I felt I needed, I was at the Louvre, where I gained early admission with a pass compliments of the French government in recognition of my father's service during World War II. Containing approximately 35,000 pieces of art, including Leonardo da Vinci's painting, Mona Lisa, and the statues of Venus de Milo, The Winged victory of Samothra, and Psyche Revived by Cupid's Kiss, there is no time for viewing and reflection. The crowds make that impossible. In summer, people may wait in line for hours to enter. Inside, there is little respect or courtesy displayed by the overwhelming number of tourists addicted to cameras, cell phones, and chatter. Everyone is talking all the time.

As I exited, I watched a group of Asians depart from one bus. Every one of the passengers was wearing a surgical mask. The group attracted as many photographers as did I.M. Pei's spectacular Pyramide du Louvre at the entrance. It was my guess that they were visiting from Communist China where breathing, like everything else, is controlled. As a condition of travel, the government must have mandated wearing protective masks in order to limit the amount of air from within a free country to which they could be exposed. What a spectacle they create when they enter a restaurant! How do they eat? Do they even know that there is no scientific or medical evidence to support that wearing those masks helps anyone avoid or not transmit disease? "Made in China" has taken on a new meaning.

Beyond the Louvre, I traveled to Les Invalides, the Pantheon, and the Musee d'Orsay and toured in a crowded, but less congested, atmosphere.

Early in the evening, I returned to the hotel. In a successful exchange of gestures with the desk clerk I succeeded in obtaining a fresh hand towel. Just for jollies I rode the metro back into the financial district where, in the early afternoon, I had walked past some cafes and pubs which were more attractive than the ones that were scattered throughout my neighborhood. I found a large, fairly sophisticated pub with fixed barstools at several service counters. That was helpful. They provided more space to eat compared with the other pubs where patrons crowded into any available space. The schedule for day five of the World Cup included a match between Belgium, where I would be arriving in two weeks, and Algeria, which I will not visit in this lifetime. I, and most of the patrons, cheered for the Belgian team. In another outstanding match, Belgium narrowly defeated Algeria, two to one.

Statistics vary depending upon the source, but the French government estimates that between 75 and 85 percent of its population are Catholics. On Wednesday, June 18th, I planned to spend the day at the Cathedral of Notre Dame and the Basilique du Sacre-Coeur (Basilica of the Sacred Heart). At noon, there would be a Mass at the Cathedral.

Notre Dame is a huge cathedral. Construction first began in the early 12th century and was not completed until 1345. After the French revolution in 1789, the cathedral suffered extensive vandalism. Many religious objects were stolen, destroyed, or badly damaged. After the new republic stabilized work began on reconstruction and restoration. Famous for its bells which tolled the hour and rang in festive occasions, detailed engineering analyses indicated that their ringing caused vibrations within the structure and was unsafe. The largest of the bells, the Emmanuel, weighs 13 tons. In 1944, its non-stop ringing alerted the residents that Paris had been liberated.

True to my experience in churches in Europe throughout the years, many tourists ignored the signs for silence, respect, and quiet. They toured the cathedral as they would tour the Louvre. The Asians remained true to their reputation as the most frequent offenders, posing for pictures on the steps of the altar, leaning against statues and sarcophagi, wiping sweat from their brows with tissues dipped in the holy water fountains.

I watched one Asian teenager pose for selfies everywhere an opportunity presented itself. She wore a Mickey Mouse hat, Elton John style oversized sunglasses; a T-shirt with the words, "Hard Rock Café New York" and sweat pants with "San Francisco" lettered on each pant leg. Over the sweat pants she wore an exceptionally abbreviated pair of blue jean cutoffs with no more than three inches of material extending below the waist. They were accented by a multi-colored, studded belt and a rainbow-colored buckle which read "Hollywood." On her feet she wore flip flops with the name "Ron Jon Surf Shop."

Mass at noon was the only opportunity I had within the cathedral to sense that I was in a church. Ushers restricted attendance to persons desiring to celebrate the Mass. Cameras and cell phones were forbidden, and the restriction was enforced. Tour groups were excluded. The Mass in French was solemn. I was able to remember many of the prayers that I had been taught in French class in second grade at St. Thomas the Apostle grammar school by the Sisters of Eternal Punishment. Years ago, the Catholic Church rejected my claim for Post-Traumatic Stress Disorder.

As I proceeded down one of several aisles to receive communion someone tapped me on my shoulder. I turned to see an older, well-dressed woman, smile at me and point down at my legs. I looked and saw that my convertible trousers had malfunctioned. The segment, at the lower two-thirds of the left trouser leg, had separated at the zipper from the upper third segment of the trouser. It was riding on my shoe down around my ankle. The right trouser leg was intact. I was walking toward the priest wearing slightly more than half my trousers, and there was an obvious contrast between the dark grey color of the trousers and the slightly tan color of my leg.

I ducked into one of the pews, and rushed to re-attach the segments. I was unsuccessful. Still sitting in the pew, I tucked the defective segment deep under my briefs and stood up. I prayed, really prayed, that this quick fix might work. To be safe, in case the Creator wasn't paying attention to me just then, I walked again toward the priest with my hands clasped low at my waist and not high at my chest. My left hand served to reinforce the trouser segment in place. My right hand was free to accept the communion wafer. When the Mass ended, I waited until everyone from the area had departed, then I left.

Outside, and at a respectable distance away from the cathedral, I removed my shoes and converted the trousers to shorts. I walked until I found a men's clothing store where I obtained several safety pins. In the changing room, I fastened the pins at the zipper on the inside of the trousers. The walk to a café for lunch and then to the Basilica of the Sacred Heart was uneventful. The repair had held.

The walk between the cathedral and the basilica was only about an hour through an attractive section of the city. Halfway along the route was the Musee Grevin, a wax museum containing figures of the most historical and famous persons from French history and others from elsewhere. There would be time to visit after my tour of the basilica.

The Basilica of the Sacred Heart is located on a hill at the highest point within Paris. Construction began in 1875, after the defeat of France in the Franco-Prussian War in 1871, and was completed at the start of another war, World War I, in 1914. Not until the end of that war was the basilica consecrated in 1919.Unlike the Cathedral of Notre Dame, which attracts far more tourists, the Basilica of the Sacred Heart bans cameras and video recorders. The faithful who seek a more contemplative atmosphere will find it here inside and throughout the grounds. At the top of the basilica is an open dome, accessible to tourists, from which all of Paris to the south is in view.

The Musee Grevin offered a pleasant transition between the solemnity of the cathedral and the basilica, and the revelry that I expected in the pubs on the sixth day of the World Cup. Within the museum are more than 400 figures depicting historical personages from the early history of France to the present. The figures are displayed in their historical context and include France's most famous warrior-emperors, Charlemagne and Napoleon Bonaparte. For some reason, actress Bridgette Bardot was easy to recognize. In addition to the French there are many international figures especially stars of stage and screen. Comedians Albert Einstein, Leonardo da Vinci, Charlie Chaplain, and Betty White are there. So are the actors Barack Obama, Vladimir Putin, Nicholas Cage and Brad Pitt.

Tonight's World Cup game pitted the Netherlands against Australia. I thought that most of the continentals would be rooting for the Netherlands. At the pub, I learned that I was wrong. If France were successful enough to advance then the Netherlands would be a powerful team to defeat if it also advanced. Any team that could knock out a threat to the French team was preferred. Similar to the game between the United States and Ghana the patrons were interested in only two things: watching a good game and consuming alcohol.

In a clever way to provide food service quickly the pub had only three meal choices: baguettes with beef, ham, or chicken. Each came layered with cheese slices, fresh spinach and lettuce, and slices of tomato and mushrooms. No special orders. I ordered a beef baguette at the start of the game. After downing two mugs of cold draught beer I was tempted to order a second. However, I knew that I would not be able to finish it all, and I had no place to store it overnight so I deferred. The game was outstanding and relatively high-scoring. The Netherlands defeated Australia in a squeaker by a score of three to two.

My father, Vincent, had one brother, Louis, older than he by 15 months. During World War II, he served in the Navy. He told me that he was willing to serve as an admiral but the Navy was unwilling to promote him 16 grades. His son, Louis, is three years younger than I. He and his bride, Kathy, would be in Paris to celebrate their 38th wedding anniversary on June 19th. We planned to meet at the northeast base of the Eiffel Tower on the morning of their anniversary.

I had not seen Louis or Kathy in 10 years, but we recognized one another immediately. They were traveling as part of a group, and would be in Paris only that day. The tour amenities included coupons to some Paris attractions. One was a cruise along the Seine. We had a short walk to the boats, and a gentle, comfortable, two-hour cruise. The air flow made the temperature feel cold enough for sweaters and windbreakers. After we docked, we visited a museum just off the Seine a few streets. There were several signs at the entrance door, the cashier's cage, and throughout the entrance foyer stating that all bags must be checked before entering the museum interior. It was ignored by almost all the visitors, and not enforced by any of the security personnel. The museum was well-organized and spacious. There was more room and more time to view the exhibits compared to the Louvre and the other larger museums.

We ate lunch nearby, and were fortunate not to have to wait for a table in an area so cluttered with tourists. I thought that our waiter was rude, his service was poor, and the few selections from the daily menu had been prepared and were waiting under heat lamps to drop at the tables of tourists almost immediately after they ordered. When Kathy asked the waiter, in English, to describe an item on the menu, he looked at her with an expression which begged the unspoken comment, "You've got to be kidding me. If you don't know what it is then order something else." My cousin does not look anything like Chevy Chase.

After lunch we took a long walk back to their hotel, crossing the Seine on the way. We stopped at a café for coffee and dessert. They had plans for their anniversary day dinner, and a very early start in the morning to visit Euro Disney. This was my only full day in Paris that I had shared with anyone. I was very happy that it was with my cousin and his wife on their wedding anniversary.

I checked out from the hotel early on Friday, June 20th. Although I was eager to check out, I was not eager to leave Paris. On the eighth day of the World Cup, France would play Switzerland. I expected that, win or lose, the revelry in Paris on a Friday night would far exceed that of Villeparisis, my next destination.

Villeparisis is a suburb on the northeast side of Paris. The distance from my hotel to the town was just shy of 15 miles. At breakfast, I re-read my notes. Half the size of Evreux, with about 25,000 residents, it supported two colleges, a conservatory, a multi-cultural arts center, several sports stadiums, and three business parks. That seemed large enough to guarantee that I would be able to find a pub in which to have a meal, relax, and watch the game. Only 10 percent of the land area was designated as forest, so I was unsure about the possibilities for camping. I had not had a problem finding a campsite to date, and I did not expect to have a problem in Villeparisis.

I found a nice bar-restaurant from which I could see a tractor trailer dispatch facility only about 200 to 300 yards further down the road. There were woods to the front and side of the facility. I decided to enter the bar with my backpack. If it were crowded and there were no space to ground the backpack and stand, then I would leave, set-up the campsite, and return. There was a small table in a corner with a good view of the wide-screen television. The match between France and Switzerland would begin in an hour. This would be a fun Friday night. I could order, eat, relax, and watch the game. The teams were evenly matched. I was rooting for France. When in France..." I was not disappointed: France, five; Switzerland, two.

Nearly midnight, the bar staff had been very busy all evening, especially after each of the five goals for France. I knew that my waiter would have preferred that I eat more than only a plate of pasta and drink more than two beers, my usual daily limit of alcohol. I felt also that he would have preferred to be watching the match rather than serving customers. When I received the bill, I saw that I had been charged for the meal and four mugs of beer. I disputed the charges for the two additional beers, but the waiter insisted that they were correct. After I asked to speak with the manager, the waiter left. The caution from Lieutenant Montreaux in Bayeux was ringing true: a bar staffer was trying to cheat me. A few minutes later he returned and told me that the manager had gone home.

"You must pay me this amount!"

In my backpack, I found my change purse and an amount of euros equal to the cost of the meal and two beers. I left it on the table.

"Go ahead and call the police. They can find me walking on the road toward the place with all the trailers."

What was his problem? I had been cheering for France, not Switzerland!

There are four towns between Villeparisis and Reims. The first of these is huge compared to the next three. Meaux supports a population of over 50,000 residents; the others only less than 2,000. Meaux was very similar to Evreux in size, city services, and conveniences. Slightly more than 13 miles from Villeparisis, I reached it in the early afternoon. There is a World War I museum and a monument to that war which was funded and built in 1932 by the Americans. During the "First Battle of the Marne," the French had halted the German advance west, thus enabling American forces to deploy and push them back east. The monument is named, "La Liberté éplorée," (The Tearful Liberty), but is referred to more commonly by the French as "The American monument." The Museum of the Great War was open late, and I was able to spend three hours touring. A permanent exhibition displays the weaponry, including aircraft and tanks, uniforms, field equipment, and artifacts, such as medical and messing supplies, personal gear, and national posters. I took an outstanding interactive tour which lasted more than an hour. The museum contained a full-service café. After the tour, I had an early evening snack and departed.

A mile past the museum, in the direction of Montreuil-aux-Lions, I found a large, wooden area and camped. The following day I would have to walk five miles further than I did this day. I went to sleep early, hoping to wake well rested for the longer hike.

Enroute to Montreuil-aux-Lions I stopped at a bakery for a coffee and roll. I read on the front page of a newspaper that on day nine of the World Cup I had missed seeing the game between Germany and Ghana. It had ended in a two-two tie.

The three towns until Reims were indistinguishable. They seemed little more than bedroom communities between Meaux and Reims. Along the route, I saw that each had at least one restaurant, a bakery, and mini market. The mini markets each had large outdoor displays full of fresh produce from the Marne region: red fruits and fruit jams, potatoes, and green vegetables. Although the scenery was somewhat sterile, the walk was not as difficult as I had expected with lengths of 18, 16 and 18 miles, respectively. From Ville-en-Tardenois, I had only a 13-mile walk to Reims.

Very close to Reims, I passed through the small town of St. Brice Courcelles with a population of only about 3,000 residents. I paused at a traffic circle where four roads converged and none of them was marked. Two roads forked towards the southeast and I did not know which one to take. A bus drove around the circle and I saw it stop about 100 yards away. There was no one waiting and no one exited, but the bus did not move away. I assumed the bus driver was ahead of schedule and had stopped for a short break. I dropped my backpack and ran toward the bus. Only about 20 yards away, the bus departed. I returned to my backpack and followed the bus.

In a small home with a large yard to the side and rear I saw a woman tending the flowers in her garden. I watched her, and when she saw me she walked over to me. A bit hesitant at first, she came alive with energy and activity after I complimented her on her garden and told her that I was an American walking from Normandy through France.

Mrs. Monique Comard ran away from me, turned off her garden hose, threw her gardening gloves on the ground, and ran into her home through the side door. A few minutes later, she came outside from the front door, fastening the button at her waist on her culottes then all of the buttons on her blouse, in a complete change of clothes.

She grabbed me by the elbow and pulled down the sidewalk and up the walkway into her house. I stopped inside as I came through the doorway to remove my shoes. While I was bent over she started to pull the backpack off me. Unbalanced and not expecting the force of her tugging, I fell on the floor.

"Pardon. Pardon. Je suis vraiment désolé. Vous êtes bien?"

"Yes, I am fine. Thank you."

Mrs. Comard told me that she had lived 40 years in the home and had never seen an American walk past it. She is the daughter of a very patriotic family who fought during the war and through the occupation.

"If the Americans had not come you would be in French Germany and I would be speaking German."

After the war, her father found a job in Reims working with the French and American military for reconstruction projects and resettlement of refuges from eastern France and Belgium. I heard from her how wonderful and how happy she and her family were while they were associated with the Americans. As a child, she would accompany her father to work on the weekends. She always came home with a chocolate bar. She had learned her English from school and from being with her father and the Americans.

"Then DeGaulle chased away the Americans and everything went to hell."

Every time she said the name "DeGaulle" she turned her head away from me, pursed her lips, and made a gesture as if she were spitting. I did not hear one kind word about the former brigadier general, leader of Free France, and president of the Republic.

She jumped up from the couch and pulled me up with her. Holding both my hands, she led me into the kitchen. She opened her refrigerator and asked me what I wanted to eat and drink. I told her that I was fine and did not need anything. Ignoring my comments she ran out of the kitchen and returned with a bottle of wine. She found an opener and handed it and the bottle of wine to me.

As I opened the bottle she put three frying pans on the stove. Into each she melted a lump of butter then added bread to one, cheese to another, and slices of ham to the third. Grabbing my hands again, she led me out of the kitchen and into the living room. From the dining table, she scooped up newspapers, mail, a fairly-full laundry basket, and a plastic bottle of detergent and threw everything into the dog's bed. Her small dog was the same soft brown color of his sleeping bed and he yelped when everything fell on top of him and woke him from his sleep.

Obviously not a guard dog, he followed me wherever Miss Monique dragged me. I caught the tablecloth she threw at me and set it on the table as she disappeared again. Remembering that she forgot something, she returned and pulled me back into the kitchen. As she cooked the meal, she handed me the plates and utensils to set the table.

My glass of wine was half full. She emptied the bottle when she refreshed my glass. I thought that she had been getting livelier for some reason. The meal was excellent. On the plate with the grilled ham and cheese sandwich she had added fresh vegetables from her garden and slices of cheeses from the region. After the meal, we cleared the table together and worked briefly in the kitchen. Miss Monique washed and I dried.

Back in her living room, she pushed the dog out of a stuffed chair, waking him just before he hit the floor. I sat opposite her and heard about everything that was wrong with France which was "decaying every day." Prices keep rising; tax money is wasted; churches are closing while mosques are being built; the Chinese and Asians are beyond annoying, always speaking "that Fu Manchu language" among themselves, never French. She made so many spitting gestures I thought that her neck and lips must hurt. But each upsetting issue justified another swig of wine and it wasn't long before she had finished the second bottle.

I learned that her husband had passed away and that her children had married and moved to larger towns where business opportunities were better. She rarely has a visitor. Miss Monique fell asleep as I was explaining "The TREK" to her. I retrieved my notebook and wrote. She awoke in less than hour, jumped up, and, waking the dog for the third time, picked him up and threw him out the side door into the garden.

She said that she had nothing in the house to offer me for dessert and asked me to accompany her to the bakery. I told her, that I was not hungry and that her kind offer was appreciated very much, but was not necessary. After some discussion, I learned that the bakery was located on the road to Reims. We could travel there together, have a cake and coffee, then I could continue my walk.

I put my backpack in the rear of her Renault. Every time she spoke she turned her head to look at me. I asked if I could take her picture and she turned and smiled. The same time that the camera snapped, we ran off the road and I got a picture of only the roof. The second picture, posed as the car was bouncing off the curb, was only half her face and all of the rear view mirror. Four tries later I finally got a good picture. We were very fortunate that there had not been any oncoming traffic.

I treated her to the dessert and added several pieces of pie, cake, and pastries for her to take home. Outside by her car, we hugged and said farewell. She told me to be safe and to have a good time in Belgium and Germany.

"But watch out for those Germans." Then she turned away, and this time for real, spit into the road.

I was surprised by the size and beauty of Reims. Slightly more than two miles from where I said "Au revoir" to Mrs. Comard, I had stumbled into the center of town in the early evening on the main road which hosts most of the bars and restaurants. The weather was clear and warm with most of the residents and tourists dressed in short-sleeved shirts and shorts or light slacks. Many of the outdoor cafes were full.

I found the hotel where I retrieved the parcel containing my next four days of rations. The hotelier and his family were eager to meet me. Our conversation was interrupted by inquiries from other guests. When they had a short break they told me that they were certain of my arrival because of the need to resupply the food. They offered me a guest room. They would not accept a fee and I was not required to register. The family asked me to visit again in the late evening when they were free after the night staff arrived. In the room set aside for me, they had placed brochures about Reims and highlighted those which would be open the following day. There were small baskets of fruit and cheese each with a note, "Monsieur Pelosi, USA. You will likes these for your walkings. Giselle, Rene."

After a shower and change of clothes, I passed through the lobby. I glanced at the father sending his daughter on an errand. He held both hands up with his ten fingers extended, then pointed to the desk. I would return from touring to meet him at 10 p.m. There were attractions along the main street and down the side streets. But on the 13th day of the World Cup France was playing Ecuador. Every facility that served alcohol and had a wide-screen television was full. I watched most of the first half then returned for my appointment with my host, Eduard Lateguin. He invited me into a small sitting room where he and I talked and watched the remainder the game which ended in a zero-zero tie. The result put quite a damper on the late night festivities.

The Lateguin family was a mixture of French and Belgian. The parents were fluent in French, German, and English. Their children were students in elementary school and only beginning to learn English. Eduard told me that they learn more English from the cinema, television, and the internet than they do in school. He added that the school curriculum still was mired in the old-school tradition, and had not advanced with the media, especially social media, opportunities. As a result, the children in school usually were further advanced in the English language than what was expected by the curriculum. I shared my oft-repeated stories about my father's military experiences during the war and the airlift, and the ceremonies at Normandy. Eduard said that children in France, if they learn nothing else, learn that France is free and they are "without war, and at peace for a record number of years" because of the Americans and the Allied victory. Before we parted company for the night he asked if I would join him and his family for breakfast at 8 a.m., and "ask my children to speak some English with you."

They did not need to be asked to speak. Shy at first, they spoke up quickly when I asked them to name the items on the table in English. I had to stifle a laugh when the boy, age seven, identified "eau" as "sea." His sister, only one year older corrected him politely, "No, Rene. It is water. Sea is the water we swimmers in."

I cleared the room for availability for another guest but left my backpack with the family in their sitting room. The next town was less than 14 miles away and I could walk there in less than five hours. If I departed Reims at two after touring for six hours, and walked in two, 2.5-hour segments with an hour's rest in between, then I would arrive at eight. There would be two hours of daylight to find and establish a campsite in Pontfaverger-Moronvilliers. According to the Lateguin family, the town was small with a population of less than 2,000 residents, no hotels, but plenty of fields and forests in which to camp.

Just beyond the hotel was a small, enclosed park, "Square Des Victimes De La Gestapo." Inside was a small pond, three benches, a sculpture, and several plaques on which were engraved the names of dozens of locals who were deported from Reims and died in concentration camps. I read every name. More than half the victims were young men in their 20's.

As I headed toward the town center, I passed through the Plaza Drouet with its monumental tower and golden angel built in honor of a former French infantryman who rose to the rank of Marshal of France. Not far away was the Cathedral of Notre-Dame of Reims. In 2011, the city celebrated the cathedral's 800th anniversary. It is a magnificent structure as attractive and ornate on the exterior as it is in the interior.

Inside, the center aisle extends almost 150 yards. Across its 30-yard width and 40-yard height are naves, alcoves and prayer recesses decorated with centuries old statues and tapestries. On the floor, not far from the main entrance, is a stone marker indicating the place where Clovis (466-511), the first King of the Franks, was baptized in 496, more than 1500 years ago. The engraving on the stone reads:

ICI

SAINT REMI

BAPTISA CLOVIC

ROI DES FRANCS

On the west side of the cathedral, just shy of the altar is a memorial plaque in English and French dedicated to the British dead from World War I.

It reads:

TO THE GLORY OF GOD

AND TO THE MEMORY OF

ONE MILLION DEAD

OF THE BRITISH EMPIRE

WHO FELL

IN THE GREAT WAR

1914 * 1918

AND OF WHOM THE

GREATER PART REST

IN FRANCE

One million British dead from four years of war in France!

I thought of Westminster Abbey where only one soldier is buried: "Beneath this stone, rests the body of a British Warrior, unknown by name or rank, brought from France to lie among the most illustrious of the land, and buried here on Armistice Day, 11 Nov., 1920."

THE LORD KNOWETH THEM THAT ARE HIS

GREATER LOVE HATH NO MAN THAN THIS

On the other side of town, I passed by the Porte Mars, built in the 3rd century and now only a ruin. It is only 500 yards from the building in which the representatives of the German Wehrmacht signed the unconditional surrender to the Allies on May 7, 1945. The building is now a museum. The older of two matrons on duty at the entrance insisted that I pay the five euros, ($7.), entrance fee. My father's contribution to their freedom had no value for her.

"What if my name were Eisenhower? Would I still have to pay?"

"Yes. Everyone must pay to visit."

While I was reading one of the surrender documents the younger woman snuck over to me and returned my entrance fee.

"She is an old crank, worried about her job and her pension."

"Her English is good. She can come to America and work for our Internal Revenue Service – the tax troublemakers. She probably could earn rapid promotions and a much better pension."

"Yes, I think so. She is mean enough. But I will not tell her that."

I departed Reims and walked without stopping directly to Pontfaverger-Moronvilliers, arriving at 9 p.m. This town was once two separate towns which were destroyed during World War I and never rebuilt. With a population of less than 2,000 residents, I did not see any pub or restaurant along the main road. There still was an hour of daylight in which to find and set up camp. The area is relatively flat fields and forests and I stopped for the night on high ground at the edge of the woods along the road to Bourcq. Perhaps it was fortunate that I was unable to find a pub. On the 14th day of the World Cup, I did not see Germany defeat the United States: one to zero.

Of the 57 cities and towns that I would visit during "The TREK," none was smaller than Bourcq. The town had fewer than 60 residents and the number was diminishing slightly every year since the turn of the century. I arrived in the middle of the afternoon and saw only seven people as I walked down the main street. The next day, I would have a 19-mile walk to Buzancy. I was not tired and, after refilling my water bottles, I walked for another hour reducing the next day's walk by three miles. The area was as desolate as what I left beyond Pontfaverger-Moronvilliers. Tonight there would be no World Cup game, not for lack of a viewing opportunity, but because the competition transitioned to the second stage, and no games were scheduled.

When I awoke, I felt more relaxed than I had any morning since I began "The TREK" 20 days earlier. For the past two days, I had walked an average of 15 miles over relatively flat farmland through an area nearly completely devoid of traffic and people. The days were sunny and warm; the nights were cool and refreshing. From the tent each night, I could hear only the sounds of owls, maybe larks, other birds, and an occasional frog. Unlike almost everywhere earlier, my sleep was undisturbed. I had walked out of the Marne region of France into the Ardennes.

I expected a third, easy day of walking through much of the same terrain and I was not disappointed. I wondered what I would do on a Saturday night in a town with fewer than 200 people. The World Cup games that evening would be played by teams only from South America. I assumed there would not be as much local interest as there would be if a team from Europe had been playing.

The hotel du Saumon, located on the road to Stenay, was the last of 21 cities and towns in France in which I would end the day. My mid-day arrival was too early for dinner and the game, but convenient to ground my backpack and have a cold beer. The hotelier, who spoke very passable English, asked me if I were expected as a guest. He was disappointed when I said no. I told him that the region was ideal for camping, and that I was enjoying peaceful nights away from the tourists and especially the late-night revelry after a World Cup match. He asked me my destination. When I told him, "Berlin," he was very surprised. He asked me from where I had started, and was equally as surprised when I said, "Normandy, on the anniversary of the liberation landings."

He suggested I visit the area close by where a great and costly battle was fought during World War I. There was a cemetery with graves for all the combatants: Americans, British, French, Scottish, and Germans, all killed as the Germans advanced toward France and the Allies tried to stop them. There also were monuments and memorials. When I had finished my beer, I secured my backpack in a cleaning closet and set out for the battlefield.

In the summer of 1918, after four years of war and only three months before its end, the Germans made a strong thrust west toward Paris. An American division of infantry had been holding the line there for several weeks. A Scottish division, one of four divisions belonging to the British Corps, moved in to relieve the Americans. Its first mission was to prepare a hasty defense, then retrieve and bury the hundreds of American soldiers whose bodies still were lying in the fields.

Together with French infantry and supported by French artillery, the Scots launched a surprise attack against the Germans and pushed them back. I could imagine the huge open battle area where cornfields provided no cover and where the forests provided concealment but no opportunity to employ artillery. The Scots advanced and maneuvered too rapidly, exposing their flanks to German counterattacks. The fighting was intense, marked by fierce hand-to-hand combat. As was true of so many battles during World War I, it ended in a stalemate. Eventually the Germans withdrew.

Impressed with the spirit, courage and fighting ability of the Scottish soldiers, the French commanding general ordered the construction of the first and only monument by the French to the British for actions during the war. The granite monument contains an image of a thistle intertwined with a rose.

At the front, the inscription in French reads, "Here will flourish forever the glorious thistle of Scotland among the roses of France."

An inscription on the side reads: "The 17th French Infantry Division to The 15th Scottish Infantry Division."

The battlefield cemetery was so very peaceful. I was its only visitor, and felt so very lonely even among all those long dead.

Major John McCrea authored the poem, "*In Flanders Fields*," on May 3, 1915, in Ypres, Belgium during the First World War It was 100 years since Major McCrea put pen to paper when I wrote these note for this narrative.

Nothing has changed. Old men will continue to send young men off to war to kill or be killed.

Man as a weapon is here to stay.

I was not any mood to be festive, and decided against watching the World Cup match between Brazil and Chile. Instead, I retrieved my backpack from the cabinet at the hotel, and set up camp within sight of, but a respectable distance from, the cemetery.

In the morning, I hoped to wake to the sound of Major McCrea's larks.

Stenay was 13 miles away. This would be the last night that I would sleep in France. The next day, after another 14 miles, I would cross the border into Belgium. The closer I came to the town, the more activity I encountered on the road. I saw several motor scooters, mopeds, couples on bicycles, adults pulling children in wooden wagons, and people strolling. There was far more activity than I would expect from a town with fewer than 3,000 people out enjoying a sunny and scenic Sunday afternoon. After two or three motorhomes passed me, I remembered that I had planned to obtain my final resupply in France at a campsite along the Meuse River.

The campsite and its location along the Meuse were ideal. For only eight euros, ($12.), I obtained a secure campsite, access to a shower and laundry facility, the opportunity to rent recreation equipment such as canoes and bicycles, and a free pass to the beer museum. A museum dedicated to beer! What better place to celebrate the last of my 27 days in France. I was certain that, if free samples were not offered, then there had to be a beer garden where I also could obtain a meal.

The campsite manager told me that he had been in business almost 20 years. In that time, no one ever had written to him describing a walk across Europe and asking to send a food parcel for support. He asked me what kind of food I had sent. After opening the box, I showed him the packets of MRE's and described the contents to him. Never having seen an MRE, he was surprised that one packet could sustain a person for a meal or even a day. I offered him the opportunity to sample as many as he would like, with the caveat that they would not taste like anything he may have eaten before. His taste buds would be shocked. He took only two.

"My boys, who think that they want to be soldiers, will taste them first. Maybe then they will decide to stay here with their family and help me with the camp."

The day was fun and festive. Like so many other small towns in this region of France there were monuments and memorials to the soldiers who died fighting in World War I. The loss of so many young men who would have married, raised families, farmed the fields, managed the agriculture, and contributed to the welfare and growth of these towns was devastating.

I thought that there should be a monument at the entrance to every military cemetery stating simply:

MANY HOPES AND DREAMS LIE BURIED HERE

After paying my respects to the memories of events which the locals honor regularly every year I toured the town in a happier mood.

The European Beer Museum at Stenay offered 60 beers to taste. My complimentary admissions ticket did not permit me to stay overnight and through the next few days until I had sampled them all. But I made a good effort to sample several in the two hours that I walked past some of the more than 40,000 objects within the museum, and then relaxed in the garden café and ate dinner.

Back at the campsite, I crowded into the field house, used for recreation during inclement weather, and watched the second half of that day's game of the World Cup. The Netherlands shutout Mexico, two to zero. Everyone had been cheering for the Dutch!

My campsite was on the far side of the campgrounds and away from the field house, so that I was unaffected by the noise as the second game of day 15 was played. Costa Rica and Greece played to a one-one tie. Penalties allowed Costa Rica to advance in the playoffs.

I went to sleep after reading my notes about the four towns that I would visit in Belgium. I was most interested in the terrain of the Ardennes, Bastogne where I would be on the Fourth of July, and the history of the Battle of Bulge.

"We have no other choice. Our submission would serve no end. If Germany is victorious, Belgium, whatever her attitude, will be annexed to the Reich. If die we must, better death with honor."
- Charles de Broqueville, Prime Minister of Belgium, responding to Germany's demand for surrender, August 2, 1914.

13. Belgium.

Belgium promised to be as interesting for me as was France. But I would be there only one-fifth as long, stopping in four towns for five nights before I crossed into Luxembourg. Of the 895-mile route, 70 miles would be in Belgium. From Stenay, Germany I would walk almost directly east nine miles, then cross the border into Belgium, and continue another seven miles east to Virton. From Virton, the route would take me approximately 70 miles north through the rolling hills and dense forests of the Ardennes region and the towns of Arlon, Martelange and Bastogne.

Although I was interested primarily in the military history of this small region of Belgium, I also was curious about the people and the strange statistics for which Belgium is noted. It ranks first in Europe for the required length of compulsory education (13 years). It also ranks first in Europe, by percentage, with the number of people living in urban areas. Those are two very respectable socio-economic indicators of the potential for social stability and prosperity. But, for some reason, Belgium also ranks first within the most densely populated countries of world in death rate, leading such underdeveloped countries as Rwanda, Burundi, and Haiti. Very surprising to me, Belgium again holds a first-place ranking in Europe for rapes and other serious crimes. Why would the citizens of an urbanized, stable, well-educated population behave so badly against one another? Why were these citizens dying younger rather than older? In only five days, I did not expect to learn the answers. However, given the opportunity to meet and speak with the citizens, I hoped that I would be able to make some helpful observations.

At the campsite, I slept well and, after a long, hot shower and a full breakfast of an MRE with fruit, I began walking about 7 a.m. The terrain of the fairly flat farmland and fields of France gradually transitioned into the hills and forests which characterize the Ardennes. I crossed into Belgium mid-morning at about 10 a.m. There was a small rest stop area beyond the border crossing point where I took a break. While I rested, I removed the small flag of France from the rear of my backpack and replaced it with the flag of Belgium alongside the flag of the United States. During the past three hours, I realized that both the volume of traffic and the number of hills were increasing as I approached Virton.

Virton.

I arrived in the late afternoon and stopped at another outdoor café. On the television screen I could see the highlights of World Cup games played to date, and the countdown for the start of the first game on day 16, in 30 minutes, between France and Nigeria. Before I entered Virton, I saw several suitable campsites at the edge of the forests. I expected to find the same opportunities at the far side of town. I decided to rest, eat, and watch my first from Belgium World Cup Championship game.

France and Belgium had been allies in the first two World Wars. I would observe the other patrons, and root for France as I expected that they would. Their sentiments during the second game between Germany and Algeria might be very different. The Belgians had suffered terribly in both wars, easily overpowered by Germany's superiority in men and weaponry. I decided to skip the second game. Instead, I would tour the town of 11,000 residents and make camp as it got dark.

France scored the only two goals of the game and shutout Nigeria. I am not a soccer player, but it appeared as if the French team easily outplayed their opponents on both offense and defense. I had been seated for a little more than two hours.

As I stood and wiggled into my backpack, I felt stiff for the first time since I had begun "The TREK." The combination of a longer, 19-mile walk and the irregular pace of climbing and descending the rolling hills had a noticeable effect on me. The next three days I would have walks of 16 miles or less through similar terrain.

As I approached the exit, a younger man in his early 20's rose from his seat and cut me off to open and hold the door for me. In English, he asked me if I were headed to one of the hotels in Virton.

I told him, "No," and said that I was on a walking and camping trip. I added that my next hotel visit would be in three days in Bastogne. He knew immediately that this would occur on the Fourth of July American holiday, and told me that he also would be in Bastogne during the weekend. He added that Bastogne would be festive, especially with many American tourists there.

"I will be there for two days. I hope this will be enough time for me to walk the terrain, study the geography, visit the museums, and understand better the historic Battle of the Bulge."

"That is the reason why there are always so many Americans in Bastogne. Whenever I visit I always have a chance to practice my English. I can understand the Americans better than I can understand the British. Most of the people make their living there because of the tourists. The Americans arrive only in the warmer weather. The weather in Belgium usually is terrible. Rain is expected tonight for the next two or three days."

I did not need to hear that news. As we were talking, we were blocking the exit, so we stepped outside to let another patron depart. I felt the rain before I saw the wet cobblestone.

"See. What did I tell you? Rain! Now it will get cold. I have a small apartment nearby. There is room if you would like to spend the night."

I probably accepted his offer too quickly. On the short walk to his apartment, I asked myself if I were being true to my original concept of "The TREK" and concluded that I was. The exceptions occurred only when I allowed myself to be spoiled by the friendship and generosity of the locals who took an interest in me and my project.

Karl Pettit, 23, told me that he was born, raised, and educated in Virton. He attended the Catholic University of Louvain where he studied Psychology and Educational Sciences. The University was founded in 1425 and is one of the oldest universities in the world. Queen Mathilde of Belgium is an alumna.

Karl's father died while he was at the university. He commuted two hours on the weekends to help his mother maintain her home. He returned to work in Virton as a school teacher, a job that was offered to him as he began his studies at the university. He said that he currently worked also for the regional public health department during the summers when school is not in session.

His one-bedroom apartment had only a single twin bed which he offered me. The living room sofa opened into a day bed. For me to not have to camp in the rain won as the better reason why he should keep his own bed. While I retrieved my shaving kit and fresh clothes from my backpack, Karl brought linens from his bedroom. We made the full-size, fold-out bed together. When we finished, he went back to his bedroom and returned with a towel.

"The shower is on and the water is hot. I will take my shower in the morning."

The shower felt great especially the hot water helping to relax my sore back and shoulder muscles. I was ready for bed but Karl wasn't. He had many questions about "The TREK," my experiences in Europe, events in the United States, and life in Texas. He said that he planned to visit one day, hoping to see the Grand Canyon, Yellowstone Park, and watch a New York Yankees baseball game. I recommended that he visit New York and see the Yankee game first.

"Get the chaos and confusion of New York City and its millions of people out of the way, then enjoy the beauty, peace, and quiet of the west and our national parks."

It was midnight when we went to sleep and just past six when I heard noise from his bedroom and the sound of water running in the shower. He came into the living room wearing only his briefs. I saw a series of scars at his upper arm, shoulder, and chest. At 16, he had fallen from behind a tractor into some machinery for baling hay. A metal rod had detached from the baler and a screw at one end penetrated his upper chest over his heart and close to his collarbone. The screw continued to rotate through his upper chest, tearing his flesh until the rod detached from the tractor and stopped at the dense mass of bone, cartilage, and muscle in his left shoulder.

The driver did not hear his calls for help, and he was dragged behind the tractor for several minutes. He spent nearly two months in the hospital to repair his broken bones and lacerated upper torso, and another several weeks at home to recover. He had to repeat a year at school. His face and arms were tanned, but his well-proportioned, shirtless torso was chalk white. He pointed to the contrast in color on his body, and said that he stays in shape by running and swimming, but always covers himself with a shirt because the patchwork of scars are an embarrassment. I felt very sorry for him.

I declined his offer to make me breakfast, and he agreed to walk with me through town where there was a bakery with a breakfast nook. The rain was heavy but was supposed to stop by noon and clear by midday.

At breakfast, Karl told me that Belgium would play the United States this night on day 17 of the World Cup. I told him my sentiments about soccer in the United States. I would be rooting for Belgium. "When in Belgium. . ."

I thanked him for his hospitality. Karl told me to be sure to visit the museum in Bastogne which is dedicated to the 101st Airborne Division, and is located only a few streets from the center of town. Then he also suggested that I visit the other attractions in the morning of July Fourth and meet him at the museum at 11 a.m. From there we could tour the museum, have lunch together, and celebrate the American Independence Day.

We made a date to meet.

Arlon.

Arlon was 16 miles north. The rain and wind were coming from the north, and I could feel the cold through my layered clothing. I wore a baseball cap to keep the rain out of my eyes and a full poncho cinched tightly at my neck to keep most of my body dry except for my face. On the road for three hours, I hoped that I had walked nine miles. The hill country was a definite physical challenge made slightly even tougher by the adverse weather and the slippery cobblestone roads.

The road between Virton and Arlon was narrow. I walked on the side of the road every time I could hear a vehicle coming up behind me. Stepping to the side where there was no shoulder and turning to see if I were out of the way of the approaching vehicle was complicated by the weight of the backpack and the uneven, slippery terrain. Twice I lost my balance and fell.

The rain was ending as I walked the long, main road up a hill which crested near the center of town. The parking lot of a convenience store doubled as the inter-city bus stop. I walked to the side of a bus where the driver was handling baggage, and passengers were exiting or entering the bus. I had passed by about 30 yards when I heard, "Hey mate! Wait up." I looked back to see someone waving. I stopped and waited.

Walking toward me, pulling a suitcase and carrying a small backpack, was a younger, tall, well-built man, with red hair. When he said, "Hello, you must be an American," I detected a strong Irish accent. Seeing the American and Belgian flags on my backpack, he correctly assumed that I was an American.

"I wouldn't expect a local to be carrying such a huge backpack with the U.S. flag."

He asked me if I were headed to town, and if I had a reservation at a hotel.

"Yes, and no," I answered.

Derek Sinnot told me that he was visiting Arlon for a three-day management committee meeting and working group workshops of the European Cooperation in Science and Technology. Representatives from 30 European countries would meet at the Arlon campus of the University of Liege.

Meeting every six months in a different host country, now in Belgium, they would discuss European regional perspectives on energy and the low carbon agenda, and how different national policies are working to meet year 2020 emission reduction targets. He explained that the member consensus is that the impacts of climate change and environmental harm associated with energy use continue to grow. The representatives would describe national and regional cooperation among science, industry and government, and emphasize research and innovation. Hailing from the Department of the Built Environment, The Waterford Institute of Technology, Derek would represent Ireland and would present a case study about the opportunities and challenges of retrofitting buildings and urban areas to reduce the emissions of greenhouse gases.

He told me that he was walking to a bed and breakfast, a multi-room three-story apartment, owned and managed by the Catholic Church in Arlon. He had a reservation obtained from the internet. A message from Father Pierre, whose additional duty was to support the facility, stated that it was located only a half-mile from the bus stop along two roads into the center of town. He suggested that I walk with him. Perhaps there would be an extra room for me. If not, he was willing to share his room.

The rain had returned.

"Let's get to the church and out of this rain. Let me get settled. Then we can find out about a room for you. Or maybe you'd want to go get a beer."

Maybe? What kind of Irishman did he think I was going to pretend to be?

"Did you know that the U.S. plays Belgium tonight in the World Cup? You won't want to miss that."

Father Pierre was not at the guest house. Bur there was an envelope at the door, addressed to "Arriving Guests," in which there was a piece of paper on which was written the combination to the cipher lock at the entrance.

Inside, the first floor contained the kitchen, combination living-dining room, and a billiards room. Off the kitchen there was a small patio and a slightly larger garden. But beyond the patio and garden there was a huge yard surrounded on three sides by a concrete wall from which were hanging multi-colored baskets of flowers. I recognized red and pink geraniums and blue, purple and white petunias. This would be an excellent location to camp.

On the second floor were two rooms, one to either side of the stairway. On one door was a yellow, sticky note with the name, "Regina." The third floor supported the shared shower and water closet. The fourth floor was similar to the second.

There were sticky notes on each door. One had the name, "Derek." He entered, found the room key on the bed, and arranged his property. I dropped my backpack near his door and removed a small, collapsible umbrella, then went down to the first floor to wait.

After Derek wrote a note for Father Pierre, we left and walked four short blocks, about half a mile, to the center of town. In the large plaza, surrounded by government buildings, offices and restaurants, there was a World War II era M-10 tank destroyer. The words, "Angel of Freedom" had been hand-painted in cursive style with yellow paint on the upper left side of its structure.

The tank was provided by the Belgian government's post-war inventory to the Town of Arlon on September 24, 1984 as part of a memorial to commemorate the 40th anniversary of the liberation of Arlon. The tank destroyer is the center point of the memorial to the 28th Infantry Division (Keystone) and the plaque adjacent to the memorial is dedicated to "Our Liberators of the Keystone."

Alongside, in front of, and on top of the tank, people were positioning themselves to watch day 17 of the World Cup. In the plaza, which normally is used for public parking during weekdays and outdoor markets on the weekends, a huge screen had been set up displaying highlights of previous games. There was no audio. Personnel working from sound trucks on either side of the screen were testing the audio equipment. Anyone who did not speak French would have learned in less than five minutes how to count from one to four. Vendors were setting up their stands. From what I could see, it looked as if only beer would be sold from those stands. The plaza was decorated with banners and posters showing the images of the Belgian team and its individual players.

Our pre-game plan was to have a nice meal away from the growing crowd and chaos in the plaza, then return to the guest house to find Father Pierre. From there we would walk back to the plaza and stand among the locals and cheer for Belgium. We visited three restaurants before we found one with an open table. We seated ourselves, ordered two ales, and exchanged stories.

I was fascinated by the fact that 30 European nations were meeting every six months in a different host country to cooperate regionally and collectively to resolve problems related to energy consumption. Goals, objectives, targets, and timelines had been established, and were the basis for their continuous cooperation. When Derek asked me if I knew of any similar effort in the United States, I almost choked on my drink.

Before I responded, I wondered if even ten American states could be as cooperative without any expectation of as productive. Certainly the world would consume its last barrel of fossil fuel oil before as many as 30 states would attempt such a project. I was in too good a mood to want to talk about the American two-party system, plagued with lawyers as career politicians, most of whom never have been responsible for the bottom line in a business. I knew of no one with a reputation as an inventor, engineer, scientist, or former Chief Executive Officer.

"Have you ever been to Texas? Do you know what a Ford F-150 is? Do you know of another country in the world where people drive pick-up trucks and never carry anything in the bed of the truck? Give up on the United States doing anything real for the international community to resolve global-energy problems."

"Now if you want someone ousted from office or something blown up then maybe you can get some suggestions from the United States," I added.

The rain had returned for a third time this day. The staff in the plaza told us that the game would be broadcast as long as the video link and sound system operated and there still were fans in the plaza.

At the guest house, we again were unsuccessful meeting Father Pierre. However, he had returned and responded to the note from Derek. The room opposite Regina's was available. There was a new sticky note with the name, "Jim" on the door.

Father Pierre wrote that he would meet us at breakfast in the morning. I could register and pay then. He had been invited to the home of one of his parishioners for dinner and to watch the game.

We returned to the plaza protected somewhat from the light rain by our small, collapsible umbrellas, and waited about ten minutes at one of eight vendor stands for a plastic cup of potent pale Belgian ale. As expected, the vendors sold only beer. Everyone was drinking something. If you wanted water, then you cupped your hands, caught the rain, and drank whatever accumulated in your handmade cup (pun intended).

The game had not started, and only a few of the 500 fans were paying attention to the pre-game commentary. Derek and I maneuvered to an area about equidistant from the screen and four of the eight beer stands. I took a second swig of ale for courage then made an announcement to everyone within hearing range.

"I just got here from Texas. Does anybody know what team the United States is going beat in this next game? Or did they already forfeit? Is there going to be a second game or am I standing out here in the rain for nothing?"

Most of the people who heard me and who understood what I had said smiled or laughed. Some of them told or interpreted for their friends who had not heard or did not understand what I had said. Other looked at me, winked and smiled. I winked back at them and returned their smiles. The boys standing next to us, 15 or 16 years of age, all with Justin Bieber haircuts, all chain-smoking, all probably drinking since the first game started three hours earlier, could not stop laughing.

"Monsieur, do you want to know who the USA plays tonight?" one of the boys said to me.

"Sure. Do you know? It better be a good team. I didn't come all the way from Texas to see some third-rate team."

"Monsieur. Tonight you play our team. The USA plays Belgium!"

"No kidding? Are your guys any good? You got guys on the team and not girls, right?"

Asking about girls on their World Cup Championship team only added to their laughter. I am certain that they thought I was serious.

"Alright, how many of you are there? One, two, three, four, five, six. Okay. I'll buy the next round so you young-uns – that's Texas talk for y'all – that's Texas talk for you - won't all be crying once you start to lose."

I bought the first round of six ales. During the game, every time one of those six boys went to refresh his beer he brought back one for me which I shared with Derek. We drank for free the rest of the night.

Belgium two! United States one. Fine by me. After all, I was in Belgium.

The rain continued as we walked back to the apartment and all night.

Noises from activity in the hallway woke me from a sound sleep provided by the firm mattress in a comfortable, quiet room. The four cups of pale ale in the late evening and the slightly longer, more strenuous walk to Arlon during the day also contributed to the ease with which I slept. The shower was occupied so I went downstairs to the kitchen. The table was set for four with a variety of juices, breads, meats, cheeses, preserves, and cakes. I put the kettle on to boil water for tea and made a pot of coffee.

Father Pierre found me and introduced himself. I explained how I had met Derek and became a guest. He told me that my room was available because of a cancellation, and was happy that I stayed so that the food he had purchased would not be wasted. We had only a short conversation when he excused himself saying that he had to prepare to say Mass in the church across the street. Two other guests arrived and needed seating so I left to make room for them at the table.

I went into the church where Mass was about to begin. There were 16 participants: Father Pierre, 14 elderly women, and I. The Mass was in French.

I used my experience of the past three weeks to participate. After Mass, Father Pierre and I returned to the guest house. Originally built as a supplemental rectory more than 70 years ago, the declining Catholic population could not support as many priests. The building was converted as a guest house for "pilgrims to the area." There is no discrimination. Everyone is welcome as a guest.

Derek was finishing breakfast and there was about an hour before his conference group would meet at 9 a.m. to begin the day. The common language for the participants was English. I asked if he thought that there would be any objection to a retired military pilot and NASA rocket scientist sitting in the back and auditing a session. Derek suggested that we could walk the one mile together to the university and ask.

The walk was easy, only one low hill to climb and descend over a very short distance. The campus is set in an idyllic location among the greenery of the forests with manicured landscaping and extensive open space. If there were a parking lot then it was hidden. We arrived during the morning welcome. Derek introduced me to the organizers. They were happy to host an American who expressed a genuine interest in their work.

I sat next to Derek for the morning session during which there were four presentations. Much of the information has global relevance although it was obvious that only Europe has taken the lead in energy conservation. Research and development and technological advances are driven by private businesses and industries, while government programs lag as a result of bureaucratic inertia, political infighting, instability, and corruption.

I already knew that energy consumption was greater in those countries which host heavy industries such as steel and aluminum production, (Belgium, Finland, Germany, the Netherlands, Russia, Spain, and the United Kingdom), compared to the service economies of such countries as Austria, Macedonia, Portugal, and Switzerland. Although Germany still depends heavily on nuclear power, I was surprised to learn that both Germany and Switzerland have created specific and binding strategies to phase out their nuclear power plants. Cyprus has mandated the installation of solar systems to satisfy the domestic hot water requirements on every new building used as a residence. I was most impressed with the interest and support from the elected officials of these European Union countries.

Unless the media in the United States is involved in a huge conspiracy with the Obama administration, no one in America has a clue, certainly not Big Oil, the automobile manufacturers, and the transportation industries.

The meeting recessed at noon for lunch. I said farewell to Derek and then walked from the university one mile toward St. Donat's Church. Built in 1626 by the Capuchin monks, the church sits at the highest point in town. From the exterior walls enclosing the church, a person may look out more than 50 miles to see the landscapes of Belgium, France, and Luxembourg.

Viewing the dense forests of the Ardennes region from such a vantage point made it easy to understand how difficult it must have been for armies, especially their armored and other mobile units, to maneuver through this terrain.

The interior of the church is quaint and stunning with 100-year old pews and kneelers, and paintings and statues more than 300 years old. One of the oldest structures on the site is a small wooden annex formerly used as a seminary, retreat and rectory. Its exact history is not well documented. It contains a beautiful garden accented in the center by a centuries-old crucifix. On the walls and along the very narrow walking path are building, farm, and garden tools once used by the Capuchins.

After retrieving my property from Father Pierre, I started the 11-mile walk northeast toward Martelange. Father Pierre was driving in the same direction to work at another additional duty, and he offered me a ride. He was enroute to work as a youth counselor for teenage boys serving terms in the prison located at the north side of Arlon. Today's topic was "Anger Management."

On the passenger seat were copies of a book, "Manuel de Communication Non Violente." I told him that I was one of NASA's distinguished "Anger Management" course non-graduates, ranked at the bottom of my group. I added that I retired from government service before NASA had a chance to recycle me a third time through the program. With the exception of the entire Astronaut Corps and most of the Flight Directors, NASA's snivel servants are in competition with Congress as the epitome of bureaucratic inertia.

Father Pierre gave me a copy of the book saying, "I will pray for you."

"Thank you, Father. Every little bit helps."

Five minutes later and a mile-plus down the road, I exited his vehicle at the north entrance to Arlon and opposite the monument erected in honor of General George S. Patton.

FROM THIS POINT

ON DECEMBER 24, 1944

GENERAL PATTON

SENT FORTH THE THIRD ARMY

INTO THE BATTLE OF THE ARDENNES

The monument is a granite column with a slightly arched top below which is a bas-relief, in bronze, of the left-facing profile of General Patton wearing a combat helmet and collar-up tanker jacket. Below the image are engraved the words first in French and then, as shown above, in English. It faces south and is bordered on the west by the American flag atop a twelve-foot metal flagpole and on the east by the Belgian flag atop an identical flagpole. Surrounding the monument was an array of multi-colored, seasonal flowers.

In an outdoor café nearby, I sipped a beer while viewing the monument and trying to imagine the battle. For the remainder of the day and the next three days I would walk across 45 miles of the battlefield. The next day I would be in Bastogne, where Patton's Third Army smashed into the city and broke the siege during the epic Battle of the Bulge. The battle secured Patton's place in history as the Western Allies' greatest combat commander of the Second World War.

Not far from the Patton monument is a second monument to another American general.

IN HONOUR OF THE

TASK FORCE STRICKLER

28TH INFANTRY DIVISION KEYSTONE

LIBERATORS OF THE

TOWN OF ARLON

10TH SEPTEMBER 1944

Lieutenant Colonel Daniel B. Strickler was the commander of a Task Force formed by different elements of the 28th Infantry Division. That division has the distinction of being the oldest division in the United States formed with its colors in 1879.

After landing at Normandy and fighting to Paris, the division marched through Paris during the liberation parade, and was the first American division to cross into Germany.

Colonel Strickler fought in the attack against the Siegfried line, in the battle of Hurtgen Forest, with his Task Force to liberate Arlon, in the Battle of the Bulge, and in the Vosges mountains. A distinguished warrior, he rapidly earned promotions. As a Major General, he commanded the 28th Infantry Division during the Korean War. In 1957, he retired as a Lieutenant General. He died in 1992 at age 95.

Walking away from the monument dedicated in his name to the men he led, I was now enroute to Bastogne where I would discover more stories about other heroes who also fought there.

Passionate military men in combat sense that love and rage make a warrior. I recalled the book by James Michener about the Korean War, The Bridges at Toko-Ri, which was made into a movie. After a scene depicting an exceptional display of self-sacrifice and heroism, one of the characters asks rhetorically, "Where do we get such men?" Yes, where do we get such men?

Bastogne.

Martelange was 11 miles northeast. I had a long day with several short walks through Arlon during the morning and afternoon. I expected to arrive in the town of 1,500 residents by 8 p.m., and have almost two hours of daylight to locate a pub and a campsite. There would be no World Cup games this night or the next while teams and their fans prepared for the quarter-finals beginning on Friday, the Fourth of July.

Martelange is a typical, small Belgian town, not famous for anything except that its main street is in two countries: Belgium and Luxembourg. On the Belgian side, residents casually walk across the street to buy alcohol and cigarettes, or drive to buy fuel, where lower taxes make the prices cheaper in Luxembourg. Belgians from Virton and Arlon, who visit Bastogne for a day trip or a weekend, stock up on these three essentials in Martelange.

I found a good campsite off a field and well into the forest. A strong wind from the north lowered the temperatures, and the trees within the dense forest helped block the wind. I slept soundly and awoke at sunrise.

Bastogne was 14 miles away, almost directly north. I would walk from Belgium, cross into Luxembourg for a short distance, then cross back into Belgium until I reached Bastogne. I finished my next-to-last MRE and hoped to pick up another resupply parcel in Bastogne. From the number of cars which passed me, I assumed that Bastogne was filling with visitors and tourists. When I entered Bastogne in the early afternoon about 2 p.m., the town looked as if it were already full.

I was surprised to see several mint-condition classic cars in the central plaza's parking area around which were located restaurants, hotels, the Bastogne Tourist Office, and three memorials commemorating the Battle of the Bulge. The clerk at the hotel from which I expected to obtain the resupply parcel was not expecting me. She did not know anything about a package addressed to me. If I returned in an hour then the hotelier would be on duty. She accepted my backpack and I left.

Sitting at a table at an outdoor café, I started to relax. From the café, I could see the traffic around the plaza, and noticed as many vehicles with license plates from France, Germany, and the Netherlands as from Belgium. I asked the waiter for any popular, light-in-color, Belgian ale. Perhaps because of my accent, he asked me if I were an American. I told him yes, and that I was visiting for two days to celebrate the American Fourth of July Independence Day holiday in Bastogne.

"Yes. The summer, especially now, is the time for the most tourists from America. I have been working here more than 20 years. I notice that the visiting Americans are becoming older and older and also fewer and fewer."

I thought about what he told me, and realized that the younger generations of Americans who are old enough to travel alone would have no special reason to visit Bastogne unless they were interested in its history from World War II. The highlights of travel to Europe for them would be Paris, the resort beaches of France and Italy, the Eternal City of Rome, and the castles of Germany along the rivers. It would not be an isolated city in the middle of a dense forest in Belgium with museums and monuments about a war which occurred more than 70 years ago.

Steffen brought me a Hoegaarden. It was smooth, refreshing, cloudy in appearance, and served with a slice of lemon. I drank the first without the lemon and the second flavored with an easy squeeze. Only five percent alcohol, I thought it was the best beer that I had tasted since I had arrived in Europe. Soon I would be drinking a rival brew in Germany.

From the café, I could see more of the classic cars driving through the streets and parking in the plaza. As a teenager, I was a bit of a classic car buff. I recognized a 1953 MG Roadster and a 1963 Alfa Romeo Spider. There also was an Austin Healy, a few Citroens, Fiats, and Jaguars, among others. When I ordered a late lunch, Steffen told me that there would be a classic car show and contest in the plaza midday tomorrow on the Fourth of July. If I were with Karl from Virton, then we would view the automobiles on display together. Certainly I could have stayed at the café, relaxed as I nursed the ale, and people-watched. But Bastogne had more to offer than I had time to experience, so I asked Steffen for my bill. The charges included only one ale, not the two as I had ordered. I told Steffen about of the error.

"This weekend, you Americans may buy the first, then we buy the next if you order a second. That is what we do every Fourth of July holiday."

I'd be back. At the hotel, I met the hotelier who handed me my parcel after I introduced myself. The next resupply would occur in seven days after I had walked through Luxembourg and 70 miles further into Germany.

Nicolas Fautre told me that he had been the person who had received and read my letter from April with the request to send a parcel to the hotel. He told me that in the letter I had written that I was camping, and that the food items were my rations which I would carry while I walked and camped.

Then he said that camping in non-approved campsites is not permitted in Belgium and that this restriction is true in most countries around Belgium. The reason is to protect people from hunters who have paid fees to the government for licenses to use the forests and land to hunt in season.

He produced a copy of a flyer, which is displayed in Belgian tourist offices, at bus stations and rail terminals, and in many places frequented by tourists.

The flyer read:

Eviter le camping sauvage.

Kamperen in het wild voorkomen.

Vermeiden Sie das wilde camping.

Avoid camping in the wild.

There had been a cancellation for a double room three weeks before my arrival. Assuming that I would arrive on schedule to obtain the parcel, Mr. Fautre had saved the room for me in case I might want it.

"When you wrote your letter to me, maybe you did not know about these restrictions. Very few persons from America or Canada do."

He offered the double room at the single room price, and told me, "The hotel always is full this weekend. If you do not want the room, I am able to offer it to others."

Since he easily could have rented it at any time after the cancellation, and since he was so very genuine in his concern for my status, I accepted his offer and registered. The guest registration card already had my name, Texas home address, and e-mail address on it.

"The information on the card I have from your letter. I knew that you would take the room. I have driven the roads between Paris and Bastogne many times. My daughter and her husband live this side of Paris in Meaux. I think how it must be to walk those roads. My little Renault works harder in the hillsides of Belgium than in the flats of France. I hope you will have a nice rest. Have you been camping in Belgium?"

I told Mr. Fautre about meeting young Karl in Virton and staying with him at his apartment, then meeting Derek the next day in Arlon and staying at Father Pierre's guesthouse. This night, and the night of the Fourth, would be my last nights in Belgium. From Bastogne, I would cross into Luxembourg and camp one night there.

"Yes. I remember. I have here your schedule. On Saturday you will walk to Troisvierges. It is not far, only 25 kilometers. I can give you a ride whenever you want. Your carrying case is very heavy."

"That is very kind. Thank you, but I will be fine walking. I need to walk a little every day. The scenery along the way is very attractive and the walk is invigorating. I may not be able to have this chance again. "

After I secured my carrying case in the room, I returned to the central plaza to view the three memorials. The plaza bears the name, "Place General McAuliffe."

On December 22, 1944, Brigadier General Anthony McAuliffe, Acting Division Commander of the 101st Airborne Division, received a note addressed "To the U.S.A. Commander of the encircled town of Bastogne," recommending, "the honorable surrender of the encircled town." General McAuliffe responded with one word, "Nuts."

His soldiers continued to fight. The 4th Armored Division from General Patton's Third Army broke into Bastogne on December 26, 1944, broke the siege, and the Germans were forced to withdraw.

The memorial contains a granite monument, approximately four feet high, on which sits a bronze bust of the upper torso and handsome face of General McAuliffe. He is wearing his bemedaled Army dress uniform. At the front, the words "General McAuliffe" are chiseled into the granite. Below his name is the Screaming Eagle crest of the 101st Airborne Division. The monument is enclosed by a rectangular garden, 10 feet by 18 feet, arrayed with seasonal, multi-colored flowers such as red wax begonias and yellow mums.

Nearby, fixed to the granite base, is a bronze plaque which is dedicated to the 406th Fighter Group and its squadrons which flew 13,612 combat missions between 1944 and 1945. There is an image of a fighter aircraft, the patch of the 9th Army Air Corps Forces, and four unit crests of the supporting squadrons. Below this is inscribed:

A TRIBUTE TO ALL THE MEN OF THIS

ORGANIZATION WHO DID THEIR PART

IN BRINGING ABOUT A SUCCESSFUL END

TO WORLD WAR II

THEY LIVE IN FAME

The third and most obvious memorial in the plaza is a Sherman tank sitting atop a huge concrete block and a tiled base. The plaque at the front reads in French, English, Dutch, and German:

This tank, knocked out in December 44,

recalls the sacrifice of all the

fighters for the liberation of Bastogne and Belgium

Within the plaza I saw a group of about 300 middle-age and senior American tourists. On their jackets, sweaters and long-sleeved shirts they wore name tags from the Best Western Hotel Melba which read, "Reunion Member, 101st Airborne Division." One of the members told me that the group visits every year over the Fourth of July for three or four days. They reside at the Best Western where they take two meals each day. The hotel provides a dedicated conference room in which family photographs and memorabilia from World War II, the Battle of the Ardennes, and the Battle of the Bulge are displayed.

On occasion there is a guest speaker from a military service, a veteran's organization, or the town of Bastogne. I was saddened to hear that every year the number of travelers in their group is smaller. The children, as they become further apart in age from their grandfathers' and great-grandfathers' World War II Greatest Generation, do not have any interest. One member told me that the Battle of the Bulge is not taught in her grandchildren's schools. She added, "I'd be surprised if any of my grandkids even know which country attacked Pearl Harbor."

Only about a quarter mile west from the plaza, on the way to view the display at the Best Western, I saw a small bronze plaque at eye level on the side of a building in which there was a restaurant and store.

The plaque reads:

IN MEMORIAM

SITE OF THE AID STATION

OF THE 20TH AIB 10TH

ARMORED DIVISION WHERE

OVER 30 U.S. WOUNDED

AND 1 VOLUNTEER BELGIAN

NURSE (RENEE LEMAIRE)

WERE INSTATLY KILLED

BY A GERMAN BOMB

DECEMBER 24, 1944

The acronym, "AIB" above, signifies Armored Infantry Battalion, which is a force composed of tanks, other armored vehicles and infantry.

In December 1944, Nurse Lemaire, born in Bastogne in 1914, was there visiting her parents for Christmas when the Germans launched their offensive into the Ardennes. With other Bastognards she was trapped in the town. She volunteered to work in the aid station. A commendation for her work states that she "cheerfully accepted the Herculean task and worked without rest or food. She changed dressings, fed patients unable to feed themselves, gave out medications, bathed and made the patients more comfortable. Her very presence among those wounded men seemed to be an inspiration."

Late at night, on Christmas Eve, the building in which the wounded were recovering and Nurse Lemaire was working was bombed, sustaining two direct hits. The aid station in the basement was destroyed. Amid the burning flames, Nurse Lemaire evacuated six wounded soldiers to safety, but died while trying to evacuate a seventh soldier. Renee Lemaire, the Angel of Bastogne, was 30 years old.

In a conference room at the Best Western the first picture I saw was of an Army private who died even younger than Nurse Lemaire at age 19. In a black and white photograph, he is shown crouching in his uniform and service cap and holding a puppy with both hands on his right knee. Hand-printed at the bottom of the picture are the words:

Born June 6, 1925

JAMES O. CUST DIED W W II 1/1/45

SON OF BRIDGET O'DONNELL AND

HAROLD A CUST   REST IN PEACE

DIED IN THE BATTLE OF THE BULGE

IN CHENOGNE NEAR BASTOGNE, BELGIUM

On several tables in the conference room were newspaper articles, family photographs, and letters received and written by members of the military who served during World War II and the Battle of the Bulge. There may have been an equal number of young men who survived and who perished at Bastogne. I could not tell for certain. However, many of the letters contained vivid descriptions of the horrors of combat, the terror of the battlefield, and the weather conditions during the winter of 1944-45. In those same letters the sentiment, "Don't worry about me, I'm fine," is almost always expressed. I doubt if it allayed the fears of their parents, wives, or sweethearts.

I returned to the plaza and found a café but I had no appetite. I nursed another ale and made some notes about what I wanted to do in Bastogne on the Fourth of July. I hoped that Karl would meet me as we had planned. It would be easier for me to pass over the ground where so many soldiers died so young if I were with someone who now was their age and was so full of life. In my notebook, I wrote, "Long life to the hearts still beating, and peace to the ones at rest."

The room which Mr. Fautre had saved for me was the most spacious accommodation that I experienced after 24 days in Europe. There were two full-size beds and a large bathroom which had both a separate shower and bathtub. I emptied everything from my backpack and placed all my clean clothing on the second bed. I took my first hot bath in months. I added my laundry into fresh bathwater with some shampoo and left everything to soak overnight. Now I was ready to eat and I thought how great it will be to have a good meal, a glass of wine and a warm bed.

In the morning, I drained the tub and rinsed the soap from the clothing with me as I showered. After everything was squeeze-dried, I draped the clothes throughout the room and opened the two windows for my clothes to dry.

Breakfast was complimentary, full and sufficient. The Fautre family was away. Later in the day I would thank them. I had a date to meet Karl at 11 a.m. and the opportunity to tour more of Bastogne until then. From outside the hotel, I could see the Place General McAuliffe and some of the classic cars positioned early for the show later in the afternoon.

A map from the Tourist Office of Bastogne highlighted the attractions in the area including the 101st museum. Enroute, I saw am M-151 jeep with the sign "M U S E E" on the windshield.

I entered and met Mrs. Suzette Grisius, the proprietor. In English, I wished her a happy Fourth of July and signed her guestbook, "Happy #238, United States of America, 1776 – 2014, James J. Pelosi, Houston, Texas." We sat side by side with the guestbook open to the page I had signed and posed for a selfie. The museum is small but packed with anything anyone would expect to find in a military museum. However, unlike most museums, everything is for sale. It is a museum-shop. The prices are expensive.

As expected, the older and rarer the item the higher price. Dress and field uniforms; unit insignia and medals; headgear and helmets; weapons, especially bayonets and knives; protective masks; field gear; load bearing equipment; and, books and documents are all available. Mrs. Grisius' museum-shop should be twice as large for visitors to see and appreciate everything which it contains. There were items I wished to purchase but no ability to carry them.

I left after two hours only because I was hoping to meet Karl. He was waiting for me when I arrived.

Karl wore a pair of relaxed jeans and a white, short-sleeved, collared shirt on which was embroidered crossed American and Belgian flags. He told me that he purchased it several years ago at the Tourist Office gift shop when white was the only color. He added that now they are available in all colors for both men and women, and in all sizes. All sizes probably did not mean 5XL for the obese Americans such as those I saw on the flight to Europe, who occupied two seats and were restrained in that additional space by an extension added to their seat belts.

The 101st Airborne Division Museum is first class. Everything within it is appropriate not only to World War II, the Battle of the Ardennes, and the Battle of the Bulge, but also to the history of the 101st Airborne Division. There are two floors and a bomb shelter. On each floor are displays in precise, nearly-perfect detail worthy of a facility that might have a director, designer, curator, manager, and full staff, which this museum does not. It is a tribute to the Belgians and Bastognards that they have dedicated time and resources to provide such a first class facility.

The displays are arranged in vertical glass-enclosed reliefs and wall units, and tabletops. Mannequins are life-life; the dress and field uniforms which they wear are accurate in every detail. The display cards provide precise information in English, French, and German.

Karl and I spent more than two hours viewing the exhibits. I explained the details of the American and some German displays; Karl described the Belgian and German units, uniforms, and weapons which he knew.

I found two errors within the displays. The American Army of Occupation medal is a simple ribbon with two colors: black on the left and red on the right as viewed by an observer. I had earned the same medal for my service in Berlin. It was correct on one dress uniform but was reversed on a second. Also, there was another display in which a signalman is holding a field radio handset to report "a SNAFU." The card described the acronym for SNAFU as "Situation Normal All Full Up." I explained why the word "full" is not the correct word for the letter, "F" in the acronym, and that the word "fouled" would be more appropriate. The actual four-letter word used by most military members is an expletive not suitable for print. The museum monitor and his maintenance tech made the two corrections.

The bomb shelter was a thrilling experience. It is the size of a small room with the appearance of a basement hideout. Inside, there are a dozen small chairs and stools and vintage clutter for effect. Every 20 minutes, a green light flashes and visitors enter. After five minutes, the light changes from green to red and no further entry is permitted. Then the bombs start falling.

As the sounds of the bombing and the explosions nearby increase, the shelter starts to vibrate and shake. Occupants can hear the sounds of debris hitting the walls and see images of explosions and smoke from the simulated windows at the top of the basement shelter. Karl and I agreed that it was very realistic, and we told the clerk as we were exiting the museum. She said that frequently children and adults come running out from the shelter during the simulated bombing because it seems so real.

From the museum, Karl and I walked about a half mile to the Place General McAuliffe. Locals and tourists were passing among the 46 classic automobiles complying with the white cardboard, signs resting on the hoods and trunks: "Look but DO NOT Touch." Those cars which were in competition had an additional sign on the driver's seat identifying the year, make and model of the vehicle, the category in which it was competing, and the name, city, and country of the owner. We liked them all. We concluded that if we pooled all our assets we could not afford any one of them.

Both of us were hungry. I could see Steffen at the café in which I was a patron the day before. As we walked over, I told Karl about my afternoon with Steffen, and drinking two ales but paying for only one. He had taken an order, saw us coming, and waited. I greeted him and introduced Karl. They spoke briefly in French. Steffen sat us at a table for two which had a "réservés" card on it, left, and returned with two glasses of Hoegaarden ales. Karl ordered a light lunch for each of us.

While we ate he recommended that we walk east to the Mardasson Memorial and Bastogne Historical Center. In the evening, a choir from Maryland would perform at a church not far from where we were sitting. Without us asking, Steffen brought two more Heogaardens and told Karl, in French, that "Jacques always has two." Karl told me what Steffen had said, and I thought that the American tourists must be pretty bad actors if the local restaurant staff keeps track of what and how much they drink.

A 30-minute walk from the café, at the traffic circle on the northeast side of Bastogne, is a large monument dedicated to the Bastognards who died in both world wars. There are three columns which make up the monument. The left column supports a wreath in which is the image of Belgian helmet from World War I. Above the wreath, "1914." Below the wreath, "1918." At the right column, in the same position, is an identical wreath in which is the image of a beret from World War II. Above the wreath, "1940." Below the wreath, "1945." At three times the width of these border columns is the central column in which are inscribed the names of those Bastognards who "died for their country." Their names appear within categories as "combatants, riflemen, partisans, and political prisoners".

Another 30 minutes in a more northerly direction is the huge Mardasson Memorial. The ground approach to the memorial passes an underground crypt reached by an open, broad staircase that descends about 30 yards into the crypt. Inside the crypt are three altars dedicated to the Catholic, Jewish, and Protestant faiths.

At the crypt is a memorial, in Latin, which reads, "The Belgian people remember their American liberators – 4th July 1946."

There is a second memorial, a block of granite on which is inscribed the words:

ON JULY SIXTEENTH

NINETEEN HUNDRED AND FIFTY

DIVINE SERVICES WERE HELD IN

THIS CRYPT IN HONOR OF THE

GALLANT OFFICERS AND MEN OF

THE ARMED FORCES OF THE

UNITED STATES OF AMERICA

WHO FOUGHT IN THE BATTLE

OF THE BULGE.

76890 WERE KILLED WOUNDED

OR REPORTED MISSING

Karl was visibly affected when he read the number of Americans who had been killed, wounded, or reported missing in less than one month of combat in so small an area as the Ardennes. When he turned toward me he was holding back tears. He reached out, hugged me, and then cried. The he stepped back, wiped his eyes and face with a handkerchief, and walked up the staircase and out of the crypt. At the top of the stairs, he kept his eyes to the ground and took a few minutes to regain his composure. During my two days at the American Cemetery at Normandy I never saw anyone as visibly upset.

"Every time I come, always once a year since I was a boy, I have the same reaction. I don't know any of these people. I have never seen any of their faces. All boys and young men like me now. All this makes me so very sad."

I asked him if he wanted to skip visiting the Mardasson Memorial and return to town. I told him that I could visit another time. But he wanted to stay. As we walked about 100 yards to the memorial, he told me that there are 84 military cemeteries in Belgium: three for the Americans; six German; nine French; 15 for his countrymen; and, 51 for the British, the majority of which are for the casualties from World War I. I asked him how he learned these numbers and what made him remember them.

"I was taught this when I was a student. I teach my own students the same now. Belgium exists as a country because of the sacrifices by others to save her. Sadly, we teach more history about what we have destroyed than about what we have created."

The Mardasson Memorial is huge covering an expanse of ground large than the Lincoln and Jefferson memorials combined. It is a 40-foot concrete structure in the shape of a pentagram with an atrium in its center. On the inner walls are 10 paintings highlighting events during the Battle of the Bulge. On the exterior walls are the listed the names of air and ground units which fought in support of the battle. At the crown of the pentagram are engraved the names of the 50 states in alphabetical order.

I was highly upset, and still remain bothered, by the fact that the air units which supported the battle were listed under the inscription, "Air Force Units." The Battle of the Bulge was fought between December 1944 and January 1945. The air units which supported that battle belonged to the United States Army Air Forces of which my father was a proud member. The United States Air Force was not formed until 1947; therefore, the inscriptions on the monument are absolutely wrong. They were not Air Force units. They were Army Air Force units. I asked to speak with someone in charge, and I met one of the assistant curators. Using websites from the internet, I showed him several sources to prove that what I said was correct.

"It has been this way for 50 years. There is nothing that I can do. As far as I know, no one has said anything before."

We parted company and I entered the Historical Center. I had not walked 20 yards in to the first exhibit hall when I read, "Atomic bomb, Nagasaki, Japan, 8 September 1945." What? Only five minutes from when we spoke I was again having another chat with the same curator.

"The United States was the first nation to invent the nuclear bomb and the only nation ever to use it, not once, but twice. That is the sort of history someone that an America who has been associated with the military for 42 years remembers."

I told him about the first bombing of Hiroshima on August 6, 1945, and then about the second bombing of Nagasaki on August 9, 1945. Different websites all confirmed these dates as correct. The poster display was wrong in all aspects. This time, he told me that it would be easier to correct the poster display about The Bomb than it would be to re-chisel the granite column about the bombing units. I received no assurance that the corrections would be made.

I asked Karl to write and tell me if anything should change. His Christmas card to me six months after our visit said, "the tourists still must read that Nagasaki was bombed on September 8, 1945."

Touring the rest of the Center became a thrill for Karl and an annoyance for me. Like a school kid, he was interested in anything else I could find wrong and show him. I was so upset that I wanted only to scan the information on the displays and look at the not-so-pretty pictures. In just over an hour, we had passed through all the exhibit halls and seen all the displays. The Bastogne Historical Center is impressive: spacious, clean, well-organized, and full of information. It would be even more impressive if all the historical information were accurate.

To the east of the Center is another small memorial. Leading to it is a narrow, slate, walking path along which are metal baskets full of seasonal flowers and the national flags of Belgium and the United States. On a square, two-foot high foundation of slate is a platform border of rectangular concrete blocks which enclose a tile base. On this base rests an image of a screaming eagle. Its talons appear to support an inverted combat helmet. The four-line white inscription on black marble reads:

May this eagle always symbolize the sacrifices and heroism

of the 101ˢᵗ Airborne Division and all its attached units,

December 1944 – January 1945

The City and The Citizens of Bastogne

Walking away from this memorial, Karl and I heard the voices of children singing. We walked back toward the Mardasson Memorial. Within the center of the atrium the Maryland State Boychoir was performing. We watched a choir of about 30 boys, ages 10 to 18, finish their first song, "*In Flanders Field.*" They performed two more songs in a six-minute presentation, "*Hear Our Prayer,*" and "*The Star Spangled Banner.*" The boys were dressed in short-sleeved, collared, pale-blue shirts with beige trousers, looked handsome, and performed enthusiastically.

Their director was undistinguished. Grossly overweight, wearing a short-sleeved, collared, black shirt with unpressed, white, chino trousers, unpolished grey docker-style shoes, and badly in need of a haircut, his appearance signaled to Karl, me, and the people with whom we spoke that this performance on America's 238ᵗʰ birthday was only business as usual. At the conclusion of the performance, he gave a short, three or four-sentence, "Thank you for hosting us," speech in English. How much more of an effort would it have taken for him to have memorized those few words in the language of the host country as a sign of respect for its citizens in the viewing audience? And how much more of an effort would it have taken for him to appear in a blue blazer, white shirt, red or blue tie, pressed trousers and shined shoes?

Maybe the nuns were wrong when they taught me that the respect you show to others is an immediate reflection of your own self-respect.

On the mile and a half walk back into town, I told Karl that I had been up and active for 10 hours. I asked him if he wanted to return to the hotel with me, refresh ourselves, and then celebrate the Fourth of July together with dinner, the choral concert in the church, and the World Cup revelry in town on day 18. Germany would play France.

"Sounds like a plan."

At the hotel, I stopped to inform Mr. Fautre that I had a guest. I did not get the chance to introduce young Karl to older Nicholas because they already knew each other. Karl's parents had referred guests to the Fautre's hotel. Karl had dated his daughter as teenagers before each of them left home to attend a university. Mr. Fautre told us, "There is plenty of space in Jacque's room for you to relax," and asked us if we needed anything.

In the room, I had forgotten about my display of laundry which I cleared from the beds and furniture, and packed. Karl used the restroom. He told me an hour later after I awoke from a nap that, when he came out, I was sound asleep on my bed. When I stood up, I made enough noise to wake Karl asleep on the bed next to mine.

After showering, Karl led me to a pub he knew on a side street away from the tourists. Almost everyone inside was a Bastognard. We drank ale and watched Germany defeat France one to zero and earn a place in the semi-finals. The locals were disappointed in the outcome. With no other reason for the Bastognards to prefer Germany or France, I assumed that it had to be the history of the world wars which again aligned the Belgians with the French.

From the pub, we had only a short walk to St. Peter's church where we again heard the Boychoir sing two of the songs we had heard earlier in addition to others. Their performance was excellent, although some of the younger boys appeared tired and not as enthusiastic as they had been when they performed at the Mardasson Memorial.

At the other pubs in Bastogne, the second game of the World Cup trumped any interest in the birthday of America. Taking advantage of the sentiment I observed in the game between Germany and France, I entered each bar with Karl and announced, in English, "Happy 238th birthday, United States of America. You all would be speaking German and not French or Flemish if it were not for my father and his Army Air Corps buddies. Who wants to buy us a drink?"

It took both time and effort before the combination of my stories in English and Karl's interpretations into French earned us some free ales.

Close to midnight and the end of the reason for our revelry, we walked back to the hotel. It would not have been safe for Karl to drive home, and there was no reason why he could not share my hotel room in the same spirit that I shared his apartment four days earlier.

At breakfast the next morning, both Mr. Fautre and Karl offered to drive me the 16 miles to Troisvierges. I declined their offers. The weather was spectacular. I had enjoyed a full day's rest from walking with the backpack and my sleep during the night had been deep and refreshing. Now I needed to resume my rhythm and my pace. After Luxembourg, I had at least 31 days ahead of me to walk through Germany.

Parting from Karl was hard because I had learned that it was a mistake to attempt "The TREK" alone. Traveling with a companion would have been safer and certainly more enjoyable. A man such as Karl, younger, healthy, enthusiastic, and with stamina, would have been an excellent companion. My French language speaking ability would have improved greatly.

Departing at 9 a.m., I hoped to arrive in Troisvierges before the start of day 19 of the World Cup. I would root for Belgium in its match with Argentina.

From the hotel in Bastogne where I said farewell to Nicholas and Karl, I started walking along the same road which Karl and I took to view the Mardasson Memorial and the Bastogne Historical Center on the Fourth. This time, I was carrying the backpack refreshed with the resupply MRE's from Nicholas, and I was not walking as comfortably.

The weather was extraordinary: bright blue skies, a few Pillsbury Doughboy clouds, light wind from the west, and low, undetectable humidity. Temperatures were in the 60's. I felt cool and comfortable in a pair of walking shorts and a T-shirt.

Just over a mile and a half, I climbed the short rise to the memorial and returned to the crypt. I paused there and pledged that I would complete the walk to Berlin and finish "The TREK." I would do so with respect for the memory of those 76,890 Americans, probably all younger than I now at age 63, who did not make it to Berlin and did not see the war in Europe end only four months later.

For another five miles, I walked along one road through the very dense forest of the Ardennes. Then I crossed the border into Luxembourg.

"Luxembourg is at the crossroads of invading armies. Conquerors have marched through this land while its people have tried elaborately to pretend that they have not been there. Rulers may make Luxembourgers a subject people, but all the while they have never forgotten their right to be free. Their birthright of freedom is a passion that centuries of occupation cannot dim."
–   Eugene Fodor, <u>Belgium</u> <u>and</u> <u>Luxembourg</u>, 1975.

14. Luxembourg.

Luxembourg is small, bordered by Belgium on the north and west, Germany on the east, and France on the south. It is only 55 miles long and 34 miles wide. The northern half of the country is dominated by the dense forests of the Ardennes through which I would pass. Luxembourg is the least populated country in the European Union. In 2013, the population was 540,000 citizens representing only five percent of the population of its neighbor Belgium at more than 11 million.

Although Luxembourg has been an independent Grand Duchy since 1867, it has been overtaken twice by German occupation forces during World War I and again during World War II. Almost 50 miles directly south of my route through Troisvierges, in the Place d'Armes at the center of Luxembourg City, is a large stone tablet on the front wall of the Cercle Municipal. An engraving proclaims Luxembourgers' gratitude to the American soldiers who helped liberate their country during World War II.

That engraving reads:

On this square on 10th September 1944

The people of Luxembourg warmly welcomed its liberators,

The valiant soldiers of the U.S. 5th armored division

And their Royal Highnesses Prince Felix of Luxembourg

And Prince John, Hereditary Grand Duke of Luxembourg.

As I moved east into Luxembourg, the vast expanse of forest began to diminish. More of the region transitioned to fields. I could not determine if the forest had been cleared to support the farmland or if I were leaving the natural area of the Ardennes. My route for next nine miles would continue along the same road. Outside the forest and across the fields, I could see that I would be walking in the manner of a sinuous river as it meandered to create an oxbow lake. Taking an azimuth and cutting across a field would trim miles from the walk. The tradeoff would be the risk of muddy or uneven terrain to slow me down and the impropriety of trespassing.

At close to three hours since the start of the walk I saw a bakery and stopped. I grounded my backpack at one of two outdoor tables, both of which were unoccupied, and entered. I ordered a cup of coffee and a pastry and refilled a bottle of water while I waited. Outside, with no one to offend, I removed my shoes and socks. I thought about the signs at some Florida beachside eateries which read, "No shirt, no shoes, no service," and the ones at Key West which read, "No shirt, no shoes, no problem."

If I continued at my regular pace of three miles an hour I would arrive at an established campsite in Troisvierges well before 5 p.m. On day 19, the last day of the World Cup semi-finals, Belgium would play Argentina. I expected that almost everyone would be rooting for Belgium. The campsite, Camping Walensbongert, was located only about 300 yards from Troisvierges, a small town of 3,000 residents. Along the main road, I saw a train station, banks, bakeries, restaurants, and signs indicating the practices of a doctor and a dentist. It was much like similar size towns I visited in Belgium and France.

At the campsite, I paid only $7. for a large pitch site shielded for privacy on three sides by hedges. In addition to the showers and hygiene facilities, there was a surprising number of amenities including: Wi-Fi hotspots; washers and dryers; a playground; indoor and outdoor lap swimming pools; and basketball, table tennis, and volleyball courts.

The managers, Andre and Vivian Lehnen, told me that the World Cup games would be shown in the recreation room on a wide-screen projection television. There would be plenty of space for viewing since many of the campers had been watching the games from their own televisions outdoors in porch extensions from their motorhomes.

After setting up camp and showering, I removed the flag of Belgium from my backpack and replaced it with the flag of Luxembourg. Then I secured my valuables and walked back into town.

In one of the hotels, I discovered a very refined brasserie with carved wooden tables and chairs, ironed linens, marble countertops, brass fixtures, and recessed lighting. Most of the other patrons were dressed as I was, informally in shorts and short-sleeved shirts. At the bar, I asked for a glass of the most-popular draft beer in Luxembourg. The bartender brought me an iced mug of Wëllen Ourdaller, a specialty grain beer from the region of the Our river which rises in south-east Belgium and flows for 50 miles through Luxembourg and Germany.

The game was exciting and, as I had expected, all the patrons seemed to be cheering for Belgium. Possession throughout the game was close to equal. Nine times both teams fired shots toward the goal but failed to score. Argentina scored the only goal of the game. In all the games I had watched in which Belgium was competing, its team performed exceptionally well allowing only three goals throughout all the matches.

There were about 90 minutes of daylight left to explore the town of the Three Virgins. The name almost guaranteed that I would find more than one church and garden to explore. I was wrong about the church but correct about the gardens.

The church of St. Andrews is more than 500 years old and its architecture closely resembles many of the churches built at that time in Europe. The inside is ornate and the Altar of the Three Virgins, (Fides, Faith; Spes, Hope; and, Caritas, Charity), is large yet simple and respectful with a tone of unaffected humility and resignation in the images of the women. There are numerous, well-landscaped walking paths throughout town which lead around, up, and over the two tallest hills in the country. The walking paths, bicycle lanes, and parks support the large tourist crowd of campers from Scandinavia, the Netherlands, Belgium, Germany, and elsewhere who visit Camping Walensbongert and Troisvierges.

I returned to the campsite to watch the second half of the second game between the Netherlands and Costa Rica. The recreation room was filled mostly with adult couples and teenagers who had the opportunity for additional free time away from the control of their parents. Most viewers cheered for the Dutch team. About ten percent of the motorhomes had NL plates and the horizontal tricolor red, white and blue flag of the Netherlands.

The game ended with neither team scoring. The recreation hall was absolutely silent as everyone awaited the judges' decision of a winner based upon the penalties during the match. The room was hushed, then erupted in cheers, hugs, and backslapping as the penalty-assessment win was awarded to the Netherlands, four to three. The Netherlands would advance to the semi-finals and play Argentina on Wednesday, July 9th.

Through the tent flap early Sunday morning, I could see a brilliant sunrise. As I cleared the campsite, I watched another spectacular day begin. At the office, I stowed my backpack then walked the short distance into town for breakfast and to attend Mass. In the church of St. Andrews, I thought about my three tours of duty with the Army in Germany, and that today I would return after an absence of 12 years.

Winterscheid was slightly more than 15 miles away. Most of the walk would be similar to that of France. The mountains of the Harz would pose more of a challenge than the hills of the Ardennes. But my proficiency with the German language far exceeded that of my French and, unlike Chevy Chase during his "European Vacation" in France, in Germany I would know when a waiter was insulting me.

A map recon of the route showed only relatively flat farmland, fields, and forest east beyond Troisvierges with two small towns about two miles distant, and the border into Belgium after another mile. The walk through Belgium would be through similar terrain for nine miles, and then there would be only another hour's walk before I would reach Winterscheid. On a few occasions, I would pass along the Our River.

There was only about one-quarter of the vehicle traffic headed in my direction toward Winterscheid. Most of the traffic, including a fair number of motorhomes, was heading west toward Troisvierges.

The weather was cloudy and cool with temperatures in the low 60's and very high humidity. I thought that it might rain and dressed in the long convertible trousers. About three hours into my walk it began to rain lightly. A small collapsible umbrella was a reliable substitute for my former Army-issue poncho. The poncho provides great protection from heavy rain but ventilates poorly and causes the body to warm up quickly. After a short rest along Belgium's Our River, I continued east. The rain stopped after another hour's walk. The humidity was close to 100 percent. The sky cleared to bright sunshine and the temperature remained cool. Just past 1 p.m., I reached the border between Belgium and Germany.

"Since the Second World War, Germany has emerged as one of the most prosperous and technologically advanced countries in Europe, a fact that can be attributed to the hard work and conscientiousness of her people. Wherever a visitor to Germany goes, he will be aware of the wealth of stories and legends that are attached to places around him."
–   From a tourist brochure, 1974.

15. Germany.

Crossing into Germany

"The TREK" route through Germany included 31 cities and towns, eight of which I had visited when they were part of the Federal Republic of Germany, and nine of which were off-limits when they were part of the German Democratic Republic before the reunification on October 3, 1990. Shortly after I crossed into Germany, I found a café and stopped for lunch. I removed the flag of Luxembourg from my backpack and replaced it with the flag of Germany next to the flag of the United States.

This day's destination, Winterscheid, has a population of only about 200 residents. The town is a tight cluster of homes and buildings. There was small sign for "Camping Bleialf 3 KM" a short mile and a half away. After lunch, I continued my walk toward the campsite.

Camping Bleialf was very small offering none of the amenities that I enjoyed at Camping Walensbongert in Troisvierges except for a shower and toilet. I was unable to negotiate a single-person price and paid the same for an individual pitch with a small tent that others paid for a double pitch with a motorhome. Meeting expenses must be difficult for the owners competing with Camping Walensbongert only 15 miles away. The finals in World Cup competition would not resume for two days on July 8th. From the television in the office, I listened to the weather report which predicted rain for the next two to three days. Steffeln, Kelberg, and Mayen were the three towns through which I would walk before I reached the city of Koblenz. Each of these three towns increased in population and services the closer I approached Koblenz.

Steffeln was the smallest with a population of fewer than 700 residents. At the end of a 17-mile walk, which began with clouds and mild, morning temperatures in the 60's, then transitioned to rain, warm temperatures in the high 70's, and high humidity, I was ready to enjoy the comfort of a pub or café.

The restaurant, Vulkanhotel Steffelberg, was an outstanding treat. It takes its name from the Eifel area which has a history of volcanic activity that includes underground gases escaping on occasion from the geological terrain features nearby. The theme of everything associated with the hotel is "A Life in Balance."

Inside the hotel was a restaurant and a tavern. I chose the tavern as the more appropriate area so as not to offend any of the guests given my rain-soaked appearance and bulky backpack. The guests were German and Dutch who returned my greeting and responded with a polite nod after I entered and said, "Guten Abend." After the waiter delivered a small, 0.2 centiliter glass of Rhineland-Pfalz Pilsner I told him that I had entered Germany at Winterscheid and hoped to walk to Berlin before the end of the month. He reached over and squeezed my shoulder and upper arm commenting that there was not enough meat on me to make it that far. He added that I would get a comfortable rest in the hotel which would help me on the walk. Pointing to the backpack which I had placed in the corner, I said that I was camping.

"Even when there is rain?"

"Yes, but I have been lucky. In more than a month there have been only a few days of rain."

He recommended a light but full meal which I chose. The portion would have satisfied any two-seater airline passenger from Houston. The meal was outstanding. The schnitzel was traditional and was accompanied by herbs and vegetables fresh from the region. Again with the waiter's recommendation, I ordered my first dessert since I began "The TREK" 32 days earlier. The apple strudel itself was almost a meal.

When the waiter brought my bill, he told me that beyond the church just outside of town was a sheltered area where it would be safe to camp. He brought me a foil-wrapped paper plate "since you ate so fast the strudel. We have breakfast here at seven if you wish to return. I am here also at seven."

The sheltered area where I camped was beneath the ruins of an aged, storm-damaged barn no longer in use. The roof and two sides were solid; the third side was fractured; and, what once was the entrance was gone completely. Inside was a rusted piece of farm machinery and broken wooden boxes. During the night, I heard the rain on the roof but no water leaked through on to the tent. It would be slightly more than 18 miles to Kelberg. I wanted to start the day prepared to walk the distance in the rain.

Tuesday, July 8, 2014, would have been my sister Kathy's 62nd birthday. One year younger than I, she died on May 24, 2013, of heart failure alone in her home in Florida. Her son Michael died suddenly five and a half years earlier at age 27, and I am sure that she died of a broken heart. I had walked past the only Catholic church in the area for 30 miles. Its name is St. Michael's. I left my backpack in the barn. On the short walk back to the hotel I went into the church. I stayed long enough to reflect on the lives of my sister and nephew both of whom I knew loved their family and loved living, but were denied the peace of a happy and healthy life. On this day, only three days after experiencing the memories of the horrors at Bastogne, I again had reasons to question my faith in a loving God.

I am a strong believer that the effect of the mind on the body is extraordinarily great. Breakfast revitalized my spirit and my body. The waiter provided me another take-away plate with two rolls, meats, cheeses, and a sliced apple.

"Kelberg is quite far. There is supposed to be rain all day and the temperatures are colder. This will help you."

Departing at nine and walking in the rain with temperatures in the mid-50's, I expected to take only a short break at the halfway point and arrive in Kelberg in the late afternoon or early evening. At 9:30 p.m. Germany would play Brazil in the first game of the World Cup "Knockout Phase" semi-finals. I was eager to arrive, get settled, and watch the game among the locals rooting for their home team. At just over three hours, I stepped off Hauptstrasse (Main Street) in the very rural village of Oberehe-Stroheich and stopped on Schule Strasse (School Street) where I found a small park with shelter from the rain and had lunch. The inside of my shoes and my socks were dry. Having them off provided substantial relief.

After half an hour, I resumed walking. The rain was steady and, fortunately, I did not have to battle a strong wind. Before I reached Kelberg I twice heard the sound of a car horn behind me. I thought that I may have been walking too close to the road or that someone was alerting me that he was about to overtake and pass me. In both cases each driver was enroute to Kelberg or beyond and offered me a ride which I declined. If I had been ill or injured I think that I would have accepted the ride. But finishing each day with the route as planned gave me a strong sense of satisfaction.

In Kelberg I saw the timber-framed houses and buildings common in some regions in Germany. I remembered them well from the north when I visited Kiel and Travemunde and also from Bavaria when I lived in Garmisch-Partenkirchen. There was another Catholic church a short distance from the town center on Pfarrkirche Strasse. The name of the church is St. Vincent's.

Vincent is my father's name. I started the day on my sister's birthday in a church with the same name as her son and ended it in a church with the same name as our father. I felt His presence with me more strongly. The family name, Pelosi, is Italian and not far from the church was Il Gabbiano Ristorante.

Throughout the long day it had been getting colder. On the television I read the temperature at nine degrees Celsius, about 49 degrees Fahrenheit. Slightly chilled, I took a seat, ordered a glass of Italian red wine, and toasted my sister on her birthday. During dinner and later during the game I drank two more glasses of wine toasting my father and my nephew. After Germany trounced Brazil by a score of seven to one, I announced to my neighbors at the bar that I had traveled all the way from the United States to see Germany win the

World Cup. Unlike in Belgium, this somewhat fraudulent announcement did not generate a free drink. Regardless, I ordered a final glass of wine to celebrate the victory. I was amazed at how much German I remembered and how easy it was for me to speak belly up to the bar with my fourth drink. When I went to pay, the waiter shook his head to the side and waived me away with a big grin and a thumbs up gesture.

In the direction of Mayern, I found a small department store with a protected delivery area and a cement and cobblestone surface large enough to support the tent. I added the rain fly to deflect any wind-driven rain. Almost immediately after I inflated the air mattress and rolled into the sleeping bag, I fell asleep just past midnight. Undisturbed by the rain, I awoke twice from a sound sleep and vowed to reduce my alcohol intake late at night, crossing my fingers for an exception in the hope and expectation that Germany would win the World Cup.

I awoke to the sound of traffic not far from where I had camped. From the tent flap I could see that it still was raining. Stepping outside I could not detect any discernible change in temperature. Thick dark clouds, low and fast-moving, almost guaranteed that I would have a fourth full day of rain. I reconciled myself to the gloom recognizing that, unlike the soldiers who moved through this area at a much slower pace while in combat, the sentiment "gloom" was not followed by "and doom." No one was shooting at me.

After three straight days of rain I did not have any dry trousers, and temperatures in the upper 40's and low 50's made it too cold to wear shorts. One advantage of the lightweight convertible trousers was that they were designed to absorb and retain body heat, and were almost completely waterproof. The poncho provided a second layer of protection from the rain and insulation against the cold.

Mayen was 16 miles almost directly east through much of the same terrain. The map showed a greater number of tributaries and streams running from the huge Rhine and Mosel rivers which converged another 18 miles away in Koblenz. I felt full of both food and beverage from the previous night at Il Gabbiano's and decided to walk for at least an hour or more before I would break for a quick breakfast. Kelberg's population at 2,000 was four times greater that of Steffeln's; Mayen's population at nearly 20,000 would be 10 times that of Kelberg's. There was no game in the World Cup this evening which would allow me two or three additional hours to explore the larger and more populous town.

During the day the rain never abated, and the temperatures remained cool between 50 and 55. On Hauptstrasse I found a small bäckerei where I stopped for 30 minutes for my standard bakery breakfast of kaffee and brötchen. I stopped again after two hours in the town of Boos as the rainfall and driving wind increased. The few cars on the road all were driving with their headlights on, and I thought is safe to wait a short while and let the squall pass. A floral delivery driver told me that the rain was expected to continue through the day but stop by morning, and that I had only 17 kilometers or about 10 miles until I arrived at Mayen.

The remainder of the walk was uneventful and I adjusted to the walk in the rain for the fourth day. The rural roads had excellent drainage. With only a few exceptions I did not have to sidestep any potholes or pass through paths of standing water.

The town of Mayen suffered almost 90 percent destruction during an Allied bombing raid on December 12, 1944, which was my father's 21st birthday. When I entered the town which had been rebuilt completely I wondered if my father had participated in that raid.

As I passed through the center of Mayen I saw the Gästehaus, Zum Alten Fritz. If there were a room available then I was going to stay. I had camped for four consecutive in the rain. Tomorrow would be my 63rd birthday, and I would be camping along the Rhine River at an upgraded, full-facility campsite. There was a vacancy, and the room was more than sufficient with a firm bed, private bathroom and small sitting area. Tonight I would treat myself.

After a shower and two-hour nap, I walked a short distance along Koblenzer Strasse where I found a Greek restaurant. The night before I had eaten pasta at Il Gabbiano's and, the night before that, schnitzel at the Vulkanhotel. Dinner tonight again would be something different. I drank a glass of Greek white wine with my meal and accepted the host's offer of an Ouzo, an anise-flavored aperitif. I fell asleep wishing for an end to the rain and a more pleasant day to walk to Koblenz.

July 10, 2014. Happy #63, James Joseph! Overnight, my prayers had been answered. I awoke not to the sound of rain falling on the top of my tent or around me but to the soft chatter of guests moving through the hallway outside my door. I opened the window into the courtyard and saw only partly cloudy skies. Although I had eaten a full dinner only 10 hours earlier, I was hungrier than usual. The long, comfortable rest during the night reinvigorated me, and I would enjoy a full breakfast before I departed for Koblenz. At breakfast, I told the waiter that it was my birthday and asked him if he and the other guests in the breakfast room would like to share a shot of Bailey's Irish Cream with me and toast the day.

"Please tell your guests this will give a good boost to the coffee and to the day."

At first, the waiter did not understand my offer. In my best German I rephrased my statement more slowly and finally he understood. Although there were six guests at three tables, only the waiter and I drank the shot neat. All I had ahead of me this day was an 18-mile walk to a city of more than 100,000 residents. Except for Paris, it would be the largest city that I would pass through after 31 days of walking.

I was in no rush to leave the comfort and the bounty in the breakfast room. As I sat enjoying the birthday breakfast and the day that was developing without rain, the guests who earlier had declined my offer of an early-morning tipple came to my table to wish me a happy birthday. I thanked them all and told them that their kind expression of a birthday greeting merited a place in my will; if they would write their names and addresses on my breakfast napkin then, given my age, in a year or two they would be very wealthy. Everyone laughed. No one signed.

As I packed to depart, I realized that I had to my advantage the prospects of a warmer day without rain along an exceptionally scenic route. To my disadvantage, I had the reality of walking 18 miles to a city of 110,000 people where I would have to be especially attentive to navigation and wary about traffic.

The Knaus Campingpark was located on the far side of Koblenz at the intersection of the Rhine and Mosel rivers approximately 18 miles east from Mayen. Without the prospect of rain and with mid-day temperatures expected around 70 degrees, I dressed in shorts and a T-shirt. I could not remember where I was or what I did on my 62nd birthday in 2013. It seemed certain that, in 2015, I would remember most of what I would do today. After three hours and just shy of 10 miles, I stopped in the fairly large town of Ochtendung, population 5,000. It is known for the discovery in 1997 of an early Neanderthal skull found with three stone artifacts used as tools or bowls. Some of the buildings in the town displayed posters of cavemen and skulls with maps highlighting archeological sites in the area. One restaurant had a poster of an early homo erectus and the words translated roughly as "even the cavemen came here to eat."

Refreshed after lunch and an hour's rest reclining on a park bench without my sweat-soaked shirt, shoes and socks, I awoke from an unintended nap to the sound of a pair of quacking ducks walking under the bench. They stopped as I sat up and faced them possibly expecting a handout. My name would be mud with the PETA people if I offered them something from an MRE. Obviously disappointed with my lack of support they walked away toward the water. I stretched, dressed, shouldered the backpack, and continued walking the route through the upper-middle Rhine valley toward Koblenz. In another hour I had reached Bassenheim where I refilled both water bottles. My destination was only six or seven miles away and the traffic continued to increase steadily. My pace was interrupted frequently waiting at lights to cross roads and reading the road signs at the more numerous intersections. I did not see the rivers until I had passed through the town and walked over the bridges which span them.

The reception team at Knaus Campingpark had both my registration documents and resupply parcel ready when I arrived just after 5 p.m. I was escorted to a single pitch campsite close to the facilities with showers, toilets, and laundry. I ran a small load of laundry as I set up the campsite. My plan was to take a short, 30-minute nap, then shower, dress, and explore Koblenz.

I overslept, not waking until just after 7 p.m. After a quick shower, there still were almost three hours of daylight to tour. I walked to the base of a funicular from which I rode a cable car over the Rhine with an incredible view of the city and the river up to the Ehrenbreitstein Fortress built around the year 1000.

A small, 30-passenger ferry brought me across the Rhine to the east access of the town center. There, in the Jesuitenplatz, part of which was a pedestrian-only area, were numerous restaurants and cafes with dining tables set up outside. Near the monument of Johannes Müller, I ate dinner having fully enjoyed my birthday and regretting only that I did not share it with anyone other than strangers.

Back at the campsite, the rain resumed just as I cleared the last item of my clothing which had been air-drying on top of my tent. It continued through the night. The one clear and comfortable day of my birthday would be bracketed by several days of rain.

The sound of foot traffic near my tent and people barking instructions to each other as they worked to decamp woke me. The noise was loud enough to trump that of the rain. I dragged the tent and its contents to an overhead shelter where I broke down the tent and packed the backpack less my shaving kit and fresh clothes. After a long, hot shower, I walked first to the office where there was complimentary coffee and hard rolls. Then I waited for the ferry to bring me to the bridge and road which would lead to Heiligenroth 16 miles away to the northeast.

With every mile I walked the crowds, congestion, and cement of the city transitioned to far fewer people and the peace of farms, fields, and forests. From a city of more than 110,000, I entered Heiligenroth with a population of only 1500. On the outskirts, in the direction of Seck, I found an isolated strip of dry ground beneath an overpass and set up camp. The tent could be seen only by someone walking out of the forest or more than 50 yards off the road and around the structure which supported the overpass. Either case was extremely unlikely, especially given the rain. I secured my valuables and returned to town for dinner. It was relaxing to sit down someplace dry and enjoy a hot meal and draught beer. After dinner, still seated in the restaurant, I reviewed my notes. On day 36 of "The TREK" I had reached exactly 500 miles after walking for 32 days. The rain continued after I returned to the tent and went to sleep.

At some time during the night the rain stopped. As I opened the tent flap and threw back the rain fly the humidity rushed in as if I had opened the door to a dry sauna. My backpack had only half the full-ration weight. The 15-mile walk northeast toward the rising sun should be no more difficult in the increasing heat and humidity than the past six of seven days in the cold and rain. At seven, the sun already had risen half a hand's breadth and would be full in my face. I applied a liberal dose of sunscreen to my face and exposed arms and legs, and started walking feeling slightly stiff but refreshed after seven hours' sleep. Halfway toward Seck, I stopped at the Bäckerei Paul Fuhr and ordered coffee, orange juice, and a sandwich. While the clerk prepared the order, I visited the restroom where I struggled to remove my T-shirt seemingly glued to my upper torso and soaked it in cold water in the sink, dressed, and returned to my seat. At 10:30 a.m. the temperature was 23 Celsius, 74 Fahrenheit. I would walk the remaining seven miles to Seck in two 90-minute segments with a short break in between to air out my shirt, shoes, and socks, and cool down.

The Camping Park Weiherhof met all my needs for the rest of the day. Arriving midday on a Saturday and without a reservation I was happy that there was more than sufficient space for me at a single-pitch site. Only a short distance northwest of the center of town, it is a spacious, scenic, and well-maintained facility bordering one side of a large lake. I selected a location as close as possible to the Großes Weiher; set up the tent; tossed everything from my backpack until I found my swim suit; changed; and, swam for 30 minutes in refreshingly cold water. Carrying a T-shirt, I walked back to the reception area and donned the shirt when I entered the snack bar to buy a beer. There were several brochures describing the Camping Park and places of interest and restaurants in Seck. Tonight, at 7:30, the Netherlands would play Brazil in the Finals of the World Cup to determine the third place winner. With almost four hours before the game started, I had time for a nap in the shade by the lake, a second refreshing swim, and a hot shower and shave.

The menu at Gästehaus Weiherhof was traditional German guaranteeing that I would not have to close my eyes, make a wish, and select one of my four remaining MRE's for dinner. After eating, I brought what remained of my second Pilsner with me to watch the match. I heard only German and Dutch spoken among the dozens of fans of both sexes and all ages. Sipping my third Pils, I became emboldened to introduce myself to some German-speaking guests. The next day, Germany would play Argentina for the championship, and I told everyone that I was confident of a victory for the German team. In this night's game, Brazil could not coordinate an effective offense and its defense did nothing on behalf of the team. The Netherlands scored the only three goals of the game. The Dutch players returned home as third place winners. That night the revelers launched fireworks over the lake. Everyone and everything settled down not too long after midnight.

Thick, fast-moving clouds were sailing low over the lake when I stepped out from the tent at sunrise. In the office Sunday morning before breakfast, I overheard a family tell the clerk that they would depart one day early because of the high probability of rain today and the next few days. As I packed and prepared to depart I hoped that I would be able to find a Gästehaus in Herborn, and treat myself to a night out of the rain to help celebrate what I was sure would be Germany's victory in the World Cup. At breakfast, one of the staff told me that checking availability for a room in Herborn would be easy using their internet service. She found a room in what she described as a "very nice hotel with breakfast included and a free sauna for relaxations." She would help me with the booking and I could return to my breakfast after I had secured the room. Fraulein Marta not only helped me secure a room but also obtained a significant discount for the price of a single room.

"There are not so many people in this hotel tonight for Sunday. Many people stay at home to watch the game. If Germany will win then not so many people will be at work on Monday."

All that worked for me. It could storm all day but I wouldn't care. This night I would sleep in a bed and have a roof over my head. The only thing that could make this night better would be the victory of the German team.

The cloud cover and wind kept the temperature cool. After only an hour enroute to Driedorf, about eight miles northeast from Seck, the rain began. Falling lightly at first, I stayed dry using only my collapsible umbrella. Half an hour later the rain increased and the wind blew stronger nearly pulling the umbrella from my hand and twice reversing the ribs and inverting the canopy. The poncho provided much better protection and required no handling. In another 90 minutes, I expected to reach town and the shelter of a café for a snack at the halfway point for today's walk. Approaching Driedorf, I was surprised to see a number of fields supporting wind turbines.

In town the waiter told me that wind power and wind turbines are becoming more popular in Germany and, although he did not know the exact number, he said that there were more than a dozen supporting the town of 5,000 residents. My German was not nearly technical enough to describe the conference that I had attended in Arlon, Belgium, where I learned that the nations of Europe were working and making substantial progress to reduce their dependence on fossil fuels and carbon emissions.

"If the taxes on gasoline keep rising then we will go back to riding with horses and carriages."

"That wouldn't bother me," I answered, adding, "With all the drivers who may be texting, tweeting, and tooting, I'm sure it would safer."

In response to his question about my destination I told him, "Herborn for today and Berlin in about a month." A resident of Herborn he knew well the Schloss Hotel and recommended the restaurant there. He suggested that I take dinner early because no one would be paying attention to the guests and customers once the game began. He reminded me that tonight the match would start one hour earlier at 8:30 p.m.

"Not far from the hotel is a terrible pub called, 'Hangover.' Everyone there will be very, very drunk no matter who is winning. We all want Germany to win. If you are in Hangover when Germany wins it will be really something special."

I had no doubt about that. My feeling was that I wanted to watch the game and not be distracted having to safeguard my beer and dodge tipsy patrons. The rain continued the remaining six miles to Herborn. At the entrance to the hotel, I dropped my backpack and removed my poncho before I approached the reception desk. The clerk, having seen my backpack, knew that I was the guest for whom the reservation had been arranged by Camping Park Weiherhof. After I registered, she informed me that the restaurant would close early to enable the staff to watch the game. She added that the bar would be open and that there would be complimentary snacks and a light menu available with bar service.

It seemed as if there were very few guests in the hotel. I passed the sauna on the way to my room which was large, airy, well-furnished, and exceptionally clean. I was embarrassed to walk in with my wet shoes, rain-soaked backpack, and clothing. From the backpack I withdrew my shaving kit, notebook, a fresh T-shirt, and shorts and went to the sauna. In traditional fashion I took a warm, soapy shower then slowly increased the heat as I stretched the muscles in my upper body. In the dry sauna I sat on a towel and leaned back against the wood-framed wall nodding off once or twice. After about 10 minutes, I took a second warm, soapy shower then reduced the water temperature to full cold. Now I was fully awake. I wrote some notes about the day and studied the route for the next few days. One more round through the sauna and shower and a few minutes for a clean shave was enough to refresh and reinvigorate me.

Back in the room, I washed out my shirts, briefs, and socks from the past three days and hung everything to dry overnight in the bathroom. In the restaurant, I enjoyed a meal of jägerschnitzel, spätzle, and red cabbage and a small glass of Pilsner. Anyone at the hotel not in his room, in the restaurant, or working was in the bar waiting for the final game of the World Cup to begin. Everyone was upbeat but not everyone was confident of a German victory. I tried to change the uncertainty sentiment by stating that I did not come all the way from Texas to watch Germany lose in the finals. It helped some. The game was thrilling. Every time the German team launched a shot and the locals knew it would miss, they cursed before the ball hit somewhere other than the goal. But every time Argentina fired a shot they held their breath and comments then roared when it missed. No one left during the first half which ended with neither side scoring. A few folks disappeared at half time but quickly returned to analyze the first half and predict the second.

I thought back to 1969 when, as a plebe at West Point without television privileges, I snuck into the day room wrapped in a blanket with shaving cream on my face, sunglasses and a baseball cap, and tried to hide in the back to watch the Miracle Mets defeat the Baltimore Orioles in game five of the

World Series. I was caught, but the upperclassmen let me stay because I had gone undetected for three innings. It was one of the first of many ill-conceived events for me as a cadet.

The second half was played at the same relentless pace as the first with the same result: no score. Now, no one left. In the overtime period, the drinking all but stopped. No one was taking his eyes away from the television to find his drink or be distracted while drinking. Finally, the miracle! Substitute player Mario Götze, age 22, scored the winning goal giving Germany its fourth World Cup victory. Tonight I would defer to my mother's Rinderknecht side of the family and be German. I headed out in the rain for one, maybe two, more glasses of beer with the Hangover crowd.

I arrived in less than ten minutes. If anyone had left when the game ended you couldn't tell from the crowd in the bar. It was standing room only and I had to wiggle my skinny, 145-pound frame between the people standing in the door. I made it to the bar only by slapping the men on the back and yelling "Good job, Germany," and other congratulatory comments in English. At the bar I discovered the reason for the crowd. Someone who slowly was spilling his beer on the front of my windbreaker told me that drinks were free immediately after Götze scored and that the bar would stay open all night. Good news on both counts. Two more glasses of beer wouldn't kill me.

The noises from the street continued all night. Having to walk more than 17 miles after a night of partying and only six hours' sleep would be a challenge. But the experience of sharing and celebrating the victory with the countrymen of the winning team easily justified the extra effort for the day.

Steaming the poisons from my system in the sauna gave a big boost to the start of the day. The victory was headline news on the television and in the local papers. At breakfast it was the dominant topic of conversation between the staff and the guests.

When I departed I thanked the reception clerk for the outstanding accommodation and extended congratulations on the victory.

"I'll come back to repeat the experience in another four years."

I stepped outside to a sparkling clear day and cool temperatures in the upper 50's. Bright sunshine and temperatures approaching 80 and possibly 90 were expected along the route for the next three to five days. There would be excellent weather for the Germans to celebrate their victory especially in Berlin where there would be a huge parade in honor of the team on Tuesday, July 15th. Many of the buildings and parked and passing cars were displaying the tricolor black, red, and yellow flag of Germany.

Regardless of the weather conditions I had been able to maintain a pace of three miles an hour for most of the past month. During that time, my experience had been that after a slow, full-body stretch before starting, I would warm up and stay on pace after about 30 minutes. The first nine miles in three hours almost always passed faster than I noticed. This day I would walk for three hours as far as Niederweidbach along what a map recon showed to be a wonderfully scenic route: wooded heights, lush meadows, orchard-lands, river valleys, and villages with half-timbered buildings and homes. After lunch somewhere in town, I would continue walking the remaining eight miles to Lohra.

From the Schloss Hotel, I walked a short distance away from the town crossing a bridge over the Dill River. The terrain was fairly flat especially along the Aar River flowing east in the same direction that I was walking and popping in and out of view along the route. After only 90 minutes, I reached the small town of Bicken. Reading my notes at breakfast earlier I was saddened to pass through such a small, quiet town which had lost 30 of its men in combat during World War I and 80 during World War II. My T-shirt dampened as the temperature continued to increase. A large lake, the Aartalsee, ran along the south side of the road and I stepped off to cool down. I splashed some fresh water on my face and soaked my T-shirt in the lake. Thirty minutes later, at 11:30 a.m., in Niederweidbach it was 75 degrees. The sun was shining brightly almost directly overhead.

At the east end of town, I found the Gasthof Brücke which I felt clean and dry enough to enter. Beneath the coatrack near the door, I grounded my backpack and took a seat at a small table. At a larger table were four men at one table whose conversation was all about the World Cup victory. Occasionally someone's comments would generate responses of "Ja, Ja, Ja," and four glasses of beer would clink together at the center of their table. After I received my beer and as I waited for my lunch I walked over to congratulate the men. From what I understood they all worked together in some sort of construction business. A sign at their place of work read, "Closed. Germany 1, Argentina, 0." They had stopped at an ATM then came straight to the restaurant. I learned that I was the first backpacker from the United States that any of them ever had seen pass through Niederweidbach.

"You have good radar or GPS systems to find the best place to eat here in town."

"Must be my radar. I do not have a GPS system."

Before my meal was served, I mentioned that I had been walking and camping in rain almost every day since I arrived in Winterscheid, and that, so far, today was my first full day of true summer weather and sunshine. I added that in Herborn I was told that good weather was expected for the next several days and asked if that were true.

"The weather will be good and the sun will keep shining until we tire of celebrating."

I took that to mean "yes." While I ate I studied my notes. Today, and for the next five days, I would have walks that would average 16.5 miles daily. The route would take me through a large valley with rolling hills, low-lying, intersecting rivers and streams, numerous lakes and ponds, and large tracts of farmland. The towns through which I would pass and try to visit would be in this scenic region of western Germany. If the days were like today, my plan would be to rise early, walk half the distance to the next town before stopping for lunch at a café or restaurant, rest for an hour while my shirt, socks, and shoes aired out, then walk the final distance and camp.

From the bridge over the Salzböde River, I could see the town of Lohra and the German flags flying in front of the buildings leading into town. At mid-afternoon, there was plenty of time for me to pass through, find a suitable place to camp, then return to explore the town and support any continuing victory celebration. Five hundred yards out of Lohra in the direction of Kirchain, I found a large sports area hosting a running track and soccer fields. There was a wooded area to the south between the track and fields which was dense enough for me to camp peaceably out of sight. There was enough room on the forest floor to pitch the tent but I decided to wait until I returned from town. Instead, I lifted the backpack and wedged it between some tree branches then climbed up the opposite side of the tree and hid the pack up higher by a few branches. It was undetectable from the ground. In town and at a pub, I would limit myself to only two victory glasses of beer and return before dark. That should allow me time to find the pack and set up camp while there still was some daylight.

Lohra was rustic and quaint. The area supported about 5,000 people, and the town only about 2,500. In the pub, in the early evening, were mostly working men at the bar and a few couples at half the tables. There were no families with children. I identified myself to the bartender as an American traveling through Germany and told him how happy I was that Germany won the World Cup and that I was in Herborn when it happened. He asked me if I was passing through. After I told him that I was staying the night in Lohra he told me that there were no hotels. I did not want to tell him that I was camping and I did not want to be deceptive so I said only that I had made previous arrangements. I drank only one beer with a plate of wurst, potato salad, and bread then drank a second beer watching the television news and weather. Tonight would be clear and 60; the next day also would be clear and slightly warmer at 80. The five-day forecast for the region was the same.

For my first time during the night I was uncomfortable trying to figure out how to sleep. I was too hot inside the sleeping bag in only my briefs. But I was too cold on top of the sleeping bag. Donning a T-shirt and shorts resolved the issue. I slept well through the remainder of the night for about seven hours. I awoke before sunrise, decamped, and started walking toward Kirchain. There was very little traffic, only an occasional automobile and a few delivery trucks. I enjoyed being on the road as the neighborhoods were coming to life. After an hour walking through terrain that was split evenly between fields and forests, I stopped in a small town and bought coffee, two hard rolls, and a banana, and refilled my water bottle which I had emptied during the first hour's walk. Maintaining my pace, in slightly more than two hours I would arrive in Schröck and stop for lunch and a rest.

In Schröck I found a small restaurant one block off the route. At the side of the restaurant and out of view from anyone I removed my sweat soaked T-shirt. I poured half the contents of a water bottle on a washcloth and washed my face, arms, and torso. The remaining water I poured over my head, then dried and combed my hair, and put on a fresh, clean shirt before I entered. After the waitress brought a small glass of draught beer I raised it to her and toasted the World Cup winners. The victory parade was ongoing in Berlin where more than 400,000, possibly half a million, fans lined the parade route for a victory celebration at the Brandenburg Gate. I expected to be in exactly the same location on the final day of "The TREK" one month later. But I did not expect as many fans. Just one would make me happy. I ordered a light meal of wurst with potato and cucumber salad. The heat and direct sun in my face would present enough of a challenge without having to deal with the lethargy following a beer and a heavy meal.

Not far from the restaurant, I stepped off into the shade of a very small wooded area surrounded entirely by acres of farmland and removed the fresh shirt, shoes, and socks and took a quick nap. Less than an hour later I awoke and put back on the still-damp T-shirt from the start of the day. There were a total of three T-shirts in my inventory. Unlike in the United States, there is more of a respectful sense of modesty in Germany and most of Europe. Even in hot and sunny weather male hikers, cyclists, runners, and athletes wear a shirt. I had one T-shirt to walk in and wash out at the campsite; a second, mostly clean and dry shirt to wear at the end of the day; and a third shirt as a spare.

Six miles ahead would be the town of Kirchain almost centered in the Hesse region. One of the largest, with a population of around 16,000, this evening it should be especially festive with pubs rebroadcasting the highlights of the World Cup victory two days earlier, and the celebration parade and revelry ongoing in Berlin. By 4 p.m., I had arrived at the hotel on the western side of Kirchain where I had sent another resupply parcel. After introducing myself, there was a short conversation between the reception staff and one clerk asked me to wait briefly.

A few minutes passed and the hotel manager greeted me with my parcel. Ernst Haltegahn's father had worked for the American military in Germany in the supply and maintenance organizations of a large logistics unit. He had been watching the parade when his staff told him that I had arrived. From my letters he knew that I had been hiking and camping since France, and asked me if I had been able to view any of the games and knew about the World Cup victory. I told him that "The TREK" daily schedule was nearly perfect; I was able to walk by day and view the games at night. During our discussion,

Ernst mentioned that the only campsite he knew was another 30 kilometers away near the next large town of Jesberg, a very long walk from the hotel. Jesberg was my destination for the following day. I was not aware that there was an established camping park there. He told me that his hotel had many vacancies, and offered me a single room with breakfast at a very good rate which I accepted. Although I was not tired and may have preferred to continue camping, I felt that I had a slight obligation to return the favor of the courtesy he had extended me by receiving and keeping the resupply parcel. Also, I would have the convenience and security of a room from which to explore Kirchain and view the televised events in Berlin.

In the room, I showered and watched the news from Berlin on the BBC and local German channels. The crowds along the parade route, near and at the Brandenburg Gate, were estimated at more than 500,000. Most of the cameras were focused on the team members, most notably the winning goal scorer Mario Goetz, passing the winning trophy among themselves and replacing their empty hands with steins of beer. Then, as I dressed, I repacked. The parcel included not only a five day resupply of MRE's but also a fresh toothbrush, tube of toothpaste, hand towel, and five washcloths.

With five hours of daylight remaining, I toured Kirchain using a tourist map from the hotel, crisscrossing through the town, and stopping in two pubs for a small beer and a local restaurant for dinner. Exploring Kirchain gave me a good sense of the customs, traditions, and some of the history of this region. Jesberg would be only one-tenth the size of Kirchain and the campsite was located outside of town. There would be far less to see and do.

The night in town was quiet and in the hotel was peaceful. If there were any other guests on the same floor as mine, I did not know it. I slept soundly with the windows open and awoke to the sound of a woodpecker. Perhaps the old, timber-framed homes and buildings hosted wood eating organisms that were meals for these birds. Closing the windows I sensed that the temperature at sunrise already was warm. At breakfast 30 minutes later, I read the temperature at over 70 degrees. At checkout, the reception clerk told me that temperatures in the 30's Celsius, (90's Fahrenheit), were expected. It would be good to be getting an early start.

The plan for the 17-mile day was the same as the day before: break up the distance into two nearly-equal lengths and stop half way for lunch and a rest to cool down. There are no distance markers between the small towns only a few kilometers apart. It would be hard to try to walk a nine-mile first leg and then an eight-mile second leg, and much easier to walk in two three-hour legs. The morning walk took me through the farmland and marshy areas of a region rich in rivers and streams. Quite frequently I saw several individual and small clusters of nesting birds, such as the red kite, black grouse, and marsh tit, pass over and around me. Near the marshes, I thought I saw an egret and a stork, definitely some kind of short, stout, wading bird with a long, knife-like beak moving slowly along the fringe between the water and the land. Stopping to find my binoculars and view these birds more closely, I confirmed that I had seen both an egret and a stork.

At about the three hour point the temperature had reached 90 degrees. I detoured a few hundred yards into the small town of Josbach where I stopped for lunch after a fast sponge bath to make myself clean and presentable enough to enter the restaurant. Inside, I again washed my face and hands and refilled both water bottles. After lunch, and outside of town in the shade by a stream, I stopped again to rest and air out my sweat-soaked clothing.

By 5 p.m. I had reached Camping Kellerwaldsteig less than two kilometers from Jesberg. It was more than sufficient for my camping needs, providing the benefit of a single tent pitch site on flat terrain and thick grass for only five euros, ($7.), and access to a hot shower, toilet, and laundry room.

At the reception, I noted that the five day weather forecast was continued sunny and hot, with temperatures remaining in the upper 80's and low 90's. After encamping, I showered, secured my valuables, and walked 15 minutes into town.

The few pubs and restaurants were supported by the campers and tourists, and it was easy to find good food and cold beer at a fair price. This night I would relax a little at dinner then return and put through a load of wash before bed. If the hot weather continued then I thought that I might have to take a hotel in four days at the next resupply city of Gottingen if for no other reason than to wash and dry my clothes in the shower. For the next three days, the small towns of the region would resemble Jesberg, with populations of 2,500 or less, but would not have an established campsite.

The inside of the tent was hot when I returned after dinner. There was no breeze to justify reorienting the tent. I kept the flap up and the screens fully extended to help cool down the interior while I was away for an hour in the laundry room. I unrolled the sleeping bag only as padding for the air mattress. The extended distance of the day's walk, the fatigue from the heat and humidity of the marshlands, and the evening meal with two iced mugs of strong beer helped me to fall asleep almost immediately.

At daybreak, I decamped and took a hot shower to wake up and a cold shower to start the day. I applied sunscreen liberally to my face and exposed arms and legs. Today's walk would be 18 miles to the northeast into bright sunshine for the fourth consecutive morning. One mile further than the day before, the terrain would be very similar along broad and deep fields used for cattle-breeding and farming a mix of vegetables and fruits. In Jesberg at a café near the restaurant where I had dinner, I ate a breakfast of two hard rolls and a bowl of fresh fruit, and drank a small pot of coffee. I stopped at an outdoor market where I bought an apple and banana then committed myself to three hours of walking before my third stop. The early morning temperature was already approaching 70, and the forecast was for 90 or slightly higher.

There was almost no shade through the extensive tracts of farmland. The occasional shade was provided by the shelter of buildings in the small villages through which I passed. After only 90 minutes, I had soaked through my shirt and finished the first bottle of water. Right at three hours I arrived in Großenenglis. The first business I saw one street off the route was the Bürgerhaus Großenenglis. Next door was the Mette Dieter supermarket where I washed up outside near the delivery area then entered and bought a third bottle of water. From now and through the usually hot and dry weather I would walk with two bottles of water to drink and a third to keep my facecloth damp.

The burger was served with cold potato salad. The meal was sufficient to negate a sense of dehydration. Großenenglis is very small. I had passed only two streets before I was at its center and, only five more streets beyond the Bürgerhaus, I was out of the town. Within Großenenglis there was no park, playground or isolated shaded area to rest and cool down. I was not ready to resume the walk. Fortunately, just as I exited at the northeast side of town, I found a clump of trees and stopped for an afternoon rest. The meal and a rest in the shade without my shirt, shoes, and socks helped me fall asleep almost as soon as my head and upper body were reclined on the backpack.

By 2 p.m. I was up, dressed and heading toward Felsberg, population about 10,000. The terrain was relatively flat. The walk continued to be peaceful. Traffic never was a threat or an issue. After 12 days in Germany, no other backpacker had crossed my path. There still was very little shade along this region of the route. Thirty to forty years earlier I had served three tours of duty with the Army in the tropics of Latin America where the sun, heat, and humidity, and the weight of the packs I had carried through triple-canopy jungle had been far more severe. This was a relative cakewalk becoming easier as I became more acclimated. The four villages of Utterhausen, Wahern, Niedermöllrich and Lohre were almost evenly spaced within the last nine miles before Felsberg. Passing through each of them gave me an opportunity to watch the people at work and the children at play most of whom paused to stare at the huge backpack and some of whom waved. The midafternoon temperature projected from the gauge at the apotheke was 92 degrees.

Safely in Felsberg, I had only three tasks for the remainder of the evening: enjoy a light, local meal and a glass of beer; locate a site and establish camp; and, study the next day's route to Niestetal only five miles and a 15-minute drive from the huge city of Kassel. I would be arriving late in the afternoon on a Friday, and traffic certainly would be increasing the closer I came to Niestetal and to the end of the work day. Felsberg is a town of more than 10,000 residents. Within the town and along the northeast route toward Niestetal I had several places to choose from in which to eat. My preference was for a small restaurant popular with the locals. As usual, before I entered I took time to make myself presentable to the other guests and wait staff. I don't remember tasting the first beer. Although the two-plus bottles of water had kept me hydrated, I must have been very thirsty or at least very thirsty for a beer. The young lady who took my order for the first beer brought me a second without my having to ask.

"Thank you. How did you know that I wanted another glass?"

"One small beer could not be enough with so big a walking case. Do you not want this?"

"Yes, thank you. I'll drink more slowly and enjoy the taste."

I was hungrier than I thought already having eaten an MRE and fruit at breakfast and a full lunch. Now I was hungry for dinner. The waitress was a resident of Felsberg. After dinner I asked her about a potential campsite. She suggested that I pass through town and the first section of woods beyond the town. At less than two kilometers, about a mile, the second section of woods would be denser, less obvious to detection, far from any noise of the town or traffic and very safe. Her younger twin brothers used to hike from their home and camp there overnight in summer when they were free from school. She told me that they would come home with stories about insects, birds, reptiles, and animals, "all of which they made up to scare my mother." I taught her the word, "critters" which she never had heard.

The campsite was perfect. The night was peaceful. Deep inside the woods the temperature dropped low enough where I needed the sleeping bag for warmth overnight. When I awoke I felt rested and refreshed and had one mile less to walk this day.

I studied the route to Niestetal before I went to sleep and planned to start walking until I found a bäckerei for coffee and a roll. Then I would continue walking for three hours. With nine miles down, lunch and a rest would provide the boost to complete the final seven miles to the hotel where I expected to obtain another resupply parcel.

The weather and most of the route would be identical to the day before. The exception was that, just beyond the halfway point, the farms and fields would transition to built-up areas of bedroom communities with short commutes to Niestetal and Kassel. Half an hour after leaving the woods, I walked between several ponds where the wildlife was becoming more active as the sun began to rise. Beyond the ponds, I crossed the Eder River. From the bridge I looked down and saw some nesting birds and a land turtle. A half hour later, I arrived at the village of Brunslar, extending east from Neunbrunslar, and stopped for coffee and a roll. Beyond Brunslar I walked for an hour with the Eder on the west. It was easier to view the wildlife along its shores when I would turn to keep the sun behind me. The Eder yielded to Ellenberg, slightly larger than Brunslar, where I bought fruit and refilled one water bottle. At two hours, I walked slowly through Guxhagen. The temperature had climbed to the lower 70's. When I stopped for lunch in Dörnhagen an hour later the temperature was pushing 80.

In the restaurant I had a pleasant conversation with the waitress who was related to the owners. Again it was the backpack which sparked the conversation when she asked my destination. Not far beyond Dörnhagen the terrain would transition from farms and fields to larger villages and towns built between the Fulda River on the west and the autobahn, E45, on the east. She could drive to Niestetal in 15 minutes at autobahn speeds which are unlimited. We guesstimated that there were three more hours of walking ahead of me. Within Dörnhagen there was no place along the route to rest in the shade, but as in Felsberg the day before, less than a mile outside of town were fields bordered by rows of trees and a long dense forest. I chose the forest for the opportunity for a more peaceful rest before the traffic, congestion, and noise of the built-up areas.

At 5 p.m. I arrived at the hotel. There was no one at the reception. While I waited I studied my notes about Niestetal and the route for the next day's walk to Scheden. A member of the housekeeping staff asked if I were being helped then told me that she would find someone to assist me. I may have been dozing when the reception clerk greeted me. Newly employed and substituting for an absent employee, she did not know anything about me or my parcel.

From my backpack, I produced a copy of the message traffic in German about the parcel and handed it to her. She read it, excused herself, and then disappeared. She told me that no one currently at the hotel knew anything that could help me. If I were willing to wait she would try to locate one of the owners or managers whose names appeared on the messages. After an hour the clerk returned to tell me that she had contacted the manager. He had the parcel in the trunk of his vehicle which was being repaired in Kassel and would be ready at 7 p.m. He would drive from Kassel to the hotel and would meet me not later than eight. The three-hour delay represented a fair amount of wasted time for me.

But the hotel was very nice with a bar and restaurant. There was a single room available at a fair price. I registered. I took a shower and dressed intending to explore Niestetal after I met the manager. A friendly man, he was overly apologetic. I tried to explain how helpful it was for me to have had his help accepting and storing the parcel and showed him a chart of the resupply locations between Normandy and Berlin. I added that my time was not wasted because I had taken a room, showered, and was ready to tour his town. He gave me a local map and indicated a few points of interest and restaurants featuring local cuisine. Surprisingly, he added, "If you want the fast foods you must go to Kassel for those places."

"Thank you. But I never visit any fast food or chain restaurant when I am in the United States. I don't even want to see one when I am in Europe."

The area around the hotel was very well-developed and the streets were full of a variety of shops supporting Kirchain's 10,000 residents. I took a leisurely walk to sightsee and found a restaurant with an outdoor dining area. At the restaurant, I planned the next day's walk to Scheden only 15 miles away. Back at the hotel I had the sauna all to myself. For almost an hour I moved between the shower and the dry sauna soaking, sweating, and scouring my body, finally feeling truly clean. In half a day I'd be gooey and grungy again. A sixth straight day of sunshine and temperatures in the low 90's was predicted for the next day's walk.

The hotel was fairly full. The fresh air in the garden, and the opportunity to enjoy the tastes of a full German breakfast there, were polluted by those guests who were smokers. I drank my first cup of coffee outside then took the second cup and my breakfast inside away from the smell of the cigarette smoke. Perhaps it's not enough for a smoker to be stupid and suicidal; he also has to be inconsiderate and rude.

Scheden was 15 miles away to the northeast. The walk today would be a mile shorter than yesterday's hike. The three water bottles had been stored overnight in the mini-fridge and were full of cold water. The side compartments of the backpack were packed with fruit from the breakfast buffet. My plan was to walk the first nine miles without stopping. If I were near or in a town then I would break for lunch; if I were somewhere rural then I would find some shade and break out an MRE.

I hardly noticed the first hour pass as I left Niestetal, then walked to the east of the Fulda River and through the village of Staufenberg, population about 8,000. At the second hour I had reached Lutterberg, a village almost identical in appearance and size. Having left the Hesse region I now was entering Lower Saxony. At the third hour I again passed along the east of the Fulda River, this time for almost 30 minutes, before I entered the southwest half of the town of Hann-Münden.

With three times the population of each of the two previous villages, Hann-Münden was a treat to enter at the lunch hour. The streets were full of people enjoying the warm, sunny weather, eating at outdoor cafes, relaxing in the parks or strolling down the streets window shopping. There were any number of nice cafés or restaurants at which to stop. I selected a small restaurant where there was an isolated area nearby to refresh myself. It would be more relaxing and enjoyable to eat indoors where the temperature was 20 degrees cooler than outside. After I ordered lunch, I told the waiter that I had crossed a river which looked different from the Fulda when I entered town. It seemed smaller, not nearly as wide, and flowed more gently. He told me that I had crossed a tributary of the Fulda when I entered, and would cross the Werra River when I left in the direction of Scheden. The town of Hann-Münden was known as the point at which the Fulda and Werra rivers merge, helping to define the border between the Hesse and Lower Saxony regions as the merged rivers flowed north.

After lunch, I walked through the northeast half of the town where I saw the Old Town Hall and the Tillyschanze, a massive stone observation tower built in the late 1800's. I crossed the Werra by the Old Werrabrücke, one of Germany's oldest stone bridges. After another 200 or 300 yards, I stopped and rested for an hour in the shade of a thick forest which ran along the route for half a mile.

When I continued, Scheden was only five miles and less than two hours away. I arrived late afternoon. For this sixth consecutive day of temperatures in the 90's, I was thirsty for a cold beer. There would be at least five hours of daylight to discover whatever was happening on a Saturday night in a town of 3,000, find and establish a campsite, and prepare for the next day's walk to Göttingen. Only 13 miles away, the shorter walk would equate to a day of rest on Sunday.

Scheden was shaped like a bat-wing-style bow tie. Broad on the southwest and northeast wings, the town narrowed toward the tie's center. From the traffic circle at the body-center a traveler could choose one of three main roads and find a sports field, a church, some small shops, and an occasional restaurant. It appeared to be a very sleepy community of farmers who worked the vast fields beyond the town and business persons who commuted primarily to Göttingen where more than a 100,000 people lived and worked.

The first road in to Scheden offered nothing of an opportunity for a pub, a restaurant, or a potential campsite. At the traffic circle I grounded the backpack. The better choice of the two remaining roads would lead in the direction of Göttingen but might also offer nothing for me for the remainder of the night. If I waited I hoped that someone might pass and I could ask for help. I did not have to wait long.

Two teenage boys on bicycles were headed toward me. They stopped when I signaled. Maybe 15 or 16 years old, they suggested I continue to Göttingen because "there is nothing here. No one ever stops." But they understood that I had been walking all day in the heat and wanted to stop in Scheden. They recommended a restaurant with a bar nearby along the road in the opposite direction from Göttingen. Without their help I would have missed the only restaurant in the town.

I asked about a church for Sunday. They told me that Saint Markus was 50 yards from where we were standing, one side street off the main road to Göttingen. That, too, was very helpful.

Finally, they told me that after leaving the restaurant, returning to the traffic circle and heading toward Göttingen, I would find a sports field with a water fountain and restroom facilities which remain open and functional. Bordered by woods, it would be safe to camp there. All that worked for me.

I was able to wash and change my shirt before I entered the Weigand's Deutsches Haus restaurant. At the door was a coat rack and umbrella bins where I left my backpack. The beer garden was quiet and rustic. If anyone was smoking I could not detect it. To be safe, I chose a small table off to the side where there were no other patrons, and drank a small draught beer. The waiter told me that the fish and game dishes were fresh and local. I ordered the fish special. The trout was served baked with almonds, parsley potatoes, and a salad. The meal was excellent; the staff was friendly; and, the atmosphere was peaceful. It was easy to understand why there was no other restaurant in competition with it within Scheden.

After dinner I walked back to the traffic circle and looked for Saint Markus. It was only 500 yards from the traffic circle and 200 yards from the road toward Göttingen. Sunday services were at ten which was two to three hours too late in the morning to attend. From the church, I found the sports field and camped within a cluster of trees between the field and the road.

Early next morning, just before sunrise I awoke to a day that seemed very similar to the mornings of the past week. While I was on my hand and knees rolling up the tent I heard, "Hallo." Startled, I turned to see the same two boys who had helped me the previous evening and who had suggested this location for a campsite. They introduced themselves as brothers, Erik and Matteus Lauter. They were visiting because they were curious about my evening in Scheden and this location as a campsite. I told them simply that the night was uneventful and that I had a good night's rest. They gave me a guide to Scheden and a detailed street map of Göttingen reminding me how much bigger Göttingen is compared to Scheden. Matteus gave me his electronic mailing address with the suffix "web.de" very common for residents of Germany. He asked me to write as I continued my trip. I had to tell him that I did not have internet access, except in an occasional hotel, but I promised to write after my arrival in Berlin.

As I started walking the early morning temperature seemed almost warmer; the sun was rising full; there was no haze or wind. Four or five hundred yards north from the campsite, I turned almost directly east on to a two-lane, well-paved road, B3, which would be the road leading directly into the southern section of Göttingen. There was very little traffic early on Sunday morning. I stepped off the road when I heard the sound of an approaching vehicle which usually passed me in the oncoming lane giving me a wide berth to continue walking. Just over an hour later I was in the village of Dransfeld where I bought coffee and a hard roll. For the 10 or 15 minutes that I sat on a bench along Route B3 drinking the coffee and eating the roll not a single person or vehicle passed by me. Ninety minutes later, I arrived in the town of Groß Ellershausen with only three miles remaining before Göttingen. Groß Ellershausen must have grown physically from the westward expansion of Göttingen and economically from the opportunities available supporting a city of more than 110,000. At the lunch hour I preferred to stop, eat and rest in Groß Ellershausen.

The Hotel Lindenhof was a wonderful facility to visit on a clear and sunny Sunday afternoon. The gaststube was furnished with handmade, carved wooden tables and chairs, and decorated with fine German linens in a rustic atmosphere. The menu items included fresh foods from the region and local wines. I ate a light meal of roast pork, potatoes, and a cucumber salad. I passed on beer or wine not wanting to be any more slowed down than I was by the increasing heat and humidity especially as I was walking along with the greater volume of traffic into Göttingen. During lunch I studied the street map which the Lauter boys had given me in the morning. I found the Hotel Rennschuh on Kasseler Landstrasse to which I had sent another resupply parcel and noted the very convoluted but scenic route from the Hotel Lindenhof to the Hotel Rennschuh through Gottingen and on to Gieboldehausen. The walk would be only an hour or so between these two hotels. At the Rennschuh I hoped to obtain my parcel, store the backpack, and then tour Göttingen for five or six hours before retrieving my gear and seeking a campsite.

Route B3 expanded occasionally to a four-lane route for short distances at the interchanges with other routes and the autobahn. The walk through those sections was a bit more perilous as the drivers who were traveling at very high speeds concentrated on negotiating the interchanges and traffic circles with other vehicles and without any pedestrians. I knew I had reached the southeastern fringe of Göttingen when I saw from an overpass the huge sign on a stand-alone building for "Burger King." There were several vehicles parked in front. I assumed that the Burger King counter clerks were having the opportunity to practice their English language skills.

The bank sign broadcasting the time also broadcast the temperature. At 2 p.m., it was 94 degrees, the hottest of the last four days with temperatures in the 90's, and the seventh consecutive day of bright sunshine, heat, and humidity. After I entered the Hotel Rennschuh, I could see the USPS red, white, and blue parcel on a counter behind the reception desk. On top of the parcel were copies of the message traffic that I had sent to the hotel. The clerk gave me the package and asked if I were planning to remain overnight as a guest. I told her that I had planned to camp. I added that if she allowed me to store the backpack and parcel while I toured Göttingen unburdened then I might be late enough returning and would take a room. She told me that there were several single rooms available. The resupply parcel did not contain food. Instead I had sent T-shirts, briefs, socks and Band Aids. In the restroom I took a quick sponge bath, exchanged old clothing for new, and dressed in a fresh shirt and shorts. The desk clerk stowed my backpack and trashed the parcel and its contents of used clothing.

Home in the United States I had read, but did not remember, that Göttingen was a university town. It is renowned for the number of famous mathematicians and scientists it has produced, sponsored, and hosted including Nobel laureate physicist Max Planck. Perhaps as a result of that status it was spared the wrath of the Allied bombing during World War II. As many other large cities in Germany struggled to rebuild after the destruction caused by the war Göttingen built on what existed and expanded. The inner city is exceptionally pleasant to visit. Except for the traffic, shops, pubs, and restaurants, the numerous walking and bicycle paths and large tracts of parks, botanical gardens, sports fields, museums, and research buildings make the Innenstadt look like a college campus. The many university students who live in the inner city give Göttingen a youthful vitality and aura of non-stop activity. Statistics from 2010 indicated that almost half the population of the inner city area were between the ages of 18 and 30. That was a heavy factor in the temptation to extend my tour and take a room for the night.

Everything changed when, in the early evening, I found a restaurant with a large outdoor area and tables full of young couples and student-age patrons. Here was an opportunity to wait for a table at the bar and practice my German. Failing that I could let these youthful strangers practice their English with me and learn about Göttingen and the area out of town to the east in the direction of the Harz Mountains. That was not to be. There was a small round table for three persons available immediately near the entrance to the garden, and I was seated there. . .alone.

I drank an Einbecker Pils from the Göttingen Brauhaus. The waiter recommended the Sunday dinner special which was a light summer fare: a plate of cold meats, cheeses, potato salad, asparagus, and cannellini beans. The portion was larger than I had expected. I ate slowly and drank a second Pils while I reviewed the street map of Göttingen and highlighted where I had been. When I had finished the waiter cleared my dinner plate from the table, and asked if wanted dessert. Ordinarily I would have declined; however, I decided to treat myself to a dish of ice cream in recognition of having triumphed over the mid-ninety-degree temperature during the day's walk. As the waiter walked away he stopped to respond to a late-middle-aged couple who asked him, in British-accented English, if there were a table for two available. I heard him say that if they would wait in the bar then there would be a table available shortly.

I left my table and greeted the couple. After I introduced myself, I told them that I had overheard their request for a table and that I had just finished my dinner. I offered them my table and told them that I would finish the ice cream, which I just had ordered, at the bar. On such a lovely Sunday night the tables were very slow to turn over. They were slightly hesitant but agreed to join me. At least they had a table without having to wait.

Alex was an active duty colonel in the British Army serving as the chief of a medical facility in Hanover about 75 miles north of Göttingen. His wife, Margaret, was a nurse, bilingual, and working in a German hospital in Hanover. They were in town for a three-day weekend through Monday. The waiter returned with my dessert, a peach melba, which was a dish of vanilla ice cream, fresh peach slices, a warm sauce from crushed peaches, and a dollop of fresh whipped cream. He took an order for drinks from Alex and Margaret who asked him for menus.

Dr. Alex asked me how I came to be in Göttingen and I told him about "The TREK." He asked me dozens of questions and I began to notice that most were related to his status as a medical doctor.

"When did you start training? How long were you in training? How did you determine what to carry and the weight of your backpack? Do you have a regimen for what and when you eat? What have you been drinking besides water? What has the terrain been like where you have walked so far? Where do you go from Göttingen?"

Margaret sat patiently sipping her glass of wine as Alex asked me questions then listened to my answers. Then he stood up and said, "Would you mind standing up for me please?"

"Stand fast and take a step forward with your right leg as far as you can reach. Recover. Now the left. Good. Recover. Now put your hands on your hips and raise your right leg. Hold it. Good. Recover. Now your left leg. Hold it. Good. Recover. Now stay standing, look straight at me and twist your torso to the left and back. Good. Now to the right and back. Good. Good."

I had a chance to look at his wife and smile.

"He does this all the time with his soldiers. But rarely in a restaurant."

"Put your hands on your head and lace your fingers." Feeling my neck and shoulder muscles he asked, "Does that hurt anywhere?" Feeling my lat, thigh, and calve muscles he asked the same question. Each time I told him that, "No. nothing hurts."

"Tell me again how far you have walked, how much further you have to go, and what your schedule is between here and Berlin."

I showed him a laminated copy of "The TREK" schedule which I had in the notebook that I always carry with me. Dr. Alex studied it for a few minutes.

"You probably are the only person on the planet, certainly the only person your age, doing what you are doing. When you first approached us and we followed you back to this table, I noticed that you had a bit of an awkward walk, almost unbalanced. I am in charge of a NATO support hospital and contract clinics in Hanover. We are standing down from our NATO support effort in Afghanistan. Hanover is a transition location for the British military supporting the NATO mission."

"I'm actually in the process of closing the hospital and completing the contract requirements. What I'd like to do is this. Come with me tonight to Hanover and I'll put you up in quarters. First light Monday morning we'll give you an MRI and a CAT/DXA scan. We'll get the results almost immediately and can be back here around noon. I'd like to be able to tell you that there are no issues with your body and that you'll be able to do everything that you have planned on the schedule you have here. Would you want to do that?"

"Sure, but what about your weekend here? You'd have to cut short your holiday to work. I don't want you to do that. Besides, I feel fine."

"You do look fine and you may feel fine, but let's make sure that you really are fine; that is, if you want to."

At last Margaret said something having watched and listened for at least half an hour. "Please go with Alex. We usually go our separate ways after breakfast and often meet up only for meals. Today, while I was at the museums he was at the Institute libraries."

From the restaurant we three returned to their vehicle then drove to the Hotel Rennschuh. I thanked the reception clerk for providing my parcel and stowing my backpack and told her that I would be driving to Hanover for the night and did not need a room. From the Rennschuh we drove to their hotel where Margaret said "Goodbye and good luck with your tests. See you tomorrow."

Alex exited the vehicle saying, "I'll be right back." He returned in about ten minutes with a dress shirt, pair of slacks and his shaving kit. In the car as we drove off, he made several calls and arranged the billeting and the testing.

We drove the autobahn to Hanover at 130 kilometers (80 miles) per hour. In Hanover, he pointed to a large gated facility and said, "That's the hospital where we'll be in the morning. Billets are just down the road."

There was a guard at the entrance to another gated facility. Dr. Alex was saluted and waved in past the raised barrier and receded tire obstacles.

"Bring your backpack and I'll get you in your room. When I have everything set for the morning I'll come back and explain what we'll be doing."

The room was a nice suite with a separate bedroom, sitting room, bathroom, and mini-kitchen. In the kitchen was a bowl of fresh fruit and a box of biscuits (cookies) on the counter. The refrigerator was stocked with beverages, breads, lunch meats, cheeses, and condiments.

"I'm sorry to tell you this but you need to fast now until we finish in the morning. The tests will start at 7:30 a.m. and will finish in no more than half an hour. I'll have the results almost immediately but I want to take some time to make copies and share the results with my staff. Just wear shorts and a shirt and have nothing metal on you: no tags, watch, or ring. You can shower and grab something to eat from the room before we head back. You and I will chat on the way to Göttingen."

Dr. Alex handed me a card with his telephone number and instructions how to dial the number from the landline in the room. I hardly had time to thank him before he made a quick exit with the comment, "I'll see that everything's in order and come get you here at 7:15 a.m., tomorrow."

Fasting would be easy because I was full from the dinner, dessert and drinks in Göttingen. Although I was tired there was now too much nervous energy circulating through my body. I wrote extensively about the events of this day in my notebook and tried to calculate how a very late midday start from Göttingen would affect the walk to Gieboldehausen 15 miles away. I took a long, hot bath in an oversized, deep bathtub, changed the water, and enjoyed a second soak. I fell asleep thinking about the next day's activities and what I would do if the test results portended issues with me physically.

A light rain was falling and the temperature was noticeably cooler when I awoke in the morning and opened the windows. I was dressed and ready at seven and left open the door to the room. Dr. Alex arrived wearing the shirt and slacks he had brought from Göttingen and a white lab coat with an embroidered crest which I did not recognize.

It was obvious to me that he was passionate about his work. He was fascinated with the effects of aging on the body and very curious about how well-trained, physically-fit, combat veterans age when they pursued a regular regimen of diet and exercise.

I met the staff after an introduction from Dr. Alex. One of the test technicians said, "If the doctor did not keep me so busy I would want to walk with you to Berlin. My grandparents live there in Zelendorf." The tests were easy for me to support. I only had to lie still while I was passed through one machine; relocate to another room; and lie still again while another machine passed over me. I felt as if I was a vehicle in a radioactive car wash. When the tests were completed I waited in a private room and read the International Herald Tribune in English.

Dr. Alex met me in the room.

"We got great results. If you're ready we can head back to your room. You can shower and get some breakfast. I'll review these results while you get ready. We can discuss them and my observations on way to Göttingen. Margaret wants to meet us for lunch at 11:30 a.m. at the hotel. After lunch we will checkout and can drive you wherever you want to go unless you want to spend another day in Göttingen. It is one of Germany's classic cities and fun to visit if you want to stay."

I told Dr. Alex that I did have a pseudo-flexible schedule. I added that I was trying to maintain my current schedule because of the dates and locations where I had planned to retrieve my resupply parcels and where I had made future hotel reservations.

"Okay. That makes sense. We may have to tweak the schedule a little but we'll discuss that later. Go ahead and get ready. I'll be back in half an hour."

I made a sandwich for breakfast, took a quick shower, and had just finished organizing and repacking the backpack when Dr. Alex returned. The mid-morning drive from Hanover back to Göttingen was more congested with the additional back-to-work Monday commuters. On the drive he told me that there was no evidence of any physical injuries or debilitation. There was, however, evidence of some physical distortions bordering on endurance wear and tear from my walking style and my favoring certain muscles. For example, walking with traffic on the right side of the roads put my balance awry since the roads usually sloped to the right to support drainage. Leading with my right foot and stepping on and off the road when traffic came up behind me over time had made the muscles in my right leg more dominant. Acknowledging that I was right-side dominant, the tests also showed that my right-side shoulder, arm and lat muscles had more mass certainly a result of my favoring those muscles to load and unload the backpack. Finally, because the weight of the backpack varied for reasons such as the weight of a wet versus dry tent and equipment, the number of MRE's, and the number and volume of the water bottles, there was evidence of stress at my hips and lower back. Before we arrived Dr. Alex strongly recommended that for the remainder of "The TREK" I change my plan from camping every night and that I take a room with a firm bed every two or three nights. He said that if I did not do that then it would be harder for me to continue walking, my walking would be slower and possibly painful, and that the continued stresses may invite a serious injury. Finally he told me that the route through the Harz Mountains and its steep inclines and declines, and the route through the towns and cities of the former German Democratic Republic with its relatively unimproved road network, would stress me more in two weeks than I had experienced in six weeks. My goal was to complete "The TREK." I was not going to act against medical advice. For the effort and expense that he and his team took to help me I would comply with everything that Dr. Alex recommended.

We arrived at the hotel shy of 11 a.m. I waited in the lobby while Dr. Alex rendezvoused with his wife.

"I hope Alex and his team was not too rough with you. How did you do?"

"I think I did fine. My results could have been better I guess if I were younger and in better shape. I have to make some changes for the next few weeks but I'll do better after I make those changes. I was very fortunate to have met your husband and his team. I'm waiting for him to ask me for an address to which to send the bill."

"Oh forget about that. His work is practically his hobby. You were a very valuable test subject for him."

Dr. Alex added, "My wife is right. My team and I just obtained 45 days of research, not counting what you told me last evening about how you prepared and trained for the walk. Your schedule with the route and distances is very valuable documentation. Let's get lunch, checkout, then get you back on the road.

I knew that Dr. Alex would put the lunch tab on his hotel bill so I ordered the least expensive item on the menu which was beef slices, diced, parsley-flavored white potatoes and red cabbage. I drank only water and we all had a coffee after the meal. While we were eating, Dr. Alex computed where I would have been at this time had he not interrupted my schedule for the physical evaluation. I may have been due a three-hour or nine-mile head start. Enroute to Gieboldehausen was a roadway network intersection that would put me back on track and orient Alex and Margaret toward Hanover. After the meal and their checkout from the hotel, we drove together for only about 20 minutes when Dr. Alex pulled off the road and stopped in Ebergötzen about nine miles away. Along the road which leads into Gieboldehausen everyone exited the vehicle and we had what a single man might describe as an emotional farewell. I was enriched as a human being and my status was enhanced as a trekker from having met this family. I wondered if I had learned more from having met Dr. Alex or if he had learned more from having met me.

Along Route 27 I had only a six-mile, two-hour walk to Gieboldehausen with much cooler temperatures in the high 70's as a result of the low clouds and occasional light rain. Nothing along the way attracted my attention. I was detached from the environment thinking about the events of the last 24 hours and how valuable this experience had been for me especially with respect to the caveats from Dr. Alex about the geography ahead of me.

The Harz Mountains.

I knew the terrain of the Harz Mountains fairly well. Between 1973 and 1976, when I was assigned in Berlin, I traveled there as often as possible during good weather on three-day holidays. When possible, I brought along two or three of my soldiers as companions and to give them the opportunity to discover Germany outside of Berlin and away from the huge training bases. The Harz was only a four-hour drive, including time for processing at the two border checkpoints, from my apartment in Dahlem to any one of the villages. The Harz is a year-round recreation area with countless walking paths, hiking and biking trails, fields for cross-country skiing and hills, and northern Germany's highest mountains with lifts for the downhill skiers.

Walpurgis Nacht is celebrated every year on April 30th when the locals gather with lighted torches to drive the witches and warlocks out of their mountains and forests and away from their homes. The tradition follows from a scene from Goethe's "Faust," in which the evil Mephistopheles takes the protagonist up the mountainside to join the witches in their revelry. Some of the Brothers Grimm fairy tales are set in the Harz. Every year I decorate my home at Halloween with souvenir witches, warlocks, devils, and creepy creatures that I bought on my travels here.

Not surprisingly this is a great opportunity to drink a beer or two for courage before setting out, sweet gluhwine for energy during the rally, and schnapps to celebrate the success after returning safely to the village. Accommodations always were available in gästehauses with big rooms and open windows to enjoy the cool, night temperatures and the smell of the Norway spruce and modified "Harz pines" in the forests. Traditional breakfasts with soft-boiled eggs, meats, cheeses, fruits, and bread were full and more than sufficient. There was enough food served with each portion to make a hearty sandwich for a snack later in the day. I hoped that the thrill of returning to the Harz would reinvigorate me and that the challenge of the rugged terrain would go unnoticed.

I thought, too, about the walk through the cities and towns of the former East Germany. In East Berlin I had only driven through sections that did not look much improved from what must have been the devastation during the final days of the war. My automobile rumbled over potholes and cobblestones that were of different levels and interlocking spaces. There were occasional bus stops in front of massive Soviet-style, dilapidated apartment buildings, few if any sidewalks, and very little pedestrian traffic off the main roads or on the side streets. I did not fear for my physical safety. My only concern was that the end of the walk would present a greater physical challenge than did the start. It reminded me of the stories from the Appalachian Trail thru-hikers who started the 2180 mile hike from the south in Georgia instead of the north in Maine, and then had to deal with increasingly stressful issues of the hard-surface granite, elevation and weather in Vermont, New Hampshire and Maine. Experienced hikers, or those who have done their homework before they start, know that the smarter way for a thru-hiker is to walk from north to south.

Perhaps less an hour had passed when I crossed over the Ellerbach River and alongside the village of Wollbrandshausen to the southeast. Within the next hour I had crossed over the point at which the Shule and Hahle rivers merge to the northwest of a large forested area within Gieboldehausen known as the Wallgarten. Turning east brought me into town. Another kilometer further and I had arrived at a nice restaurant near the town center. The rain had stopped; there was a mix of sun and clouds. It was late enough in the afternoon to stop for a drink and order a meal. "Kein Bier vor vier." (No beer before four is a German expression with which I often was not compliant.

I was more thirsty than hungry not having consumed as much water in the cooler temperatures and rain, and having eaten a good breakfast and a great lunch. Inside the restaurant there were several tables and a bierstube in a side room. Only two of the larger tables were occupied. I sat near a window at a table for two with my backpack between the wall and the table. After the waiter took my order for a beer I retrieved my map and my notebook and did some homework.

I had estimated the distance between Gieboldehausen and the next town of Clausthal-Zellerfeld at 17 miles. I knew that this leg of the route would be the start of the Harz region. Beyond Clausthal-Zellerfeld I had planned only a six mile walk to Hahnenklee which was my favorite town within the Harz and where I had a reservation for a room in a gästehaus along the lake. Coincidentally, and in support of the advice from Dr. Alex, I would sleep in a bed and not on the ground after two days of camping. After dinner, with more than five hours of daylight remaining, I would push beyond Gieboldehausen until I sensed that it was time to stop or the rain resumed. Setting up camp and having shelter from the rain was far more preferable than having to decamp, attend to hygiene, pack, and start the day in the rain.

The waiter described three specialties of the house prepared, in part, on Sunday for the hungry townsfolk who returned to work this Monday. He told me that many residents work in Göttingen. The two large tables were occupied by single men from town just home from work in companies in Göttingen. I asked him to surprise me with a selection he favored. When the meal came I was served roulade, a flat piece of baked beef rolled into a spiral over a hard-boiled egg, bacon slices, green peppers, onions, pimentos, and served with quartered white potatoes, brown gravy, carrots, and green beans. I did not think that I was hungry, but I surprised myself when I started eating. Toward the end of the meal I asked for a glass of local red wine. Everything was excellent. While I was paying the bill, I asked the waiter about the terrain beyond Gieboldehausen and the distance to the next town. He told me that outside of the town was an open area of fields and mostly forest and that the village of Hattorf am Harz was five-minutes by car toward Clausthal-Zellerfeld. Five minutes by car (assuming 30 miles per hour) translated to 50 minutes by foot (assuming three miles per hour). I decided to walk 30 to 45 minutes, camp, then have only a 30 to 45 minute walk in the morning before I would stop for coffee and a roll.

When I left the restaurant the temperature still was warm and there were patches of clouds passing, but it was not raining. After a comfortable walk of about half an hour I was deep in the middle of a dense forest. I stepped off the road and set up the tent, adding the rain fly for the first time in weeks. Inside the tent I was writing my notes about the day's activities when I heard the rain.

In the morning, the sky was clear. It was slightly humid and I guessed the temperature at around 60. The rain had passed and the day was developing nicely as I entered Hattorf am Harz and stopped for breakfast. It was not necessary for me to read "am Harz" after "Hattorf." I could tell from the changing terrain that I had entered the mountainous area of northern Germany. Four hours later I entered Osterode am Harz where I had visited during a weekend 40 years earlier. Walking through the middle of town to find a restaurant for lunch I could not be sure if I recognized any of the main or historic buildings. In town I read the temperature at 78 degrees. The sky was bright blue. I was sure that there was no chance of rain for the remainder of my walk that day.

I was very happy to be back in the Harz. At the restaurant I ordered a Gose beer named from Goslar's Gose River and exempt from the strict German beer-brewing purity laws because it is considered a specialty of the region. With it I tried the local Harzer Käse which I remembered as an old, very traditional, and potent type of cheese considered very healthy because of its high-protein and low-fat content. After the first four-hour walk through the more rugged terrain, and while I waited for a light meal of wurst and potato salad, I adjusted my plan for the remainder of the day and the following day.

Instead of walking to Clausthal-Zellerfeld, this day's objective would be a campsite after only another five miles or more at or just beyond Buntenbock. The next day I would have only an hour's walk of three miles to Clausthal-Zellerfeld for breakfast, then another two or three hours for five or six miles until I reached Hahnenklee. I knew that I had eaten more of a meal than I needed after I left restaurant and stepped outside. Either the cheese plate or the wurst would have been more than sufficient. The temperature seemed warmer, and I was more tired than usual after lunch perhaps because of the heavier meal or the more rugged walk or both. Not far from the restaurant I found a patch of woods located between Hauptstrasse on which I was walking and a second major road. The area was too small to support a building and lot of any respectable size so it was left as a green area. It was ideal for me to relax in the shade minus my shoes and socks. I fell asleep immediately and slept undisturbed for more than an hour. Starting the walk toward Buntenbock after this rest was much easier than when I had started out from the restaurant.

By 4 p.m. I had arrived in town. I found a rustic gaststätte overlooking a park and sat at a table outdoors in the shade. I drank my second beer of the day and confirmed the distances to Clausthal-Zellerfeld and Hahnenklee with the waiter. I also asked about the weather, and learned that it was expected to be sunny and seasonably warm in the low 80's for the next two or three days. From the gaststätte I walked only about 20 minutes across the six streets which intersected the main road and I was gone from Buntenbock. To my right was a large lake typical of the many which characterize the Harz region. Ahead of me was thick forest. As I walked, to my left was another lake not more than 300 yards from the road where I was entering the forest. I set up camp in a clearing about 20 yards west of the road. Wearing only a T-shirt, gym shorts, and walking shoes I secured my valuables and a towel and walked to the lake. There were no obvious obstacles and easy access to the water. I undressed completely and waded in. The icy cold water on my feet and ankles sent a shiver up the rest of my body. Taking a deep breath I dove under the water and swam to get acclimated. A slow breast stroke for 50 yards brought me to the center of lake where I tried to stand but could not. On my back I stroked back toward shore, turned over, stood, and then walked naked out of the water. That was a first-time experience. Sitting on my towel I watched the sun reflect on the water and waited for any signs of wildlife but there were none.

Back at the tent I reorganized my equipment. There were two shirts, pairs of briefs, socks, and worn washcloths that were not very serviceable and added only weight and bulk. I added them to a plastic hotel laundry bag at the top of the backpack to trash as soon as I located a container in Clausthal-Zellerfeld. I went to bed early, so that, in isolation, I could hear the sounds in the forest as the day ended and wake early to take another swim.

I heard nothing through the night. The day broke clear and cool with every indication of as comfortable a day as was the previous day. At the lake there still were no signs of wildlife. The swim was so refreshing that I felt as if I could run to Clausthal-Zellerfeld. Having skipped dinner and slept for eight hours I was hungry for breakfast which I would find after only a two or three-mile walk. Clausthal-Zellerfeld was less than an hour away. Like Osterode am Harz, I knew the town from previous visits. There would be any number of Bäckereien and cafes in which I could enjoy coffee and a traditional Harz breakfast.

From the campsite I returned to the road and continued to walk north. After only 100 yards, I walked out of the forest and across the Hasenbach stream which emptied into the Hasenbach Lake in which I had taken the two swims. I walked into town earlier than I expected and trashed the laundry bag. The reduction in the weight of the backpack was negligible. In the early morning the Bäckerei counter service was busy but only a few of the dozen tables were occupied. At a corner booth for one or two persons I sat and ordered a pot of coffee. The hot coffee melted the ice that had formed inside me during the morning swim. I ate a full breakfast looking forward to working it off as I walked many of the same trails over which I had passed 40 years earlier.

There was very little of this once-favorite Rest and Recreation (R&R) area that I remembered or recognized as I walked out of Clausthal-Zellerfeld to Hahnenklee. For three miles I noticed that the roads were more numerous off the main highway and that the highway itself was much improved and widened. Along some lengths of the highway there were designated turn-outs to allow traffic to pass slower-moving vehicles. There also were painted white lines running along the shoulders which seemed too narrow to designate bicycle lanes or walking paths. There were many new buildings, especially gästehauses and restaurants, near the entrances to these newer roads and expanded communities. Only a mile from Hahnenklee I recognized Bocksweise, the hamlet with one hotel and one restaurant and one exceptionally unique ice-bath spa open to the public and free of charge. It is called the "Am Wassertretbecken" (at the water pool). Here hikers remove their walking shoes and socks and step into a tiled, shoulder-width culvert through which runs freezing water from a source deep underground in the mountains. The sensation at the feet and ankles is like stepping on to dry ice. All feeling is lost immediately and the shock rockets through the calve muscles to the knees. Walking settles the sensation. There are hand rails at both sides of the culvert to make walking safer and faster. Stepping out and drying off gives the feeling that a person has had his legs exchanged with those of a teenage athlete. The weight of the walking shoes is undetectable for 15 to 20 minutes. The small area is decorated with carved wooden name plaques, such as "BOCKSWEISE" and "FOR THE BATHING OF FEET," and wooden sculptures of mushrooms, love totems, and curiosities. I do not know how the water source was discovered or why the culvert and comfort area were created. But it obviously is maintained as not only a respite for the hikers but also as an attraction for the tourists. Everyone whom I have met and who had endured the experience was thrilled with having tried.

I knew the route from Bocksweise into Hahnenklee as only one or two trails which would lead to the main street along the Kranicher Teich (Crane Pond) and park area near which I knew there had been several hotels and gästehauses. There, in an ideal location and at an incredibly reasonable daily rate, I secured a single room at Parkstraße 12 in the wonderfully charming Blackcoms Erika, owned, managed, and operated by hoteliers Marion and Ralph Schwartz. I did not know this hotel and caféhaus, but future events would prove that I was blessed by my choice.

I had assumed from the expansion and growth which I had seen in the other towns and villages of the Harz that Hahnenklee would be no different. I was right in some respects and wrong in others. Some existing hotels had been bought by large corporations and expanded. Some smaller hotels had changed ownership with varying degrees of success or failure. Some hotels had transitioned to time share properties or condominiums. What I learned from the local merchants was that the reunification of Germany in 1990 had placed a tremendous financial burden on the formerly-prosperous business owners when taxes skyrocketed to support the reunification. The former East Germany had little to offer financially. Taxes were raised to upgrade the infrastructure and to improve the standard of living for the West's former countrymen who had been separated only as a result of the post-war realignment of Europe. These taxes were passed to hotel guests and tourists who subsequently reduced the number and the length of their visits or stopped visiting completely. I noticed that the prices for everything which I needed, such as lodging, food, and incidentals, were as expensive in Hahnenklee as they had been in Paris.

At the reception office, Marion had given me the keys to three single rooms and told me to select the one which I preferred. All were more than sufficient for my needs, especially after the routine of camping. I selected the simplest to defer to other, possibly more demanding, future guests. The second-floor room had two windows with views toward the lake and the town.

Temperatures were cool and comfortable. There were no issues with insects, and I kept the windows open. Opposite the single bed was a wall unit with space to hang my trousers, shirts, and windbreaker, and shelves to sort my other clothing and equipment. In the sitting area was an overstuffed chair and an end table on which I placed my maps, guides, and notebook. I was ready for a short nap, but I slept soundly for almost two hours.

After a shower I dressed in clean jeans and a short-sleeved shirt with a collar, then left the hotel to reacquaint myself with Hahnenklee and its surroundings after a 40-year absence. Around the corner from my hotel was a huge sterile Ramada with a formal staff and all of the amenities of a hotel in a large city and none of the charm of the smaller, privately-owned hotels and gästehauses for which Hahnenklee is famous. Next to it was an Italian restaurant and pizzeria with an outdoor ice cream stand. It was owned by Arabs from North Africa who also were the waiters, bartenders, cooks, and dishwashers, and all of whom were dark-haired, bearded men. Respect for the country which had provided them a new homeland and an appreciation for their improved quality of life seemed to me to be factors which would justify the employment of a German worker. I'd withhold my business until I saw someone, male or female, with blond hair, blue eyes, and not in need of a shave, waiting tables or serving ice cream cones.

Down the street was the pedestrian-only area which I remembered, but now was expanded with additional tourist attractions, shops, restaurants and pubs. A modern sports shop, which sold and rented a variety of gear for walkers, hikers, cyclists, swimmers, and skiers was full with tourists. In the bright sunshine, at an outdoor café, I nursed a Hasseröder bier while I studied a map of the town and read the guides which Marion had provided me. Today, in the afternoon, I wanted only to walk away from the shops and tourists and get lost down the rural side streets where I knew I would find another less crowded and less noisy outdoor pub, and continue reading. I found the police station, which was a single-family home with a small sign, "POLIZEI" attached to the wooden letter-box in front, the new-and-improved Tourist Office and library, a Catholic church, and the grocery store. On the trail to one of the large lakes I found another café and stopped, this time for coffee and cake.

At the lake, the swimming facility had been expanded to include a guarded swimming area 50 yards long, a unisex locker room with private cabinets for changing and storing clothes, separate bathrooms with hot shower facilities, and a restaurant which provided daily food specials for take out to the tables or grounds. Curry wurst with pommes frites was the most popular snack. There also were canoe, row boats, and paddle boats for rent. Within my daily, night-touring, mini-backpack I had stuffed a pair of gym shorts in addition to my sunglasses, reading glasses, notebook, pen, maps, guides, spare T-shirt, and a washcloth. In the locker room I changed, secured the backpack in a locker, and then swam free-style across the lake in what must have been record time in order to keep warm. When I came out of the water shivering and unable to uncup my hands, the veteran Schwimmen-Master met me and, smiling, told me that the water temperature was only 68 degrees.

"Du bist ein sehr mutig und ein sehr schneller Schwimmer." ("You are a very brave and a very fast swimmer.")

I stayed longer than usual in the shower slowly making the water temperature hotter and hotter trying to restore my body temperature. The fast-paced mile walk back to the hotel was invigorating. In my room I stripped to my briefs and took a second nap, this time only for about 30 minutes after which I rose and annotated my notebook for the day. At 8 p.m. I took a short walk to the town center and ate dinner outdoors at a restaurant with the sun setting over the natural beauty of the Harz. I ate heartily and drank two glasses of red wine, my preferred beverage at dinner when I truly can relax. With the aid of my notebook and the landkarte for Hahnenklee I planned the day for Thursday, July 24th.

After dinner, I walked in isolation along the trails leading to the ski lift summit and then back to the hotel. I heard birds, but saw none. Only a couple of squirrels crossed my path during the walk home. By 10 p.m., when the sun had set, I was in bed expecting to get a good night's rest for a full day of touring after breakfast.

The excellent food served by Marion and Ralph and the view from the hotel made that morning my best to date. From my booth I could see the lake with the ducks and waterfowl crisscrossing paths on the water as they moved and munched. Early morning strollers paused to watch their antics; some stopped to feed them. Huge carp raced to snatch the pieces of bread and spooked the ducks into short-distance flights when the fish bumped their bottoms and flat, webbed feet. The joggers and cyclists skirted the strollers, detouring off the walking paths. Over the lake and across the park gardens, dark slow-moving clouds were forming. My experience in the Harz was that there was a 50-50 chance for rain.

On the table there was a pot of coffee in Bavarian china kept hot over a ceramic sterno warmer, a glass of fresh-squeezed orange juice, a soft boiled egg, a plate of cheese slices and meats, a dish of fruit, and a basket with two hard rolls, jam and butter. Marion came to the table, and I complimented her on the breakfast which she had prepared. She told me that she was a vegetarian but provided breakfast meats for the guests because, "In Germany, it is expected to serve meat."

She told me that the hotel was fairly full and asked if I had been disturbed by any of the other guests. I told her, "No," and she added that, when the hotel was built, the rooms had been designed intentionally to provide space for peace and privacy. In response to her question about what my plans were for the day, I told her weather permitting, I hoped to ride a cable car up the mountain then walk down along the network of trails and have lunch in the town center. After lunch I wanted to find a different trail to the lake for a second swim and, on the way back, visit the market to buy some personal hygiene items which I needed. Regardless of the weather, in the evening I planned to visit another restaurant which offered a view of the parks and gardens. Marion told me that she thought it would rain but probably not the entire day. We parted company when other guests arriving for breakfast required her attention. As a snack for after the swim I made a ham and cheese sandwich slopping on some jam for flavor.

From my room I retrieved the day pack and my reliable collapsible umbrella and walked only 200 yards to the town center. The lift was not yet open. I wandered down a logging trail and discovered a small apartment complex where it appeared that guest workers and their families lived. Nothing about the area looked German. There were no gardens or boxes of flowers; trash was everywhere; car panels were rusted; children's bicycles and toys were in disrepair; inoperable televisions and other electronic items were scattered near the woods behind the buildings. Certainly it was better for tourism that this area was concealed from the public.

Back at the lift, I paid $2. for a one-way trip to the top of the mountain. For about 10 minutes I had a panoramic view of almost all of Hahnenklee and the expanse of this Harz area. At the top, there were several trails on which to hike, color-coded by their lengths and degrees of difficulty for walking. The trails were mostly natural. Very few trees had been sacrificed to create the paths. The width of the trails varied frequently; the ground was rugged and uneven. Common sense and good judgment suggested a slower rather than a faster pace with attention to tree roots, protruding rocks, and slippery ferns to prevent falling. Some sections of the trails were treacherous enough to justify the construction of wooden, concrete-based handrails for safety. Walking uphill was less dangerous. The naturally slower pace invited more observations.

Along the trails, I had stopped by the ponds to watch the waterfowl and fish along the edges and by the fields hoping to see deer, wild pigs or birds of prey circling overhead. I saw only squirrels, mostly grey with small, round ears, others, large and puffy, and a small number of reddish-brown critters which were less skittish than their grey cousins. In one area which formed a fire break between the town and the forest, there was a group of teenagers racing motorbikes up and down the slopes. Three hours later, I was back at town.

In town, the pavement was damp, but no one was using an umbrella. If it had rained when I was on the trails, I could not detect it because of the thickness of the trees. Shy of noon the temperature was only 70 degrees. Most of the older tourists were wearing jackets or sweaters. At the restaurants and cafes with outdoor eating areas, the tables were set for service. There always were far more tables inside. I decided to eat a light lunch after which I would return to the hotel for my swimsuit and then hike to the lake.

Outside, the tables were fairly close together. I could hear only German spoken. I had been in Hahnenklee a full day and only now realized that I had not heard any English or seen any other Americans. Hahnenklee is a Kur-Stadt, a town where people come to regain, improve, or enhance their health and their physical fitness. In a Kur-Stadt, health and fitness are the focus, and walking is the primary means of transportation. There is not a single drive-through fast-food restaurant.

The sun broke out during lunch. I ate slowly. After lunch I was eager to hike to the lake for a second, longer swim. At the lake there were only about 30 visitors, mostly older couples and two or three young families. The children seemed unbothered by the cold water. Wearing small plastic floats on their arms, they were running in and out of the water carrying water guns, toys, plastic pails, and floats. They left the water only if their parents called them or if they wanted something to eat. I swam 200 yards within the protected area, ducked under the plastic lane markers and border barrier and swam another 200 yards across the width of the lake. I felt as if I was warming up as I returned and stopped near the ladder to exit near where I had entered. The sun was shining when I went into the locker room for a hot shower. When I finished it was raining lightly. At a table with an overhead umbrella, I drank a cup of black coffee and ate the sandwich that I had prepared at breakfast.

I hiked back in light rain shirtless through the forest and put on my dry T-shirt as I broke out into town three short blocks from the market. The corner market was about the size of a 7-Eleven. At the entrance was a small sitting area and a bakery on one half of only four aisles. The first aisle had breads, cheeses, fruits, energy bars, and candy. The second aisle had canned goods, boxed products such as cereals and snacks, and home essentials such as batteries and light bulbs. On the north side of the third aisle were detergents, bleaches, polishes, gloves, sponges, and mops for cleaning anything inanimate and non-human, (homes, cars, bicycles, sporting goods, and pets). On the south side of the same aisle was almost everything for personal hygiene and home health. I noticed that the products were stocked in alignment with the body. At the top shelf were products for the head, including hair colorings, hair sprays, brushes, combs, shower caps, bathing caps, sunglasses, curlers, and a lot more stuff which must be for women since it was unrecognizable to me.

The next shelf had products for the face, eyes, ears, nose, and mouth, and over-the-counter medications and vitamins. Below that were products for the torso and limbs such as body lotions, soaps, creams, sunscreen, and nail polishes. It was on this shelf that the differences between the sexes were obvious. Except for soap and sunscreen, there was nothing on this shelf that I recognized and used.

On the bottom shelf was everything for young children and babies.

The last aisle was stocked on one side with beer and wine, and on the other side with bottled water, soda, soft drinks, and juices. Along the back wall were all the fresh products: fruits, vegetables, spices, dairy, meats, fish, and flowers. After I made the tour I returned to the third aisle. From the second shelf I took a small bottle of ibuprofen, a tube of toothpaste and a large container of contact lens solution. I assumed that I was purchasing a generic brand. Different brand names of other smaller containers cost five euros, ($7.), for only three fluid ounces. The brand I selected cost four euros, ($6.), for nine fluid ounces. I was buying three times as much solution for a dollar less.

It turned out for me to be not so good a deal.

From the market I walked roughly 300 yards in light rain back to the hotel, climbed the stairs to my room, put down my gear and took a nap. It still was raining slightly when I awoke and continued to rain while I was in the shower. At the sink I shaved and then opened the newly-purchased container of what I thought was contact lens solution, removed the bottle, placed a drop of solution on the lens for my right eye, and inserted it.

I immediately felt as if I had pointed a lit blow torch at my right eye.

The italicized text which follows is an excerpt from a message, (with all the spelling and grammatical errors), that I sent to my family and friends three days later from a computer at the desk in the office of a finance and accounting clerk at a hospital in Braunschweig, 40 miles away to the north:

I went back to the gastehaus and took a shower. Then I cleaned my contact lens with the new solution and inserted the lens. My eye was on fire and I could not extract the lens. I went back into the shower and got out the lens but I could not see. It turns out that I did not by contact lens solution but bought acid to add to laundry to kill head lice. My hotelmeister has determined that ut was stocked incorrectlon. But I saw it next to other cntact lense solutions brands and it had a picture of a smiling face with words , wasche and rinse. So I am blind now in my right eye whch, after four days in the emergency eye klinikum in Braunschweig still will not open without^the aid of pain medication and a cold water bath. The hospital s taff woked on my eve everz minute for the first 12 hours then everz 15 minutes for the next 12 hours then everz hour for the next 2 days but the sight is gone for now. I lost almost all my let eye and left ear hearing from the head trauma incidentin San Francisco in 1987. Now I cnnot contiue this TREK. My hotelmeister will keep me at her hme until I have enough sight in the left eye ´- which for some reason does nt want to open ´to change flights and return to the USA probably within the next 2 weeks. It has taken me 8 hours to type this. I am so soory that I made so stupid an error which has compromised me and this project and which must be a disappointment for you also. Jakob"

(Jakob is the German name for James.)

I needed emergency medical attention immediately. I had undressed at the bedside and fumbled to find my briefs, jeans, T-shirt, socks, and shoes. With a cold wet washcloth on my eye, I felt my way to the door, down the stairs, and into the office where I called for Marion. Fortunately for me she was in the back and reacted immediately after I told her what had happened. She consulted with her husband Ralph.

While he was calling the closest doctor in a town 12 miles away, she led me outside, down another set of stairs, and to the family car. Marion was very sympathetic constantly reassuring me that everything would be fine. I knew that I was riding in an automobile made in Germany especially for these sorts of roads and road conditions. But given the speed that Marion was negotiating the S-turns, curves, and construction detours, I began to wonder in what kind of vehicle we would arrive at a clinic or a hospital and if it would be me and my eye that would require attention or both of us and our broken bones and mangled bodies.

The doctor was waiting for us when we arrived at his clinic in Clausthal-Zellerfeld. Marion walked me from her car up the stairs into his office. We followed the doctor to an examination room.

In English, he asked me to explain the circumstances of the accident, which I did, while he read the information from the box which had contained the solution to kill hair lice. He spoke English exceptionally well, and I had no problem understanding his instructions. I had great difficulty complying with them however. Neither of my eyes would open. After a few minutes of trying to relax I was able to open my left eye well enough to see the machine on which he told me to place my chin and lean my forehead inward. But I could not open the right eye even when he tried to lift the eyelid with his fingers and some sort of instrument which I could not see.

"I am going to try to put some drops in your eye which will help it to open. It will sting at first then your eye should open easily. This will work for only 10 or 15 minutes then the pain will return. Please listen closely and do as I ask."

The doctor put the drops in my eye and for a few seconds the sensation felt as if he had added more acid. Then I relaxed and felt as euphoric as if I had been partying with Janis Joplin and John Belushi. I think I remember seeing the doctor opposite the machine and Marion standing next to him. The examination was over very quickly. I understood his German well enough to hear him tell Marion that he could not do anything for me, and that I had to go immediately to the Klinikum Braunschweig where there were specialists in a medical unit dedicated to eye illnesses and injuries. I heard Marion say that she knew the location of the hospital and would drive me there immediately. The doctor told her that he would call ahead and alert the appropriate personnel. We thanked him and left as the medication began to wear off and the pain returned.

Back in the car, sweet Marion told me in English much of what I thought I had understood the doctor told her in German. Again, she assured me that everything would be fine. She added that Braunschweig was 40 miles away and that we would need to make a quick stop to buy fuel. That was fine with me.

I sensed the car move from the parking spot then race away. I also felt the car slow, turn, and stop, and I heard Marion tell me to wait and that she would be right back. I heard the click of the fuel flap and the bang of the nozzle as it was inserted into the cylinder to the gas tank. Then I heard the rattle of the nozzle as it was removed. Marion came back into the car and we were off.

"Here, Jim. Drink this. It should help you with the pain."

I felt something cold and hard on my left kneecap. My hand grasped a cold bottle. Marion told me it was a Harzer beer fresh from the cooler. When I finished the first there were two more. Before I took my first swig I asked if it was legal to have an open container of alcohol in the front seat of a moving vehicle.

"Oh, sure. As long as the driver is not the person doing the drinking. Anyone but the driver, then that is okay."

Fine by me. That was the tastiest pain medication I had ever been given. I finished the third Harzer as Marion parked the car somewhere at the Klinikum. There was not an appreciable effect on the pain, but my concern about my status had diminished. With typical German efficiency, we were met at the hospital entrance then guided through a maze of ground-floor hallways to an elevator, up four floors, then down two more hallways to the medical ward.

Several of the attending staff met us. I could hear voices of both sexes speaking with Marion. Relatively quickly someone took me by my wrist and forearm and led me to a hospital bed where I was told to sit. I had enough experience as a trauma patient in hospitals that I knew to ask to detour first to the restroom. Once I was in bed and the staff started their work with me, I did not want to interrupt the process with Marion's mobile medications moving at my bladder.

Seated on the bed, my sneakers and socks were removed, and I was pivoted to my left as my legs were raised onto the bed. I was covered with a sheet and light blanket. There were at least four people at my bedside. All of the voices were female. One team to my left cleaned my forearm and hand and started one or two IV's. Another team to my right began some kind of flush for my eye.

I felt a very slow flow of room-temperature liquid pass over my closed right eye. I think that whoever was conducting this procedure was ever so gently touching and trying to move or open my eyelid to allow better access of the fluid to my eye. I felt her finger first at the top of my cheek pulling down to create an opening, then at the left to expand the cavity where sinus fluids collect, at the top which still seemed firmly shut, and last at the right with two fingers to open the lid at the top and bottom. She continued the effort in the same clockwise routine.

Directly beside her was a second nurse holding a metal pan with her right hand flush below my jaw and against my neck to catch the fluid which was running over and into my eye, across my cheek and face, and into the pan. Occasionally, I felt her pet the top and back of my head and the sides of my cheeks with her left hand. Every so often I sensed a pause in the irrigating and heard the sound of the fluid being spilled into a bucket. It is only speculation, but I think that this two or three-person duty was rotated with one or more teams of nurses throughout the procedure. The sound of the voices beside me were different and then, after a while more familiar again.

There were intermittent pauses when the plastic bag of irrigating fluid ran dry and had to be replaced, and whenever someone came in and exchanged information.

The events of the day and the effect of the pain medication in the IV and in the flush fluid, if there were any, made me drowsy. At some time during all this Marion, said goodbye to me as she squeezed my shoulder and rubbed my upper arm. I remember hearing her tell me that she would return the next day after she finished her work at the hotel.

My next awareness of anything happening around me must have been early the next morning, a Friday. A nurse still was irrigating my eye and a second nurse still was catching the runoff. But now I was able to open the injured eye and see them. When I greeted them and said, "I can see you," they immediately stopped the process and summoned additional staff.

In response to several questions from another woman, who may have been a doctor or another nurse, I said that I was able to open my eye only slightly but not completely. Looking toward bright light was almost impossible. I was able to distinguish between light and dark objects in the room. I could make out the figures of the three women beside me, but could not describe their hair color or facial features. Even their physical images were a blur and a blend between the white color of the nurses' caps and their hair and the hospital scrubs and their arms and hands. I said that I was not hungry and did not need to use the restroom; however, I was very warm and asked to have the blanket removed or permission to extend my arm with the IV infusion to reach down and remove my jeans. One nurse helped me to shed my jeans. Another changed the blanket, bed sheet, wet pillowcase, and pillow.

Time passed quickly. The eye-irrigation procedure was now only once an hour for 15 minutes. The IV continued. It must have contained primarily pain medication. It no longer hurt as much to try to open the eye as it did to look toward the light.

When the nurses were away from the bedside, I pulled the sheet and blanket over my head to make it dark then looked at my hands and fingers separately with each eye then with both eyes. I got a different view with each of the three efforts, which concerned me, and which I described to the nurses when they returned.

Around 5 p.m., I was given a dinner tray with juice, two slices of black bread, slices of cheese and processed meat, and a dish of diced fresh fruit. Although I did not feel hungry, I ate and drank everything quickly. I stopped eating when another nurse entered the room to give me a status report.

After asking how I felt, she told me that Marion had called and would return this second night between nine and ten. She would bring anything that I thought I needed. I asked for only a fresh T-shirt, briefs, toothbrush, and toothpaste. She explained that my eye had been injured badly. The team was trying to counter the effects of the acid after studying the product information from the hair lice packet. The solution in the irrigation bags was a mixture of base fluids and chemicals to counteract the acid.

She said that she thought my progress to date was better than expected. The flush would continue for a second full day, and I again would be evaluated. If everything continued to progress, on Saturday, the third day, the IV would be stopped. I would have an eye examination on the ward, and reevaluated.

On Sunday, with continued improvement, she said I would have a final evaluation to determine if I could be discharged for outpatient care. The nurse said that Marion had the same information.

What a remarkable heath care system! Strangers and medical professionals were working together to help me without any concern for my signature on a single piece of paper authorizing any care or access to information. In two days of extensive treatment, no one had asked for any identification or said word one about payment. Wake up, America!

For a second day, Marion made the 80-mile round-trip drive to the hospital to visit me after having started her day at 5 a.m. to prepare breakfast for her hotel guests and ending it after 7 p.m. when the outdoor café closed. Ralph managed everything about the business during her absence. This night was a kick for me. Marion was exuberant even after having worked a full day and driven 40-plus miles.

She told me that I was a changed person after only 24 hours: my eyes were open, a pleasant pallor had returned to my face, and I was smiling. She had stopped at the nurses' station before she came to my room and repeated much of the same information I had been told earlier. The only detail she added was that the evaluation and discharge processes might move slower because of the reduced staff on the weekends.

I continued to be surprised that Marion would drive 80 miles for only a 30-minute visit to check on me. She left close to 10 p.m., saying that she would return on Saturday after she had finished her work at the hotel.

I fell asleep almost immediately after she left. I awoke when the nursing staff alerted me to the start of another eye flush which I assumed was about 15 minutes every two or three hours. One of the nurses brought a tray with my breakfast and pills in a paper cup and placed it on a small table in the room. She removed the IV in my left arm and cleaned it, and told me that the irrigation procedures would be discontinued if my evaluation later in the morning justified the termination. She guided me to the door of the restroom then from there to the table for breakfast. She cautioned me not to move from the table without assistance.

The breakfast was excellent and I felt full when I finished. I counted four pills then swallowed them.

While I waited to be escorted to the bed, I looked around the room. The wall unit had three lockers but I could not see the doors or door handles. The ceiling had removable paneling, but I could not see the separations. I could not detect the seam between the wall and ceiling. The floor color changed depending on how much light was in the area. All the views looked different when I used only my left eye (strongest and clearest), then my right eye (weakest and most blurred), then both eyes (constantly changing images).

I expected the examination and evaluation in the morning. It was not until after lunch, served again at the table. A nurse asked me to walk with her to an examination room. She gave me permission and accompanied me to the restroom to wash my face and blot my eyes before we left. A doctor and nurse were in the examination room. Everyone spoke English. I did not remember seeing or speaking before with this doctor. As he started the examination, he asked me to explain the circumstances of the accident. In German, he reviewed the care I had been provided although everyone spoke too quickly and too technically for me to understand very much. There was a clock in the room which I could see and read. The examination took almost two hours using two machines and the normal eye chart. I was compliant with all of the doctor's instructions and spooked only when he added drops to my right eye. The doctor told me that the damage had been contained and that the eye was showing signs of healing. He said that I would remain in the hospital at least another 24 hours after which I would receive another examination and evaluation.

As I had heard earlier, there was a strong chance that I could be discharged to outpatient care midday on Sunday. Everything I heard was very good news for me.

The nurse escorted me back to the bed. She told me that a nurses' aide would visit later to help me practice walking unassisted for short walks from the bed to the restroom and to the dining facility where coffee, drinks, fruit, and cookies always were available. I was unusually tired for this time of day, having done nothing but sleep, eat breakfast, and sit through an examination. I concluded that my condition was a result of the injury, the treatment, the medications, and the body's natural healing processes which had slowed down certain systems for resources to repair the damage to my eye. I fell asleep and was awakened by the nurses' aide.

Angelika was a nursing student during the week and an aide at the Klinikum on the weekends rotating among the various clinics and wards wherever the need was the greatest. She would walk with me and then provide the staff her evaluation of my ability to walk unassisted. She told me that the longer I walked with activities such as recognizing persons and obstacles in the hallways, opening doors, turning corners, and climbing stairs the easier it would be to provide an evaluation.

I told her that I was willing to do everything she described. We walked for about an hour. During the walk, I occasionally closed my left eye to determine how well I could see with only my right eye. That was not a good idea. At much greater distances than the short spaces within my room everything was a blur, and I was not able to distinguish objects and colors, moving or fixed. Angelika gave me a favorable evaluation and told me that she would inform the nurses at the station. One of them would instruct me further on the frequency and limits of my walks.

I slept uninterrupted until one of the nurses woke me to tell me that my dinner tray had arrived. I could eat either in the room or in the dining facility. While we walked together down the hall, she told me that I had no restrictions on walking except to inform someone at the nurses' station when I departed and how long I expected to be gone. She told me that the hospital had several outdoor gardens, a gift shop, chapel, and a lending library all of which I was free to explore. After dinner, I told the staff that I wanted to walk to the see the gardens and locate the chapel. There might be an opportunity to attend a Sunday morning service the next day. I said that I would be back within an hour. It was 6 p.m. I did not expect Marion for another three or four hours.

Exploring was more difficult than I expected. I kept to the right while walking. Crossing an intersection of two hallways, I focused to the left on a couple with young children and did not see peripherally another couple coming toward me from the right. I walked into the woman then apologized in German saying, "I have a problem with my eye."

At the library, I found a small guide book for the Harz region. There were pictures and, if I took some extra time to focus, I could read the text. After the library visit, I found one of the gardens and sat alone on a bench. There may have been four more hours of daylight, but the difference in light between indoors and outdoors was startling. Everything was more of a blur. With both eyes open I could not read anything in the guide book or make out anything in the pictures. If I used only my right eye, the pages and pictures were black. With only my left eye, I could see almost normally. I am sure that the garden had a colorful mix of seasonal flowers and green boxwood hedges as borders, but, to me, it was all one swirl of mostly dark colors resembling any one of my paintings in kindergarten that Miss Kenny took one look at then put in the trash and not on the wall. That was alright with me. I wanted to be a fireman and not a painter.

Back in the room I sat at the small table and tried to process what I had learned from this walking tour. The more objective and honest I was with myself the more I was convinced that I could not continue "The TREK."

If I were to be discharged to outpatient status, what would my future medical requirements be? How long would it take before I could see clearly outside, especially in the bright sun at high noon? How would I be able to navigate and walk when the pavement, curb, and sidewalk all appeared as one color? How could I differentiate among them? How much longer would a 15-mile walk each day take? How would the weather, camping, and attending to washing and hygiene affect the healing process for my eye with greater exposure to dirt and debris? How would these sorts of concerns affect my motivation?

Like Scarlett O'Hara in *"Gone with the Wind,"* I wouldn't think about it just now. "Tomorrow is another day."

Although I wanted to stay awake and alert until Marion arrived, there was not much that I was able to do. I assumed that the less stress and more rest I gave my eye the better it would be for the healing process. Until the next examination and evaluation in 18 hours, I would rest in bed with my eyes closed for as long as I was able to endure the boredom. Marion arrived with fruit and a box of cookies, and my hairbrush which I forgot to include when I had asked for the toothbrush and toothpaste. She had been a bit longer at the nurses' station where she provided her contact information and attempted to understand and coordinate the sequence of events which could result in my discharge. The news was that she was planning to host me in my outpatient status because the staff was trying to locate and schedule my outpatient appointment with a doctor in or around Hahnenklee and not in Braunschweig. Also, her address at the hotel would serve to receive mail from the hospital about the hospitalization, medical records, outpatient instructions, and billing if I were not contacted by anyone on Sunday which seemed highly unlikely to both of us. Marion continued to encourage me and exaggerate how well the doctors said that I was doing. Ralph was prepared to accept the workload any time on Sunday if she were called to collect me. I had proposed going by taxi, but she insisted that the fare for the 40-mile trip would be prohibitive and that she wanted to be on hand to understand the discharge instructions.

After Marion left, a nurse entered carrying a tray containing a paper cup with two pills and a glass of water. After I took the pills she told me that one pill was for pain and to help the eye heal; the second pill was to help me sleep. Certainly I did not need the second pill. At age 63, it was the first time in my life that I had taken anything to help me sleep. Another first.

Surprisingly, Sunday morning was slightly hectic for me. I awoke to the sound of voices in the hallway. The meal cart was in motion and breakfast was being delivered to the patients. After washing my face and brushing my hair, I found a tray with my name on it "PELOZ" and brought to the dining room. I took a seat at a table with several other patients all of whom had remained overnight following cataract surgery. I was the only person in the room without a patch over one eye. I poured myself a cup of coffee and then asked around where I saw empty or half-full cups if anyone wanted another hit. Only one woman accepted. My gesture was not usually demonstrated among strangers in Germany.

I had enough time after breakfast to return to my room, brush my teeth, notify the nurses' station, and depart for the chapel. Mass was to start in 10 minutes. I felt as if I needed every minute to keep the Creator on the team and working to help heal my eye. Perhaps because I looked healthier than most of the 14 other attendees, the priest asked me to do the readings. In my best German, I told him that I was an American and could not read German very well. In English, I added, "I'm sorry."

The Mass was formal, but the frequent activities of standing, sitting, and kneeling, (designed, I'm sure, to keep everyone awake), were waived. Everyone remained seated. The sermon was short. The comments which I could understand had to do with loving life, bearing crosses, avoiding anger, and keeping the faith.

At the nurses' station where I reported my return my primary care nurse, Head Nurse Rienster, told me that my appointment with the doctor would be in 30 minutes at 10 a.m. She would meet me in my room and escort me to the examination room. In Germany, when something is scheduled to happen at 10 a.m. it happens at 10 a.m. A different doctor introduced himself and his assistant to me and asked me to describe how I injured my eye. I had told the story so many times that I did not leave out a single detail. In response to his question about my present status, I told him that I felt healthy, that I thought my eye was healing, that there was no pain except when the eye was exposed to direct light, and that I had three spectra of vision depending upon which eye or both eyes I was using to see.

"Please take a seat," he told me.

I read the eye chart, almost perfectly with my left eye and both eyes, but not at all with my right eye. I could not even see the huge "E" which I knew was at the top of the chart.

The examination routine seemed identical to that of the day before, including the application of eye drops and the sequence of events at both machines for almost two hours. But, at the conclusion, I was happy to hear that the results were better than they were at the first examination, that the eye was healing, that no further treatment was necessary from the hospital, and that I should expect to be discharged later in the day. The doctor asked if

I had any questions and I replied, "No. Thank you. Thank you for your time with me this morning."

On her way out of the examination room, Head Nurse Rienster told me that my lunch was ready, and that she would alert Marion as to my status for discharge later in the day. While I was eating, Head Nurse Rienster came and sat beside me. My discharge would be effective at 6 p.m. Marion was expected to arrive about 8 p.m. The hospital would provide dinner for me. I could wait wherever I wanted, but if I left the ward, then I still was required to inform someone at the nurses' station. I told her that I had not had a shower in more than three days and asked if I could shower in my room adding that I would feel safer showering here than at the hotel. Head Nurse Rienster approved. She told me to adjust the water temperature before I entered the shower, to lather my hair with my head leaning back toward the shower head so no soap could come near my eye, not to use any soap on my face, and to use a soft hand towel to gently pat my face dry.

It was not only my body which required a good washing. I had worn my T-shirt for four straight days. I had saved the clean one which Marion had brought me for the day that I would be discharged. My briefs had two days' wear. I had the room to myself and a set of high quality German windows facing south and the sun at midday. One set of windows, four feet high and two feet wide, were installed the length of one side of the room at four feet from the floor and above a broad wooden counter.

They opened to the inside of the room similar to a door by turning the handle and pulling. Above them was a second series of windows, only two feet high and also two feet wide. They opened differently. After turning a handle they canted open to the inside laterally the width of the window. In this way fresh air, but not rain, snow or debris, could enter. The four-foot counter, four-foot vertical windows and two-foot horizontal windows formed one side of the room with 10-foot ceilings.

My plan was to take all my worn clothing, except for my jeans, into the shower with me and wash them. I had done this a few times before in hotel rooms, showering and washing my clothes and hanging them to dry in the room. Then I would climb on to the counter, open and hold the frames of the lower vertical windows for balance and safety, then open the upper lateral windows and drape my clothes from them. There would be at least six hours before Marion would arrive and plenty of time for the clothes to dry using Mother Nature's natural blow-dry process.

At least that was my plan.

The shower felt wonderful. I kept a washcloth at my face and was unaffected by the water passing over my head and hair and into my eyes. I did not lather my hair but soaped and scrubbed all of me from the neck down. I washed and rinsed my T-shirt, briefs and socks. I used the metal safety grab bar to wring out my clothing, exited the shower, and dried myself using a bath towel for my body and gently patting my face and eyes with the soft hand towel as Head Nurse Rienster had instructed.

Dressed in only my jeans, I collected my washed clothing and came out into the room and opened two of the tall, lower vertical windows. I moved a chair in front of one of the opened windows and used it as a platform to stand on the counter and open the two upper lateral windows. I stepped down, retrieved my clothing, and began hanging my one pair of socks, two pairs of briefs, and one T-shirt.

From out of nowhere I heard a blood-curdling scream and turned, half naked and barefoot, to face Head Nurse Rienster. In as loud a whisper as she could manage using words interrupted by protracted labored breathing, Head Nurse Reinster was slowly tiptoeing toward me with her arms flexed forward and her fingers spread widely gesturing as if she were patting the air much like a conductor, calmly signaling his orchestra for a slower tempo and gentler sound.

"Herr Pelosi. Bitte nicht aus dem Fenster springen."

("Mister Pelosi. Please do not jump from the window.")

Still on the counter and securely inside the room I answered,

"Krankenschwester Rienster. Ich lege nur meine Wäsche trocknen. Ich bin nicht aus dem Fenster springen."

("Nurse Rienster. I only am hanging my laundry to dry. I'm not jumping out the window.")

But, clearly, she was in shock. She kept tiptoeing toward me, gesturing and imploring me not to jump even when I was standing next to her beside my bed. It had not occurred to me that her screams upon seeing me at the window ledge had alerted other members of the staff.

Into the room raced two nurses carrying a deflated fire hose which they proceeded to wrap around my hips, waist and lower chest and tie in a knot (minus a bow).

After them came more nurses, hospital security personnel, two uniformed firemen minus their helmets and fire axes, some orderlies, folks from the cleaning crew, and even the priest who had said Mass that morning.

While I remained bound and fixed by the bed watching the room fill to capacity I did not notice that Head Nurse Rienster had collapsed on my bed where she was fanning her face with one hand and sipping water with the other. Throughout all the chaos which continued for at least half an hour, all I could think was, "Is any of this going to affect my discharge?"

Head Nurse Rienster was unable to convey any information. In English and my best German I explained what I had done from the time I washed my clothes in the shower until Head Nurse Rienster saw me standing on the window ledge and hanging the laundry by the open windows. After the room had emptied, two nurses stayed behind to comfort Head Nurse Reinster, still prone on my bed. They told me that the eye clinic shares the floor with the terminal cancer ward. Three years prior, Nurse Reinster was on duty, again as Head Nurse, when one of the cancer patients sneaked out from his room and came into this same room, where he opened the same window where I had been standing, and jumped to his death. They knew this tragic story because Head Nurse Rienster had just completed two years of Post-Traumatic Stress Disorder counseling mandated by the hospital as a result of her experience. After they explained that she might have to be re-enrolled not two weeks after she just finished the counseling, one of them asked me, "Are you sure someone is coming to get you?"

"I hope so. And the sooner the better."

When Marion arrived, I was standing still shirtless and barefoot next to Head Nurse Rienster immobile on the bed, holding her hand and petting it. It's hard to describe the look on Marion's face after she called, "Jim?" and I turned to look at her.

I told her the story as we drove away toward the hotel. We laughed all the way home.

When we arrived at the hotel, Ralph was waiting for us. Although it was close to 11 p.m., he had set three places with a dish of home-made torts for each of us. We sat together while I listened to Marion tell Ralph the story of Head Nurse Rienster. We spoke briefly, mostly about what my plans might be for the future. Marion told me that I could keep my room for as long as I needed it, and I asked that she extend me for one week. I thanked them for everything and excused myself to go to bed. Marion told me to get the extra sleep I might need and come to breakfast whenever I wanted. I told her that I always am awake early and should be at breakfast at eight.

My room was exactly as I had left it. Marion did not rearrange any of the mess that I had made stumbling and rushing to get out of the room for help four days earlier. Even the bottle of hair lice acid still was on the sink. Most people who have spent time in a hospital know that it is not a place to get much sleep with interruptions for doctor visits, medications, and health status checks. My sleep was undisturbed until I awoke just before seven.

At breakfast, Marion made several stops to my table. With each visit she told me something new about my outpatient status. Later this day, Detlev and Ilona Gebhard, my friends of 30 years from Berlin, would visit. They would stay the night. The next morning they would take me to a 9 a.m. appointment with an eye specialist in Osterode am Harz, near the town where Marion had rushed me after the accident. The hospital had called and asked for an address for me in the States. Marion assumed it concerned the bill. I told her that I would make sure that the bill was paid before I left Germany, ideally before I left the Harz.

Back in my room, the reality of my status began to sink in. I started to brush my teeth with a tube of bacitracin. I could not distinguish between the multi-colored tube of the antibiotic and my toothpaste. I was only able to tell a pair of black dress socks from brown hiking socks by the difference in thickness. I could not see white briefs, white socks, or handkerchiefs on the bedsheets. This morning's fresh-cut flowers at the breakfast table were one blend of pastels. The brown outside and buttered white inside of a hard roll looked identical. When I picked up what I thought was the outside of the roll my fingers grasped the buttered inside. The cakes, torts, and pastries all were beige with gray toppings.

Perhaps I had panicked when, on Sunday, I sent my family and closest friends the convoluted message about my status, my very limited vision, and my inability to continue "The TREK." When I re-read the message, the events were factual but my enthusiasm to continue was missing. It was raining lightly and I stayed in the room to reacquaint myself with my possessions and reorganize them. I also wanted to rest before Detlev and Ilona arrived.

I awoke to a knock at my door. Detlev and Ilona greeted me. I was very happy to see them. The 200-mile trip from Berlin had taken almost four hours in Monday morning traffic. After inviting them into the room and walking into the open door of the wall unit, Detlev asked me, "Can you see us?"

"Yes, but not as well as when we were together last. I cannot see any difference in color between your jacket (brown) and your trousers (beige) and Ilona's jacket (Navy blue) and her slacks (black)."

I showed them my room, the container and bottle of the hair lice acid, and the clothing and equipment which I had carried from Normandy to Hahnenklee. The room was too small and crowded. We relocated to the breakfast room where Marion served us coffee. I praised Marion's support for me over the past five days. She dismissed my comments as if it all were routine. Everyone was interested to know if I were going to continue or quit. Quitting was not characteristic of my behavior in adverse situations. But there were many factors that weighed heavily suggesting that it may not be possible to continue. They dominated the conversation.

"The TREK" was a very important personal challenge for me. With more than 40 years' work experience shared between the military and NASA, I often had heard General of the Army Douglas McArthur's comment that "there is no substitute for victory," and the comment, which he did not say but that Hollywood attributed to Gene Kranz, NASA's Flight Director for the Apollo Thirteen mission, "failure is not an option." I promised everyone that, at the doctor's examination and evaluation the next day, I would explain to him "The TREK," and comply with his professional recommendations. If he determined that it would be unsuitable for the healing process, and that my sight and safety would be at risk, then I would not continue. If he had no objections, but only requirements and recommendations that would affect my schedule or routine, then I would comply completely and continue.

We left the breakfast table and secured their luggage from the car. Marion provided them a room on my floor down the hall from me. We spent the remainder of the day together at meals, walking within the town, around the lake, and through the parks. Whenever possible, I walked between them or behind them. At dinner I said that walking with them had been very valuable for me. I could not distinguish the very similar colors of the sidewalks, curbs, or cobblestone streets, and could not see the curbs or detect the change in elevation between the streets and the sidewalks. During our many conversations I sensed that Detlev thought that I was underestimating the extent of the injury and overestimating my ability to continue. I am sure that he was right. With more of a gesture of friendship than a concern that I might not tell the whole truth or something other than the truth, Detlev told me that he and Ilona not only would take me to the doctor but that they also would stay with me during the examination. Detlev kept insisting, and I kept agreeing, that the doctor's decision would be final.

Tuesday morning I was up early, showered, dressed, and ready to start the day. I sat in the easy chair opposite the open door to my room and wrote in my notebook as I waited for Detlev and Ilona. At 7:30 a.m. we went down to breakfast together. The sky was dark and it was raining steadily. Marion told Detlev the directions to the doctor's office only a 15-minute, 10-kilometer drive from the hotel. She gave us a one copy of all the documentation from the hospital for the doctor and two additional copies for ourselves.

We arrived ten minutes early and checked in together. Ilona and I took a seat while Detlev spoke with the office administrator. Their conversation was about the billing for this visit. Detlev had told her that I had private insurance and personal funds but that he would guarantee the payment with a credit from his bank in Berlin. After the examination, she would tell us what I needed to do about payment.

Exactly on schedule a nurse called for "Herr Pelosi." We left our seats and followed her into an examination room. Dr. med. Rainer Baumann, Augenartz (Eye doctor), introduced himself to us in English. I introduced myself to him, and then introduced Detlev and Ilona as my friends from Berlin who had traveled to help me after they heard about the injury to my eye. Dr. Baumann asked how we came to know each other and I told him. He said that he had read the information sent from the hospital and which Detlev had provided the nurse when we arrived. Then he asked me about the incident. I described how I had purchased the hair lice acid, stocked accidentally by a school-age boy working at his first summer job, and used it thinking it was contact lens solution. I also told him about Marion rushing me to an eye doctor in Clausthal-Zellerfeld before traveling to the Klinikum in Braunschweig where I was admitted, treated, and discharged on Sunday evening. Finally, I said that his examination today was important for his decision about my ability and the prudence of continuing the remaining 200 miles of the walk to Berlin which began seven weeks earlier at Normandy.

Dr. Baumann asked me far more questions about "The TREK" than I thought were necessary as background for the eye examination. I was very happy to tell him, hoping that the more he sensed how important an event this was for me the more it might influence him to approve my continuing. My last comment was that I had promised Detlev, Ilona, and others that I would comply with whatever he recommended concerning my ability to continue.

Dr. Baumann's examination took slightly more than two hours using two nurses in three different examination rooms. He confirmed a serious injury to the eye. I learned that the eyes, with more than two million working parts, follow the brain as the most complex organ in our bodies. Dr. Baumann added that the damage could have been far worse. Showering to get the lens out of my eye and keeping a wet washcloth over the eye enroute to the hospital started the flush which, after I was admitted, the doctors continued using very potent medication. He felt confident that my eye would heal, but said that it would take a very long time, perhaps three to six months.

When Dr. Baumann said that camping at night would not be advisable because of my potential isolation from immediate medical care and my long-term exposure to dust, dirt, and the elements, I thought that he had doomed me. But I was thrilled to hear him say that as long as I continued to walk by day, as safely as I had walked to date; protect the eye from overexposure to direct sunlight by wearing a hat and sunglasses; and, sleep in a hotel with a shower at least once a day, then he would not recommend termination of "The TREK." I thanked him profusely.

In the examination room he shook hands with all of us, wished me luck with the continuation of "The TREK", and said that he would walk us out. At the reception desk, Detlev said that he would pay the bill for my visit and that I would reimburse him. Dr. Baumann shook his head.

"His father flew in the airlift for Berlin and to do something for the Berliners. You both drove from Berlin to do something for him. He served with Army in Berlin to keep Berlin free after the war and before the wall came down. I, too, should do something now. There is no charge."

"Surprised" is too mild a word to express our reaction to Dr. Baumann's comments. Again I thanked him and told him how fortunate I was to have been cared for by his countrymen and him. Outside, Detlev and Ilona told me that they had never seen something like this happen between strangers. I said that it was a sign of only good things to happen to me for the remainder of my time in Germany.

On the drive back to Hahnenklee, Detlev offered to help me comply with Dr. Baumann's instructions and modify my original plan. With his copy of "The TREK" route he proposed to locate hotels in the cities and towns between Hahnenklee and Berlin. He would make reservations and send Marion an electronic message with the names of the hotels and walking directions provided from MapQuest links between the hotels. Back at the hotel, we told Marion the details of our visit with Dr. Baumann and his reasons for waiving the fees for my examination. Detlev described his re-routing plan and Marion agreed to collect and print his message traffic for me.

We invited Marion and Ralph to join us for lunch but both declined because of obligations at their hotel. There was no one to take their places at work. Temperatures had warmed to the low 80's, but the rain continued and we were forced to take lunch indoors. At lunch, we discussed a plan and schedule to support my rehabilitation while continuing with "The TREK." Detlev and Ilona would transport my tent, sleeping bag, air mattress, and other camping equipment back to the apartment in Berlin. I would find it all there when I arrived. The weight of my backpack would be reduced by almost ten pounds. The remaining gear, which was far less bulky, could be distributed more evenly in the backpack which would minimize the load-bearing stresses. For the remainder of today and the next four days I would make short-distance practice walks to evaluate my ability to navigate and avoid obstacles. On Sunday, August 3d, I would depart Hahnenklee for Goslar, only 10 miles away. Based upon the revised schedule that Detlev would create for me I could expect to arrive in Berlin around the middle of August, a week or two later than originally planned.

Back at the hotel I gave them the gear that I no longer needed. From the trunk of their automobile, Ilona gave me one of her cross-country ski poles to use as an aid for walking. I knew immediately that it would be a great help to locate curbs and feel for steps. Before they departed I promised to do my best to walk slowly and deliberately the remaining 200 miles to Berlin and to see them next at the Brandenburg Gate when I arrived. Upon reflection, I know that the intervention of Marion immediately after the accident and the visit by Detlev and Ilona immediately after my discharge helped me as much the medical care which I received to continue and finish "The TREK."

The remainder of the day I took two short walks through the main streets and town navigating with the use of the ski pole to find curbs and obstacles and an umbrella to protect my eye from the rain. At a restaurant for dinner the print on the menu was too small and blurred for me to read using both eyes. It was better for me to close my right eye and read using only my left. Best of all was reading the specialties printed with white chalk on a blackboard. Back in my room I made my notes from the day's events and organized what was left of my gear in the wall unit. The rain continued through the night. It still was raining, but not as heavily, when I awoke.

At breakfast, Marion informed me that she had received a message from Detlev and Ilona. They had arrived safely in Berlin after a slower drive as a result of the rain. Detlev wrote that he would send the revised route and hotel information before the end of the next day, Thursday, July 31st.

After breakfast, I retrieved the ski pole and umbrella and walked the more uneven terrain through the gardens, parks, and streets on the outskirts of town. It had taken a day for me to notice that the street signs all were lettered in black on a white background which made it very easy for me to read. However, the words were a blur until I was close enough to touch the sign post. Off a paved road and less than a mile away on a wide dirt trail was the hamlet of Bocksweise and the "Am Wassertretbecken" spa. I walked there and throughout Bocksweise trying to determine if there was any difference in walking between familiar and unfamiliar streets. There was none.

I was hoping for the rain to end and the sun to shine. Bright light had caused me the most problems and I wanted to practice walking with a baseball cap and sunglasses. In Bocksweise, I asked the waitress about the weather. She told me that the rain was expected to stop later in the day and that it should be sunny and much warmer beginning on Thursday and continuing through the weekend. That was exactly what I wanted to hear.

Back in my room I ate an MRE for lunch and took a nap. When I awoke in mid-afternoon the rain had stopped. The skies were clearing and the temperature and humidity were increasing. After a shower, I placed my notebook, sunglasses, baseball cap, and collapsible umbrella in my daypack and went outside. Walking on the narrow dirt trail to the lake required more attention than on the wider dirt trails to Bocksweise. I easily could see the green vegetation which grew out onto the trail but I could not see the brown tree roots. However, the roots had not grown very high or very thick, and I did not stumble when I missed seeing them. Even as the hours were passing, the light was increasing as the clouds disappeared almost completely. It was my first opportunity to walk the streets during daylight and twilight. Just for practice, I walked until 8 p.m., far later than the daily walks before Hahnenklee. Although my abilities may not have been improving, I felt as if I were becoming more confident and walking more naturally.

At dinner, I tweaked my rehab plan to take advantage of the sunny weather. For the next two days I would stay based with Marion in Hahnenklee. After breakfast, I wanted to walk locally to adjust to the light and then ride a local bus, which stopped only block from the hotel, to someplace new. There, in completely different surroundings, I would walk for three or four hours and then return by bus to the hotel.

Thursday morning, at breakfast, Marion told me that a good day and a good weekend were in store for me. The weather was expected to be sunny and warm. From the hotel I walked three miles to the hamlet of Lautenthal. The first half of the walk was along paths and trails within the dense, shaded forests where I did not need the sunglasses. The second half was along paths and roads in more open terrain. A baseball cap with the brim resting on my sunglasses absolutely was essential. I had a heightened awareness of the sun reflecting from white buildings, car windshields, and everything else that was glass. Ilona's walking pole was an added advantage.

From Lautenthal I rode the bus to Goslar which is the train and bus hub for the region. This was my parents' favorite town in the Harz. We stayed at the Hotel Kaiserworth, a 500 year old medieval guildhall, in the Market Center during both of their visits. The center had been built up significantly after 40 years, and now was far more congested. Much of its charm must have faded away over time. At a new Tourist Office there I obtained a guide and street map. I ate lunch outdoors at the Kaiserworth and listened to the huge glockenspiel chime, and watched its cast of laborers perform, exactly at 12 noon. While I ate, I plotted a six to eight-mile course from the town center to the outskirts and back. The afternoon was a great test of my ability to read a street map and street signs, and to navigate through the town and its structures. I fell walking up about a dozen steps to the entrance to the Kaiserhaus, one of several buildings which make up the Kaiserpflaz, the Old Imperial Palace of Goslar. I did not see the top step, assumed that I was walking on a flat surface, tripped, and fell forward. Had I used the walking pole more diligently I would have detected the step, and probably not have fallen. I recovered quickly and committed myself to using the pole especially when descending steps or stairs in places unknown.

I rode the bus back to Hahnenklee with a group of teenage soccer players still dressed in their muddy uniforms. One or two exited at each stop. When we arrived in Hahnenklee only one boy remained and exited with me. I asked him about the game. He told me that the other team was a no-show, wrongly assuming that the game had been canceled because of all the rain. His team won by forfeit. After I asked him how he and his teammates got so muddy, he told me that the coach made them use the time for practice and drills.

"Our coach hates losing."

"Yes, I know the feeling. Do your best – in school, too."

The outdoor café at the hotel was open and Marion and Ralph were serving to guests who filled six of their eight tables. I wanted to taste one of their torts but they had done so much work for me every day at breakfast that I decided not to add to their work. In my room I removed and stowed the contents of my daypack except for my notebook, undressed, and took a nap with the windows open fully and a gentle breeze blowing over me. After a shower, I spoke with Marion and Ralph to tell them about my first day's long walks and how the sunlight had affected me. I also told them about my fall at the Kaiserhaus in Goslar. We all agreed that it was better to have fallen going up the steps rather than on the way down. I promised them a more active use of my walking pole. At dinner, I made notes about the day's events and planned the next day's walk with greater distances both in the morning and the afternoon.

Marion greeted me at breakfast with good news about another spectacular day for evaluating my walking skills. Today would be sunny with temperatures a few degrees warmer in the lower 80's.

By 7:45 a.m., I was off enroute to Wolfshagen im Harz, a small hamlet nestled between two of the larger lakes in the Harz, the Innerstestausee and the Granestausee. The walk would be right at five miles almost directly north through areas of thick forest. Just shy of 10 a.m., I arrived and drank a cup of coffee while I rested and waited for the bus. Near the terminal in Goslar, I visited the Tourist Bureau for guides and maps of the towns where I could plan and plot routes for the next two days of training. Beyond there was the Market Square. Prices were expensive except for certain grocery products. For five euros, ($7.), I bought a sewing kit to the replace the one I had lost. Outdoors, at a hotel near the Kaiserworth opposite the statue of the Golden Eagle in the Fountain at Market Square, I drank a beer and people-watched. Directly overhead, the figures in the glockenspiel performed again as the chimes rang at high noon.

I paced lunch saving time to return to the terminal and catch the bus for Vienenburg, seven miles away. With a population of 10,000, it was one-fifth the size of Goslar and unfamiliar to me. I hoped that navigating through it would provide challenges that I could recognize and overcome. The ride took only 15 minutes and I exited at the second stop in town. I started walking on the sidewalk on the same side of the street as the traffic. At the sign on a bank I read the temperature as 82 degrees. Fifty yards away I heard a loud ringing to my right coming from what I thought was a side street. My view was blocked by a row of tall hedges. The loud ringing was constant. I thought that it was a signal from a fire station that emergency vehicles were departing the station and entering traffic.

I was wrong. I leaned forward and turned my head to use both eyes to see to the right. Using my walking pole I moved back part of the hedge at the corner for a better view before I was closer to the road. As I looked I felt tentacles hit the top of my head above my injured eye, then at my neck and my shoulders. I was standing beneath a railroad train crossing barrier which was lowering as a train approached. The tentacles were wire segments which were part of the barrier pole and hung from the barrier down to the ground. The impact of the tentacles and the barrier knocked me down and forward in the direction that I was leaning just in front of the tracks. I remained on the ground until the train passed. After the barrier raised, people on either side of the tracks ran from their cars to help me up. With my dark sunglasses and white ski pole some people thought that I was blind. (I may as well have been.) Others thought that I was both blind and deaf. I struggled to explain my status, and most of those nearby understood me. Everyone left after one young man in his 20's with a bicycle said that he would walk me to wherever I was going.

We crossed the tracks together and I had more time to explain why I was in Vienenburg. He said that it was smart to walk with the traffic, but that I was walking on the main street, and all the traffic into town came from the right (south), the side on which I had no sight. He suggested that we cross the street together and that I continue walking in Vienenburg on the left (north) opposite any threat from the traffic. I was expecting challenges but I had no intention of deliberately creating any.

"Your ski pole is a good help for you. When people see you with it they will make room for you. You should keep it with you for this walking. You were with luck. I think if you had made another step and looked past the trees the machine would have hit you in the back and knocked you on to the tracks. Yes. You were with very much luck."

Yes, I was. Now I wanted to be with very much beer and think through what just had happened. A few hundred yards away I found "Eis Ecke Vienenburg" (Ice cream corner Vienenburg). An ice cream and a coffee would be a respectable substitute for beer.

Outside the ice cream shop was a sofa, tables, and chairs facing the street. I preferred to sit inside with the cooler temperatures and away from the traffic. There were three or four steps at the entrance and, for the second time, I missed the last step. This time I only stumbled and did not fall. The color of the painted steps outside, the carpet inside, and the light made it difficult for me to see the distinction. A young, male employee, 16 or 17 years old, dressed sharply in clean jeans and a short-sleeved, collared shirt embroidered with the words, "Eis Ecke Vienenburg," asked me if I was alright. I told him that I was and I asked him if there was a menu. He told me, "Yes," and said that he would bring it to my table. I walked away from him and tripped a second time, forgetting to use my walking pole indoors, and not seeing the one step which set off the cashier's area and work station from the sitting area. The boy left the work station, came to my side, and asked me if I needed help to be seated at a table. I declined his offer and asked his name. He told me, "Sven."

I was getting very frustrated very quickly. I wanted to continue "THE TREK" and start out in two or three days. Now I was making inexcusable errors which were avoidable if only I were more diligent and attentive.

Sven returned to the table with a menu. This time I was more polite and introduced myself to him. I said only a little about having walked from Normandy to Hahnenklee, the eye accident, and my time now on self-imposed rehab to practice walking. He did not take his eyes off me for the few minutes that I was speaking which I thought was unusually attentive for someone who might be more concerned about the needs of other customers or the observations of his boss. He told me that his father had been to the United States and that he spoke English very well. He, his older brother, and his younger sister were strongly encouraged by their parents to master their lessons in school and learn English to help them with their future. He did not need to tell me that he was very interested in visiting the United States one day. I asked him for a dish of ice cream with two scoops of anything to surprise me: "something you would order for yourself if you were sitting here."

Sven returned with a dish of strawberry and vanilla. It probably was not what he would have had for himself. I think he deferred to something neutral and conservative that is universally a favorite and does not exact complaints. He served me with a sweet smile on his face and the comment, in English, "I hope you like it." Sven returned to my table more times than was usual, especially for servers in Europe. I sensed that I presented him an opportunity to speak English in a very practical situation and, more importantly, that while he had time away from other customers, he would improve his English speaking with a native speaker with whom he shared some common interests. Old enough to be his grandfather, with no children or grandchildren of my own, I had this brief shining moment to help a young, intelligent, high school student practice his English and hone his speaking and comprehension skills. Certainly there were other customers in the shop with whom he could relate more easily, without struggling with a foreign language. Perhaps there even other boys or girls his own age with whom it would be easier and more fun to chat. But, for some reason I did not understand, he moved my way when he was not busy. He had the physique of an athlete and told me that he rode his bicycle to work in all weather conditions a distance of seven miles through the hills one way from his home in Hornburg. He also was a martial arts competitor and trained with his brother, Nils, one year older at 18, who now was a new recruit in the German Army.

After I finished the ice cream, I asked Sven for a cup of black coffee, which gave us more time to be together and more of an opportunity to communicate. When I felt that I had been too much of a distraction for him for too long I asked for my bill and followed him from the table to the work station. While I paid I told him that I again would be walking through the same area the next day and perhaps I would meet him if he were working. Sven told me that Saturday was his day off and that he had plans to be with his family.

From the Eis Ecke Vienenburg I walked through and out the town for an hour then turned around and retraced my steps back to a bus stop. Enroute to the bus stop I passed by a stream flowing alongside the street beyond the sluices of the mill bridge. Nearby the bus stop was a bookstore and I bought a book on the history of Vienenburg and the region. The distance from Goslar to Hahnenklee is 11.5 miles by car along roads which curve around the mountains. However, the distance by foot is less than half as far at only five miles along the trails through the forests. There still were six hours of daylight. I walked, entering Hahnenklee at the north side of town and passing through the parks and around Crane Pond to the hotel.

This afternoon I accepted Marion's invitation to have a cake and coffee with her. I sat at one of only two unoccupied tables and waited for Marion to bring me a surprise: a rich and sweet fruit tort made with fresh blackberries, blueberries, raspberries, strawberries, and whipped cream. Marion told me that Detlev had sent a detailed message to her containing his recommendation for a revised route and schedule and the names of hotels between Hahnenklee and Berlin. She had printed his message and the 15 pages of attachments and placed them on the table in my room. She responded and told him and Ilona that I was continuing to improve.

Marion was not expecting to hear anything like my stories about falling near a passing train or stumbling twice in the ice cream shop. With the sensitivity of a mother with three children, she suggested that I take more time to re-evaluate my condition and train before I continued. She knew that I had no deadline to arrive in Berlin, that I was not pressed for time, and that Detlev's revised route could remain the same with only changes to the schedule. I admitted that in my eagerness to continue walking and sightseeing I was careless and not as cautious as I should have been. I promised to be more attentive.

Marion told me that seated at the table across from us was a man and his wife who had just come from his graduation ceremony at Clausthal University of Technology, earning a degree in metallurgy. He was 84 years old. After I heard some of his story from Marion, and when she departed to tend to other customers, I left the table to extend my congratulations. After I did so in German, Herr Konrad Aschendorff said to me, "I heard you and Marion speaking English. I learned my English from the American army during and after the war."

The words "during the war" confused me. In 1944, Herr Aschendorff was a 14-year old conscripted member of the Hitler Youth living with his family in the Harz. After the D-Day invasion, he and a group of other young teenage members of the Hitler youth were driven by truck by a representative of their local Gauleiter, (a political official who governed a district under Nazi rule), to Normandy.

"There were 20 or 25 of us. We had no uniforms and no weapons. I had only my clothing from home and a cap. When we arrived in Normandy, the German soldiers told the Nazi official to stay and fight with us boys. He tried to flee in the truck and they shot him. Two of the soldiers ordered all of us back into the truck and they drove us home the same day. We were told to stay and take care of our families, and not to fight against the Americans, only the Russians if they should come first. I think that they must have shot the other Nazi party officials because no one could find them some days after we had come back home. Our families gave the soldiers some food and clothing to take back with them to France."

"Much later, the American army did come first, but there was no German army in the area to fight. Most units had surrendered. No one wanted to fight any more. Our families had no money and very little food. We boys received some treats from the American soldiers. I stayed near them to do work for food. I cleaned pots and pans in the field kitchens, cleaned mud from their boots, and even cleaned weapons. I was allowed to do that because, a few times the soldiers were busy cleaning, carrying, and moving things and walked away from their rifles. I returned them to them. Many months near the Americans helped me to learn English."

"After the war, there was no work, but the Americans had workers with the huge Krupp factory which made weapons during the war and then was making equipment to rebuild Germany. I started to work there. My English improved. My jobs were better and better over time. I finished my minimum schooling. In later years, after I was married, I started studies again, but work and raising my family made too many demands. Now, 70 years after I was brought home from Normandy, I have earned my university degree."

I listened to stories that almost were unbelievable, but some were similar to narratives I had read at West Point and beyond and while conducting research for "The TREK." His stories about conditions in Europe sounded like what I had heard from my father and, more recently, from other strangers whom I had met since Normandy. New to me, and truly shocking, was his story about German soldiers returning from combat on the eastern front. There had been a "scorched earth policy" by both sides to deny the other food and resources. Orphaned and homeless Russian children were everywhere scrounging anything they could to survive. Boys between the ages of six and 12 had the best chances, possessing strong survival instincts and exceptional physical endurance. A year or two older they would have been vulnerable as combatants. They did almost anything for food, clothing, and comfort. They stole rations and clothing from the dead and slept in the hulls of destroyed vehicles. Some German units kept groups of these "feral children" almost like mascots. In areas of close combat they could disappear into Soviet villages and towns, wander among the disoriented population, and return with information or sketch maps. Their status was known at the highest levels of the German military. On the retreat from the Soviet Union, Himmler ordered that all these children be executed. He did not want the Russian untermenschen returning with the army and entering Germany. Many units, most notably the SS, complied with Himmler's order. However, other units, especially those that had been decimated and were returning piecemeal under the leadership of noncommissioned officers, spared the children from execution. After the war, dozens of these survivors living in Austria, East

Germany, Hungary, and Poland described the horrors of their struggles for survival.

It had been a very long day for the Aschendorff family. More than hour after we finished our cake and coffee together they excused themselves to return home. This had been a truly historic and memorable day for their family and for me.

Before dinner, I told Marion that I would read and study everything which Detlev had sent and that I had planned much the same day for Saturday as I did today except that I would carry my backpack. If I were to trip or stumble I needed to know the results of an impact while carrying 35 to 40 pounds. At dinner, I ordered a light meal and studied the route revisions. Detlev's work was meticulous. There was nothing I needed to do differently with the route or the schedule, except to do my best and get to Berlin.

In bed, I read the book that I had bought that afternoon in Vienenburg. I learned much about the town and the region. Almost immediately after the war, the townspeople renamed many of their streets. "Adolf-Hitler Straße" became "Goslarer Straße"; "Hindenburger straße" became "Osterwiecker Straße"; Hermann-Goring Straße" became "Lierestraße"; and, "Horst-Wessel Straße" became "Okerstraße."

Saturday morning Marion gave me more good news about the weather for the day: continued sunny with slightly warmer temperatures approaching 85 degrees. I told her that I would catch a first bus from Hahnenklee to Goslar and then a second to Vienenburg. From there I would walk during the morning the seven miles to Hornburg where Sven lived, and discover the route along which he rode his bicycle when he came to Vienenburg to work. From Hornburg I would take a bus to Goslar then walk back in the afternoon to Hahnenklee. If everything went well then I would check out from the hotel on Sunday and begin the last leg of the walk to Berlin.

None of that happened after I stepped off the bus in Vienenburg. I moved away from the bus stop to put on the backpack. Then I took the street map and my compass to orient myself. While I was looking at the map I felt two gentle taps on my right shoulder. I turned and saw Sven smiling broadly.

"Hello Jim. How are you? What do you do now in Vienenburg?"

I told him my plan for the day.

He said that he was riding in the family car with his mother and sister when he saw me standing on the sidewalk. His mother had driven to a parking place from which he had walked to meet me. He wanted me to meet his mother and sister. Mrs. Anette Küppers and her daughter Maren met us as we walked toward them. Sven made a very polite introduction and I said that I was very happy to meet them both. I told them that my spirits had been uplifted after a difficult day when I had the opportunity to meet and speak with Sven while he worked at the ice cream shop. Miss Anette asked me about my plans for the day and I told her. She asked me to join them on the drive to Goslar where we could shop and take lunch together. I accepted and sat in the front next to Anette. Miss Maren was a bit shy only because she did not have the command of the English language that her brother and mother had. I tried to involve her by speaking slowly in English or in German.

At the central parking plaza we decided to part company for two hours while the Küppers family shopped for clothing and school supplies before the start of the new academic year. I needed to retrieve another resupply at the Hotel Kaiserworth and make a reservation for the next day. After that, I needed to buy a back-up pair of sunglasses. I was waiting in the Market Square when Sven found me. Nearby we sat together outdoors at Café Galileo for cake and coffee. The family had several questions about "The TREK" which Sven had described to them after he returned home from work. Essentially I confirmed what Sven had related and provided some family information about my father's support of the Berlin Airlift. Miss Maren was a good listener. Miss Anette surprised me when she invited me to return with them to meet her husband and see their home. I gladly accepted.

We arrived in the early afternoon. Steffen Küppers, together with the two family pet dogs, met us in the enclosed courtyard which led to the home, garage, barn, yard, and gardens. Eighteen years my junior, Steffen is a very distinguished and accomplished man who exuded pride in his family and his home, and who immediately made me feel welcome among them. One of his first comments was to thank me for helping his son practice his English.

Sven walked away with my backpack. Anette and Maren disappeared. Steffen led me up a short flight of 18 steps outdoors and into the house. The foyer led to the center of the home which split into the family rooms. Steffen told me that the home was built in 1748. He said that there was not a straight corner anywhere in the original structure and proceeded to show me. Huge wooden cross timbers at the ceilings joined the walls at noticeably different heights when traced across the rooms. But the differences are not noticeable to the casual observer, only when studied. There was a large library with books in both German and English. I read some of the English titles and discussed the subjects briefly with Steffen.

Sven joined us and his father suggested that he and his sister show me their rooms. I saw Sven's room first. It looked like a typical room for a 16 year old boy, except that everything was exceptionally neat and well organized. It was obvious to me that he took his studies very seriously. His textbooks, notebooks, reading, and writing materials all were set as if it were a work station at a business.

From his room he took me to his brother's room where he had placed my backpack. Because Nils was away in the Army, his room would be available to me for this night. The room was very similar to Sven's except that there were several models of aircraft and boats which Nils had built. In a bookcase were a variety of books, many of which were of technical subjects.

Sven passed me to Maren who struggled with her English to describe her room to me. At 14, she is every bit a real girl. Lots of clothes, dolls, stuffed animals, teen idol posters, and keepsakes. I was enjoying her guided tour when Anette called us to lunch which she served to all five of us at a table outdoors beyond the top of the steps and the entrance. The children each had the same size room with windows, a desk and chair, a computer, a stacked bookshelf, and filled clothes closet. There was no indication of favoritism or excess.

I was thrilled to have my fourth home-cooked meal in 56 days. The family had many questions about "The TREK" and what I saw as the differences between Europe and the United States. There were a few, such as Europeans having a more relaxed and patient lifestyle, their extensive use of a better mass transportation system, and far more smokers of both sexes and all ages. For similarities, all I could think of was the overwhelming use of cell phones invading everything that once was private and personal, young teenage males with Justin Bieber haircuts, and hordes of tourists from Asia all clueless about host-nation customs and courtesies. As I write this narrative, the national news is reporting that a 16 year old exchange student from Taiwan was gored by a bison in Yellowstone National Park after she ignored warnings from Park Rangers and moved too close to the wild animal to have her photograph taken. Clueless.

After lunch, Anette and Maren cleared the table and started work in the kitchen. Sven brought me back downstairs to show me the garage, barn, workout area with pull-up bar, and sauna. I saw also the large property line bordered by trees, shrubs, and flowers. His grandmother, Steffen's mother Suzanne, lives with them in a suite adjacent to the main structure of the home and, in her late 70's, does all the work to maintain the gardens. She hosts friends who visit her regularly and she enjoys traveling.

Steffen met us outside and invited me back inside for a tour of the first floor of his home. He showed me his mother's residence, the basement cold storage area which, when the house first was built, was used to stock fresh-killed game. Built with thick mortar and below ground it still is cold enough to keep groceries without refrigeration.

As a side business the family hosts an outstanding and pristine hostel named "Hornburg–Hostel," a description for which can be found on the internet, Facebook, and through internet travel services. There are nine beds available in three separate rooms: one room with six; one room with two, and one private room, together with all amenities necessary for a visit of any length. As Steffen was showing me the facility, a group of four with reservations arrived to check in. Steffen excused himself and I went back outside to the courtyard.

Maren was on hand with Blacky, a Scottish terrier or close enough to be called one. I sat and watched while Maren put Blacky through a series of responses to commands, tricks, and stunts done on two or four legs. Maren is a sweet teenager possessing a calm and gentle manner. She told me that she trains her animals with love and not with discipline.

Steffen joined Sven and me at the table where we continued to watch Maren with Blacky. He told me that when Maren was born in 1999 he and Anette were informed by the doctors that she had a congenital spinal deformity and probably never would walk. With two other seemingly perfect older children, this was not acceptable to Maren's parents. Steffen told me that he knew the story of the American 101st Airborne Division commander who was surrounded by superior German forces at Bastogne and refused to surrender. "I basically said, 'NUTS,' and we committed ourselves to proving the doctors wrong."

Steffen was so committed to this effort that he had the image of the 101st Airborne Division's screaming eagle tattooed on his arm. Maren had just spent the last two years of her life, from age 11 to age 13 in a hospital and wheelchair. Eventually the doctors and the Küppers family triumphed. Maren was able to walk. After she left the hospital, the family built a bonfire and burned her back and leg braces, her wheelchair, and everything else that she had needed to support her. Her parents bought her all kinds of pets, mostly guinea pigs, dogs, and a pony so she would be forced to be outdoors, standing, walking, and running while she cared for them. Training the dogs, Tom and Blacky, and the pony, Anton, grew into a hobby for Maren. She earned a special privilege from the German government and a special license to allow her to use a pony-driven carriage on the rural roads. Her goal is to be a school teacher.

Happy Hour arrived and the saga of Miss Maren was a story to make anyone feel happy. Drinking laws in Europe are much more relaxed and there are far fewer underage drinking incidents than in the United States. We finish two Harzer beers before Anette and Maren brought dinner outside for everyone. At dinner, I was invited to spend the night with the family, and sleep in Nils' room. I accepted without hesitation. After dinner, I asked Steffen or Anette to call to Marion in Hahnenklee so that she knew I would absent from my room that night and from breakfast in the morning. There is another room in the family residence that is a dedicated entertainment center. I saw home movies of the family, mostly of the children, as they grew up in this region of Germany. Given Maren's earlier severely handicapped status it was not possible for the family to travel far or often. I had a sound night's sleep in Nils' bed. With the windows open through the night I heard nothing from the street below.

Early next morning there were no sounds within the home. I took my shaving kit and tiptoed from the bedroom. In the hall, I met Sven, both of us in our briefs and carrying a bath towel. He guided me to the shower which he and his brother used, and then he showered at an annex to the hostel. The family knew that I was departing this day to resume "The TREK." At breakfast I told them that I wished I could stay longer. I had a sad departure from Anette and Maren and then Steffen and Sven drove me to Hahnenklee.

We have kept in close contact since I left their home. This year, in 2015, Sven will discover the United States and its national parks with me between July and September. In September, I will return with him to Hornburg. At the end of the month, his brother Nils will return with me through November for his discovery tour through Texas, the Gulf states, and Florida. He is a school-trained certified windsurfing instructor and very eager to test his skills. I am hoping that the boys will enjoy visiting the United States as much as I always have enjoyed visiting Germany.

Back at the hotel, I had a second sad departure, this time with Marion and Ralph. They were a part of everything good that had happened to me in the Harz before and especially after my eye accident. I know that Marion fudged the bill in my favor. I could not thank them enough and I promised to return. At that time I did not know that I would be returning 13 months later when I escorted Sven home to his family. Marion has my room reserved again.

As I waved goodbye to Marion and Ralph and walked away from Blackcoms Erika I knew that I had 200 miles to walk in the next 13 days averaging 15.5 miles per day. I also knew that the closer I came to Berlin the easier the walk would seem. What I did not know was anything about the ten cities of the former German Democratic Republic which I would visit other than what I had read. That I would discover after I left Goslar and arrived in Osterwieck.

The five and a half mile walk to Goslar was familiar having been twice down the same route within the week. I walked slightly slower than the other treks probably because of the weight of a full pack. It was only the middle of the morning when I arrived at the Hotel Kaiserworth. The clerks at reception were busy checking out departing guests, and I dropped my backpack to help myself to my third cup of coffee. After I introduced myself to the reception clerk, she told me that she knew my name because she had been sending me messages about my status when I failed to arrive on time to retrieve my resupply parcel. One of her coworkers told her that I had visited the day before to inquire about the package and to make a reservation for today. The room was ready. While I checked in she brought the parcel with a note still attached to it, "Halten Sie für James Pelosi, USA." The room was on the top floor facing the Marketplatz. I opened the windows and had a commanding view of the market square and town center. I had no agenda for the day other than to play tourist, relax and make notes about my visit with the Küppers family and the departure from Hahnenklee, and get sufficient rest for the 18 mile walk to Osterwieck the next day.

At high noon I was seated at a café in the Market Square to watch again the eight-minute performance of the figures at the glockenspiel. The children stood fascinated and attentive with their eyes fixed on the variety of workers moving in close order behind one another in a parade simulating the end of the work day. Every day there are a total of four performances. Three more followed every three hours at three, six and nine. Within Goslar are 1,800 old houses, the highest number in all of Germany. Many of them are half-timbered adding greatly to the character of the town nestled deeply within the Harz. For the remainder of the day I walked away from the Hotel Kaiserworth and the Market Square and fanned out along the side streets visiting the shops, bookstores, churches, and other attractions. I found two pubs hidden away from the main tourist routes and drank a Harzer in each listening to only German being spoken among the locals, not hearing a single cell-yell phone conversation, and not watching anyone snap photographs. I ate dinner early and returned to the hotel before ten. I had packed hastily before leaving Hahnenklee which was not an issue for this day's short walk. But the next day's walk of 18 miles, through more rugged terrain, would be more of a challenge for me. Before bed, I removed and reorganized the contents of my backpack and then repacked everything.

During the night I awoke to the sound of rain hitting the panes of the open windows in my room. It still was raining when I awoke and when I went downstairs for breakfast. At the reception desk the "Daily Events" notice described the day's weather as "mostly cloudy with rain." The temperature was 71 degrees. I ate heartily from the breakfast buffet and took away two hard rolls with meats and cheeses and an apple as a snack for later in the day. My previous visit to the Hotel Kaiserworth was with my parents in July, 1974. At checkout I told the receptionist that I hoped to see her again when I returned in another 40 years at 103 years of age.

She said, "I hope not. I do not want to be working that long. But I can make the reservation for you."

"That would be fine. But, next time, not for the top floor. Three flights of stairs with a backpack may be too much for me."

It was raining lightly when I departed using both an umbrella and the walking pole. I walked slower leaving the town because the cobblestone streets are slippery when wet. For the first hour beyond town and through the outskirts of a semi-industrial area there was relatively heavy traffic along the main road. The traffic diminished and the route transitioned to longer stretches of forest, fields, and farmland as I approached Vienenburg. After my experience stumbling at the train tracks three days earlier I remembered to walk on the left (north) side of the main street. I passed the Eis Ecke Vienenburg which was closed. My experience of having met Sven there on Friday and his family at their home in Hornburg on Saturday and Sunday was personally very rewarding. They are a very close and loving young family whose shared experiences with Maren's physical handicap defines their character.

Beyond Vienenburg, along Route 241, the Radius and Oker rivers flowed to the north. I passed over an autobahn and then a small bridge over the Ecker River into the town of Wiedelah. I saw several shops for newspapers, tobacco, clothing, computer repair, and groceries but I could not find a restaurant. One of the residents told me that the only restaurant was about two miles south and west of where we were standing. It was exactly in the opposite direction that I was headed. The clouds remained thick, low, and slow-moving, and the continuous rain made the morning walk especially dreary. Although I was not hungry and could have continued to walk, I was conditioned to stop at or beyond the halfway point now in Wiedelah. I did not want to risk slipping, tripping, or falling because, as I tired, I may have becoming less attentive to the terrain or obstacles. Near a commercial building I found an annex with overhead cover, protection from the rain, and surrounded by trees. The street was named, "In den Pappeln," (in the poplars). It was sufficient as a place to eat lunch and rest for an hour.

<u>Through the former East Germany.</u>

The rain continued as I departed Wiedelah and the German state of Lower Saxony, and crossed into Saxony-Anhalt. This area is part of the fertile Harz Foreland which extends from the Harz foothills in the southwest to the Elbe at Magdeburg along the route of "The TREK." I was nearing the central portion of Saxony-Anhalt which is occupied by the Fläming Hills and the fertile Börde region.

In two hours I arrived at the half-timbered hotel Bruner Hirsch (Brown Deer) near the center of the medieval town of Osterwieck. There were many indications that this historic town was once a part of the former East Germany. Hahnenklee, with a population just under 12,000 was only 30 miles west of Osterwieck with a population of just over 12,000. It was difficult to comprehend how much these similar-sized towns, both in the Harz district, grew apart during the years that Germany was divided. Many of the buildings and homes appeared as if they had been in need of repair for quite some time. The structure of the hotel itself was quite old, but the owners had made a herculean effort to upgrade the rooms, dining area, and kitchen. Despite the radical difference from the five-star Hotel Kaiserworth I was just as happy and comfortable here feeling more like a guest than a tourist.

There was not much outdoor activity to observe in the rain; however, there were a few hours to tour before dinner. In the hotel I left everything behind except the umbrella a baseball cap to protect my eye, and the walking pole. The Mühlgraben stream runs east alongside the Bruner Hirsch which is located on the same street as the Saint Stephen church. It dates from the Romanesque era, and was closed, as usual, on Mondays when I arrived. I was able to see only the exterior which boasted an impressive tower front from the year 1150. Inside there are Protestant emblem iconography in stonemason reliefs on pillars, arcades, and keystones, and galleries with biblical pictures dating back to 1589. It was not long before I realized that there were too many potential physical hazards to negotiate and, combined with the rain, it would be more judicious to stop for dinner and then return to the hotel.

At the hotel I used the empty breakfast room to make my notes for the day and plan the route to Huy, only 14 miles away. I was up early and saw from the window in my room that the rain had stopped. There was a local newspaper at a table in the breakfast room. On the front page was the weather inset, indicating a mix of sun and clouds but no rain for today, and temperatures between 67 and 80 degrees. The rain was expected to return the next day. During checkout I asked the hotelier about the route to Huy. She told me that Dardesheim was 10 kilometers (six miles) to the east and Huy was perhaps another 10 kilometers. She added that, although Huy was only two-thirds the size of Osterwieck, along the Romanesque Route there were attractions such as a castle, old town hall, historic church, and memorials.

On the road before eight, I arrived in Dardesheim mid-morning and stopped for coffee and a roll. My backpack contained two more MRE's than I needed until Magdeburg where I would obtain the last resupply parcel. That weight was insignificant now that I was not carrying any of the camping equipment. Maybe a troop of German Boy Scouts would cross my path and I would have the opportunity to give the boys a true appreciation for mama's home cooking.

The walk may have been the easiest two hours to date. The road passed through predominantly farmland over relatively flat terrain. About two-thirds of the landscape is farmland. The vistas across the fields of wheat, rye, barley, sugar beets, and fodder crops extended for hundreds of yards in various stages of cultivation. Only about one-fourth is covered by forests which I passed alongside and did not walk through.

Enroute to Huy, I expected the terrain to remain the same for the next two or three hours until I arrived. The day was warm and cloudless. The views looking across the fields were exceptionally peaceful, flat, wooded lands with a few scattered farm homes and buildings leading up to the town. Upon entering the city I could not tell that it was smaller by two-thirds than Osterweick. There seemed to be much more space between clusters of buildings and homes. I learned later that this was because the town was formed by the merger of several small villages to conserve and consolidate resources for infrastructure development and to provide for community services.

There are no hotels or gästehauses in Huy. An internet travel service was the source for a room in a private farmhouse located slightly north from the center of town. When I arrived, both parents were away at work, but one of the children, a girl of 12 or 13 with blond hair braided in pigtails, was expecting me. Louise showed me a very clean room on the second floor, similar in size and furnishings to my room at Blackcoms Erika in Hahnenklee, except that there was not a private bathroom or shower which did not concern me. She told me that the family rooms all were on the first floor and that I would be alone on this floor. In the absence of her parents, I did not want to be the source of any worry for her. I told her that I would leave my backpack in the room and then tour the several attractions in the area. Louise smiled when I told her that, if I did not get lost, I would return by nine. Before I left I gave her 20 euros, ($30.), for the room which was advertised for only 14 euros but had a much greater value. She had not given me a key to the room and I did not ask her for one. I left the door to the room open and then left to explore Huy.

Not too far away, along one of the Romanesque routes, is the Castle Westerburg. It is the oldest castle in Germany that was built with a moat. Unlike the Alamo in San Antonio, Texas, which is surrounded by concrete and in a neighborhood characterized by streets with bumper-to bumper traffic, high-rise hotels, tourist traps, and fast-food facilities, the Castle Westerburg stands alone. Its original medieval stone and timber-framed construction could have been the inspiration for any one of the many castles created by Hollywood's set makers. Again, unlike the Alamo, it has a commanding view of the area from which a tourist can envision its defenders looking out across the moat at an approaching enemy.

I visited an early 19th century manor house, The Röderhof, built entirely of stone and mortar with a sloping clay-tiled roof and more in the image of a church than a castle. Lacking a moat, the small fence which encloses part of it, with its wooden, weather-worn slats, offers no protection from anyone or anything. The local parish Church of St. Trinity was built two centuries earlier. The door was open. Inside was a spectacular display of artwork. I was surprised that anything of quality and value had survived the years of war and administration by the godless bureaucrats of the former East Germany.

Quite by accident I discovered the Heinrich Meutefin Museum, created in honor of shoemaker Heinrich Meutefin (1745-1816), who collected herbs and flowers and preserved them in small displays with short poems written about each of his exhibits. His intention was to provide a work of art tribute to the variety and beauty of the flora in his native Huy. This little museum is a one room, one story stone structure, possibly only 15 yards wide by 10 yards deep at most. The small door at the front is locked; however, there is a key code and any visitor at any time may enter, view the displays, and read the poems. Visiting hours are described as "12:00 a.m. to 11:30 p.m."

Five hundred yards south, along the same road as the museum, was the small "Landhaus" restaurant. It was the only restaurant in Huy. I was fortunate to have found it before the end of the day. During my walking tour of Huy, in which there were only four, short, north-south and east-west streets, I had become resigned to reducing the number of MRE's in my backpack by one after I returned to my room.

When I arrived, there was only one light on in the house upstairs, perhaps in my room. I did not want to knock and disturb the family who might be sleeping. The front door was not locked. I entered, locked the door behind me, and went upstairs. On the bed was a penciled note in a schoolchild's handwriting which read, "Guten Abend. Das Frühstück ist von 0700. Danke. Die Familie Meyer." As the only guest I did not want the Meyer family to wait on me. I wrote a note stating that I would be at breakfast at 7:30 a.m., and placed it on a counter in the kitchen.

The bed and fresh air from the open window made for a very comfortable night's sleep. When I awoke at six, it was raining lightly. I hoped that the 18 miles to Oschersleben would not be all in the rain. But at breakfast Frau Meyer dashed my hopes. She told me that a cold front was passing through and that, in addition to the rain, temperatures would drop between five and ten degrees. However, the front was predicted to be fast-moving, and the following day would be clear, maybe sunny, and with warmer temperatures. Herr Meyer had departed earlier with Louise to take her to a summer camp for swimming and outdoor sporting events for school-age girls. I drank only one cup of coffee and ate quickly so that Frau Meyer could leave for her place of business. After I cleared my room I set out for Oschersleben using the umbrella, baseball cap, and walking pole to assist me while walking in the rain. The first mile beyond Huy was through fields and farmland nearly identical to the approach of the town. But then next two miles were through dense forest so thick that the volume of rain blowing across the walking path was reduced as it was deflected and absorbed by the trees. One hundred yards beyond the forest was the village of Dinglestedt am Huy where I stopped at a small gaststätte for a second cup of coffee. The waitress confirmed that the rain was expected to continue throughout the day, and told me that the next village of Wulferstedt was approximately 12 kilometers, or just shy of eight miles, further east. After 62 days, she was the first service person in any facility to tell me that she liked seeing both the USA and German flags displayed side by side on my backpack.

"Since, for 20 years now, we have our freedom because of the American army and the NATO, I think America is as important as one Germany again."

Within a mile of Wulferstedt I could see a huge forested area across the vast tracts of farmland. When I reached the town I had been walking just over four hours. It was time for lunch and I was ready to eat and rest away from the rain which now was no more than an annoying drizzle. I saw a poster for a restaurant only 50 yards off my route to the north and went inside. Instead of a beer, which is my beverage of choice when I am hot and sweaty, I ordered a glass of wine. I was the only customer. After I introduced myself to the waiter, I asked him what the huge expanse of greenery was that I saw as I approached the town.

The waiter told me that it is an expansive natural forest and wetlands called the "Großes Bruch bei Wulferstedt" which extends approximately 45 kilometers, about 27 miles, between Hornburg in Lower Saxony in the west, where I had been three days earlier, and Oschersleben in Saxony-Anhalt in the east, which was my destination for this day. It covers a depression that had been formed from a glacial valley. Until the region began to be drained in the Middle Ages it was impassable, crossed only by wooden ferries. Leading into the nearby town of Neudamm (New dyke) is a road called "the old ferry way," and the oldest structure built of rubble stone in Neudamm is "the old ferryman's house." After World War II, the Großes Bruch became the natural inner border between The Federal Republic of Germany and the German Democratic Republic. Following the German reunification in 1990, all of the Großes Bruch was declared a protected area with meadows containing numerous species of fauna and homes for rare birds such as the hen harrier, Montagu's harrier, Eurasian curlew, short-eared owl, common snipe, and corncrake. The route for next five miles to Oschersleben would be alongside and then through the Großes Bruch.

Oschersleben sits at a junction where the Großes Bruch ends in the west and where the Bode River flowing to the north-northeast turns at its northernmost point to flow east-southeast. In addition to agriculture and farming, Oschersleben hosts a variety of industrial enterprises including breweries, brick works, iron foundries, manufacturing shops, and sugar refineries. Before World War II, an aircraft manufacturing plant was located there. It expanded to support the war effort producing Focke Wulf 190-series aircraft after 1941. The factory, many aircraft, and the protective anti-aircraft batteries were destroyed almost completely by a series of Allied bombings during the war. What the Western Allies did not destroy was blown-up by the Soviet Army of Occupation in 1947.

I arrived at 3 p.m., and had checked into the Pension Da Gigi by 4 p.m. With two and a half times the population of Huy, it would be the second largest city in the former East Germany behind Magdeburg that I would visit. In the city of almost 20,000 residents there were several attractions that I was eager to see. My plan was to explore Oschersleben through the remainder of the afternoon and evening until lunch the following day. The next town of Wanzleben was only 10 miles away to the east and I could walk that distance easily after lunch the next day.

I left my backpack in the room and took only my valuables, umbrella, and walking pole outside. My destination was the Oschersleben City Museum less than half a mile away. Inside I found a city guide and street map. There also were posters and notices about events throughout the summer and during August but nothing special for this day, Wednesday, August 6, 2014. Inside were many small but professional displays about the history of Oschersleben. Sadly, there were many displays concerning the activities in the city and the area during World War II, including narratives about the 10 raids conducted by the Allies to destroy the aircraft manufacturing facilities, airfield, and defenses. There was as much information about the surrounding region, nature trails, hiking routes, and sports clubs as there was about the city itself.

From the City Museum, I followed the guide book to a location near the library where I found the statue to "The Seed Man," or "The Sower," constructed between 1913 and 1914. It is the town icon inspired by the especially fertile soil of the area which is dominated by farmland. Once I discovered the pedestrian-only zone in the center of town the rain was no longer a factor influencing my tour. Free from the potential threat of traffic and the chores of trying to read street signs and find curbs, the difficulty I still had seeing with my right eye was diminished. I could follow other pedestrians and guide on them to avoid obstacles that might blend in with the color of the streets, sidewalks, or buildings. Only 10 days since my discharge from the Klinikum Braunschweig, I knew that my eye was healing; however, the colors black, brown, grey, Navy blue and purple still all blended as one. So did the lighter colors of orange, yellow, green and blue.

I sipped a glass of local wine while I people-watched and annotated the guidebook with a route for the attractions I hope to see. The picturesque Town Hall dates from 1698. The Protestant church to Saint Nikolai followed almost 200 years later constructed between 1867 and 1869. The Catholic Marienkirche followed near the end of 19th century. Not far from these churches, on a half-acre plot, is a Jewish cemetery with memorials to the victims of the holocaust and forced labor service. Around the town also are memorials to Soviet soldiers who died either as prisoners of war or as combatants during the final days of World War II. Although there were several public and private schools for primary-age children I did not see any technical institutes or universities.

In the early evening, I stopped my walking tour and found a quiet restaurant at which I enjoyed a traditional German meal of beef, roasted potatoes, red cabbage, and some kind of boiled white beans. I drank a second glass of the same white wine I had tasted earlier. During dinner, I decided to trade the shorter, 10-mile route directly east past the Motorsport Arena and Museum for the longer, 14-mile route north then southeast past the Ampfurth Castle to Wanzeleben. This castle dates from the 12th century and has an unfortunate history of being destroyed and reconstructed several times since then. Having lived 60 miles south of the Speedway in Daytona, Florida for almost 10 years, I had more of an interest in this castle. The only castle in Florida is at a Disney attraction in Orlando, not quite the same thing.

At the Pension Da Gigi the hotelier saw me arrive with my umbrella. Smiling, she told me that a cold front would pass through this evening and clear away the rain. The next day would be clear and sunny. Back in my room, I soaked in a hot bath in a traditional oversized tub, made my notes from the day, and my plan for the walk to Wanzleben. The bathtub was so large that, for no reason other than to try, I was able to spin around completely inside it. The whirling water went all over me but managed to stay in the tub.

For the second straight day I was the only overnight guest, and there was an abundance of food at the breakfast table. When my host brought me the kännchen kaffee she told me that I had a much more pleasant day for my journey to Wanzleben: clear skies, bright sunshine with a high dappled sky, and temperatures starting out in the low 60's and rising into the 80's by mid-afternoon. This kind of day presented an entirely different set of threats to my ability to see and focus on objects. With rain I had to contend with airborne particles streaming into my eye and slippery walkways. With bright sunshine, the glare from windows, vehicle windshields, and anything shiny tended to make objects appear blurry or cause my eye to close. My preference, after 10 days' post-hospitalization experience, was for a clear, dry day rather than a cloudy day with rain. I expected very little vehicle traffic along the rural route through the forest to the castle and an easy walk. I made a sandwich and packed an extra piece of fruit with it for a snack along the way.

At 10 a.m., I arrived at a path leading to the Schloss Ampfurth. The exact date of construction, sometime in the 12th century, is unknown. The guide book and historical data describe multiple ownerships throughout the centuries ranging from regional royalty, local bureaucracies, entrepreneurs, and public organizations. In 1997, the castle was sold to a private family. Two wings of the castle are used for apartments. Part of a former barn is used as a meeting hall for local organizations.

The structure is unique to the area and it is very hard to tell what parts are original, what original parts have been restored, and what parts have been added and then restored over the years. The primary supporting structure of the castle and its walls, two towers, and the moat have been restored and preserved. On the property are large garden areas. When I visited there were hundreds of sunflowers at full height and bloom throughout the grounds. On a bench within the gardens I relaxed and ate the sandwich I made at breakfast.

Twenty minutes east from the castle I passed out of the forest into the fields and farmlands stretching toward the village of Klein Wanzleben. The terrain was flat; there was almost no traffic; and, I adjusted to walking full-face into the sun using both a low-brimmed baseball cap and aviator sunglasses to shield my eye from the direct sunlight. Within an hour I had reached the town of 2,500 residents. At the approach, the sign bearing the name Klein Wanzleben also includes an image of the town's coat of arms: a silver sugar beet with silver leaves.

One of Europe's largest and most modern sugar beet factories was built there in 1994, and employs the majority of the townspeople. It replaced the sugar mill company that was founded by the local sugar beet farmers in 1838. There was an unusually large number of small businesses and services located within the town and supported by the residents and employees of the factory. In the area of the factory, a sweet, non-chemical odor was easy to detect. In the market where I stopped to replace my water bottles, I learned about the sunflower gardens I had seen at the Castle Ampfurth. Sugar beets had been planted there for hundreds of years and, over time, robbed the soil of most if its nutrients. Over the years the harvests returned fewer and less viable sugar beets. The sunflower beds grew in the less fertile soil and helped to restore the nutrients. The sunflowers were more attractive to the tourists and were retained in the gardens. It seems as if the sugar beets are everywhere else. When I asked how important sugar beets were for the area and the economy I was told that Germany produces as much tonnage as the United States and ranks behind only France and Russia in global production. It is the cash cow for the population and must have absorbed a huge proportion of resources when managed centrally under the five-year plans by the government of the former East Germany.

Wanzleben, my destination for this day, was only another two hours east-southeast from its smaller (kleiner) sister city. The hustle and bustle of the sugar beet center was too active for the pace which I was pursuing. My hope was that the four-mile distance closer to Wanzeleben would add a greater element of peace so characteristic of the rural and rustic region through which I was walking.

I had a reservation at the four-star Hotel Burg, located at the northern side of Wanzleben less than three-quarters of a mile from the center of the town. The modern hotel boasts as the foundation for its structure a former castle as old as the Castle Ampfurth but smaller in size and land area. Similar to Ampfurth, space in the former structures on the castle grounds such as the manor house, barns, and storage areas were transformed into suites and rooms, and decorated with antiques from the old German and Prussian states. The interior sports the character of a former castle emphasizing long dark halls, thick walls, isolation, and privacy. The window ledges in the suites and rooms are so long and deep that an adult can sit comfortably on a ledge, look out at views of the fields, forests, and town, and listen to the sounds of nature. Inside there is a fine dining restaurant, the "Philippe Auguste," with a terrace, fireplace, separate bar, and lounge. Although I did not have fine dining attire I did have clean, business-casual jeans and a shirt with a collar. I also had status as a guest, which I hoped would gain me entrance this evening at least as far as the bar.

After I checked in, there were five hours of daylight to tour. One of the brochures at the reception area described the "Spaßbad Wanzleben," a huge water park with an oversized lap pool for the adults, and chutes, slides, and a simulated ocean with waves and underwater tidal currents for the children. The park supported volleyball and badminton courts, ping pong tables, and jungle gyms. I returned to my room for my swimsuit and goggles. I walked the half mile to the Spaßbad along the east side of the Wanzleben which is bisected by the Sarre River. I read the sign for a street, "Hospitalstraße," which surprised me. The German word for hospital is krankenhaus. "Krankenhaus Straße" is the name I would have expected on the sign. Not surprisingly, there was a pharmacy, (Apotheke), on this street. Three couples were browsing in an antique shop down the road and around the corner. Everything which I saw from the window was displayed very stylishly and all without price tags. The Catholic Church of Saint Boniface was closed. There was a schedule for Masses only on Wednesday and Sunday mornings at 8:30 a.m.

The outdoor temperature was 84 degrees when I arrived at the Spaßbad. The water temperature was 10 degrees cooler. For 15 minutes, I relaxed in the hot tub and then shared a lane in the lap pool and swam for half an hour. I remained poolside watching the swimmers and the children at play for another hour. A soccer ball ricocheted off a wooden chair a few feet away from me, and I caught it before it hit me right at chest level. A man brought his young son, four or five years old, over to apologize to me. "No harm. No foul." The boy's older companion rushed over to claim the ball, and then they both ran away.

I returned to the Hotel Burg by the west side of the Sarre, passing two boutiques, a restaurant, a pizzeria, and the high school. Perhaps because of the prosperity generated from the sugar beet industry and the trickle down of income from businesses and tourists in neighboring Magdeburg, Wanzleben appeared to be an especially prosperous and vital town.

The dinner was exceptional, rivaling, if not exceeding, anything I had eaten in restaurants in France, Belgium and elsewhere in Germany in terms of taste, quantity, and value. The menu selections offered food entirely raised or grown within the region. I selected an appetizer of smoked breast of quail, and sliced hard-boiled quail egg with baked bread. For the entrée I chose the grilled "Netlitzer" ostrich fillet with celery mousseline, rhubarb, green asparagus, and potato pyramid cake. I almost never eat dessert but made an exception for the marinated raspberries with vanilla raspberry brandy sauce. Together with two glasses of local red wine, the entire bill was only 38 euros, ($ 45.).

The lounge proved an excellent retreat to sit comfortably among the antique furnishings, write my notes, and plan my route for the next day. The weather was expected to be a mix of sun and clouds with a 50-50 chance for rain in the afternoon and evening. Magdeburg, the capital of the state of Saxony-Anhalt, was huge, a city of a quarter of a million residents, and historic. Only

14 miles almost directly east of Wanzleben, I planned to start out early in the better weather, and arrive at a hotel in the early afternoon before the weather deteriorated.

At the end of a good day's walk in sunshine and fresh air, a few hours poolside and a swim, almost four hours of sightseeing and a fabulous dinner, I fell asleep hearing only the occasional sounds of songbirds. I heard the same sounds when I awoke. They were heralding the start to a beautiful day.

The morning newspaper in the hotel lobby displayed the weather forecast on the front page and predicted bright sunshine with temperatures from the mid-60's to the mid-80's, about 10 percent higher than normal, with average humidity. When Detlev was revising my walk between Hahnenklee and Berlin he had planned a short walk from Wanzleben to Magdeburg so that I would have more time to tour the historic city. Magdeburg was only a nine-mile, three-hour walk northeast from the hotel. I easily would arrive by noon. With 225,000 residents, it had 40 times the population of Wanzleben and, following the reunification of Germany, now served as the capital of the state of Saxony-Anhalt. There would be more attractions to visit than I would have time to see.

I followed my normal routine at breakfast, eating as much as I could at the table and packing a sandwich and fruit to eat along the way. Only 30 minutes beyond Wanzleben through the fresh farm fields was the small hamlet of Schleibnitz to the north; 90 minutes later, I crossed over the A-14 autobahn, and the fields melted into the outskirts of Ottersleben.

I slowed my pace through the center of town and window shopped. Some of the shops and market entrance doors had poster displays of summer events in Ottersleben and Magdeburg. At a bus stop along the route I read that the time between the stop in town and the arrival at the bus station in Magdeburg was only 20 minutes. In another hour I expected to be at my hotel. But when I saw a group of children and their pet dogs chasing the ducks across the grass and in and out of the Ottersleber Pond I stopped to watch.

The walk for the final part of the day was through an entirely built-up area. Viewing only the roads and the structures, I was not able to distinguish between the centers and outskirts of either Ottersleben or Magdeburg. As I continued east I saw the road signs for the "Magdeburger-Ring" which I knew from the map was a loop around the city much like the roadway rings which circle such cities as Moscow, Houston and Washington, DC. Only one mile northeast from the five-point, nine-lane traffic circle was my hotel, "The Maritim Hotel Magdeburg," a four-star hotel that was undergoing renovations and offered a great rate of less than $100. a night in the middle of the Altstadt (Old City). I had to negotiate only two of the five points and only three of the nine lanes and was able to do so without incident.

The Maritim Hotel Magdeburg was spectacular. It boasts the largest and tallest entrance and lobby of any hotel in Germany, and contains 514 rooms, two restaurants and two pubs in addition to other amenities most of which were being renovated. At noon, there were seven clerks at the reception desk at the time when I was the only person checking in. Affixed to each of the clerks' nametags were the flags of the countries representing the languages which he spoke. Everyone displayed the flags from Germany and Great Britain. I saw flags from France, the Netherlands, Italy, Spain, Denmark, Greece, and Turkey. All of the remodeling occurring within the hotel was in areas that did not affect my stay. The swimming pool, sauna, fitness center, locker rooms, guest laundry, parts of the kitchen, banquet rooms, and business center were closed and under construction. After checking in, I was provided a pass to the café adjacent to one of the restaurants where lunch items, such as paninis, pasta dishes, salads, soft drinks, juices and water were provided without charge. There was a charge for alcohol, and I bought a Diamant Tafelbier which is brewed in Magdeburg.

My room was on the seventh floor and I had a commanding view of the city. I could see the Elbe River, the City Hall, the Cathedral of Magdeburg, the Saint John church, the Kloisters, the outdoor cafes of the Old City, and the pedestrians-only zone within a 90 degree arc from my window and all only a short walking distance from the hotel. I decided to take a hot bath and a short nap, and then tour the town for three or four hours before dinner and another two or three hours after dinner.

When I was assigned in Berlin, Germany still was divided and Magdeburg was the highlight of the former German Democratic Republic. East Berlin, the capital, was its rival. Both had been destroyed significantly during World War II: East Berlin almost completely by the Soviets and Magdeburg very heavily by the British Royal Air Force (RAF). In January 1945, during one night of heavy bombing by the RAF, much of the city was destroyed; 16,000 people were killed; and, the cathedral suffered severe damage. I wanted to see the cathedral 70 years later and it was my first stop beyond the hotel.

The cathedral was huge as seen from my hotel room and majestic in appearance as I walked around it and through it. It is the oldest Gothic cathedral in Germany, dating from 1520. Unlike the typical Gothic cathedrals, the Magdeburg Cathedral does not have flying buttresses supporting the walls which rise to a height of 100 feet and to 300 feet within the two towers. The antique pillars, made from marble and granite, date from 937. A baptismal font, transported from Egypt and still used today, is said to be thousands of years old. A similar age is associated with the grave of Otto I, Holy Roman Emperor from 973, but nothing within the grave, including the skeleton, exists to supports this. There is a sculpture of Saint Catherine and an incomplete sculpture of Saint Maurice, each created around 1250 by the same artist, and for whom the cathedral once had been named, "The Cathedral of

Saints Catherine and Maurice." The most interesting and remarkable piece of art is said to be the sculptures of the five wise and the five foolish virgins, each different in appearance and created some time in the early 13th century. All of the art which had survived is ornate, simple in design and structure but complex in detail, color, and beauty. More than an hour had passed before I left to visit the "Kunstmuseum Kloster Unser Lieben Frauen (The Art-museum Monastery of our Women."

From mid-year 2015 through 2016 the museum would celebrate its 40th anniversary. At the entrance were brochures in several languages which described the museum's mission and the exhibits. I read that "Our intention is to make children, adolescents and adults curious about art. Watching exhibitions together in the Kunstmuseum Kloster Unser Lieben Frauen and discovering art promotes personal, cultural and creative skills." It is dedicated to national and international contemporary art. Before the reunification of Germany the focus was sculpture and drawings from artists within the German Democratic Republic. It seemed to me that there was too much to see in too small an area, and that the atmosphere was too interactive, more conducive to touching, feeling, talking, and creating than it was to viewing, studying, contemplating, and reflecting. After viewing most of the exhibits I concluded that this museum was not a place that made me want to spend time in it and was an attraction that I would not re-visit or recommend.

I thought that I might fare better back in a church. There were 65 churches or temples in Magdeburg from which I could choose. I chose the closest, Johannes Kirche (St. John's Church), a quarter mile to the north in Old Town and a stone's throw to the Elbe River. Everything was typically Gothic from the outside: a massive structure, rebuilt many times for many reasons, most notably war; tall, stained glass windows; two towers at the front with crosses at the highest points. There was the façade of what once must have been the original entrance framing the base to the larger, restored entrance. But there was nothing Gothic inside, only the outline of what once were framings and supports. Now the church is used as a city concert hall and meeting place. The interior has a polished floor and a wide open space where once there must have been pews, apses, naves, sanctuaries, and altars. I saw cubicle desks and chairs set up around an educational display for energy conservation. Off to the sides and corners were high-dollar microphone stands, amplifiers, speakers, and related electronics on hand for the next choral or concert performances. Later I learned that the church congregation had merged with one of the 64 other churches to form the Church of the Trinity somewhere in town.

Still in Old Town I moved slightly northwest and stayed outdoors to view the Rathaus and the Alter Markt (Old Market). The Rathaus dates from 1244 and, like most structures built then and later, it was destroyed as a result of fire and war, and rebuilt several times. A completely new Rathaus was built after the war in 1950. There now are two buildings which provide similar government functions and administrative services. Facing the front of the old Rathaus is the gilded statue of the Magdeburg Horseman. At the entrance is a beautiful bronze door with engravings which depict scenes from the history of Magdeburg. The Alter Markt is the landmark for tourists to find and ride the City Tour bus and discover the attractions of Magdeburg. During the first 11 months of the year the area hosts several small shops and restaurants and the atmosphere is relaxed and sleepy. But it comes to life for the annual Christmas Market and fills with tourists and locals in a shopping frenzy. The area is reorganized and a mini-carnival with rides is provided as a distraction to the shopping. Vendors set up stands offering hand-made gifts, ornaments, curios, food, and drink. This night, at dinner in a quiet restaurant in Old Town, I only could imagine the Christmas crowds wandering in winter through the Markt in the spirit of the season.

I lost all interest in exploring the last section of Old Town as soon as I saw the McDonald's hugging a corner of an intersection. Walking southwest toward the hotel I could hear rock and roll and heavy metal music blaring from somewhere not too far away. Perhaps there was a Friday night concert in the park. I found the event at the Hauptbahnhof (Main train station) only four long blocks from the hotel. There were more police than there were revelers. Uniformed officers on foot, on horseback, in squad cars and armored vehicles, and crews at fire trucks and ambulances formed a ring around about 200 mostly younger protestors who had assembled to demonstrate against government cuts in social welfare programs. The two bands alternated providing the entertainment to the protestors and the curious. I watched and listened for more than an hour. Possessing and drinking alcohol from an open container in public is legal and, given the crowd, the environment, and the potential for an incident, there was none. Only one person, who was excessively inebriated, was led away by a team of police to an ambulance. From the open window in my hotel room I could hear the sounds from the bands. But the room was absolutely quiet once I closed the window and turned on the air conditioning. After all the noise and excitement, this night ended very differently for me compared to almost every other day. Until I arrived in Berlin, I expected that the next six towns would be more representative of my earlier experiences both by day and by night.

I was on the road east 17 miles toward Möckern at 8 a.m. the next morning. There was a mix of sun and clouds and high humidity. I sensed that it would rain sometime in the morning or later that day. Not far from the hotel, I passed the Johannes Kirche and then crossed the Elbe and two of its parallel tributaries, the Zollelbe and Alte Elbe, by way of the Anna-Ebert-Brücke. I saw a cargo barge heading north on the Elbe and watched two fisherman in a rowboat bounce up and down in its wake. A quarter mile away was the huge GETEC Arena capable of hosting 7,000 people for a variety of events.

Sports, such as boxing, wrestling, gymnastics, tennis, handball, and table tennis, are most popular. The arena can be converted to host trade shows, exhibitions, seasonal pageants and celebrations, as well as concerts, dances, theater, meetings, and rallies.

A light rain began to fall just as I passed the arena. In less than two hours, I arrived in the town of Königsborn where I stopped for a cup of coffee which I did not need, and to ask the locals about the weather for the day. My waitress informed me that there would be only a few brief showers in the morning and then the skies would clear for the next few days. She was disappointed because she said her husband was a farmer and that the fields needed the rain. Before I left, she told me that she and her family reside in Königsborn and that she had a married daughter with children in Möckern which is the fourth largest land city in Germany, more than 300 square miles, and a composite of more than 60 villages. She assured me that the walk would be easy and that I would enjoy the town.

The route for the next 10 miles beyond Königsborn along Route 246 into Möckern was predominantly farmland. I could see fields recently harvested or tilled for planting and they appeared especially dry. The baked earth easily absorbed the rain. There was no runoff or patches of standing water. One year earlier, in late May and early June 2013, there had been several days of heavy rainfall resulting in record flooding. In Magdeburg the water level rose more than 15 feet above normal and more than ten percent of the city's residents, about 25,000 people, were evacuated mandatorily and forced to flee their homes. Now, this woman was wishing for more rain.

When I entered Möckern about four hours later, I had walked 10 miles mostly through fields and farmland, except for the tiny hamlet of Nedlitz which I passed in less than 10 minutes. With such a vast amount of territory dedicated to farming, and with so many people dependent upon the weather for their livelihood, it was easy to sympathize with the farmer's wife.

Like many other cities in Germany, Möckern, founded in the year 950, has a history plagued by war. However, unlike many of the other larger cities in Germany, Möckern frequently ended up on the winning side until the First World War. After its most prestigious victory supporting Prussian forces to defeat Napoleon in 1813 in the Battle of Möckern, the city was transformed. The population of farmers and beer brewers who traded at open-air markets and their local administrators were rewarded by the government with an expansion of infrastructure which included saw and steam mills, malt and starch factories, and a rail line. Möckern suffered during both world wars, especially after World War II when it came under Soviet occupation and then became part of the German Democratic Republic.

The Soviets dismantled the mills and factories and sent the materials back to the Soviet Union. Residents survived by maintaining an agrarian economy with limited resources provided in accordance with Soviet and East German five-year plans and directives. Under the communists, land reform was instituted and private property was seized. The uncompromising work ethic and community spirit of the residents paid off after the German reunification. Today Möckern is prosperous as a farming community, and operates one of the largest poultry factories in Germany. It contains another huge factory which produces laminate flooring with customers throughout the European Union.

The hotel which Detlev had recommended, the "Schützenhaus Möckern," was absolutely consistent with the Google reviewer's comments which read, "Very clean hotel with a very friendly staff." The hotel was small and, at check-in, I was the only overnight guest. The receptionist offered me the opportunity to view and select my room but I told her that it was not necessary. The smallest room with a bed and bathroom would suit my needs just perfectly. She gave me a second-floor room with a view west to the courtyard and garden. To the east was the main street and a large and busy market, "EDEKA Weiss."

After I checked in, I took a shower and had a short nap. Then I dressed and crossed the street to EDEKA Weiss. The work day was ending and there were many shoppers passing through for groceries. Everything was well organized and sale items were displayed prominently at each aisle. For at least six more nights, plus whatever amount of time I decided to stay in the apartment in Berlin, I had the convenience of a bed and light by which to read. At the aisle with school supplies, newspapers and magazines, I found two shelves of books and selected a paperback about the history of aircraft development. I walked through the market for almost an hour but purchased only the book, a tube of toothpaste, and two bars of chocolate. In the morning I would return and buy some fruit if none was provided at breakfast. From the EDEKA, I walked through a small neighborhood of five streets and perhaps 50 homes exactly in the opposite image of a Levittown community from the 1950's. The five roads curved and twisted; none was straight. No two homes were built the same or even at the same time. From very old to very new most sat on the same size quarter-acre lot. Others sat on larger lots and three or four sat in front or alongside large fields. Every home had a garden and flowers to the front and one or both sides. I saw only two people outside in the neighborhood: a man washing his Volkswagen station wagon and a woman retrieving laundry from clotheslines on the side of her home. I did not see anything that gave evidence of children such as bicycles, toys or jungle gyms. Except for automobiles and the occasional display of laundry, personal property was kept out of sight.

I did not want to burden the staff at the hotel with preparing two meals for me, and so I walked further through the town to a small restaurant for dinner. At 7 p.m. on a Saturday, I noticed that only about one-third of the tables were occupied. I ordered a beer and nursed it while scanning the book about aircraft and waiting for my meal. Not surprisingly, there was more food presented on my plate than I thought I would be able to finish. The 18 miles to Schopsdorf the next day would provide an opportunity to burn off most of the calories.

Back at the hotel I wrote in my notebook about the day's activities and then read the aircraft book until I fell asleep. The evening and night had been one of the more quiet Saturdays throughout "The TREK."

From my window, I could see clusters of broken clouds moving easterly high overhead as the day began. "Weather from the west" was a common expression for forecasting the next day's weather. If there was a newspaper available at the breakfast room then I would look to see what the weather had been the day before in the Harz region. It might foretell what I could expect for the day. There was no newspaper; however, the hotelier told me that the forecaster from the morning television news was predicting a mix of sun and clouds with no chance of rain and with warmer temperatures in the mid-80's.

While I was studying the route to Schopsdorf which Detlev had planned for me, the hotelier brought the breakfast tray to my table. She told me that Schopsdorf was a town of fewer than 400 residents, however, there were two hotels. She recommended the "Hotel A2." It was located one mile deeper into Schopsdorf and closer to the next town of Golzow and had very good reviews from internet users. I made the Hotel A2 my objective for the day.

Shortly after I left the Schützenhaus Möckern, I realized I had forgotten to ask if there was a Catholic church in Möckern, Hohenziatz, Drewitz, Magdeburgerforth or Schopsdorf. I already had walked out of Möckern and, in the three small hamlets between Möckern and Schopsdorf, there was little chance of finding one. I arrived in Hohenziatz at 9:45 a.m., an hour and a 45 minutes after I started walking, and assumed that I had walked about five miles. The walk had been entirely through fields and farmland. It was not until I reached Hohenziatz that I saw a home or building. I entered the town at the intersection of Karl-Marx Straße and Alt Frose Straße, crossed over the Ihle River and four small streets, and was out of the town in less than 15 minutes. Beyond Hohenziatz all I could see for a mile or more were more fields and farmland.

In another five miles I would reach Drewitz, population less than 400. I was hoping to find a restaurant there. If not, then I would look for some sort of isolated and shaded area in which to stop, dress down slightly to cool off, eat an MRE, and take a rest. Failing that, I would push on another hour to Magdeburgerforth. With temperatures nearing the mid-80's it would be prudent to stop, eat, and rest after having walked 12 or more miles with another four or five to follow.

One block north off the main street into Drewitz, I was fortunate to find the Gaststätte Rüscher. It had been quite some time that I had walked so far in such hot, dry weather and I reverted to my routine of finding an alley in which to remove my shirt, take a quick, upper-body sponge bath, put on a clean, dry shirt, and then enter a restaurant. This one was a delightful surprise, nearly full at just past noon with couples and families who looked as if this were the place to gather mid-day on Sunday. I was concerned that I might look out of place and attract attention dressed in only shorts and a T-shirt and toting a large backpack over my left shoulder. But no one seemed to notice me. All that was available were tables for four persons and, after I asked, the older hostess told me that there was nothing smaller. She guided me to an empty table and waited while I set down my backpack. Then she patted my cheek and touched my forehead and said, "Your face is very red and your head is very wet. You must want a cold beer."

"Ja, bitte."

In the restroom, as I was refilling my two water bottles, I looked into the mirror. My face was very red. I had forgotten to apply sunscreen before I started out and had walked full-face east toward the rising sun for five hours with only my baseball cap and sunglasses as protection. The beer was on the table when I returned. Half of it was gone before I sat down. Now I could relax and order lunch.

There were three "Sonntag-Spezial" handwritten on a chalkboard. I ordered a second mug of beer and the pork schnitzel. The fresh-baked black bread was delicious, but I knew not to eat too much before I saw the size of the meal. The schnitzel was served with a seasoned cucumber and red beet salad, spätzle (soft egg noodles), and asparagus. As usual, I would have no room for dessert.

After lunch I made a second trip to the restroom to apply sunscreen to my face. Once back on the main street, I found a cluster of trees on the north side at the end of town just before the area opened up again into acres of farmland. Out of view from the road, I removed my shirt, shoes, and socks and was asleep almost as soon as I placed my head on the backpack. I slept soundly for about an hour. Nothing like a heavy mid-day meal followed by a nap.

I entered Magdeburgerforth along Friedenstraße (Peace Street). Much like Hohenziatz but narrower, I crossed over five streets, passed by the large Gloine Pond and through about 300 yards of forest, and once again was walking between the fields in less than 15 minutes. Earlier than I had expected, I arrived in Schopsdorf passing by the Hotel Jerichower Land-Hof and turning north off Route L52 to Heidestraße and the hotel.

There are approximately 300 residents in Schopsdorf and it seemed very surprising that such a small town would have two hotels. There were several automobiles, all but one with German license plates, parked at the hotel, and I was slightly apprehensive that there would not be an available room. However, the hotelier told me that several rooms were available and that most of the cars belonged to the hotel staff and two or three patrons at the

Rosenkrug (Rose jug) restaurant and bar. The room was on the second floor, small but comfortable, with two single beds, a private bathroom with shower and a mini-refrigerator which is very rare in small, privately-owned German hotels, pensions, and gästehauses. I had walked about 18 miles this Sunday and had a walk of 19 miles ahead of me on Monday. After checking in, I decided to take a long, hot shower, bring my notebook and map to work at the bar, and then eat dinner and go to bed early.

Enroute to the bar, I found a brochure about Schopsdorf and the Hotel A2. At the bar, I read that I was located almost exactly on the border of the German states of Saxony-Anhalt and Brandenburg. This was my first real indication that I was closing in on Berlin. I felt good and began studying the map and reviewing the revised route which Detlev had created for me.

I knew I had only three towns and less than 60 miles before I reached the outskirts of Berlin, then only 14 miles to Wannsee and another 13 miles to the Brandenburg Gate. My spirits were lifted, not as much from the effects of a second glass of wine, but more by the comments from the bartender who told me that clear skies, lower temperatures and no rain was the forecast for the next week. He served also as a waiter and asked me if I were planning to eat dinner in the hotel. Exactly as in Drewitz at lunch, the Rosenkrug restaurant offered three "Sonntag-Spezial." I asked him to surprise me and bring what he would have ordered if he were eating alone here on a Sunday evening.

Hans Krugerman, a resident of Schopsdorf, worked three jobs to support his family of seven. His wife Gretta was a stay-at-home mother. He told me that he was 10 years old when the Berlin Wall fell and Germany was reunited. He was able to see the changes for the better as he was coming of age. After he married he wanted to have a large family with many children who could grow up in freedom and opportunity. He told me all this and more as he sat next to me after he brought my meal and the remainder of the bottle of wine which I had been drinking.

We finished the bottle together while we talked. Hans told me that as long as his children were living at his home they would learn from him and his wife about how difficult everything was for everyone of all ages when Germany was divided and when their parents were living in the German Democratic Republic. They would learn also how much more of things of value, "including life itself," now was available to them. Our conversation was cut short by the demand of the Sunday-evening customers. I felt fairly certain that much of his sentiments are shared by many of his countrymen close to his age and with similar experiences.

After dinner I went for a walk to explore the large forested area behind the hotel. However there were no trails leading into the forest and the surrounding area was very industrial with large truck parking areas, storage facilities, and commercial buildings. I went back to the hotel and read before falling asleep.

Monday morning I awoke early to the sounds of diesel engines idling and the industrial park coming alive with the start of a new work week. I would have preferred the sounds of songbirds. Hans was not at breakfast. The day was developing much like he described to me the night before: sunny with cool temperatures and very little humidity.

I remembered to apply sunscreen before I set out for Golzow 18 miles almost directly to the east. There was no walking route to the southeast. The area there was one huge forest called the "Belziger Landschaftwiesen" (Belz Countryside Meadows). The six-hour walk slightly northeast would be divided into two three-hour segments with a break in between for lunch and a rest.

The first 300 yards from the hotel was through the built-up and industrial areas and across Highway 30. Then the road opened up to tracts of fields and farmlands for the next 2.5 miles to the town of Ziesar, population 2,500.

In the middle of town, just one block south of the route on Schloßstraße (Castle Street), was the historic "Bischofsresidenz Burg Ziesar," (Bishop's residence, Castle Ziesar). It was opened as a museum 10 years earlier and contains exhibits from the Middle Ages to the present. Inside there also is a 100-foot-tall tower from which one may view the town and its surroundings. For five euros, ($ 7.), there is a guided tour of the castle, museum exhibitions, and the chapel.

Before the start of a tour, I was able to secure my backpack with the staff and refill one bottle of water from the indoor fountain. I understood less than half of the information on the tour. The statistics about the Middle Ages, the types of machinery and tools used then, and the details about the politics and culture were too technical for my level of proficiency in German.

After the tour, I returned to the route and passed by the Town Hall and the City Church. Near the church I saw a group of senior citizens who I knew were not Germans and guessed from their girth, clothing, and inscriptions on the men's baseball caps that they were Americans. I confirmed my guess as I passed them and saw "AARP Travel" on several day packs. At least they weren't wearing surgical masks.

At noon I entered the village of Glienecke from the west on Dorfstraße and, after passing five intersecting streets, at 12:10 p.m. I was exiting to the east. I did not see a single store, café, restaurant, or pension. Months later, at home in the United States, I researched "Glienecke, Germany," to see if I had missed anything. From the "AOL Travel" website I read:

"Sorry, we don't have any 'Things To Do' located in Glienecke but please check out nearby cities for 'Things To Do'."

"Sorry, we don't have any Restaurants located in Glienecke but please check out nearby cities for Restaurants."

"Sorry, we don't have any Hotels located in Glienecke but please check out nearby cities for Hotels."

"Sorry, we don't have any Nightlife located in Glienecke but please check out nearby cities for Nightlife."

One hundred yards beyond Glienecke was a large forested area where I stopped for lunch and a rest. I had two full bottles of water and used half of one to wash my face and hands and take a quick sponge bath before I ate. Lunch was a mystery meat MRE, an apple, and a "Nature Valley Dark Chocolate Peanut Butter" protein bar containing 190 calories, by far the most nutritious and tastiest snack I was consuming during "The TREK."

If there were traffic along the road near where I was resting I did not hear any, and I woke myself up after napping for almost an hour. I washed my face again using the remaining half of the first water bottle and liberally applied additional sunscreen.

I could have saved the sunscreen. For the next 90 minutes, I walked comfortably through the shade of the forest, sensing only the warm temperature but not the direct sun on my face, arms, and legs. Wollin appeared about a quarter mile east of the forest. Two more hours and another six miles behind me, I entered Golzow from the southwest. Crossing over the Plane River along Hauptstraße I had a difficult choice to make. If I wanted to exercise my right arm and hand I could deter one block to the left to the "Whiskyzone" and sample whatever was available. If I wanted to exercise both arms and hands and the rest of my body I could detour one block to the right to the Schwimmbad Golzow and swim laps. I did neither. The long walk this day, the MRE for lunch, and the thought of another long walk the next morning compelled me to find the "Bürgers Pension and Restaurant." It was less than half a mile away.

This was a small (four rooms) but very stately facility, exceptionally furnished more for the business traveler than for the day tourist. I selected a single room for 30 euros, ($45.). It was much larger than I had expected, with a private bathroom and shower, and furnished with a writing desk, two sitting chairs, and a television. Except for the time that I had watched the World Cup playoff games in France, Belgium and my first 10 days back in Germany, I had not watched any television and did not care to do so.

After a shower I was very thirsty for a cold beer. Although it still was very warm I dressed in a short-sleeve shirt with a collar and clean jeans and went downstairs to the pub. I drank half the beer rather quickly then realized that I had forgotten to bring my map and notebook to write my daily notes and plan the next day's activities. I told the bartender that I was departing only to return to my room and would be back shortly. He just nodded. When I returned my mug had been refilled.

"You drank this first beer so quickly. I think that you must have much thirst."

Wasn't that nice? Too bad for me that I am so blatantly obvious when I am thirsty for a beer. Juggling papers and turning a map over and over and inside and out always sparks an offer of assistance from a bartender, especially when there are no other customers. We had a nice talk.

Lawrence Hermann was more interested in talking about what I had done between Normandy and Golzow. I was more interested in hearing what to expect on the walk to Kloster Lehnin and Caputh, the last two towns before I arrived in Wannsee on the outskirts of Berlin. I guessed that the closer I came to Berlin the more obvious the transition would become between the towns of the former German Democratic Republic and the former free West Berlin. Lawrence told me, "Certainly, Berlin spends its money on its own. Then it helps us if there is something left over."

Now I regretted not having spent more time before I began "The TREK" studying the towns along the route that had been in the former East Germany. It would have been a valuable history lesson to know those towns as they once were and then to know them now, 24 years after the reunification.

The restaurant and outdoor terrace also were much larger than I expected viewing the pension only from the front as I entered. The restaurant had wooden tables which seated between two and six persons with a capacity of 50 or more; the terrace had several circular wrought-iron tables which seated four persons with a capacity of 28 or more. Lawrence would be the waiter at the terrace so I sat outside for dinner although I would have preferred eating indoors with the air conditioning. I finished my second beer at the bar and then moved outside.

After telling Lawrence that I had eaten an Army MRE for lunch I asked if he could recommend something to tilt the scales in favor of edible cuisine. He suggested a four-course dinner: wild turkey soup with onions and carrots; a spinach salad with tomatoes, asparagus, and feta cheese; a beef filet with mushroom sauce, seasoned boiled potatoes, and steamed broccoli; and carrot cake with fresh whipped cream."

"Sounds very much like the MRE I had for lunch. That will be fine, please." Lawrence did not understand my attempt at humor and I was sorry that I tried to make a joke about the food. When he returned with a glass of wine, I tried to explain to him what I had said. This time his smiled. The meal was excellent. Back in my room it was an effort to undress and tend to my personal hygiene. In bed, I didn't turn a single page of my book before I fell asleep.

The morning looked and felt the same as the day before: clear skies and cool temperatures. Hans was spot on with his weather prediction.

Breakfast was a buffet with baskets of rolls and breads, trays of meats and cheeses, and bowls with varieties of yogurt and fresh fruit. Today I planned a very different walk.

First, I would walk for about three hours the nine miles to the Hotel Markgraf in Kloster Lehnin. Then I would check into the hotel and leave my backpack in the room. In my daypack I'd carry a swimsuit and goggles, sunscreen, a bath towel, binoculars, a compass, the sandwiches and fruit from breakfast, and water. Kloster Lehnin had a huge area to explore which included a castle, a monastery, a library with books hundreds of years old, museums, and at least a half dozen churches. If that were not enough, there are more than 7,500 acres of protected area which surround and include three huge lakes and an abundance of nature.

The second nine miles for the day would be a hike four or five miles northwest on the nature trails within the protected areas along the western side of the Klostersee and the Netzener See. From there I would turn to the northeast then south and walk on the trails another four or five miles along the eastern side of these two lakes until I returned to town.

I passed the Lehnin Abbey, also referred to as the Monastery Kloster Lehnin, as I entered town. One of the most visited sites in town, it was built in 1180 in a style known as "German Brick Gothic" and different from the Baroque style of the churches. As is true of most structures, especially castles, forts, churches, and monasteries built that early in old Europe, most were damaged severely or destroyed by wars and pillaging. The first serious restoration of this monastery took place in the late 1870's. The property contains a museum with structures and tools used when the monastery was active and supported a bakery and a distillery. There is also a farming museum annex which portrays the agricultural life of the area from the mid-19th Century.

Only a five-minute walk from the Kloster was the Hotel Markgraf. Stately from the outside, the inside was equally presentable, very attractive and modern. At noon, there was not a single-bed room available, but the staff accepted my backpack, minus the contents for my sightseeing tour, until a room was ready.

Leading to the Klostersee was a network of hiking and biking trails which passed through both fields and forested areas. Walking along the water I could see individuals in canoes and rowboats circumnavigating the lake, and others beachside with blankets and chairs relaxing, catching rays and swimming. There did not seem to be a designated or guarded swimming area which made the thrill of being a part of nature and the environment much more personal and private.

The Autobahn E-30 bisected the quarter-mile separation between the Kloster See and Netzener See but did not interfere with the trails leading between them. The Netzener See was much larger: broad at both the southeast and northwest ends and narrow in the center. The shape gave me the impression that this was once two lakes which had merged over time. Perhaps because of its greater size there was far more activity on and around the lake. There were campsites, restaurants with outdoor-eating areas, cafes, and ice-cream shops at the intersections of roads and trails leading to the lake.

I stopped at an ice cream shop for a two-scoop ice-cream treat and a glass of ice water. At the shore, near what looked like the center of the lake, I changed into my swimsuit and stepped into the water. The water temperature was refreshingly cool, chilling at first and perhaps 70 degrees. But I warmed up as soon as I started moving. It was possible to swim across the lake, but I did not want to be so far from my valuables and property although I had no fear that they would be disturbed by anyone. When I finished swimming I rested lakeside and read the brochures about Kloster Lehnin which I had obtained earlier at the monastery. I could see what looked like deer blinds and knew that there could not be hunting in any protected area. Then I saw a family standing atop one and sharing a pair of binoculars. These structures were observation towers. The family seemed to be watching the birds wading along the shoreline.

There were two more lakes northwest of the Netzener See. One of the brochures which described these lakes noted that at the fourth lake, the large Rietzer See, there was a bird sanctuary which hosted almost 300 different species of birds, such as the kingfisher and white-tailed eagle. There also was a large diversity of plants such as reeds, sedge, lime-dry grass, fever clover, beach-centaury, Troll flowers, and Broad-wing marsh orchids. The Rietzer See was too far away for me to visit and I turned east then south from the end of the Netzener See to sightsee and return to town.

The views from the east westward toward the lakes were magnified with the sun from the west highlighting the activities of the people and the wildlife as if they were spotlighted for filming. I was only about two weeks too early to witness the annual August "Creative Raft Contest" when homemade rafts are built, decorated, and floated along the Klostersee in competition for prizes; and, four to six weeks too early to witness the thousands of migrating birds, especially the large European cranes and storks, which would use these lakes as a stopover and rest area. Also in September I would miss the International Pumpkin Festival located nearby at the Lehnin Institute for Arts and Crafts.

Beyond the Netzener See the trails returned to the west of the Klostersee which I had seen already. To get a different view from the east, I stayed on the thickly-wooded shore or walked in the water 300 or 400 yards until I came upon a trail at the "Havellandkanu" canoe rental facility near the southern section of the lake. At the Gästehaus Am Klostersee I stopped for cake and coffee and watched all the activity near and on the lake continue unabated.

Signs along the trails guided me to the center of town and the monastery near the hotel. Back at the Markgraf, the staff informed me that my room was ready and that my backpack had been placed in the room. The room was on the second floor facing away from the street and overlooking the courtyard where there was a dining area with tables shaded by large umbrellas. With the windows open, I was able to hear the guests, a sound preferable to that of the traffic on the street side. After a shower I was ready for dinner.

The Hotel Markgraf is located at Friedensstraße 13. At Friedensstraße 21 is the Café Restaurant Klosterhof. I walked the 20 yards to the Klosterhof carrying only my notebook and map. The restaurant itself is in one of the oldest buildings built outside the monastery walls. A brochure describing the facility noted that the trees surrounding the terrace where I was seated "are almost 100 years old. . ." hardly impressive considering some of the buildings in and around the town were more than a thousand years old.

The menu was extensive. I ordered a traditional German dinner and sipped on a glass of red wine from the region while I waited for the meal. Having only snacked for lunch while I walked around the lakes I was hungry. However, the dinner portion was typically large, almost excessive, and I struggled to finish.

Back at the hotel, after I undressed for bed, I looked in the mirror and could not understand why I did not appear as if I were gaining weight. The answer had to be that my activities during my typical 16-hour days were burning an average 4,000 calories consumed daily in three meals, two snacks and a ration of alcohol each day.

Good luck with the weather continued through the night and the next morning. For the third consecutive morning, I awoke to a very promising day. Perhaps because of the nature trails, lakes, and outdoor recreation opportunities in the area the weather forecast and water temperatures were posted on a "Täglichen Aktivitäten" (Daily Activities) sheet at the reception desk. The water temperature was noted as 21.5 C, (70.0 F). As invigorating as it might have been, I had no plans to swim today.

Caputh, the location of the summer home of Albert Einstein, was 13 miles almost directly east over relatively flat terrain through two large forests and across the Schwielowsee. A quarter mile from the hotel I passed the Muehlenteich (Mill Pond) to the south, and another quarter mile beyond the pond I entered the forest, part of the "Lehniner Wald and Seengebiet" (Lehniner Forest and Lake Region). Although I was walking east as the sun was rising in a cloudless sky, the thickly-wooded forest provided good protection from the bright sun. In just over an hour I had walked out of the forest and saw across the fields the Autobahn E30 exchange, as large a traffic network as I had seen in Göttingen and Magdeburg. Here was where the east-west traffic routes to and from the major cities of Potsdam and Berlin merged with the routes from those cities to north and south of Germany. From the safety of an overpass I watched the traffic negotiate the exchanges with most of the vehicles moving in the east and west directions.

Two hours from the start, I entered the village of Elisabethhöhe where I stopped to peek into the "Evangelische Kirchengemeinde und Kirche" (Evangelical Parish and Church) and eat a pastry at the Linde Café next door to the church. At the third hour I entered the second forest within the "Potsdamer Wald und Havelseengebiet" (Potsdam Forest and Havel Lake Region." I knew from my four years living in Berlin that almost one-third of the city was forested. Now, as I was within 30 miles of the city, I was learning how much of this area of the former East Germany so closely resembled what I remembered about Berlin.

Reaching the Schwielowsee at late morning was a delight. It includes a huge lake almost 3.5 miles long and 1.5 miles wide to the south and west of Potsdam, which I had never seen and which I planned to visit after I was settled in Berlin. For half an hour, I walked along the northwest half of the lake and then crossed the bridge over the Havel River. There I stopped at the Gaststätte Baumgartenbrück and ate lunch while I watched leisure and commercial watercraft move over the lake and river. The view was so pleasant and the weather so perfect for a mid-August day that I decided to relax with a second glass of wine and people-watch.

From the gaststätte I walked southeast then south and crossed a second bridge, again over the Havel, which led me to the outskirts of Caputh. One quarter mile later I was at the Hotel Müllerhof and checked in at 2:30 p.m. I had the rest of the day to explore Caputh, the final former East German city before Wannsee on the outskirts of Berlin, and the last 13 miles to the Brandenburg Gate.

The Müllerhof was a 125-year old hotel that had been completely modernized. Although it boasted 29 rooms, only two were single rooms and I was lucky to secure the last available one. The room was very well furnished but I did not plan on spending any time there except to shower and sleep. The next day's route would take me northeast past the Schloss Caputh and the Einsteinhaus. For the remainder of the day I decided to tour the outdoor attractions to the south through the town and along the water.

In the room I reapplied some sunscreen and stuffed the daypack with the same items as I had packed in Kloster Lehnin except for the compass. With the binoculars I would be able the view the lakes and rivers from the bridges. I had my swimsuit, goggles, and a towel in case I found a beach or pool.

From the hotel I walked west toward the Havel river and through a marina where the Havel narrowed and joined the Templiner See. In the marina were about 100 watercraft mostly single-engine motorboats, small sailboats, and several rowboats. Half the slips were empty which was understandable on a summer day with temperatures in the mid-70's. South of the marina, I strolled along the Uferpromenade where a walking path at led to the pedestrian bridge across the Havel and into the area referred to as the "boot" of Caputh-Geltow. At the base of the bridge on the northwest side was the Trattoria del Sole restaurant. Only a few yards beyond the restaurant was the Seebad Caputh (Seaside resort, Caputh). The resort extended for about 300 yards by the Schwielowsee and had a swimming area, cabanas, locker rooms, and a pier with a restaurant which extended into the lake.

There were no restrictions for swimming within 100 yards of the shoreline. I changed and swam 30 or 40 yards out from the shore and then across and back the length of the resort. I had the energy for a longer swim but, unlike the lakes in which I swam, the Schwielowsee hosted motor craft and I preferred a more sterile environment. There were no other swimmers but there were several adults and groups of children in the water at the shoreline. Back on shore, I rested and studied Detlev's route to the Wannsee for the next day.

In the early evening I left the Seebad, crossed the pedestrian bridge and toured Caputh through the center of town. The Hotel Golden Anker (Anchor) was a second family-owned hotel claiming more than 100 years in business. Like the Müllerhof, these hotels must have suffered badly during the years of the war, especially during the Soviet assault on Berlin. I'm sure that if anything of value survived it was stolen by the occupiers. Below the image of a golden anchor I saw a sign for a bar and restaurant and went inside. The bar was designed with a mariner theme. On its walls were several large framed black-and-white photographs of the lakes and watercraft. Over the bar were a variety of nautical instruments used for navigation and sailing. I ordered a Berliner Kindl and took it outside on the terrace. The menu was inviting and I stayed for dinner and the opportunity to have a meal some place different from my hotel where I would have breakfast the next day.

After dinner I walked back to the Hotel Müllerhof crossing only four short streets before I arrived. I was very surprised to hear from the reception clerk that there was a message for me. Having re-planned the route, Detlev knew that I was due in Caputh and at the Müllerhof. He had called and left a message that he and Ilona would meet me on Friday, August 15th at 3 p.m. at the Brandenburg Gate. I was elated by the message.

At breakfast I read the brochures describing the three attractions I planned to visit along the route from Caputh to Wannsee: the Heimathaus (Heritage House), the Schloss Caputh (Castle Caputh), and the Einsteinhaus (Einstein House). The weather this day promised to be every bit as delightful as it had been the first three days of the week.

The Heimathaus is one of the oldest former residences in Caputh. The town obtained the property 40 years earlier in the 1970's and began converting it in 1992 to a small museum depicting the historical character of the town and describing the occupations and activities of its early residents. The physical work of restoration and construction was completed by the tradesman of Caputh. Many of the exhibits displaying the lifestyle of the Caputhers were designed and produced by students and members of youth clubs in the area. Volunteers bake brownies for the visitors. Brownies are my number-one lifetime favorite snack or dessert. I took one as soon as it was offered and was tempted to ask for a second.

Five minutes further to the east was the Schloss Caputh. Built in 1662, ravaged, and destroyed many times over the centuries, it is the only structure of its kind to survive in the Potsdam and Berlin areas. It was restored after the reunification of Germany between 1995 and 1999. The interior is spacious and ornate, extending from a basement to upper floors with several rooms of varying size. There is a ballroom and dining room each large enough to support hundreds of guests. The floor of the dining room is constructed of 7,500 blue and white tiles which were imported from the Netherlands. The interior molding in the great rooms and the ceilings are Baroque style but the furniture, paintings, sculptures, and artifacts on display reflect many different styles and eras.

Another 10 minutes away, in the direction of Wannsee, is the Einstein House. In the early 1920's, the Berlin government proposed building a home for Albert Einstein for his 50th birthday in March 1929. However, near the water in Caputh, Einstein had his own home built entirely of fixed and half-timbered wood and bricks with ceilings made of wooden cross-beams. He occupied the home as a summer residence beginning in 1929, and was quoted as saying, "The sailing ship, the distant view, the lonely fall walks, the relative calm, it is a paradise."

After the Nazis came to power in the early 1930's, Einstein fled Germany in 1933. He lived in the Caputh residence for only three summers. The home served several organizations and purposes before, during and after the war, as a part of the German Democratic Republic, and as a part of the reunified Germany. It now is the property of the Hebrew University of Jerusalem and serves as a tourist attraction and museum.

For the next hour I enjoyed a comfortable and scenic walk on Templiner Straße almost directly northeast along the eastern shore of the Templiner See and within and to the west of the Potsdam Forest South. The city of Potsdam had sprawled south, and I was forced to negotiate a major autobahn exchange leading to and from Potsdam. Turning east, I arrived in the town of Bablesberg walking for about a mile on Friedrich-Engels-Straße and crossing a second major autobahn exchange. The traffic, noise and congestion were increasing noticeably. I was passing an S-Bahn train station about every 400 or 500 yards.

Away from the traffic exchanges, Bablesberg seemed as sleepy as Caputh, but with many more businesses and professional office buildings near its bus and train stops unlike the cafes and parks in Caputh near its lakes and rivers.

After almost four hours of touring and walking, it was close to noon as the Griebnitzsee came into view on the west. I found the Avandi Hotel am Griebnitzsee, right at the waterside. The hotel was five stories tall with a restaurant and terrace overlooking the water at the second level. I knew that I was no more than two hours away from the Hotel Grunewald, not far from the beach at the Groß Wannsee (Large Wannsee). Now I could enjoy a meal in a very scenic and relaxed environment and then walk off the calories enroute to the next hotel.

I ordered a small Pilsner and a meal of whitefish with boiled potatoes. Tempting fate, I asked the waiter about the weather for the rest of the day and the weekend. Odin would not be kind to me. The waiter told me that the weather would continue to be nice through the afternoon. Then clouds would develop. Rain was forecast through the night and intermittently through Friday. What would be the chances that it would be raining on Friday at 3 p.m. at the Brandenburg Gate? Again recalling Scarlett O'Hara's comments in "*Gone with the Wind*," I would worry about that tomorrow.

The next five miles took me to the east of the Grienbnitzsee and over a canal which led to the Machnower See. Here the pavement on which I had travelled since Bablesberg ended and I began to walk on an improved trail through the Groß Fenn Forest with a section, "Hundeauslaufgebiet Wannsee-Düppel" (Dog run area Wannsee Düppel). Just beyond the Pohlesee the forest and trail ended and I broke out onto pavement in an open area with a view of the Kleiner Wannsee to the west.

One mile later I reached the pedestrian crossing under the four-lane Autobahn A1 which meshed with Autobahn E51 linking Berlin to Magdeburg and Leipzig. When I read the sign for "Kronprinzessinnenweg" (Crown Princess Way) I thought I knew where I was. Many times in good weather, I had transported my bicycle on the metro to the Wannsee U-Bahn station and then ridden through the forests and around the lakes. At the far end of the underpass I saw signs for "The American Academy in Berlin" and "The American Yacht Club, Berlin." Now I knew for certain where I was, and I had a strange almost peaceful feeling that, after 38 years, I was home.

There still were about 15 miles to the Brandenburg Gate but I felt as happy as if I were already there. Soon I would be near Lake Groß Wannsee. The Hotel Grunewald could not be too far away. In another 30 minutes I was at the front desk and checking in to my last hotel room for the final night after 71 days on the road.

Across the street to the west and down the road no more than a quarter of a mile was the Strandbad (Bathing beach) Wannsee. Many times during my four years in Berlin I had driven my automobile or ridden my bicycle the 5.5 miles from my apartment on Flanaganstraße in Dahlem to spend time at this beach. This afternoon I walked there carrying only my swimsuit, towel, and notebook. In between soaks all I did for almost three hours was re-read my notes and make additions, deletions or corrections for the time when I would use it later as a reference to remember details to write about the walk.

The Hotel Grunewald is located near a major autobahn leading in and out of Berlin. There is a gas station and fast-food establishment adjacent to the hotel. More than half the guests were truck drivers. Their big rigs, which were aligned in the oversized parking spaces behind the hotel, had license plates from as far away as Sweden, Romania, and Italy. Across the street to the south is the large restaurant, Andis Imbiss Easy Rider, with an outdoor eating area and small park. It is very popular with motorcycle enthusiasts. Spanische Allee which runs east-west in front of the Easy Rider is lined on good-weather evenings and weekends with bikers and their machines in the image of Bike Week at Daytona Beach, Florida. At an outdoor table in the park I drank two mugs of draft beer, ate a light dinner, and returned to the hotel as it began to get dark and started to rain. In my room, I emptied my backpack completely and discarded items that I would not need for the final day's walk in the morning. I looked at my worn-out socks, briefs, extra washcloths, and tattered baseball caps that I had worn and carried these 880 miles, and then threw them all into the trash.

I awoke at 4:30 a.m. to the sounds of doors slamming closed. The truckers were getting ready for an early start. The hallway, elevator, and lobby smelled of cigarette smoke. Service for coffee and a continental breakfast began at 5 a.m. and a full breakfast was available at 6 a.m.

I decided to eat early, get out of the hotel, and have a more relaxed breakfast at a café I knew I'd find near one of the intersections leading into the Grunewald.

Outside, daylight was trying to break through the thick, scattered clouds. It still was raining lightly, and the roads were wet. I started the final day's walk dressed in shorts and a T-shirt, wearing a baseball cap, and carrying an umbrella for protection in case the rain began to fall more heavily.

On the trail leading to the Strandbad Wannsee I turned north into the Grunewald, Berlin's largest forested area covering almost 7,500 acres in the southwest sector. Despite the early hour, rain and slippery pavement, the 10-yard wide trail had a fair number of joggers and bicyclists. Many of them waved to me as they passed me from the front. In less than an hour I came to Am Hüttenweg and recalled that this is where I would enter the Grunewald on Saturday mornings when I came to exercise more than 40 years ago. It was only two miles from my apartment on Flanagan Straße. The recollection slowed me down. I looked for a few minutes, as if I were going back in time, at nothing more than the overpass, trees, trail signs, markings on the pavement, and the people.

Just shy of 8 a.m., I walked by the Café Scheune and stopped for breakfast. I figured that I had walked between four and five miles with only eight miles more to go. I would be at the Brandenburg Gate easily before 3 p.m. and my scheduled rendezvous with Detlev and Ilona.

Beyond the café I broke out into the affluent suburb of Charlottenburg best known for the magnificent and beautiful Charlottenburg Palace. This was the first attraction that I had brought my parents to tour when they made their first visit to Berlin 40 years earlier in the summer of 1974. I crossed over Highways 100 and 101 and a set of S-Bahn tracks and then walked northeast with the Lietzensee and Lietzenseepark to my right until I reached Bismarkstraße. Now I knew exactly where I was. Before I reached age 40 I tried to run between two and four marathons a year, almost never missing the Marine Corps Marathon in Washington, D.C. in the late fall. Now I had a feeling similar to running a marathon when the finish line is in sight. I thought that I felt a rush of adrenaline and my heart begin to race.

Bismarkstraße would change names several times but the remaining walk was directly east. I just did not know how far.

The rain had stopped and the sun was breaking through the clouds. On a side street near the German Opera House and the Shakespeare Park I found a unisex barbershop. One of the female barbers saw me enter and waved me to her chair. She struggled to relocate my backpack out of her work area. Tapping me lightly on the arms and shoulders she told me that I was "all wet" and asked me to take off my shirt. She put a barber's cape over my shirtless torso and then put the sweat and rain-soaked shirt into a dryer used for towels. She gave the shirt back to me after she finished the haircut.

Beyond the park at the Ernst-Reuter-Platz traffic circle, Bismarkstraße changed into Straße des 17 Juni (17th of June Street) re-named by the West Berliners to commemorate the uprising by East Berliners who were shot and killed by Soviet soldiers and East German police during a workers protest on June 17, 1953. Having driven my automobile and ridden my bicycle numerous times down this historic street, I knew that I only had to pass the Charlottenburger Gate, cross over the Landwerkskanal, walk through the Tiergarten, and around the Victory Angel monument before I would be able to see the Brandenburg Gate only 1.5 miles beyond the Angel.

When I reached the monument and saw the Brandenburg Gate I felt so dizzy and light-headed from the thrill that I thought I could fly like an angel right up to the Gate.

I walked slowly, occasionally stepping off the pavement on Straße des 17 Juni on to the dirt trails parallel in the Tiergarten. When I reached the intersection of Straße des 17 Juni and Ebertsstraße, only 20 yards from the Brandenburg Gate, I decided that I did not want to arrive alone. This intersection is a major stopping point for tour buses and tourist vehicles to discharge passengers at the base of the Gate. Each time a bus stopped and unloaded passengers I called out, "Is anyone here an American? Does anyone here speak English?" Everyone from three buses ignored me.

From the fourth bus a group of especially attractive female college students approached me and said, "We're from England, will that work?"

I responded, "I've been asking, are there any very pretty young ladies from England here," and they all laughed. Then I told them that I had just walked 895 miles from Normandy, France, starting on June 6th, 71 days ago, to commemorate the 70th anniversary of the Allied landings on D-Day, and that I did not want to arrive and touch the Brandenburg Gate, my final destination, alone. I asked them if they would walk together with me. Holding hands with one girl on each side of me and two other girls on each side of them we crossed the street and touched the Brandenburg Gate together. The girls took a series of photos and selfies of all of us shaking hands and exchanging pecks on the cheek. When they left to go off to tour I took out the copy of the "Arrival Prayer" prepared by my West Point "Proud and Free, 73" classmate, Father Richard Wilson, ordained a Roman Catholic priest on May 29, 2015, and recited it.

I was exhilarated emotionally and spiritually at having arrived, but physically I felt like a survivor from the retreat from Moscow.

Beyond the Brandenburg Gate is the American Embassy. In May 2014, I had sent a detailed letter describing "The TREK" and my plan to arrive at the Brandenburg Gate after the walk which began at Normandy. I introduced myself to the security guard at the American Embassy and produced a copy of the letter I had sent. Like Dorothy from Kansas who traveled a good distance and then asked to see the Wizard of OZ I received the same courteous response, "Go away."

Because I did not include a specific arrival date and time and because I did not have an appointment with a staffer, no one in the American Embassy was available to meet with me for a comment or a media release statement. After closing down the World War II memorials to the veterans during the November 2013, federal government shutdown, the American Embassy in Berlin only added insult to injury when its staffers told me to leave.

As I walked away in disgust I saw Detlev and Ilona. Detlev was holding a bottle of champagne and Ilona was holding three glasses. We embraced and hugged and kissed. Detlev held me and looked closely at my eye. I told him and Ilona that everything was fine. They told me that I was one crazy man.

That I already knew.

Detlev opened the bottle and filled the three glasses. While we drank the contents then finished the bottle, I told them briefly about the walk beyond Hahnenklee, where we had parted company on July 29th, and in much detail about this last day's walk. They gave me a statue of a male German wanderer wearing an Alpine cap, carrying a backpack, and using a walking stick. The inscription reads:

James Joseph Pelosi
Trek to Honor the Legacies
Normandy – Berlin
June 6th – August 15th 2014

It stands on a bookshelf in my library at home next to a picture of my father wearing his World War II Army Air Corps uniform.

They led me back to their car just as the rain returned and many of the tourists sought some form of shelter. We had a short drive to the apartment in Wilmersdorf where I left the backpack and changed clothes to have an early dinner with them at a local Italian restaurant. Throughout the remainder of the evening I could not tell them enough how thrilled I was at having completed "The TREK" and how thankful I was for the support that they and so many others had provided me. I know in my heart that everything I was able to accomplish after two years of planning, organizing and conducting "The TREK" pales in comparison to the contributions made by our combat veterans.

"Overcoming the Cold War required courage from the people of Central and Eastern Europe and what was then the German Democratic Republic, but it also required the steadfastness of Western partners over many decades when many had long lost hope of integrating the two Germanys and Europe."
–   Angela Merkel, Chancellor of Germany.

16. Legacy Events at Seventy Years.

"The TREK," as a personal project in 2014, was the result of an observation I made in 2013 while reading a biography about President Franklin Delano Roosevelt. I learned that there would be four significant anniversaries of events related to international sources of war and conflict, all of which would be recognized in 2014, and all of which occurred in Western Europe. The year 2014 would herald the 100th anniversary of the beginning of World War I, which began after the assassination of Archduke Franz Ferdinand and his wife, Sophie, by 19-year old Serbian nationalist, Gavrilo (Gabriel) Princip on June 28, 1914. June 6, 2014, would be the 70th anniversary of the Allied landings at five beaches along the coast of Normandy, France. The 65th anniversary of the end of the Berlin Airlift would occur officially on May 12, 2014, (although the Allies continued to supply the Berliners with food, fuel and provisions through September 1949). On November 9, 2014, Berliners, other Germans, most Europeans, and many people throughout the world would celebrate the 25th anniversary of the fall of the Berlin Wall.

Americans played a critical role in the successful outcome of all four of these events. The American taxpayers funded the salaries and expenses of more than 16 million service members who deployed from the United States to Europe during both world wars. They also funded, produced, and transported all of the aircraft, ships, vehicles, weapons, equipment, hardware, and food used to support the American combatants. Almost half a million American military members were killed in Europe during seven years, 1917-1918 and 1941-1945, of the two world wars.

American pilots flying relief supplies from American and Allied bases in Europe helped to save the lives of almost three million Berliners during 1948 and 1949 after the Soviets closed all rail and road traffic routes to and from Berlin. During that effort, 31 Americans gave their lives.

Before and after the creation of NATO in Western Europe, designed to check the Soviet and Warsaw Pact threat from the east, Americans of all services and their families served on duty at bases throughout Europe. They were assigned initially as part of the Occupying Powers following the end of World War II, and then as members of units of NATO and independent commands. Since the fall of the Berlin Wall, the collapse of the former Soviet Union, and the reunification of Germany, the American and Allied military presence has been reduced significantly.

My family is of European descent: German, Italian and Irish. During World War II, my father served in the US Army Air Corps and his brother served in the US Navy. Their six first cousins also served in the military in both the European and Pacific Theaters of war. My father was the only one of those eight men to serve and support the Berlin Airlift.

I came of age during the Vietnam War, but I did not serve there. From July 1969, through June 1973, I was a cadet at the United States Military Academy at West Point. In early 1973, Henry Kissinger and Le Duc Tho declared a "peace with honor" for Vietnam, and the United States stopped sending troops to Vietnam in April 1973, two months before I was graduated. Saigon fell two years later in April 1975. As an Infantry Lieutenant, I chose Berlin as my first duty assignment because I wanted to live and work in Europe where my family had lived and where my father served during and after the Second World War.

A book review, which I was reading in the spring of 2013, described the deplorable conditions at the Veterans Administration's (VA) hospitals and medical facilities, and the inability by the VA to provide adequate and timely care for veterans in need of medical attention. This was especially true for combat veterans of the most-recent conflicts in Iraq, Afghanistan, and elsewhere who served in support of the War on Terror after September 11, 2001.

When the federal government shut down in November 2013, many veterans were stranded at their memorials which were closed, including those overseas in such places as the American Cemetery at Omaha Beach, Normandy, France, and the other cemeteries and memorials throughout Europe. World War II veterans were incensed. So were their children, grandchildren, family, and friends. When the government spent money to employ personnel to erect barriers at these places of honor it only added insult to injury. The outcry by veterans critical of the Commander in Chief and his administration resounded in the media, in veterans' organizations magazines, military weekly newspapers, and the meeting halls of military service organizations such as the American Legion and the Veterans of Foreign Wars.

After consulting with my classmates from West Point, fellow veterans, and friends, I decided that the time was right to demonstrate support for all veterans, especially those in need. "The TREK" would be the vehicle by which I could demonstrate that support. The intent was to bring an awareness to the contributions made by veterans, their families, and support groups who served and sacrificed to preserve, protect, and defend this country and its allies in time of war or conflict. Perhaps with a successful event, popular support, and an interest by the media I might be able to generate a publication for profit, and donate those funds to the veterans in need. It would be a goal worthy of our veterans.

At Omaha Beach, in the towns of Bayeux and Caen, and in the region of Normandy, I was interested in speaking with Allied veterans and their family and friends and with tourists who had traveled to attend the 70th anniversary of the D-Day landings. I wanted to hear from as many people as possible what their sentiments were for those who fought and survived and for those who fought and died. There were fewer than 60 surviving Allied World War II veterans who I saw, mostly from Great Britain. All were wearing some form of unit insignia and their medals. They were in great demand.

I was able to speak separately with four of these heroes: two from the United States and two from England. No one was younger than 88. After I introduced myself, I told them about my father's and family's service during World War II, and then briefly described "The TREK" which would begin at Omaha Beach. Without exception, all four men felt as if their service during the war was the singular accomplishment of their lives. They were too young to care about any politics or the reasons for the war; too young to comprehend the threats facing them; too young not to trust the men who led them into combat; and, at the end of the war, still too young to appreciate how much they had accomplished.

After the war, all four men worked at careers, married, sired children, and helped raise grandchildren. I was surprised to learn that, after their retirements, all four remained active in some form of volunteer community service. I was not surprised to hear that, after their experiences in combat at Normandy and beyond until the end of the war, everything that they experienced at work and at home seemed easy in comparison. Challenges always were compared to their wartime experiences, and nothing in civilian life ever proved as difficult as combat. The most common sentiment which each veteran shared with his fellow veteran was that the lives of his buddy, his team, and his unit were more important than his own life. They all were willing to risk their lives to protect or save the men on their left or their right. Upon reflection, they gave thanks that the Allies were victorious and that they, their families, and their friends continue to enjoy the benefits of their victory.

If their families or friends were present then they smiled and radiated pride as they listened to the men speak. The children commented that they always knew there was something special about their fathers.

Most of the tourists, especially those who lived in countries liberated by the Allies, said that they could not imagine life had the Allies not been victorious. Many German tourists commented that after the Nazi invasion of the Soviet Union their countrymen began to despair about the war. As casualties mounted, especially on the Eastern Front, the despair intensified and the concerns were no longer how to win but about how badly they would lose.

After the invasion at Normandy, soldiers returning home as casualties or during a unit rotation told their family members that the size of the Allied opposition was huge and unstoppable. After viewing the destruction of their homeland and property, most of these men were hoping to surrender to the Allies in general and the Americans in particular. They feared surrendering to and an occupation by the Soviets in retaliation for the casualties and destruction in the Soviet Union.

Throughout France after the D-Day anniversary, and in Belgium during the 4th of July weekend, the French and Belgians were extremely polite, pleasant, gracious, and hospitable to me. An introduction and brief description about "The TREK" was the trigger for a strong response of sentimentality. Perhaps because France and Belgium had suffered so much during two wars with Germany and under the administration of their occupying forces, the people who respected the liberation, bought with the lives and sacrifices of young Americans such as my father, treated me as if I were the returning hero. There were many times when I was embarrassed by their attention and affection having done nothing to earn it. There also were many times when I reflected upon my meeting and touring Bastogne with elementary school teacher, Karl Pettit. His young students knew the names of the American commanders who liberated their cities and towns and whose names are inscribed on monuments throughout Belgium. Yet the 101st Airborne Division's reunion-tour coordinator complained to me that her American granddaughter in high school in Michigan did not know which country attacked Pearl Harbor.

Certainly when I entered Germany I had no intention to broadcast my participation at the D-Day invasion 70th Anniversary events. I did not want to open any old wounds with anyone who was a stranger to me. Instead, when I described the route of "The TREK," I emphasized my father's support of the Berlin Airlift along the three corridors from England, France, and Germany. I did not meet a single German who may have harbored any ill feelings toward an American for any reason who did not respect and appreciate the fact that the Airlift helped rescue Berlin, saved starving Berliners, and helped create the unity and cooperation that one day would bring down the Berlin Wall.

When I walked through Germany, the Wall had been down for three months shy of 25 years, and Germany had been reunited for almost as long. There was a sense of only one Germany even when some Germans would review my route, read the names of the cities within 100 miles of Berlin, and tell me, "Those are in the East. There's not much there," as if there still were an East Germany. It was like someone saying "upstate" for northern New York, or "East Texas" compared to the "Panhandle." I noted that there was far more pride with how far the cities of the former East Germany had progressed among the residents of those cities and towns, than there was among the residents of the former West Germany whose increased tax burdens had helped to promote progress and provide prosperity for their countrymen in the east.

In Berlin, many of the Berliners had always believed there was only one Berlin. The West Berliners with whom I lived between 1973 and 1976, 12 years after the Wall was erected in August 1961, knew that two such disparate systems could not exist so close for very long. I remember visiting a pub not far off the Ku'damm and paying 10 marks ($2.50) to buy a Lotto ticket on which I guessed the date that the Wall would come down. After I returned 40 years later, I did not remember the name or the location of that bar. It would not have mattered. I did not remember the date I had predicted, but I am sure that it was not November 9, 1989.

I am very proud of the experiences I gained during "The TREK." I learned more European history in three months on the ground than I did in six years of classroom instruction. I may even have learned as much military history and tactics in those same three months as I did in four years at the Military Academy. But the greatest lesson learned is the desire of all people to live in freedom, free from oppression, persecution and prejudice. The Europeans I met throughout 73 days in four countries, who now live in freedom, reminded me daily of their respect and admiration for their American liberators.

James Vincent Pelosi, (1923-1996), flew an American B-24 "Liberator" over Normandy in June 1944 and later C-47 and C-54 cargo aircraft in support of the Berlin Airlift between 1948 and 1949. It was for him, his World War II Army Air Corps veterans who liberated Europe, his Berlin Airlift Air Force veterans who kept Berlin free and alive, and all Allied veterans who served anywhere during these four Legacy Events that I walked.

"One day the great European War will come out of some damned foolish thing."
– Otto von Bismarck, 1888.

17. One Hundred Years. World War I, 1914-1918.

The number 100 has a variety of special significances. For longevity, 100 years of age merits recognition for a life long lived and almost certainly well lived. In math, it is the basis of percentages. In science, it is the temperature at which water boils at sea level using the Celsius scale. In business, it is the basis for most of the world currencies. In sports, it is a standard for the length of a race, the 100-yard dash; the length of a football field; and, the record number of points scored in a single basketball game by Wilt Chamberlain as a player for the Philadelphia Warriors on March 2, 1962. The number 100 is also the basis for Centennial activities which recognize and celebrate events of historical importance.

Centered in Europe, World War I began on July 28, 1914, and ended on November 11, 1918. Memorial services for the Centennial anniversary of the start of World War I were held throughout the world during 2014. The war raged for more than18 months before the entry of the United States after Congress declared war on April 6, 1917.

Although the physical scope of World War I was vast with Theaters of Combat on Western, Eastern, Serbian, Italian, and Turkish Fronts, the narrative of "Normandy to Berlin: The TREK to Honor The Legacies" is focused only on the Western Front and the participation of the United States American Expeditionary Force. Many of the battlefields, cities, and towns through which the American armies maneuvered and fought during this war were along the route of "The TREK."

The causes for the start of World War I began two generations earlier with the defeat of France by the combined armies of the northern states of Germany, united as the North German Confederation, and Prussia during the Franco-Prussian War which began on July 19, 1870. German superiority in men, materiel, and battlefield tactics easily defeated the French. Paris fell on January 28, 1871, and the war ended on May 10, 1871. The German states united under Kaiser Wilhelm I. The Treaty of Frankfurt, which formally brought an end to the war, ceded the French territories of Alsace and Lorraine to the new nation-state of Germany and inflamed French sentiment against the Germans.

The ever-industrious Germans took full advantage of the technologies, inventions, and prosperities as a result of the Industrial Revolution. Germany expanded its trade and built up its industries extending its influence beyond the borders to colonies which provided both raw materials and markets.

Germany's construction of a navy to protect her trade flow was considered to be a threat to Great Britain's naval superiority which was recognized as the strongest in the world. Great Britain possessed 30 battleships and battle cruisers. Germany had only 17.

By the early 1900's, France had made a rapid recovery both economically and militarily. Within Europe, only Germany was a more dominant nation.

On the other side of Europe in the east there was the constant conflict of national interests between the Austro-Hungarian and Russian empires. These conflicts were exacerbated by clashes within the much smaller Balkan states which rejected any form of foreign domination. Before the start of World War I, these antagonisms resulted in alliances which formed The Triple Alliance among Austria, Germany, and Italy, and the Triple Entente among England, France, and Russia. A condition within these alliances pledged each country to come to the aid of another if it were attacked. The nations all mobilized, and by 1914 tensions were tight.

Consistent with the terms of these and other pre-war alliances, war began shortly after Austrian Archduke Franz Ferdinand and his wife Sophie were assassinated by one member of a group of six Serbian terrorists in Sarajevo, Bosnia on June 8, 1914. The Austro-Hungarian Empire declared war on Serbia. By August 4, 1914, Germany and Austria (the Central Powers) were at war with Belgium, Britain, France, Serbia, and Russia (the Allies). Then, as the war continued, other nations entered.

For the Central Powers, Germany was the powerhouse. Its strategic plan of battle had been prepared in 1905 by the Chief of the German General Staff, Count Alfred von Schlieffen. The plan for the Western Front called for an attack into France from Germany and through Belgium, and the complete destruction of the French well before their Allied partner Russia could prepare for and join the war. Germany's plan for the Eastern Front assumed a slow Russian mobilization during which France would be defeated, and German forces could be concentrated in East Prussia against Russia.

In the 11 years since the Schlieffen Plan had been prepared, the Allied armies of Britain, France, and Russia all had improved their armies significantly. The French plan for war was to concentrate their forces and then attack the Germans from France through Belgium and into Germany. In the west, approximately two million Germans faced almost 1.4 million French including relatively small units of British and Belgians.

The first German attack failed. So did the first French attack. The Germans regrouped and responded with long-duration, massed artillery fire followed by well-coordinated infantry attacks. Most French defenses were destroyed by artillery and then were occupied by enemy infantry. Following the initial attacks and counterattacks by both sides, and amid the chaos and confusion of battle, the early results strongly favored the Germans. French Commander in Chief Joseph Joffre's armies had collapsed. By late August 1914, after three weeks of combat, the French had suffered more than 300,000 casualties. Allied with the French, the British Expeditionary Forces fought valiantly but suffered defeats and lost territory to the rapidly moving and tactically superior German ground forces.

By mid-September 1914, the Germans were closing in on Paris but were stopped by the combined forces of the French and the British. Both the Germans and the Allies then conducted numerous combat actions to envelop each other's flanks. However, the flanks were bordered to the north and west by water and to south by Switzerland whose neutrality neither side intended to compromise. Indecisive minor offenses along the front and flanks resulted in a general stalemate. The forces of both sides, which had been closing with the enemy by means of fire and maneuver over extensive territory, slowed the pace of combat, established defensive fighting positions, and began a period of protracted misery in combat deadlocked and defined by trench warfare. This was the battlefield status through the remainder of 1914 and almost all of 1915.

Major offensives during 1916 included the Battles of Verdun and the Battle of the Somme. Beginning on February 21, 1916, and continuing for 300 days, the Battle of Verdun was the longest single battle fought during World War I. Initially, more than 140,000 German soldiers attacked an opposing force of only 30,000 French. This became a battle of attrition where territory was exchanged numerous times between the combatants. It was the first time that the tank was used in combat when, as part of the Somme offensive, the British employed nearly 50 tanks in the battle of Flers-Courcelette. It also was the first time that flame throwers were used in combat. In December 1916, at the end of the fighting in positions close to where hostilities had begun, the French had lost almost 540,000 soldiers and the Germans approximately 340,000.

To relive the pressure on the French, the British began the Battle of the Somme on July 1, 1916, attacking along a 25-mile front. German opposition was fierce. Trenches, outlined by barbed wire and with insufficient overhead cover, fixed soldiers in locations vulnerable to massive artillery fire and gas attacks. Frontal assaults, out of the trenches and "over the top" where maneuver was impossible, drove combatants directly into the barbed wire and lines of withering machine gun fire. On the first day of the attack, many of the overwhelming number of British casualties estimated at 60,000, including almost 20,000 killed, were a direct result of machine gun fire.

Like the Battle of Verdun, the Battle of the Somme was a battle of attrition. Each side persisted in the slaughter of its enemy in the backward belief that an intolerable number of casualties would force a surrender.

American interests in the war took hold not long after it started. There was general economic concern about the increased dangers and costs of conducting trade with any of the numerous belligerents. On May 1, 1915, a

German U-boat torpedoed, but did not sink, an American flag-carrier cargo ship belonging to Gulf Oil. There were three fatalities including the Captain of the ship. On the same day, the British passenger liner, Lusitania sailed from New York bound for Liverpool. Six days later, on May 7, 1915, she was torpedoed by another German U-boat and sank 18 minutes after the explosion. Of 1960 passengers, 1198 perished including 128 Americans. An enraged population strongly supported United States protests to Germany. But the United States took no military action. Then, after Germany began conducting unrestricted submarine warfare in February 1917, the United States broke off diplomatic relations. The discovery of a copy of a cable from Germany's Foreign Minister to the Mexican Ambassador offering Mexico help to reclaim former territory in the United States in return for help with the war in Europe led American President Wilson to request a declaration of war. Congress declared war on Germany on April 2, 1917.

The Selective Service Act was passed by Congress on May 18, 1917. Together with enlistments and conscriptions, the United States mobilized an Army of four million men. From these young men, 1,400,000 were trained and assigned to the American Expeditionary Force in Europe under the command of General John J. Pershing. The political and military leadership of the Allies did not seek America's large and independent Army as a new and additional fighting force, but instead sought to split the American Expeditionary Force into smaller units as parts of their own armies. The European Allies were desperate to fill the ranks of their decimated ground forces with fresh troops from the United States. Much to the recurrent consternation of the Allies, neither President Wilson nor General Pershing would deliver any fighting force that was not an autonomous American unit fighting under its own commander and flag.

Just over two months after declaring war on Germany, the first American soldiers arrived in France on June 26, 1917. Pershing and his field commanders rejected the failed strategy of attrition through trench warfare, and incorporated the concepts of mobility, offensive spirit, and combined arms operations involving infantry, armor, artillery, and air support to set the combat tempo for a future Allied victory.

Initially, and together with the Allies, Pershing's divisions drove back the German assault just shy of Paris forcing a retreat of the enemy that would end in Germany. Then, in 1918, after more than six months' combat experience in combined combat operations with the Allies, the American Expeditionary Force conducted two great offensives. The first was the St. Mihiel offensive; the second, the Meuse-Argonne offensive. The battlefields were 60 miles apart over ground which America's allies earlier had considered impregnable.

Pershing and his Allied commanders expected these offensives to be fierce and costly in treasure. In a battle on July 19, 1918 a Marine Corps First Lieutenant Clifton B Cates, company commander, sent the following message up his chain of command: "I have only two men out of my company and 20 out of some other company. We need support, but it is almost suicide to try to get it here as we are swept by machine gun fire and a constant barrage is on us. I have no one on my left and only a few on my right. I will hold."

Lieutenant Cates survived, earned the Navy Cross and two awards of the Distinguished Service Cross for his valor, and later served as the Commandant of the U.S. Marine Corps.

Pershing planned the St. Mihiel offensive as a double envelopment. Beginning on September 12, 1918, the offensive lasted for 48 hours. By the time that the two pincher arms of the envelopment, the U.S. 1st and 26th Divisions, linked at Vigneulles most of the Germans had escaped. However, they had been driven from a fixed position which they had held for almost four years despite repeated attempts by French forces to dislodge them.

Less than two weeks later, on September 26, 1918, First Army turned north to begin the second major effort, the Meuse-Argonne offensive. The main effort was initiated in the Verdun Sector near the town of Verdun. Two years earlier in 1916, the Battle of Verdun had been the longest battle of the war, fought between February 21st and December 16th.

Now and for 47 days until the end of the war in November, the Americans fought in, through, and around the Argonne Forest pushing toward and eventually across the Meuse River. The Germans fought tenaciously knowing full well that a defeat in this critical sector would result in the failure of offensive operations on the Western Front and the loss of the war. At that time, the American offensive was the largest in its military history involving approximately 1.2 million soldiers.

Having the cleared the Germans from the Argonne Forest, the American forces reorganized into the First and Second Armies and continued the offensive east. Seizing the initiative, Pershing conducted the offensives in a series of deliberate, fast-moving, increasing-in-intensity operations which disrupted the German forces, broke their lines of communication, and gave them no time to reorganize or conduct counterattacks of any real tactical value. The final Allied offensive was launched on November 1, 1918. It broke through the heavily fortified former Hindenburg Line which had become reconstituted as the Siegfried Zone, and two final strong points along lines of resistance which the Germans held. On November 10, 1918, the Kaiser abdicated. On November 11, 1918, the "War to End All Wars" to an end.

World War I is significant for three reasons. First, it was a war which saw the introduction of new and lethal weapons as a result of technology and its applications to the armaments industry. The airplane, the machine gun, and the tank all came into existence as weapons of combat. Artillery became more powerful over longer ranges and accordingly became more deadly. Poison gas, heavier than air, lingered in the trenches, and was the most feared weapon during the war because it killed either immediately upon contact or slowly and painfully over time.

Next, it was a war which proved victory would belong to the nation with the best technology, the strongest industrial base with which to build weapons, armaments and defenses, and the best organizational infrastructure to deliver men and materiel to the battlefield.

Finally, it was a war which taught little to the elder statesmen and generals who prosecuted and fought it. Many of the countries which fought in World War I would fight each other again in World War II, changing nothing with respect to sentiments and very little with respect to tactics.

When World War I ended, 30 million people had perished.

June 28, 2014, was the 100th anniversary of the start of World War I.

"You will enter the continent of Europe and, in conjunction with the other United Nations, undertake operations aimed at the heart of Germany and the destruction of her armed forces."
–   Directive, Combined Chiefs of Staff to General Eisenhower.

"I have full confidence in your courage and devotion to duty and skill in battle. We will accept nothing less than full victory! Good luck! Let us beseech the blessing of Almighty God upon this great and noble undertaking."
— Dwight D Eisenhower.

18. Seventy Years. The Invasion of Normandy, June 6, 1944.

In Europe, after the end of World War I in 1918, all of the countries which had fought each other were struggling to recover from the physical and economic destruction caused by the war. Casualties from the war, which represented the loss of millions of young men from the labor pool, were an almost insignificant factor in the economies of the countries which had been disrupted during the war, had curtailed production after the war, and now were suffering staggering unemployment.

In the United States, the crash of the Stock Market in 1929 helped bring on the Great Depression. Poverty was epidemic. Approximately one-fourth of all American workers did not have a job.

In Europe, the Great Depression of the 1930's helped to create the conditions which brought to power such leaders as Hitler in Germany, Mussolini in Italy, and Stalin in Russia. In rallies and demonstrations, their fervent orations exhorting public spirit and nationalism won favor with their citizens. Adolf Hitler, an obscure World War I veteran who between 1915 and 1918 had earned seven military decorations from the grateful nation of Germany, including two awards of the Iron Cross and the German equivalent the Purple Heart, founded the Nationalist Socialist German Workers' (NAZI) Party in 1920. By 1929, NAZI Party membership grew to more than 100,000 Germans. Hitler had capitalized on the fears and desperation of more than five million unemployed Germans while touring Germany, promoting himself and the Party, and condemning the terms of the Treaty of Versailles. He offered his leadership through the increasingly more popular NAZI Party and he promised to reinvigorate the German economy, rebuild her military, and make Germany the dominant power in Europe. In time, Germany's defeat in the last war and its humiliation under the terms of the Treaty of Versailles would be avenged.

When the German states unified in 1871, the population of the new nation of Germany was approximately 41 million. Within 50 years, by the mid-

1920's, the population was approximately 70 million. Hitler believed that Germany needed space for its increasing population – space that had been lost by the terms of the Treaty of Versailles.

With Hitler's Nazi party dominant in the German government, Hitler succeeded in having himself appointed Chancellor of Germany in 1933. Less than two years later, on January 13, 1935, Hitler's government regained control of the former German territory of the Saarland, which had been governed jointly by the British and the French since 1920. Fourteen months later, on March 7, 1936, more than 30,000 German troops and police marched into the Rhineland which, as a result of the Treaty of Versailles, had been designated as a demilitarized zone to buffer France from Germany. Nothing was done to confront Hitler who concluded that the international community still was militarily war weary and politically impotent.

Emboldened by these successes and still focused on the intolerable and humiliating terms of the Treaty of Versailles, Hitler moved to unite Germany with Austria which had a large pro-German and pro-Nazi population. Two years after reclaiming the Rhineland, he forced the resignation of the Austrian Chancellor; replaced him with a strong supporter of Germany and the Nazis; and, deployed troops into Austria on March 12, 1938.

Later that same year, Hitler set his sights on Czechoslovakia, which not only bordered Germany on the southeast but also had a large population of ethnic Germans who resided primarily in an area which came to be called the Sudetenland. His threat of an invasion on the pretense of protecting the rights of its German minority caused the Czechs to mobilize. It sparked a response by the British and French who were obligated by treaty to protect and defend Czechoslovakia.

Britain's Prime Minister, Neville Chamberlain, flew to Munich to defuse a crisis that had the potential to lead to a new war. Together with other leaders in Europe and excluding any representation by anyone from Czechoslovakia, Chamberlain produced an agreement which ceded the Sudetenland to Germany. He informed the Czech government that it should be prepared to go to war alone against Germany or accept the terms of this Munich Agreement. Czechoslovakia yielded, knowing that it had been betrayed by its allies. All of Europe knew that Hitler had been appeased and further emboldened.

Still, the world was shocked when, less than six months later in March 1939, Hitler marched his troops beyond the Sudetenland into the Czech provinces of Bohemia and Moravia, in effect seizing the country of Czechoslovakia.

Only 20 years, 9 months, and 23 days after World War I ended, World War II began. There had been no formal declaration of war before 62 divisions of the German army and 1,300 of its aircraft attacked Poland from the east on September 1, 1939. Hitler believed that Germany easily could defeat Poland before either Britain or France could react. Two days later, on September 3,

1939, both Britain and France declared war on Germany. Each began a surprisingly slow mobilization. On September 17, 1939, Russia, having signed a non-aggression pact with Germany on August 28, 1939, only three days before Germany's attack on Poland, attacked her from the west and seized almost one-third of the country. Unlike Czechoslovakia, which surrendered without a fight, Poland fought back on both fronts. Poland was overrun within the month, and surrendered on September 27, 1939, before receiving any aid or assistance from either Britain or France. Having declared war on Germany, their plan of engagement included economic sanctions, naval blockades, and the failed World War I tactic of manning and maintaining fixed defensive fortifications.

Hitler and his military slowed the pace of aggression and offensive actions during the winter of 1939-1940 to consolidate gains, develop a strategy based upon their initial successes, and plan tactical operations to support the strategy as it evolved. On April 9, 1940, Denmark and Norway were invaded. These two relatively defenseless nations fell quickly. Hitler and the Germans secured not only land and naval bases from which to block threats from Britain and her navy but also obtained new sources of raw materials, such as iron ore, much needed and very valuable for Germany's armaments and transportation industries.

On May 10, 1040, Germany resumed offensive operations with simultaneous combined arms invasions into Belgium, the Netherlands, and France. Although the number of opposing ground forces was about the same, almost all of the German tactical commanders and most of their units were experienced in combat which emphasized shock, mobility and speed. German air forces included more than 3,500 aircraft which were opposed by only 2,000 among the Allies and all of which were located in France.

Almost immediately after the surprise attack, the Dutch government fled for England. The Netherlands fell in only five days on May 14, 1940.

In Belgium, the Belgian military fought with support from both the British and the French. The Luftwaffe overwhelmed Allied air forces and supported German ground troops in concentrated attacks on the Allies who conducted mostly defensive delaying actions. Against vastly superior forces, the Belgians fought throughout their country to defend it. Allied forces composed primarily of French units fought and then withdrew to the west and south. Other Allied forces composed mostly of British units fought and then withdrew to the west and north.

On May 27, 1940, it appeared as if the entire British Expeditionary Force and other Allied units would be trapped along the northern beaches in the vicinity of the town of Dunkirk, France. Surprisingly, and for reasons which still are unknown to this day, and over the protests of his senior field commanders and advisors, Hitler gave orders for a halt to the combined arms panzer-infantry units which were in pursuit of the Allies. Between May 27th and June 4th an armada of more than 850 Allied vessels, 693 of which were British and which were protected in part by Britain's Royal Air Force (RAF), successfully evacuated 338,225 Belgian, British, and French combatants. Losses as a result of the evacuation included nine Allied destroyers, more than 200 civilian vessels, and 145 RAF aircraft.

Prior to the end of the evacuation and the resulting rescue of the Allies from Dunkirk, Belgium's King Leopold had surrendered unconditionally on May 28, 1940.

German forces, having been released by Hitler, reached Dunkirk on June 5, 1940, one day too late to close with and destroy their enemies. Instead of conducting combat operations, the units reorganized and refit while they waited for orders to conduct the next offensive. They did not have to wait at all.

That same day, June 5, 1940, the Battle of France began. For almost a month, French forces had been fighting alongside their allies in Belgium and Holland. Now they were withdrawn to defend their homeland. The German main attack massed 45 divisions east and north of Paris; the secondary attack massed another 50 divisions west and south of Paris. An additional 24 divisions attacked across the length of the Maginot Line. To defend against an attack of almost 120 divisions, which did not include the more than 20 additional reserve divisions, the French fielded only 65 divisions of which only three of which were armored. The Germans crushed the French opposition for the same reason that they had succeeded elsewhere since the start of the war: combat characterized by surprise, shock, speed, mobility, overwhelming firepower concentrated at the center of each attack, and superior coordination of combined arms which employed air power, artillery, armor, and infantry.

Surprisingly, German infantrymen proved able to follow their mobile artillery and armor in forced marches as far as 20 to 35 miles and then continue to fight. Even more surprising was the fact that since the start of the war in 1939, German tank officers had followed closely the British theories, writings, and field manuals about "armoured" warfare.

France petitioned for an armistice after only 18 days on June 17, 1940. From London, on June 18, 1940, General Charles de Gaulle announced:

"To all Frenchmen, France has lost a battle! But France has not lost the war! The men who happen to head the government may have capitulated, yielding to panic, forgetting honor, delivering the land over to servitude. Yet nothing is lost! Nothing is lost because this is a world war. In the free universe, tremendous forces have not yet made themselves felt. Someday these forces will crush the enemy. Our country is in mortal peril. Let us all fight to save her. Vive la France!"

The armistice was signed five days later on June 22, 1940. All hostilities ceased on June 25, 1940. After only six weeks Germany's campaign in the West ended.

In June 1941, Hitler took another gamble. This time he lost. Deliberately violating his non-aggression pact with the Soviet Union, Hitler launched Operation Barbarossa on June 22, 1941. German forces attacked from the west on a wide front catching the Soviets by surprise. They achieved a series of quick victories and penetrated deep into the Soviet Union. Within three weeks, the Soviets had lost 28 divisions; another 70 divisions had lost half of their men and equipment. Ferocious resistance by the Soviet military and civilians, aided by all the debilitating aspects of a Russian winter, stopped the German advance just shy of Moscow in January 1942.

Between 1941 and 1945, German lines into the Soviet Union had been extended too deeply, and men and equipment had been attrited too severely. In the winter of 1942-1943, the German defeat at Stalingrad resulted in a catastrophic loss of men and equipment. The entire German Sixth Army had been destroyed. Of 91,000 Germans who were taken prisoner, only 6,000 survived the conditions of Soviet captivity to return home after the war. In the largest land battle in history, the Germans again were defeated by the Soviets at the Battle of Kursk in the summer of 1943.

Following the sneak attack on Pearl Harbor by the Japanese on December 7, 1941, Hitler declared war on the United States. But the war in Europe retained a greater priority for America ahead of the vengeance to be wrought upon Japan later. Within a year, on November 8, 1942, American forces numbering 100,000 men landed in North Africa. They were supported by 260 aircraft. This American force added to the pressure on German military forces which had been battling the British across North Africa. At the same time, the Germans continued to occupy most of Western Europe and Scandinavia, and they continued to fight a tenacious enemy defending its homeland across the western expanses of the Soviet Union. On May 10, 1943, German forces suffered their last defeat in combat in North Africa.

On July 10, 1943, using ports in North Africa as bases, Allied forces numbering 180,000 troops invaded Sicily for the dual purposes of protecting Allied shipping in the Mediterranean and establishing a base for support for the invasion of Europe. Led by General George S. Patton's U.S. Seventh Army and General Bernard Montgomery's British Eighth Army, the Allies were opposed by an Axis force of 230,000 Italians and two divisions of Germans. Fighting was fierce, but the key cities of Syracuse, Palermo, Catania, Messina, and their surroundings were cleared of defenders. In just under two months, the Axis forces in Sicily and Italy were defeated. Mussolini was deposed. The new Italian government surrendered unconditionally to the Allies on September 3, 1943 and one month later, on October 10, 1943, Italy declared war on Germany.

In 1944, it became clear that the Allied invasion of Europe would be launched from England because of the scale of the American forces and their equipment which were being transported and stationed there. Since the beginning of the war in Europe, troops had been training, their leaders had been planning, and their units had been equipped and supplied continuously with everything that senior planners thought would be needed to support the invasion. The mission was to invade Europe, defeat Hitler's "Fortress Europe" and his armed forces, and liberate the occupied countries.

By May 1944, more than 1.5 million men and women of the air, sea, and land forces of the United States were assembled in England. Together with other Allied military, the invasion force would include six battleships, 22 cruisers, 90 destroyers, and hundreds of troop transport ships and beach landing craft. Support from the air would include a force of 2,000 bombers and 170 squadrons of fighter aircraft. General Dwight D. Eisenhower, in his capacity as Supreme Commander, Allied Forces Europe, would command this force of more than 2,800,000 personnel throughout "Operation Overlord" within his European Theater of Operations (ETO).

Opposing General Eisenhower and his Allied forces was the German Commander-in-Chief, Field Marshal Gerd von Rundstedt. He commanded 60 divisions, eight of which were in Belgium and Holland. Only 27 of the 60 were maneuver divisions and only 10 of those 27 were armored divisions. The 33 other divisions were coastal defense divisions in relatively fixed locations, and training divisions which hosted recruits as young as 14 years old. Von Rundstedt had over 3,000 miles of coastline to defend, from the Italian frontier in the south to the German frontier in the north. Even if all 60 divisions were at full strength, equipped, supplied, and maneuverable, Field Marshal von Rundstedt had an average of 50 miles of coastline to defend in width and in depth with each division.

The invasion began on Tuesday, June 6, 1944. Just after midnight, approximately 25,000 American, British, and Canadian paratroopers conducted an airborne assault into France along the Normandy coast in the midst of strong German defenses. Both Hitler and one of his best Generals, the Desert Fox, Field-Marshal Erwin Rommel, expected the Allied invasion at Normandy. Six hours later, at dawn, approximately 160,000 American, British, and Canadian ground forces, on board history's largest amphibious invasion fleet from eight different navies, began landing on five beaches: Sword, Juno, Gold, Omaha, and Utah.

The Americans were assigned to the right at Omaha and Utah; the British and Canadians were assigned to the left at Sword, Juno, and Gold. The landings came as a surprise to the Germans whose radar systems had been compromised by Allied bombings and whose leaders thought that the weather was too rough for a landing. However, along the beaches where the invasion had been expected, enemy resistance was fierce. Underwater obstacles had been emplaced, coastal defenses had been reinforced with concrete pillboxes and strongpoints, and reserve forces had been placed on alert.

Although German units in Normandy were understrength, short of equipment, and manned with mostly inexperienced soldiers and very young recruits, more than 5,000 Americans became casualties that first day on Omaha Beach alone. Most of the casualties occurred during the early hours of the invasion in the airborne and waterborne assaults to secure the beaches. Along the beaches, the assault force was caught in the open and vulnerable to artillery and machine gun fire which sank the landing craft and slaughtered the troops as they exited and trudged under the weight of their weapons and load-bearing equipment through the surf toward the beach.

By the end of the day, eight Allied Divisions and three armored Brigades had come ashore. Landing these 55,000 men had been no easy task. At the end of D+1, 177,000 troops were boots on the ground on four beachheads.

Within three days, Omaha Beach was secured and the German defenders had been driven inland. At the end of the first week, 7,000 tons of supplies were arriving daily. These supplies were essential to sustain the pace of combat operations in the continuous Allied offensives aimed at the heart of Germany.

The Germans mounted counterattacks with armored and combined arms armored-infantry units, moved forward great quantities of mobile artillery and heavy field guns, and placed interlocking fields of machine gun and mortar fire along Allied avenues of approach. Allied advances were slowed and made more difficult by the terrain which favored the German defenders. The extensive network of hedgerows were yards thick, averaged six feet tall, and were cluttered with thickets and trees. They provided thick cover and dense concealment. Seven weeks had passed before the Allies had gained a lodgment in Normandy. Then, the build-up of troops and supplies, most importantly weapons and ammunition, took effect. One hundred days later Allied forces were nearing the German border.

In September 1944, the Allies suffered a significant setback when Operation Market Garden, planned and commanded by British Field Marshal Montgomery failed. A combined force of three divisions of Allied paratroopers and additional divisions of ground units attacked into Holland. They were unable to seize and hold the bridges and terrain that, if captured and held, would have opened up a northern corridor into Germany. Instead, because of Montgomery's over-ambitious and defective plan, another six months would pass before the Allies would cross the Rhine River into Germany.

Following the Market Garden failure, the Allies experienced a second far more serious setback when the Germans launched a huge counteroffensive through the Ardennes forest just before Christmas on December 16, 1944.

The attack by four German Armies, including two Panzer Armies, targeted lightly fortified segments of the U.S. line. The intent was to break through the Allied lines, separate the British from the Americans, split their lines of communications and logistics support, and seize the port of Antwerp. By capturing Antwerp and encircling the Allies, the Germans effectively would cut off their supplies. Taking advantage of bad weather and a false sense of security in the area, the Germans succeeded in a breakthrough at the weakest part of the Allied lines and forced them on the defensive.

However, when the weather cleared and the Allies were reinforced with men and resupplied by air, their resistance stiffened and they checked the German advance. Allied bombers supported their ground forces. Patton, who joked that he was "touring Europe with an Army," led his Third Army in a breakthrough. His attack helped relieve the siege at Bastogne and support the "Battling Bastards" of the 101st Airborne Division who were fighting there. For the Germans, when their fuel ran out their advance halted. Lacking air support, suffering unacceptable losses in men and equipment, and without supplies for their troops, the German forces withdrew.

Then, every mile that the Allies moved east and inland drove the enemy defenders closer to their homeland. German defenses stiffened in direct proportion to the proximity of Allied forces to Germany.

Eisenhower had 85 full-strength divisions composed of five airborne, 23 armored, and 57 infantry pressing the attack. Of the four million Allied soldiers who were in Germany three million were Americans.

In March, 1945, the Allies crossed the Rhine River at four locations into Germany. More than 60,000 German defenders were killed and another 250,000 taken prisoner, resulting in the destruction of the German Army in Western Europe.

In April, as more and more German soldiers deserted, units surrendered. The Russians, who outnumbered the German defenders by almost 15 to one, closed in on Berlin. There, in his underground bunker, Hitler committed suicide on April 30, 1945. Hitler's successor, Grand Admiral Karl Doenitz surrendered to the Allies in the French city of Reims on May 7, 1945.

As was true with the Allied victory in World War I, the Allied victory in World War II was a result of superiority in the numbers of combatants, aircraft, naval vessels, weapons and logistics.

June 6, 2014, was the 70th anniversary of the Allied landings along the beaches in Normandy, France.

"If we mean that we are to hold Europe against communism, we must not budge. We can take humiliation and pressure short of war in Berlin without losing face. I believe the future of democracy requires us to stay here until forced out."
–   General Lucius D. Clay, Commander-in-Chief, U.S. Forces in Europe and Military Governor of the U.S. Zone in Germany.

"There is no discussion on this point. We are going to stay. Period."
–   President Harry S. Truman.

19. Sixty-five Years. The Berlin Airlift, 1948-1949.

World War II ended after the Allied forces of Americans, British and French crossed into Germany from the west, passed through the heartland and swept to its eastern borders. The Russians simultaneously crossed into Germany from the east attacking with 20 Armies, 6,300 tanks, and 8,500 aircraft. They reached the capital city of Berlin on May 2, 1945. Berlin fell, and Germany surrendered on May 7, 1945.

In retaliation for the German destruction and devastation of their homeland after the invasion in 1941, the Russian soldiers who captured Berlin destroyed it and savaged its people. It is estimated that more than 100,000 women between the ages of 12 and 80 were raped by Russian soldiers. They looted Berlin of its treasure and robbed Berliners of their valuables. Berlin's largest power plant, its biggest radio station, (bigger than any other in Europe), more than 3,500 factories, and more a million pieces of industrial hardware and machinery were dismantled and sent to the Soviet Union. Also seized and transported east were thousands of German machinists and their managers who possessed the skills to reassemble and operate the pillaged property back within the Soviet Union.

At Yalta in 1945, Churchill, Roosevelt, and Stalin agreed on a joint military occupation of Berlin at the end of the war. But there was no discussion and no agreement for a common policy for recovery for Germany.

Following its unconditional surrender, Germany not only had to face the loss of its sovereignty, but also its partition into divided zones of occupation. Germany was divided into two countries: the Federal Republic of Germany (FRG), or West Germany, and the German Democratic Republic (GDR), or East Germany. Berlin is located in what became and once as East Germany. It morphed into an island-state in the middle of the continent of Europe, seemingly so isolated that the Berliners began to refer to themselves as "The Islanders." The 346 square miles of Berlin were divided into four sectors through a Four-Power Agreement among the Allies.

The free Western sector, encompassing 12 districts and 54 percent of Berlin, was under the protection of the United States, Great Britain, and France. The communist Eastern sector, encompassing eight districts and 46 percent of Berlin, was under the control of the Soviet Union. Within Berlin is an area known as the Grunewald which contains 25,000 acres of canals, rivers, lakes, parklands, farms, and forests. It is the largest forest within city limits anywhere in the world.

The 12,000 troops of the Western Allies served in the role as a "protective" power compared to that of an "occupation" power. They maintained a presence consistent with post-war agreements in their respective sectors of West Berlin. These 12,000 troops were encircled by a half million military members of the Warsaw Pact that included 350,000 Soviets and 150,000 East Germans. Overwhelmingly outnumbered, the presence of the Allied forces within West Berlin was as symbolic and as practical as the presence of Swiss Guards at the Vatican.

At the end of the war, the Soviet Union had emerged as one of the four Allied victors and as the world's second ranking military and industrial power. In less than two years, there was almost no common meeting ground between the Soviet Union and its former allies. Winston Churchill, Great Britain's former Prime Minister between 1940 and 1945, stated in a speech in 1946 that an "Iron Curtain" had descended in Europe separating the free West from the communist controlled East. Stalin and the Soviet Union no longer were an ally of the West, but were an enemy.

Shortly after midnight, June 24, 1948, the Soviets cut off all communications with West Berlin. Using Soviet troops, trucks, tanks, motorboats, and watercraft, they blocked the road, railway, and canal routes in and out of Berlin for all sources of transportation except for military convoys. These routes had been supplying the Berliners with approximately 15,000 tons of food, fuel, and supplies daily which were needed to operate the city and feed its citizens. In addition, the Soviets cut the electric power which was delivered from their Eastern sector to the free Western sector.

Attempting to render a shattering blow to the Western prestige in Germany, the official Soviet justification was its effort to prevent the entry of West German currency into the Soviet sector of Berlin after the Soviets and East Germans had enacted their own first post-war currency reform. Simply a pretext, the reality of the blockade was a deliberate effort by the Soviets to drive the Western Allies out of their sectors in Berlin and then to seize control of all of the city. By denying access to food, fuel, and supplies, as well as access to services necessary to live and work, the Soviets hoped to force the three Western Allies to submit and ultimately to abandon Berlin. On the safe side for the Soviets, it always remained a possibility that they could lift the blockade if ever it appeared that it, or an incident related to it, might lead to a shooting war. Stalin did not want a war. He wanted the entire city of Berlin.

At that time, the population of West Berlin was estimated at 2.1 million citizens, the majority of whom were women, the elderly and children. In 1938, before the start of World War II, the population had been twice that, estimated at 4.3million. The people were dependent upon the West Berlin military and civilian administrators to provide for and maintain their basic needs.

In an attempt to defeat the blockade an idea for an airlift was proposed by the Commandant of the British sector of Berlin. He believed that the Western Allies were capable of controlling the air space in the three corridors of Berlin as completely as the Soviets were capable of controlling the road, railway, and canal routes which they were doing. He sold the idea to his two Allied counterparts.

The Americans believed with certainty that the American Air Force could do anything that the Royal Air Force could do. The Commander of the United States Air Force in Europe, General Curtis LeMay, stated that "The Air Force can deliver anything, anytime, anywhere."

Under the leadership of American General Lucius Clay, the Allies initiated an airlift to fly in all supplies essential to operate the city and to keep its citizens alive. During World War II, General Clay had been responsible for logistics, supplying the materiel that supported the invasion forces from Normandy east across Europe. He was instrumental in unclogging the backup of Allied supplies at the French port of Cherbourg, and for providing tons of ammunition to the Allied defenders at Bastogne. In March 1947, General Clay was appointed to the dual roles of Commander-in Chief, U.S. Forces Europe, and Military Governor of the U.S. Occupation Zone in Germany.

Ordered to take no action that would risk a war with the Soviet Union, Clay and the British agreed that an Allied airlift of food and provisions should be able to sustain the occupation forces and their families. The number to support was approximately 25,000 military members and their dependents.

Provisions aboard 32 C-47 cargo aircraft, in the very first Allied Airlift into Berlin, landed at Templehof Airport on June 26, 1948. Throughout the summer of 1948, when the weather was mostly favorable, the Airlift was able to provide only about 1,500 tons of supplies. That amount represented 25 percent of what was needed to keep the Western sectors functioning and only 10 percent of what had been delivered before the blockade began.

More than 3,000 companies closed. More than 4,500 companies reduced operations because they could not obtain the resources, most importantly supplies and power, which their operating capacities demanded. Because the Allies were unwilling to ignore the plight of the citizens of Berlin, and because the tonnage of supplies required to support them was so large, the scope of the Airlift problem grew dramatically. The ability to deliver all the supplies needed exceeded the capacity of the entire Air Force C-47 cargo fleet in Europe. The C-54 was a bigger, better, faster version of the C-47 and could carry three times the amount of cargo. But at that time, there were only two of 400 C-54's which belonged to the Air Force that were in Germany.

General Clay recruited a fellow West Point alumnus, Major General William H. Tunner, who during World War II, commanded the Air Transportation Command's "Ferrying Wing" which delivered all types of aircraft to U.S. and Allied forces in every theater of the war. He distinguished himself in the Burma–China "Hump" Airlift by tripling the amount of supplies to the Chinese, who were battling our enemy the Japanese in their homeland. Supplies provided increased from 23,000 tons to 69,000 tons a month. General Tunner, as Commander of the new "Military Air Transport Service" which integrated the Air Transport Commands of the Air Force, Army, and Navy into a single unified Command, became the man in charge to make the Allied Airlift work.

Generals Clay and Tunner together were a formidable team. They shared the same motivation to prove to the Soviets, the Allied politicians, their military superiors, and, most importantly, the Berliners that Berlin would remain viable, that Berliners would not starve, and that the Western Allies would not be driven out of Berlin. Together they built an additional airport, Tegel, in the French sector. Before World War I, Tegel had been a facility to build and test dirigibles. During World War II, it was a base used to build and test rockets, and to train crews of Hermann Goering's Luftwaffe.

Beginning in July 1948, it again was converted and rebuilt. The conversion was completed in only 92 days. The first aircraft in support of the Allied Airlift landed at Tegel on November 5, 1948. It touched down on what then was the world's longest runway at 2500 yards. To build Tegel, the Allied and civilian leadership recruited an estimated 20,000 local men and women from the three Western sectors.

In 1945, more than 60,000 "rubble women" dug Berlin out of its wreckage with their bare hands, brick by brick. Now, many of were tasked to assist the military in the construction of new runways and with the upgrades and reinforcement of old runways at the three Allied Airlift bases: Templehof in the American sector; Gatow, a former Luftwaffe base in the British sector; and, Tegel in the French sector. Needed also were maintenance hangars and support facilities, flight operations buildings, and housing for the pilots, crews, and base maintenance and support personnel.

To meet the demand for workers the Allies went beyond Berlin to recruit and hire skilled personnel from the United States, England, and West Germany. The former Chief Transport Officer for the Luftwaffe, Major General Hans von Rohden, was hired together with many of his former Luftwaffe aircraft maintenance personnel to support the Airlift. Some of these men arrived for work with their own personal toolboxes. Eventually, the workforce numbered in the tens of thousands worldwide.

Contending that any aircraft on the ground, that was not off line or was not in maintenance for routine inspection or repair, was a wasted aircraft, General Tunner instituted a system of strict flight procedures and schedules. Eventually there were hundreds of aircraft following identical deployments and flight routines every hour of every day, in all types of weather. The flights were flown and supported by Air Force pilots and support personnel who were on active duty; members of the Air Force Reserve who had been recalled to active duty; and, civilians who had volunteered to support the Airlift. The Navy also provided aircraft, pilots, and maintenance crews. Allied Airlift pilots transported food, fuel, clothing, and domestic necessities which helped to keep the population alive. They also transported cargo that included industrial components, spare parts, tools, and equipment which kept open the factories, facilities, mills, farms, and shops where the Berliners worked.

In December, 1948, the Allied Airlift delivered 4,500 tons of supplies to their three Western air bases. But throughout the winter of 1948, the Allies failed to meet the 12,000-ton objective. With only 8,000 tons of food and fuel delivered, many of West Berlin's displaced, elderly, sick, disabled, and children died from exposure and starvation. The Soviets, knowing all too well how "General Winter" had defeated Napoleon and the Nazis, fully expected Winter to defeat one more enemy one more time.

Doubling his efforts, General Tunner, with the full backing of General Clay and his resources, pushed himself, his crews, and their flight control teams to increase the tonnage being flown into Berlin. They added the greater capacity C-54 cargo aircraft to the Allied Air Fleet. Pilots flew round-the-clock sorties.

To his personal and professional credit, and with the overwhelming support of his staff, pilots, air, and ground crews, General Tunner successfully instituted reforms, supervised improvements and established efficiencies that gradually increased the tonnage arriving in Berlin. These supplies helped keep the population alive and their places of work functioning.

Tunner reorganized flight patterns which brought larger and faster aircraft into Berlin from closer airfields in England and ahead of smaller and slower aircraft further away at bases deep within West Germany. Recognizing the unacceptable number of pilots and crews who were suffering from fatigue, he ordered and enforced regular flight schedules for everyone flying or supporting Airlift flights. That meant fixed hours for flight, meals, sleep, rest, and recreation. With crew safety as his first priority and aircraft maintenance as his other first priority, he reorganized flight paths, patterns, and schedules within the three corridors ensuring that every aircraft which had arrived safely and unloaded its cargo either was in the air again to fly another mission or was in maintenance in preparation for another mission. Flying with the use of radar guidance by means of cockpit instrumentation became mandatory for all flights.

Believing that "everyone loves a winner," General Tunner created forms of competition among the Allies and their pilots and crews to reward best units and outstanding performers within the units. Most significantly, during the spring of 1949, he created and organized "The Easter Parade," an event intended as an Easter present for the citizens of Berlin. It pitted ally against ally, air crews against air crews, and pilots against pilots with the purpose of delivering a record tonnage of supplies in the 24 hours between noon on Holy Saturday and noon on Easter Sunday. The event was a morale booster for everyone involved. As General Tunner predicted, 1,398 flights delivered a record 12,941 tons of supplies. The amount of coal transported was equal to that which could have been carried by a train with 650 freight cars loaded with coal. In a one-week period after "The Easter Parade," the Airlift delivered more tons of supplies than had been delivered by freight trains before the blockade.

The Airlift Commanders, their flight crews, and their support personnel truly distinguished themselves as professionals. One Pilot, Air Force Lieutenant Gail Halvorsen, met several children who were watching the flights near Templehof Airfield. He shared some sticks of gum with them. Sympathetic to their smiling faces, he promised to fly over the same area the following day and drop gum and candy from his aircraft to the children. That night at Rhein-Main in West Germany, together with some of the members of his crew, Lieutenant Halvorsen and team used their rations cards at the Base Exchange to purchase gum, candy, and handkerchiefs to create mini parachutes. As promised, he returned and, approaching the area where the children were waiting, tipped or wiggled the wings of his C-54, and then had his crew release the parachutes. Many of the children who recovered these mini parachutes containing treats never had seen or tasted "candy."

Halvorsen and his crew repeated the candy drop twice within the next two weeks to ever-increasing numbers of children. Fearing criticism by his commanders and unwilling to risk potential disciplinary action, he stopped. The next day, back at Rhein-Main, the Base Operations Officer was waiting for him with an order to report immediately to the Base Commander.

In the office he found dozens of letters addressed to "Wiggly Wings," "General Bonbon," and "The Chocolate Flyer," among other names. He also found the Base Commander who congratulated him on behalf of the more senior Allied Commanders for an activity that was an Allied Airlift public relations bonanza.

Soon, he had his own office complete with secretaries who managed his mail and stocked the candy and the handkerchiefs which came from everywhere, but mostly from other personnel who were supporting the Airlift. Eventually, after appearing in the press internationally and on television in the United

States, Halvorsen's supply of candy increased to tens of thousands of pounds. The huge increased was provided by the American public and the candy manufacturers. There was so much of it that the candy was delivered not only by aircraft but also by trucks to the children within Berlin and throughout West Germany.

On April 4, 1949, the North Atlantic Treaty was signed in Washington, D.C. Shortly afterwards, on May 4, 1949, all four powers jointly announced that the blockade would be lifted. The blockade proved to be a massive failure. The Soviets had relented. At midnight, May 11, 1949, all regular traffic flow along all the rail, road, and canal routes through all corridors of the Western sectors resumed.

Even though the blockade had ended, the Western Allies did not trust the Soviets to comply with the agreement that they had signed. As a contingency, the Allied Airlift continued to fly supplies in Berlin, especially food, fuel, medicines, and spare parts for machinery which were stockpiled.

The airlift ended on September 30, 1949. For 321 days between June 26, 1948, and May 12, 1949, 277,804 flights in 690 Allied aircraft flew more than 92 million miles,(the distance from the Earth to the sun), to provide more than 2.3 million tons of life support to Berlin. The Allies suffered the losses of 17 American and eight British aircraft, and 73 military service members. There were approximately 32 civilians who died performing duty directly related to the support of the Allied Airlift.

Once the focus of the world for more than a year, Templehof Airport, from which American and British aircraft sortied to sustain Berlin and its citizens, was converted into a park. Gatow Airport was transferred by the British to the Germans in 1994. It closed as an airport and was converted to a German military base which hosts a German Air Force museum. Tegel Airport again expanded. It is Berlin's largest airport for commercial aviation and international flights. Rhein-Main Airport was transferred by the United States to the Germans in 2005. It closed and was converted to an office park.

September 30, 2014, was the 65th anniversary of the end of the Allied Airlift into Berlin.

"Niemand hat die Absicht, eine Mauer zu errichten!"
"No one has the intention to erect a wall!"
– Walter Ulbricht, State Chairman and First Secretary of the Socialist Unity
Party, German Democratic Republic (East Germany).

"There are many people in the world who really don't understand what is the
great issue between the free world and the Communist world. Let them come
to Berlin. There are some who say that communism is the wave of the future.
Let them come to Berlin."
– President John F. Kennedy.

20. Twenty-five Years. The Berlin Wall Falls, November 9, 1989.

After the end of World War II, between 1945 and 1961, Berlin was the focus
of the cold war which divided Europe. The West was restored relatively
quickly with money provided for recovery as part of the Marshal Plan. But
the East was ravaged by a vengeful Soviet Union that continued to exploit
resources, pillage industries, loot property, and ignore reconstruction. In
1945, more than half of all the housing in East Berlin was destroyed, and
more than a billion cubic feet of rubble clogged the streets. Surprisingly, with
the division of Berlin, all the major public and historic buildings, with the
exception of the Reichstag, remained in East Berlin.

Located 120 miles inside East Germany, West Berlin was a zone of military
occupation governed in three sectors by the United States, Great Britain, and
France. Beginning primarily after the war, the division of Germany, and the
creation of the German Democratic Republic (GDR or East Germany) in
1949, more than three million people fled to the free West in a "referendum
of the feet." That number was equivalent to one of every six persons. They
had been fleeing at the rate of 20,000 citizens a month. More than half of
those who fled were under 25 years of age. They represented a variety of skills
and occupations: doctors, dentists, lawyers, teachers, students, craftsmen,
laborers, and farmers. After 1958, the exits by professionals and persons with
in-demand, high-tech skills increased steadily. Their mass exodus posed a
serious threat to the foundations of the new state.

In Berlin, in order to prevent an economic disaster, the Soviet-controlled
East German leadership decided to build a wall to enclose the population
within the Soviet sector of Berlin. During the night from Saturday to Sunday
on August 13, 1961, the East Berlin population was sealed off from
everything and everyone in West Berlin. Approximately 50,000 Russian and
East German men, many of whom were soldiers, went to work that night and
constructed an interlocking barrier of fences and barbed wire. At the
Brandenburg Gate, six companies of men from a variety of military and

paramilitary units stood shoulder to shoulder against a crowd that had formed. Passersby gathered together with drivers standing beside their vehicles to watch in numb disbelief as their city was walled off. Most people were shocked but far fewer were surprised at the activity. Berliners had been expecting a response to the mass exodus of talent and manpower. At the worksites, the laborers, guards, and their overseers worked the entire day.

On August 14, 1961, West Berliners formally were prevented from entering East Berlin. The Brandenburg Gate was closed "until further notice" which was 25 years later. The Four-Power agreement which guaranteed the free circulation of people within all four sectors of Berlin had been violated. In 24 hours, everything about the city of Berlin was changed. The creation of the wall ended the opportunity for East Berliners to work, study, and relax in the West. Jobs vanished. The wall struck at the heart of many German workers' sentiment: "my life is my job." Without work there no sense of living. Access to the Free University and to the West's culturally diverse theaters, concert halls, cinemas, and expositions ended.

Two days later, on August 15, 1961, Berliners observed an East German border guard desert his post and flee into the West by scaling the barbed wire. They also saw work begin to reinforce the relatively fragile barrier when concrete structures approximately six feet high were substituted to replace the barbed wire and supplement the fences. The barbed wire that had been placed in the rivers and lakes remained.

Within two weeks, the Communist East had succeeded in closing every crossing point that previously had permitted transit between the East and West sectors. The first wall followed the exact boundary lines between the Tiergarten and the Mitte districts. A subway entrance there was closed then blocked with concrete slabs which sealed the entrance.

In the first two months following the construction of the wall, some 150 guards fled to the West. Less than one year later, in June 1962, work began on a second wall to reinforce the original wall and to help reduce the number of successful escapes. In the East, nearly all the houses near the wall were demolished in order to give the guards better sight and greater range to intercept anyone attempting to flee to freedom. At the end of the first year, there were 130 observation towers along the two mile length of the wall.

During the week of the anniversary recognizing one year since construction of the wall began in 1961, an 18 year old bricklayer named Peter Fechter, who was unwilling to be drafted into military service with the East German army, attempted to escape. On August 17, 1962, he was shot by border guards and left where he fell for almost an hour without any medical assistance. Rescuers were prevented by the guards, still in their hiding places but brandishing their weapons, from coming to his aid. The West Berlin police were unable to do anything more than toss First Aid packets to him. Mortally wounded, young Fechter was too weak to respond and he bled to death. The event was witnessed and recorded by the Western media which were travelling around Berlin reporting on the events and ceremonies to commemorate the first anniversary of the wall.

Before the end of the first year, more than 30,000 people in East Berlin had been arrested and charged with "attempting to flee from the Republic." The average punishment for this offense was 22 months at hard labor or "penal servitude" in the words of the court authorities in the East. For assisting someone who escaped successfully the average punishment was five years at penal servitude. For conspiring to organize an escape the penalty was the most severe that could be imposed: penal servitude for life. This spectrum of penalties also applied to an additional 500 people from as many as 30 countries who had been arrested, charged, and found guilty of participation in some degree with an attempted or successful escape.

On June 26, 1963, the President of the United States, John F. Kennedy, sited Berlin reinforcing American solidarity with West Germany and West Berlin and giving a huge morale boost to their citizens. After visiting the Allied crossing point at the now-famous "Checkpoint Charlie," he told an audience of almost 120,000, including West German Chancellor Konrad Adenauer and West Berlin Governing Mayor Wily Brandt, that all free persons everywhere are citizens of Berlin, and that he himself is a Berliner, "Ich bin ein Berliner." President Kennedy did not live to see an agreement, signed on December 17, 1963, one month after his assassination, which allowed West Berliners to visit their family members in East Berlin under certain conditions and restrictions.

A third-generation wall was constructed in 1965. It replaced the earlier barriers and was superior in its ability to prevent crossing. The concrete contained reinforced steel supports. The top of the 12-foot wall was capped with a circular, 1.5 foot concrete tube which made scaling the wall nearly impossible.

In 1966, after almost five years, there were now 210 observation towers and 245 bunkers with rifle pits along the five mile length of the wall. In spite of all this effort, at a trial before the Peoples Court in East Berlin, the statement was recorded that there was an average of 5,000 successful escapes yearly from East Berlin. In 1961, before the wall was erected, an average of 1,500 persons escaped from East Berlin each month during the months of June and July. Supposedly, according to East Berlin authorities, these escapes were orchestrated by persons who "organized in labor groups for the purpose of human trafficking by means of transit through other countries of the East."

The existence of such a wall triggered negotiations not only among the leadership in West and East Berlin but also among the leadership in West and East Germany concerning the free flow of information, technology, trade, and people. There were similar discussions within the leadership of NATO and also the Warsaw Pact whose military members were stationed in both Berlins and both Germanys.

Ten years following the construction of the wall, a Quadripartite Agreement among the Four Powers, (United States, Great Britain, France, and the Soviet Union), was signed on September 3, 1971. It opened the way for West Berliners to travel into East Berlin, East Germany, and West Germany. The East agreed to permit Westerners unimpeded access through East Germany. West Berliners were permitted to visit relatives and friends in the East up to 30 days annually.

This Quadripartite Agreement was supplemented just over six months later when in May 1972, East German citizens also were granted the opportunity to visit family members in West Germany but only on an emergency basis.

Still, escapes continued, especially whenever an international conference failed to produce results.

Within West and East Germany, political reconciliation among former countrymen began to advance more rapidly. In December, 1972, a Treaty between the two Germanys was signed in which each country pledged to normalize relations with the other in recognition of each country's status as sovereign and as independent of the other. Diplomatic missions were created in Bonn and East Berlin. Less than six months later, in May 1973, West and East Germany established full diplomatic ties.

As long as the wall remained in place for the same purposes for which it had been built, the East German secret police still had a job to do. After spying on its own citizens, its next priority mission was to prevent escapes into the free West. Although relations between West and East Germany gradually were improving after the establishment of full diplomatic relations it was not relevant to the mission of the secret police. Their members who belonged to the cadre of border guards were given a directive on October 1, 1973 with specific orders to "challenge or liquidate the border breacher." Agents were ordered to "not hesitate to use your weapon even when border breaches happen with women and children traitors."

Their job was made somewhat simpler when a stronger, more reinforced, and technologically enhanced fourth-generation wall was constructed between 1975 and 1976. This new "antifascist protective barrier," as it was called in the East, was a more formidable deterrent to escape. At 12 feet tall and four feet deep, it supported a touch-sensitive, self-exploding surface. This monstrous structure was the primary obstacle to freedom along its 102.5 mile length. It enclosed a no-man's area up to 300 yards deep that was protected also by floodlights, armed patrols, 267 dog runs, tank traps, fakir beds of upturned spikes, flares set off by hidden wires, and electrified fences with listening devices and alarms. This "security zone" existed between inner and outer walls, and was monitored by guards armed with machine guns on duty in 260 fixed watchtowers. Other guards patrolled in vehicles, on foot with dogs or in pairs along stretches of open ground that offered no concealment from their observation and no cover from their lethal weapons. The death zone was seeded with anti-personnel fragmentation mines that were powerful enough to blow off the feet and legs of a person.

In the late 1980's, Soviet General Secretary Mikhail Gorbachev instituted a period of reform and reconstruction within the Soviet Union. Outside the borders of the Soviet Union, his priority concern was the stability of the Soviet allies who were members of the Warsaw Pact within Europe. East Germany slowly and steadily was bettering its relations with West Germany.

Beyond the issues which occupied the politicians in both countries, a majority of Germans sought reunification into one country under one flag with one economy and one currency. There already was a common language. Although the Soviets had sent tanks to crush rebellions in Hungary in 1956, then in Czechoslovakia in 1968, and finally in Poland in 1979, Secretary Gorbachev decided not to interfere with the processes of reconciliation leading to unification. He declared that the reunification of Germany was an affair internal to each country.

On June 12, 1987, President Ronald Reagan visited Berlin to participate in the celebrations for the 750th anniversary of the founding of Berlin. In a speech in front of only 45,000 Berliners he implored the General Secretary of the Communist Party of the Soviet Union, "Mister Gorbachev, tear down this wall." The speech was simple and polite, and did not receive much media attention. Later, in a little more than two years, hundreds of thousands of people again would listen to President Reagan's words which were repeated by the international media when the wall did come down.

Before then, however, on February 6, 1989, Christopher Geuffroy, age 20, would be the last person killed by border guards during his attempt to flee to freedom. He was shot twice in the chest and died from his wounds.

One month later, on March 8, 1989, Winfried Freudenberg, age 32, would be the very last person to die in an escape attempt. He succeeded in crossing the border into West Berlin in a homemade balloon made of canvas strips and lifted by lighter-than-air natural gas. Aloft for several hours at an altitude as high as 2500 feet, he apparently was unable to control his landing. He died of severe internal injuries after impact with the ground in a garden near a private home in West Berlin.

On August 23, 1989, slightly more than two years after President Reagan's speech in June 1987, Warsaw Pact member Hungary removed all the border restrictions with its free neighbor Austria. On September 10, 1989, it did the same for its communist neighbor East Germany. More than 13,000 East Germans fled across the open border into Austria.

The momentum to escape communist domination continued to build. In East Berlin's main square, more than one million demonstrators attended a pro-democracy rally. The numbers were so great that the security forces and police could only watch. Within one week, the East German government resigned. Finally, on November 9, 1989, the government announced that visits from East Berlin into West Berlin and also West Germany were free and without conditions or restrictions. The wall was open and the Berliners began the process of tearing it down. It took until December 22, 1989, for the Brandenburg Gate to open just in time for a joyous Christmas celebration in Berlin.

During its time, the wall was considered to be the most closely guarded and most difficult to cross border in the world. Approximately 25 people escaped every year that the wall was in place but hundreds more died in failed attempts.

The wall was destroyed in 1990. On October 3, 1990, West Germany reunited with East Germany.

November 9, 2014, was the 25th anniversary of the fall of the Berlin wall.

Appendix 1. "The TREK" Patch.

Appendix 2. The TREK Route. 895 miles. Omaha Beach, Normandy, France to the Brandenburg Gate, Berlin, Germany. June 6, to August 15, 2014.

DATE	WALK DAY TOTAL MILES	ROUTE DISTANCE BETWEEN CITIES	AVERAGE MILES WALKED / DAY
Jun 6	1 10.2	Omaha Beach → Bayeux 10.2	10.2
Jun 7	2 17.4	Bayeux → Caen 27.6	13.8
Jun 8	3 15.0	Caen → Mery-Corbon 42.6	14.2
Jun 9	4 15.3	Mery-Corbon → Lisieux 57.9	14.5
Jun 10	5 17.4	Lisieux → Bernay 75.3	15.1
Jun 11	6 12.0	Bernay → Barc 87.3	14.5
Jun 12	7 16.2	Barc → Evreux 103.5	14.8
Jun 13	8 14.4	Evreux → Breuilpont 117.9	14.7
Jun 14	9 13.2	Breuilpont → Septuil 131.1	14.6
Jun 15	10 17.4	Septuil → Bois d'Arcy 148.5	14.9
Jun 16	11 17.0	Bois d'Arcy → **PARIS**[1] 165.5	15.0

DATE	WALK DAY	ROUTE	AVERAGE MILES WALKED / DAY
	TOTAL MILES	DISTANCE BETWEEN CITIES	
Jun 17	11	Paris	
	0.0	165.5	15.0
Jun 18	11	Paris	
	0.0	165.5	15.0
Jun 19	11	Paris	
	0.0	165.5	15.0
Jun 20	12	Paris → Villeparisis	
	14.2	179.7	15.0
Jun 21	13	Villeparisis → Meaux	
	13.4	193.1	14.9
Jun 22	14	Meaux → Montreuil-Lion	
	18.1	211.2	15.1
Jun 23	15	Montreuil-Lion → Crezancy	
	16.0	227.2	15.1
Jun 24	16	Crezancy→ Ville-en-Tardenois	
	18.5	245.7	15.4
Jun 25	17	Ville-en-Tardenois → **Reims**[2]	
	13.2	258.9	15.2
Jun 26	17	Reims	
	0.0	258.9	15.2
Jun 27	18	Reims→Pontfaverger-Mor'ers	
	13.8	272.7	15.2
Jun 28	19	Pontf-Moronvilliers → Bourcq	
	14.0	287.4	15.2
Jun 29	20	Bourcq → Buzancy	
	19.1	306.5	15.3

DATE	WALK DAY	ROUTE	AVERAGE MILES WALKED / DAY
	TOTAL MILES	DISTANCE BETWEEN CITIES	

| Jun 30 | 21 | Buzancy → Stenay | |
| | 13.2 | 319.7 | 15.2 |

| Jul 1 | 22 | Stenay,FR → Virton, BE | |
| | 19.2 | 338.9 | 15.4 |

| Jul 2 | 23 | Virton → Arlon | |
| | 16.5 | 355.4 | 15.5 |

| Jul 3 | 24 | Arlon → Martelange | |
| | 11.4 | 366.8 | 15.3 |

| Jul 4 | 25 | Martelange → **BASTOGNE,BE**[3] | |
| | 16.3 | 383.1 | 15.3 |

| Jul 5 | 26 | Bastogne → Troisvierges,LX | |
| | 16.1 | 399.2 | 15.4 |

| Jul 6 | 27 | Troisvierges → Winterscheid,GE | |
| | 15.0 | 414.4 | 15.3 |

| Jul 7 | 28 | Winterscheid → Steffeln | |
| | 17. | 431.7 | 15.4 |

DATE	WALK DAY	ROUTE	AVERAGE MILES WALKED / DAY
	TOTAL MILES	DISTANCE BETWEEN CITIES	

DATE	WALK DAY / TOTAL MILES	ROUTE / DISTANCE BETWEEN CITIES	AVERAGE MILES WALKED / DAY
Jul 8	29 18.2	Steffeln → Kelberg 449.9	15.4
Jul 9	30 16.2	Kelberg → Mayen 466.1	15.5
Jul 10	31 18.0	Mayen → Koblenz 484.1	15.6
Jul 11	32 15.9	Koblenz → Heiligenroth 500.0	15.6
Jul 12	33 14.8	Heiligenroth → Seck 514.8	15.6
Jul 13	34 16.0	Seck → Herborn 530.8	15.6
Jul 14	35 17.3	Herborn → Lohra 548.1	15.7
Jul 15	36 16.6	Lohra → Kirchain 564.7	15.7
Jul 16	37 17.0	Kirchain → Jesberg 582.1	15.7
Jul 17	38 18.0	Jesberg → Felsberg 600.2	15.8
Jul 18	39 16.8	Felsberg → Niestetal 617.0	15.8
Jul 19	40 14.8	Niestetal → Kreideberg-Gilerode 631.8	15.8
Jul 20	41 13.4	K-berg-Gilerode → Gottingen 645.2	15.8

DATE	WALK DAY	ROUTE	AVERAGE MILES WALKED / DAY
	TOTAL MILES	DISTANCE BETWEEN CITIES	

Jul 21	42	Gottingen → Gieboldehausen	
	15.6	660.8	15.7
Jul 22	43	Gieboldehausen → Claus-Zellerfeld	
	17.0	677.8	15.8
Jul 23	44	Claus-Zellerfeld → Hahnenklee	
	6.0	683.8	15.5
Jul 24	44	**Hahnenklee[4]**	
	0.0	683.3	15.5
Jul 25	44	Braunschweig Klinikum	
	0.0	683.3	15.5
Jul 26	44	Braunschweig Klinikum	
	0.0	683.3	15.5
Jul 27	44	Braunschweig Klinikum	
	0.0	683.3	15.5
Jul 28	44	Hahnenklee	
	0.0	683.3	15.5
Jul 29	44	Hahnenklee	
	0.0	683.3	15.5
Jul 30	44	Hahnenklee → Bocksweise	
	0.0	683.3	15.5
Jul 31	44	Hahnenklee → Lautenthal	
	0.0	683.3	15.5
Aug 1	44	Hahnenklee → Wolfshagen im Harz	
	0.0	683.3	15.5
Aug 2	45	Hahnenklee → Hornburg	
	0.0	683.3	15.4

DATE	WALK DAY TOTAL MILES	ROUTE DISTANCE BETWEEN CITIES	AVERAGE MILES WALKED / DAY
Aug 3	46 10.0	Hahnenklee → Goslar 693.3	15.4
Aug 4	47 17.9	Goslar → Osterwieck 711.	15.5
Aug 5	48 14.3	Osterwieck → Huy 725.5	15.4
Aug 6	49 19.2	Huy → Oschersleben 744.7	15.5
Aug 7	50 13.5	Oschersleben → Wanzleben 758.2	15.5
Aug 8	50 14.0	Wanzleben → Magdeburg 772.2	15.4
Aug 9	51 17.5	Magdeburg → Möckern 789.7	15.5
Aug 10	52 18.9	Möckern → Schopsdorf 808.6	15.6
Aug 11	53 19.6	Schopsdorf → Wollin 828.	15.6
Aug 12	54 19.8	Wollin → Kloster Lehnin 848.0	15.7
Aug 13	55 18.4	Kloster Lehnin → Caputh 866.4	15.7
Aug 14	56 14.8	Caputh → Wannsee 881.2	15.7
Aug 15	57 13.5	Wannsee→**Brandenburg Gate**[5] 894.7	15.7

Footnotes to Appendix 2, The TREK Route. 895 miles. Omaha Beach, Normandy, France to the Brandenburg Gate, Berlin, Germany. June 6, to August 15, 2014.

[1] **Paris.** Mile 165.5. Liberated August 25, 1944.

[2] **Reims.** Mile 258.9. WWII surrender documents signed May 7, 1945.

[3] **Bastogne.** Mile 383.1. Key battlefield city during the Battle of the Bulge.

[4] **Hahnenklee.** Mile 683.3. Town for rehabilitation following eye accident.

[5] **Brandenburg Gate.** Mile 894.7. Objective. August 15, 2014.

Appendix 3. Page 1 of 2. TREK Route. Equivalent Distance between Cities in North America. 895 miles + / - 20 miles. Alphabetical by distance.

Boston, MA to Columbia, SC	915
Detroit, MI to Portland, OR	915
Grand Junction, CO to Des Moines, IA	915
Kansas City, KS to New Orleans, LA	915
Little Rock, AR to Pittsburg, PA	915
Memphis, TN to Baltimore, MD	915
New Orleans, LA to Columbus, OH	915
Norfolk, VA to Memphis, TN	915
Omaha, NE to Pittsburg, PA	915

Atlanta, GA to Salt Lake City, UT	910
Charleston, SC to Chicago, IL	910
Charleston, WV to New Orleans, LA	910
Houston, TX to Omaha, NE	910
Jackson, MS to Miami, FL	910
Milwaukee, WI to New York City, NY	910
Minneapolis, MN to Memphis, TN	910
Savannah, GA to Houston, TX	910
Shreveport, LA to Orlando, FL	910

Raleigh, NC to Milwaukee, WI	905

Brownsville, TX to Wichita, KS	900
Charleston, WV to Minneapolis, MN	900
Columbia, SC to Milwaukee, WI	900
Fargo, ND to Denver, CO	900
Hartford, CT to Chicago, IL	900
Jacksonville, FL to St. Louis, MO	900
Miami, FL to Jackson, MS	900
Nashville, TN to New York City, NY	900
Philadelphia, PA to Birmingham, AL	900
Philadelphia, PA to St. Louis, MO	900
Phoenix, AZ to Cheyenne, WY	900
Tampa, FL to Washington, DC	900

Appendix 3. Page 2 of 2. TREK Route. Equivalent Distance between Cities in North America. 895 miles + / - 20 miles. Alphabetical by distance.

Atlanta, GA to Buffalo, NY	895	**Omaha**
Calgary, AB to Salt Lake City, UT	895	**Beach**
Cheyenne, WY to St. Louis, MO	895	→
Cincinnati, OH to Boston, MA	895	**Brandenburg**
Cleveland, OH to Jacksonville, FL	895	**Gate, Berlin**
New York City, NY to Atlanta, GA	895	=
Omaha, NE to Billings, MT	895	**895 miles.**
Savannah, GA to Detroit, MI	895	
Albuquerque, NM to Houston, TX	890	
Billings, MT to Portland, OR	890	
Charleston, SC to Chicago, IL	890	
Chicago, IL to Norfolk, VA	890	
Hartford, Ct to Louisville, KY	890	
Albuquerque, NM to Little Rock, AR	885	
Charleston, WV to Portland, ME	885	
Columbus, OH to Portland, ME	885	
Dallas, TX to Denver, CO	885	
Detroit, MI to Little Rock, AR	885	
Great Smoky Mtns Park to Dallas, TX	885	
Raleigh, NC to Little Rock, AR	885	
Baltimore, MD to Orlando, FL	880	
Big Bend Park, TX to Little Rock, AR	880	
Cheyenne, WY to Minneapolis, MN	880	
Dallas, TX to Indianapolis, IN	880	
Great Smoky Mtns Park-Des Moines, IA	880	
Milwaukee, WI to Oklahoma City, OK	880	
Quebec, QC to Dallas, TX	880	
St, Louis, MO to Seattle, WA	880	
Washington, DC to St. Louis, MO	880	
Cleveland, OH to Little Rock, AR	875	
Indianapolis, IN to Jacksonville, FL	875	
Memphis, TN to Washington, DC	875	
Mexico City, MX to San Antonio, TX	875	
Tampa, FL to Louisville, KY	875	

Appendix 4. Page 1 of 4. TREK Route. Equivalent Distance between Cities in North America. 895 miles + / - 20 miles. Alphabetical by City.

Albuquerque, NM to Houston, TX	890
Albuquerque, NM to Little Rock, AR	885
Atlanta, GA to Buffalo, NY	895
Atlanta, GA to Salt Lake City, UT	910
Baltimore, MD to Orlando, FL	880
Big Bend Park, TX to Little Rock, AR	880
Billings, MT to Portland, OR	890
Boston, MA to Columbia, SC	915
Brownsville, TX to Wichita, KS	900
Calgary, AB to Salt Lake City, UT	895
Charleston, SC to Albany, NY	890
Charleston, SC to Chicago, IL	910
Charleston, WV to Minneapolis, MN	900
Charleston, WV to New Orleans, LA	910
Charleston, WV to Portland, ME	885
Cheyenne, WY to Minneapolis, MN	880
Cheyenne, WY to St. Louis, MO	895
Chicago, IL to Norfolk, VA	890
Cincinnati, OH to Boston, MA	895
Cleveland, OH to Jacksonville, FL	895

Appendix 4. Page 2 of 4. TREK Route. Equivalent Distance between Cities in North America. 895 miles + / - 20 miles. Alphabetical by City.

Cleveland, OH to Little Rock, AR	875
Columbia, SC to Milwaukee, WI	900
Columbus, OH to Portland, ME	885
Dallas, TX to Denver, CO	885
Dallas, TX to Indianapolis, IN	880
Detroit, MI to Little Rock, AR	885
Detroit, MI to Portland, ME	915
Fargo, ND to Denver, CO	900
Grand Junction, CO to Des Moines, IA	915
Great Smoky Mtns Park to Dallas, TX	885
Great Smoky Mtns Park to Des Moines, IA	880
Hartford, CT to Chicago, IL	900
Hartford, CT to Louisville, KY	890
Houston, TX to Jacksonville, FL	875
Houston, TX to Omaha, NE	910
Indianapolis, IN to Jacksonville, FL	875
Jackson, MS to Miami, FL	910
Jacksonville, FL to St. Louis, MO	900
Kansas City, KS to New Orleans, LA	915
Little Rock, AR to Pittsburg, PA	915

Appendix 4. Page 3 of 4. TREK Route. Equivalent Distance between Cities in North America. 895 miles + / - 20 miles. Alphabetical by City.

Memphis, TN to Baltimore, MD	915
Memphis, TX to Washington, DC	875
Mexico City, MX to San Antonio, TX	875
Miami, FL to Jackson, MS	900
Milwaukee, WI to New York City, NY	910
Milwaukee, WI to Oklahoma City, OK	880
Minneapolis, MN to Memphis, TN	910
Nashville, KY to New York City, NY	900
New Orleans, LA to Columbus, OH	915
New York City, NY to Atlanta, GA	895
Norfolk, VA to Memphis, TN	915
Omaha, NE to Billings, MT	895
Omaha, NE to Pittsburg, PA	915
Philadelphia, PA to Birmingham, AL	900
Philadelphia, PA to St. Louis, MO	900
Phoenix, AZ to Cheyenne, WY	900
Quebec, QC to Dallas, TX	880
Raleigh, NC to Little Rock, AR	885
Raleigh, NC to Milwaukee, WI	905
St, Louis, MO to Seattle, WA	880

Appendix 4. Page 4 of 4. TREK Route. Equivalent Distance between Cities in North America. 895 miles + / - 20 miles. Alphabetical by City.

San Antonio, TX to St. Louis, MO   910

Savannah, GA to Detroit, MI   895

Savannah, GA to Houston, TX   910

Shreveport, LA to Orlando, FL   910

Tampa, FL to Louisville, KY   875

Tampa, FL to Washington, DC   900

Washington, DC to St. Louis, MO   880

Appendix 5. Page 1 of 2. Military Ranks, Titles and Abbreviations used within the Text.

RANK	TITLE	ABBREVIATION
	OFFICERS	
0-10	General	GEN
0-9	Lieutenant General	LTG
0-8	Major General	MG
0-7	Brigadier General	BG
0-6	Colonel	COL
0-5	Lieutenant Colonel	LTC
0-4	Major	MAJ
0-3	Captain	CPT
0-2	First Lieutenant	1LT
0-1	Second Lieutenant	2LT

RANK	TITLE	ABBREVIATION
	SENIOR NON-COMMISSIONED OFFICERS	
E-9	Command Sergeant Major	CSM
E-9	Sergeant Major	SGM
E-8	First Sergeant	1SG
E-8	Master Sergeant	MSG
E-7	Platoon Sergeant	PSG
E-7	Sergeant First Class	SFC

Appendix 5. Page 2 of 2. Military Ranks, Titles and Abbreviations used within the Text.

NON-COMMISSIONED OFFICERS-NCO's

E-6	Staff Sergeant	SSG
E-5	Sergeant	SGT
E-4	Corporal	CPL

JUNIOR ENLISTED

E-4	Specialist Fourth Class	SP4
E-3	Private First Class	PFC
E-2	Private	PV2
E-1	Private	PV1

Appendix 6. Graduates of the United States Military Academy on duty during World War II in Europe and North Africa. (Rank at retirement or death.) Page 1 of 5.

CLASS	RANK and TITLE
1904	**LTG Leslie McNair** [3], Commanding General, Army Ground Forces
1906	**LTG Frank Andrews** [2], Commanding General, U.S. Forces, Europe
1907	GEN Henry Arnold, General of the Army, General of the Air Force
1909	GEN Jacob Devers, Commanding General, U.S. 6th Army
1909	LTG John Lee, Commanding General Services of Supply
1909	GEN Alexander Patch, Commanding General, U.S. 7th Army
1909	GEN George Patton, Commanding General, U.S. 3rd Army
1909	GEN William Simpson, Commanding General, U.S. 9th Army
1910	MG John Millikin, Commanding General, III Corps
1912	COL Harry Flint[3], Commmander, 39th Infantry Regiment, France
1912	**BG William Wilbur** [1], Commanding General, 36th Infantry Division
1914	LTG Harold Bull, Chief of Staff, Operations, Allied Forces Europe
1914	MG Robert Crawford, Chief of Staff, Supply, Allied Forces Europe
1914	LTG Frank Milburn, Commanding General, XXI Corps
1914	GEN Carl Spaatz, Commanding General, Army Air Forces
1915	GEN Omar Bradley, Commanding General, 1st Army Group

Appendix 6. Graduates of the United States Military Academy on duty during World War II in Europe and North Africa. (Rank at retirement or death.) Page 2 of 5.

CLASS	RANK and TITLE
1915	GEN Dwight Eisenhower, Supreme Commander, Allied Forces Europe
1915	LTG John Leonard, Commanding General, 9th Armored Division
1915	MG Leland Hobbs, Commanding General, 30th Infantry Division
1915	LTG John Leonard, Commanding General, 9th Armored Division
1915	COL Mason Young, VII Corps Engineer Officer
1916	GEN William Hoge, Commanding General, 4th Armored Division
1917	GEN Mark Clark, Commanding General, 15th Army Group
1917	GEN Joseph Collins, Commanding General, VII Corps, Normandy
1917	MG Norman Cota, Commanding General, 28th Infantry Division
1917	MG Ernest Harmon, Commanding General 2nd Armored Division
1917	MG Robert Hasbrouck, Commanding General 7th Armored Division
1917	GEN Matthew Ridgway Commanding General, 82nd Airborne Division
1918	GEN Anthony McAuliffe, Commanding General, 101st Airborne Division
1918	MG Walter Muller, A/Chief of Staff, Logistics, U.S. 3rd Army
1919	GEN Nathan Twining, Commanding General, 15th Air Force
1922	BG George Taylor, Commander, 16th Infantry Regiment, Normandy

Appendix 6. Graduates of the United States Military Academy on duty during World War II in Europe and North Africa. (Rank at retirement or death.) Page 3 of 5.

CLASS	RANK and TITLE
1922	GEN Maxwell Taylor, Commanding General, 101st Airborne Division
1923	BG Alexander Reid, Commander, 424th Infantry Regiment
1924	COL Demas Craw[1], Air Officer, Operation Torch, North Africa
1924	LTG Richard Nugent, Commander, XXIX Tactical Air Command
1924	MG George Smythe, Commander, 47th Infantry Regiment
1924	LTG Richard Nugent, Commander, XXIX Tactical Air Command
1924	MG George Smythe, Commander, 47th Infantry Regiment
1925	GEN Bruce Clarke, Commander, Combat Command, 4th Armored Division
1926	MG Charles Canham, Commander, 116th Infantry Regiment, Normandy
1926	COL Russell Reeder, Commander, 12th Infantry Regiment, Normandy
1928	**BG Nathan Forrest III [4],** Chief of Staff, 2nd Air Force
1928	BG John Upham, Commander, 743rd Tank Battlion, Normandy
1928	LTG James Gavin, Commanding General, 82nd Airborne Division
1929	COL Paul Thompson, Commander, 6th Engineer Brigade, Normandy
1930	**BG Frederick Castle [1,7],** Army Air Corps, 487th Bomb Group
1933	BG William Darby, Battalion Commander, 1st, 4th, 6th Rangers

Appendix 6. Graduates of the United States Military Academy on duty during World War II in Europe and North Africa. (Rank at retirement or death.) Page 4 of 5.

CLASS	RANK and TITLE
1936	GEN Creighton Abrams, Tank Battalion Commander
1939	**LTC Robert Cole** [1, 3,] Battalion Commander, 101st Airborne Division
1940	COL Sidney Bingham, Commander, 2nd Battalion, 106th Infantry
1941	**CPT Robert Rosen** [3], Company Commander, 82nd Airborne Division
1941	**CPT Thomas Norwood** [5], Company Commander, 326th Airborne Engineers
1941	**CPT Thomas Norwood** [5], Company Commander, 326th Airborne Engineers
1942	**LTC John Leonard** [6], Commander, 405th Fighter Squadron Army Air Corps
1943	**1LT Jarrett Huddleston** [7], 424th Infantry Regiment

Footnotes to Appendix 6. Graduates of the United States Military Academy on duty during World War II in Europe and North Africa. (Rank at retirement or death.) Page 5 of 5.

[1] **Congressional Medal of Honor**

[2] **Killed, aircraft crash, England, 1944.**

[3] **Killed in action, France, 1944**

[4] **Killed in action, Germany, 1943.**

[5] **Killed in action, The Netherlands, 1944.**

[6] **Killed in action, Germany, 1945.**

[7] **Killed in action, Belgium, 1944.**

Appendix 7. Graduates of the United States Military Academy with duty during the Berlin Airlift, 1948-1949. (Rank at retirement or death.)

CLASS	RANK and TITLE
1918	GEN Lucius Clay, Commander-in-Chief, U.S. Forces Europe and Military Governor, U.S. Forces Germany
1923	LTG Joseph Smith, HQs Commandant, U.S. Air Forces Europe
1923	GEN Hoyt Vandenberg, Chief of Staff United States Air Force
1928	LTG William Tunner, Commander, U.S. Air Forces Europe
1945	**1LT Charles King,** Pilot, C-47B [1]

[1] Killed, Berlin Airlift Support, Templehof Airport

Appendix 8. Airlift Personnel Killed in Support of the Berlin Airlift, 1948-1949. (Rank or title at death.)

BE THOU AT PEACE

First Lieutenant Ralph H. Boyd, USAF, Fort Worth, Texas [1]

Air Mechanic-3 Harry R. Crites, Jr., USN, Lafayette, Indiana [2]

Captain Joel M. DeVolentine, USAF, Miami, Florida

Major Edwin C. Diltz, Fayetteville, Texas [1]

First Lieutenant Eric S. Erickson, USAF, Collinsville, Illinois

Mr. Karl V. Hagen, New York City, New York

First Lieutenant Willis F. Hargis, Nacogdoches, Texas [1]

Technical Sergeant Herbert F. Heinig, USAF, Fort Wayne, Indiana

Captain William R. Howard, USAF Gunnison, Mississippi

First Lieutenant Charles H. King, USAF, Britton, South Dakota

First Lieutenant Craig B. Ladd, USAF, Minneapolis, Minnestoa

Second Lieutenant Donald J. Leemon, USAF, Green Bay, Wisconsin

First Lieutenant William T. Lucas, USAF, Wilson, North Carolina

Private First Class Johnny T. Orms, USA, Rhein-Main Air Force Base

Captain Billy E. Phelps, USAF, Long Beach, California

Technical Sergeant Charles L. Putnam, USAF, Colorado Springs, CO

Captain William A. Rathgeber, USAF, Portland, Oregon

---

[1] Texas. State with the greatest number of casualties, 7: 3-military, 4 civilian
[2] Lafayette, Indiana. Hometown service buddies. Army and Navy.

Appendix 9. Prayers. Prepared in support of The TREK by Father Richard Wilson, United States Military Academy Class of 1973, Lieutenant Colonel, U.S. Army Retired, Diocese of Charleston, South Carolina.   Page 1 of 2.

Prayer at Normandy, June 5th and 6th, 2014

Almighty and ever-living God, I stand here today before the hallowed graves of thousands of Allied soldiers who gave their all to defeat the forces of tyranny. We truly cannot know the sacrifices that they have made, but you, Oh God, know and understand.

Help us, Oh Lord, to appreciate the sacrifices that these brave men and women have made.

Now, Oh God, I dedicate "The TREK" to you.

Allow me to walk in honor of those many brave men and women who sacrificed so bravely for freedom on the beaches of Normandy. Allow me to walk for my father and the hundreds of airmen who served honorably and well during the Berlin Airlift. Allow me to walk to celebrate the fall of the Berlin Wall that so unjustly divided the German peoples and deprived them of their basic human freedoms.

Eternal God, I ask that You bless this walk and make my sacrifices serve in some small way to bring honor and glory to those men and women who served so bravely. May my walk cause men and women everywhere to reflect upon the sacrifices of these members of the military, remember them, and honor them.

I humbly ask this before the Almighty ever-living God who lives and reigns forever and ever.

Amen.

Daily Prayer, June 7th through August 15th, 2014

Heavenly Father, as I begin this day, I thank You for the life and the health with which You have blessed me. I ask for your special protection and guidance as I walk.

Help me to see your Son in the people whom I meet today. May I be a powerful witness to the brave sacrifices of countless soldiers, sailors, airmen and marines.

As Mother Mary points us to her Son, may I be an instrument to many to reflect and remember the sacrifices of these brave men and women.

I ask this in the name of the Lord Jesus Christ, your Son, who lives and reigns with You and the Holy Spirit, one God, forever and ever.

Amen.

Appendix 9. Prayers. Prepared in support of The TREK by Father Richard Wilson, United States Military Academy Class of 1973, Lieutenant Colonel, U.S. Army Retired, Diocese of Charleston, South Carolina.   Page 2 of 2

Prayer upon arrival at Brandenburg Gate, August 15th, 2014

Almighty and ever-living God, I thank You for your guidance and protection throughout this trek. I dedicate every step to the courageous men and women who sacrificed all at Normandy, served so gallantly throughout the Berlin Airlift and faithfully persisted in the cause of freedom to tear down the Berlin Wall.

For the sacrifices made by all the military at Normandy, we give you thanks, Oh Lord.

Lord, hear our prayer.

For the sacrifices made by the peoples of the allied nations in support of the Normandy landings, we give thanks, Oh Lord.

Lord, hear our prayer.

For the heroic efforts made by my father Captain James Vincent Pelosi and all of the Allied airmen and soldiers throughout the Berlin airlift, we give thanks, Oh Lord.

Lord, hear our prayer.

For the yearning for freedom which You have instilled in the hearts of all, that caused free men and women to persist in seeking freedom and justice until the Berlin Wall fell, we give thanks, Oh Lord.

Lord, hear our prayer.

Eternal Father, it is your desire that all men and women live in freedom. May my trek serve to remind the world that our liberties are not free, and that we must be ever vigilant to maintain our freedom.

We humbly ask this before the one eternal God, who lives and reigns forever and ever.

Amen.

Appendix 10. Diet. Average Calories.

MEAL	CALORIES / APPROXIMATE (~) CALORIES
BREAKFAST:	~1500
Meal Ready to Eat (MRE):	1250
Roll	~150
Apple, Banana, Pear or Strawberries	~100
SNACK:	~290
Nature Valley Protein Bar	190
Apple, Banana, Pear or Strawberries	100
LUNCH:	~875
One-half MRE or restaurant meal	~750
Fruit juice or beer, 8 ounces	~125
SNACK II:	~290
Nature Valley Protein Bar	190
Apple, Banana, Pear or Strawberries	~100
DINNER:	~1000
One-half MRE or restaurant meal	~750
Wine, 8 ounces	~250
TOTAL DAILY CALORIES:	~3955

Appendix 11. Strength Training Exercise Routine.   Page 1 of 2.

A strength training exercise routine was performed daily, Monday through Saturday, for between 45 and 60 minutes, for only one body part which included chest, back, shoulders, arms (triceps and biceps), legs and abs. Each week the body part routine was scrambled to aid in strength training and to reduce muscle adaptation to a standard regimen.

The training period was two months. During the first week, a minimum weight was used for three sets of eight repetitions. During the 7th and 8th weeks, the maximum weight that I could lift without strain was used for three sets of eight repetitions.

BODY PART	EXERCISE	EQUIPMENT
Chest	Bent-over flys	Cable X-over machine pulleys
Chest	Bench press	Smith machine bar & bench
Chest	Dumbbell press	5# - 35# dumbbells
Back	Lat pulldown	Smith machine & cable grips
Back	Dumbbell rows	10# - 45# dumbbells
Back	Bent-over rows	45# bar & weight plates
Shoulders	Seated flys	5# - 20# dumbbells
Shoulders	Seated press	Smith machine bar & weights
Shoulders	Narrow-grip press	Smith machine bar & weights
Arms	Cable push-down	Cable X-over machine
Arms	Bicep curl	Curling bar & weights
Arms	Single arm curl	5# - 30# dumbbells

Appendix 11. Strength Training Exercise Routine. Page 2 of 2.

BODY PART	EXERCISE	EQUIPMENT
Legs	Lunge	45# bar & weights
Legs	Squats	Smith machine bar & weights
Abs	Crunches	3 sets of 20
Abs	Cable crunches	3 sets of 20 w/40# weight
Abs	Hanging leg raises	3 sets of 20
Abs	Incline sit-ups	3 sets of 20

Appendix 12. Aerobic Exercise Routine.

An aerobic exercise routine was performed daily, Monday through Sunday, for eight weeks in April and May 2014. I began the first week walking six miles with a minimum weight of 10 pounds in the backpack.

During the final two weeks, I walked 15 miles with the maximum weight of 45 pounds. The pace at which I conditioned myself to walk was three miles an hour regardless of the weight of the backpack.

This chart reflects that routine.

WEEK	DISTANCE (Miles)	BACKPACK WEIGHT (Pounds)	TIME (Hours)
1	6	10	2
2	9	20	3
3	12	25	4
4	12	30	4
5	15	35	5
6	15	35	5
7	15	45	5
8	15	45	5

ABOUT THE AUTHOR

James Joseph Pelosi is a retired Army officer, university professor and aerospace engineer with 42 years government service. He earned a Bachelor of Science degree in Civil and Mechanical engineering from the United States Military Academy at West Point, New York with the "Proud and Free" class of 1973; a Master in Business Administration degree from Pepperdine University's Presidential and Key Executive program in Los Angeles, California in 1982; a Master of Arts degree in Russian Area Studies from Georgetown University's overseas extension program at the U.S. Army Russian Institute in Garmisch-Partenkirchen, Germany in 1985; and a Doctor of Philosophy degree in aerospace biomedical engineering from Moscow State University in 1988. With an academic's fluency in several European languages, he conducted much of the research related to the four Legacy events from sources in France, Belgium, Germany and Russia. He is a 38-year member of the American Legion and an advocate for all veterans especially those injured and disabled by combat. He spends his time conducting research for future publications and as a volunteer for medical research investigations related to healthy aging. He resides among homes in the United States, Germany, Italy and Russia where he writes. His book, <u>At War</u> <u>with</u> <u>Parkinson's</u> <u>Disease</u>, which relates the story of his at-home care for his disabled mother between 2000 and 2010, will be published in 2018.

Made in the USA
Columbia, SC
06 August 2017